DERIVATIVES AND ALTERNATIVE INVESTMENTS

CFA® Program Curriculum
2015 • LEVEL I • VOLUME 6

CFA Institute | WILEY

Photography courtesy of Hector Emanuel.

ISBN 978-1-939515-37-7 (paper)
ISBN 978-1-939515-58-2 (ebk)

10 9 8 7 6 5 4 3 2 1

Please visit our website at
www.WileyGlobalFinance.com.

WILEY

CONTENTS

Derivatives

◙ indicates an optional segment

Alternative Investments

◙ indicates an optional segment

Contents

How to Use the CFA Program Curriculum

Congratulations on your decision to enter the Chartered Financial Analyst (CFA®) Program. This exciting and rewarding program of study reflects your desire to become a serious investment professional. You are embarking on a program noted for its high ethical standards and the breadth of knowledge, skills, and abilities it develops. Your commitment to the CFA Program should be educationally and professionally rewarding.

The credential you seek is respected around the world as a mark of accomplishment and dedication. Each level of the program represents a distinct achievement in professional development. Successful completion of the program is rewarded with membership in a prestigious global community of investment professionals. CFA charterholders are dedicated to life-long learning and maintaining currency with the ever-changing dynamics of a challenging profession. The CFA Program represents the first step toward a career-long commitment to professional education.

The CFA examination measures your mastery of the core skills required to succeed as an investment professional. These core skills are the basis for the Candidate Body of Knowledge (CBOK™). The CBOK consists of four components:

- A broad topic outline that lists the major top-level topic areas (www. cfainstitute.org/cbok);
- Topic area weights that indicate the relative exam weightings of the top-level topic areas (www.cfainstitute.org/level_I);
- Learning outcome statements (LOS) that advise candidates about the specific knowledge, skills, and abilities they should acquire from readings covering a topic area (LOS are provided in candidate study sessions and at the beginning of each reading); and
- The CFA Program curriculum, readings, and end-of-reading questions, which candidates receive upon exam registration.

Therefore, the key to your success on the CFA examinations is studying and understanding the CBOK. The following sections provide background on the CBOK, the organization of the curriculum, and tips for developing an effective study program.

CURRICULUM DEVELOPMENT PROCESS

The CFA Program is grounded in the practice of the investment profession. Using the Global Body of Investment Knowledge (GBIK) collaborative website, CFA Institute performs a continuous practice analysis with investment professionals around the world to determine the knowledge, skills, and abilities (competencies) that are relevant to the profession. Regional expert panels and targeted surveys are conducted annually to verify and reinforce the continuous feedback from the GBIK collaborative website. The practice analysis process ultimately defines the CBOK. The CBOK contains the competencies that are generally accepted and applied by investment professionals. These competencies are used in practice in a generalist context and are expected to be demonstrated by a recently qualified CFA charterholder.

A committee consisting of practicing charterholders, in conjunction with CFA Institute staff, designs the CFA Program curriculum in order to deliver the CBOK to candidates. The examinations, also written by practicing charterholders, are designed to allow you to demonstrate your mastery of the CBOK as set forth in the CFA Program curriculum. As you structure your personal study program, you should emphasize mastery of the CBOK and the practical application of that knowledge. For more information on the practice analysis, CBOK, and development of the CFA Program curriculum, please visit www.cfainstitute.org.

ORGANIZATION OF THE CURRICULUM

The Level I CFA Program curriculum is organized into 10 topic areas. Each topic area begins with a brief statement of the material and the depth of knowledge expected.

Each topic area is then divided into one or more study sessions. These study sessions—18 sessions in the Level I curriculum—should form the basic structure of your reading and preparation.

Each study session includes a statement of its structure and objective and is further divided into specific reading assignments. An outline illustrating the organization of these 18 study sessions can be found at the front of each volume.

The reading assignments are the basis for all examination questions and are selected or developed specifically to teach the knowledge, skills, and abilities reflected in the CBOK. These readings are drawn from content commissioned by CFA Institute, textbook chapters, professional journal articles, research analyst reports, and cases. All readings include problems and solutions to help you understand and master the topic areas.

Reading-specific Learning Outcome Statements (LOS) are listed at the beginning of each reading. These LOS indicate what you should be able to accomplish after studying the reading. The LOS, the reading, and the end-of-reading questions are dependent on each other, with the reading and questions providing context for understanding the scope of the LOS.

You should use the LOS to guide and focus your study because each examination question is based on an assigned reading and one or more LOS. The readings provide context for the LOS and enable you to apply a principle or concept in a variety of scenarios. The candidate is responsible for the entirety of the required material in a study session, which includes the assigned readings as well as the end-of-reading questions and problems.

We encourage you to review the information about the LOS on our website (www.cfainstitute.org/programs/cfaprogram/courseofstudy/Pages/study_sessions.aspx), including the descriptions of LOS "command words" (www.cfainstitute.org/programs/Documents/cfa_and_cipm_los_command_words.pdf).

FEATURES OF THE CURRICULUM

OPTIONAL
SEGMENT

Required vs. Optional Segments   You should read all of an assigned reading. In some cases, though, we have reprinted an entire chapter or article and marked certain parts of the reading as "optional." The CFA examination is based only on the required segments, and the optional segments are included only when it is determined that they might help you to better understand the required segments (by seeing the required material in its full context). When an optional segment begins, you will see an icon and a dashed vertical bar in the outside margin that will continue until the optional segment ends, accompanied by another icon. *Unless the material is specifically marked as optional, you should assume it is required.* You should rely on the required segments and the reading-specific LOS in preparing for the examination.

END OPTIONAL SEGMENT

Problems/Solutions *All questions and problems in the readings as well as their solutions (which are provided directly following the problems) are part of the curriculum and are required material for the exam.* When appropriate, we have included problems within and after the readings to demonstrate practical application and reinforce your understanding of the concepts presented. The questions and problems are designed to help you learn these concepts and may serve as a basis for exam questions. Many of these questions are adapted from past CFA examinations.

Glossary and Index For your convenience, we have printed a comprehensive glossary in each volume. Throughout the curriculum, a **bolded** word in a reading denotes a term defined in the glossary. The curriculum eBook is searchable, but we also publish an index that can be found on the CFA Institute website with the Level I study sessions.

Source Material The authorship, publisher, and copyright owners are given for each reading for your reference. We recommend that you use the CFA Institute curriculum rather than the original source materials because the curriculum may include only selected pages from outside readings, updated sections within the readings, and problems and solutions tailored to the CFA Program.

LOS Self-Check We have inserted checkboxes next to each LOS that you can use to track your progress in mastering the concepts in each reading.

DESIGNING YOUR PERSONAL STUDY PROGRAM

Create a Schedule An orderly, systematic approach to exam preparation is critical. You should dedicate a consistent block of time every week to reading and studying. Complete all reading assignments and the associated problems and solutions in each study session. Review the LOS both before and after you study each reading to ensure that you have mastered the applicable content and can demonstrate the knowledge, skill, or ability described by the LOS and the assigned reading. Use the LOS self-check to track your progress and highlight areas of weakness for later review.

As you prepare for your exam, we will e-mail you important exam updates, testing policies, and study tips. Be sure to read these carefully. Curriculum errata are periodically updated and posted on the study session page at www.cfainstitute.org. You can also sign up for an RSS feed to alert you to the latest errata update.

Successful candidates report an average of more than 300 hours preparing for each exam. Your preparation time will vary based on your prior education and experience. For each level of the curriculum, there are 18 study sessions. So, a good plan is to devote 15–20 hours per week for 18 weeks to studying the material. Use the final four to six weeks before the exam to review what you have learned and practice with topic and mock exams. This recommendation, however, may underestimate the hours needed for appropriate examination preparation depending on your individual circumstances, relevant experience, and academic background. You will undoubtedly adjust your study time to conform to your own strengths and weaknesses and to your educational and professional background.

You will probably spend more time on some study sessions than on others, but on average you should plan on devoting 15–20 hours per study session. You should allow ample time for both in-depth study of all topic areas and additional concentration on those topic areas for which you feel the least prepared.

An interactive study planner is available in the candidate resources area of our website to help you plan your study time. The interactive study planner recommends completion dates for each topic of the curriculum. Dates are determined based on study time available, exam topic weights, and curriculum weights. As you progress through the curriculum, the interactive study planner dynamically adjusts your study plan when you are running off schedule to help you stay on track for completion prior to the examination.

CFA Institute Topic Exams   The CFA Institute topic exams are intended to assess your mastery of individual topic areas as you progress through your studies. After each test, you will receive immediate feedback noting the correct responses and indicating the relevant assigned reading so you can identify areas of weakness for further study. The topic exams reflect the question formats and level of difficulty of the actual CFA examinations. For more information on the topic tests, please visit www.cfainstitute.org.

CFA Institute Mock Exams   Mock examinations mimic the actual CFA examinations not only in question format and level of difficulty, but also in length and topic weight. The three-hour mock exams simulate the morning and afternoon sessions of the actual CFA examination, and are intended to be taken after you complete your study of the full curriculum so you can test your understanding of the curriculum and your readiness for the exam. You will receive feedback at the end of the mock exam, noting the correct responses and indicating the relevant assigned readings so you can assess areas of weakness for further study during your review period. We recommend that you take mock exams during the final stages of your preparation for the actual CFA examination. For more information on the mock examinations, please visit www.cfainstitute.org.

Preparatory Providers   After you enroll in the CFA Program, you may receive numerous solicitations for preparatory courses and review materials. When considering a prep course, make sure the provider is in compliance with the CFA Institute Prep Provider Guidelines Program (www.cfainstitute.org/partners/examprep/Pages/cfa_prep_provider_guidelines.aspx). Just remember, there are no shortcuts to success on the CFA examinations; reading and studying the CFA curriculum is the key to success on the examination. The CFA examinations reference only the CFA Institute assigned curriculum—no preparatory course or review course materials are consulted or referenced.

SUMMARY

Every question on the CFA examination is based on the content contained in the required readings and on one or more LOS. Frequently, an examination question is based on a specific example highlighted within a reading or on a specific end-of-reading question and/or problem and its solution. To make effective use of the CFA Program curriculum, please remember these key points:

1   All pages printed in the curriculum are required reading for the examination except for occasional sections marked as optional. You may read optional pages as background, but you will not be tested on them.

2   All questions, problems, and their solutions—printed at the end of readings—are part of the curriculum and are required study material for the examination.

3   You should make appropriate use of the topic and mock examinations and other resources available at www.cfainstitute.org.

4   Use the interactive study planner to create a schedule and commit sufficient study time to cover the 18 study sessions, review the materials, and take topic and mock examinations.

5   Some of the concepts in the study sessions may be superseded by updated rulings and/or pronouncements issued after a reading was published. Candidates are expected to be familiar with the overall analytical framework contained in the assigned readings. Candidates are not responsible for changes that occur after the material was written.

FEEDBACK

At CFA Institute, we are committed to delivering a comprehensive and rigorous curriculum for the development of competent, ethically grounded investment professionals. We rely on candidate and member feedback as we work to incorporate content, design, and packaging improvements. You can be assured that we will continue to listen to your suggestions. Please send any comments or feedback to info@cfainstitute.org. Ongoing improvements in the curriculum will help you prepare for success on the upcoming examinations and for a lifetime of learning as a serious investment professional.

Derivatives

TOPIC LEVEL LEARNING OUTCOME

The candidate should be able to demonstrate a working knowledge of the analysis of derivatives, including forwards, futures, options, and swaps.

Derivatives

Derivatives—financial instruments that derive their value from the value of some underlying asset—have become increasingly important and fundamental in effectively managing financial risk and creating synthetic exposures to asset classes. As in other security markets, arbitrage and market efficiency play a critical role in establishing prices.

This study session builds the conceptual framework for understanding the basic derivatives (forwards, futures, options, and swaps), derivative markets, and the use of options in risk management.

READING ASSIGNMENTS

READING

57

Derivative Markets and Instruments

by Don M. Chance, CFA

LEARNING OUTCOMES

Mastery	The candidate should be able to:
☐	**a.** define a derivative, and distinguish between exchange-traded and over-the-counter derivatives;
☐	**b.** contrast forward commitments with contingent claims;
☐	**c.** define forward contracts, futures contracts, options (calls and puts), swaps, and credit derivatives, and compare their basic characteristics;
☐	**d.** describe purposes of, and controversies related to, derivative markets;
☐	**e.** explain arbitrage and the role it plays in determining prices and promoting market efficiency.

INTRODUCTION

1

Equity, fixed-income, currency, and commodity markets are facilities for trading the basic assets of an economy. Equity and fixed-income securities are claims on the assets of a company. Currencies are the monetary units issued by a government or central bank. Commodities are natural resources, such as oil or gold. These underlying assets are said to trade in **cash markets** or **spot markets** and their prices are sometimes referred to as **cash prices** or **spot prices**, though we usually just refer to them as stock prices, bond prices, exchange rates, and commodity prices. These markets exist around the world and receive much attention in the financial and mainstream media. Hence, they are relatively familiar not only to financial experts but also to the general population.

Somewhat less familiar are the markets for **derivatives**, which are financial instruments that derive their values from the performance of these basic assets. This reading is an overview of derivatives. Subsequent readings will explore many aspects of derivatives and their uses in depth. Among the questions that this first reading will address are the following:

■ What are the defining characteristics of derivatives?

- What purposes do derivatives serve for financial market participants?
- What is the distinction between a forward commitment and a contingent claim?
- What are forward and futures contracts? In what ways are they alike and in what ways are they different?
- What are swaps?
- What are call and put options and how do they differ from forwards, futures, and swaps?
- What are credit derivatives and what are the various types of credit derivatives?
- What are the benefits of derivatives?
- What are some criticisms of derivatives and to what extent are they well founded?
- What is arbitrage and what role does it play in a well-functioning financial market?

This reading is organized as follows. Section 2 explores the definition and uses of derivatives and establishes some basic terminology. Section 3 describes derivatives markets. Section 4 categorizes and explains types of derivatives. Sections 5 and 6 discuss the benefits and criticisms of derivatives, respectively. Section 7 introduces the basic principles of derivative pricing and the concept of arbitrage. Section 8 provides a summary.

DERIVATIVES: DEFINITIONS AND USES

The most common definition of a derivative reads approximately as follows:

> *A derivative is a financial instrument that derives its performance from the performance of an underlying asset.*

This definition, despite being so widely quoted, can nonetheless be a bit troublesome. For example, it can also describe mutual funds and exchange-traded funds, which would never be viewed as derivatives even though they derive their values from the values of the underlying securities they hold. Perhaps the distinction that best characterizes derivatives is that they usually *transform* the performance of the underlying asset before paying it out in the derivatives transaction. In contrast, with the exception of expense deductions, mutual funds and exchange-traded funds simply pass through the returns of their underlying securities. This transformation of performance is typically understood or implicit in references to derivatives but rarely makes its way into the formal definition. In keeping with customary industry practice, this characteristic will be retained as an implied, albeit critical, factor distinguishing derivatives from mutual funds and exchange-traded funds and some other straight pass-through instruments. Also, note that the idea that derivatives take their *performance* from an underlying asset encompasses the fact that derivatives take their value and certain other characteristics from the underlying asset. Derivatives strategies perform in ways that are derived from the underlying and the specific features of derivatives.

Derivatives are similar to insurance in that both allow for the transfer of risk from one party to another. As everyone knows, insurance is a financial contract that provides protection against loss. The party bearing the risk purchases an insurance policy, which transfers the risk to the other party, the insurer, for a specified period of time. The risk itself does not change, but the party bearing it does. Derivatives allow for this same type of transfer of risk. One type of derivative in particular, the put option, when combined with a position exposed to the risk, functions almost exactly like insurance, but all derivatives can be used to protect against loss. Of course, an insurance contract must specify the underlying risk, such as property, health, or life. Likewise, so do derivatives. As noted earlier, derivatives are associated with an underlying asset. As such, the so-called "underlying asset" is often simply referred to as the **underlying**, whose value is the source of risk.[1] In fact, the underlying need not even be an asset itself. Although common derivatives underlyings are equities, fixed-income securities, currencies, and commodities, other derivatives underlyings include interest rates, credit, energy, weather, and even other derivatives, all of which are not generally thought of as assets. Thus, like insurance, derivatives pay off on the basis of a source of risk, which is often, but not always, the value of an underlying asset. And like insurance, derivatives have a definite life span and expire on a specified date.

Derivatives are created in the form of legal contracts. They involve two parties—the buyer and the seller (sometimes known as the writer)—each of whom agrees to do something for the other, either now or later. The buyer, who purchases the derivative, is referred to as the **long** or the holder because he owns (holds) the derivative and holds a long position. The seller is referred to as the **short** because he holds a short position.[2]

A derivative contract always defines the rights and obligations of each party. These contracts are intended to be, and almost always are, recognized by the legal system as commercial contracts that each party expects to be upheld and supported in the legal system. Nonetheless, disputes sometimes arise, and lawyers, judges, and juries may be required to step in and resolve the matter.

There are two general classes of derivatives. Some provide the ability to lock in a price at which one might buy or sell the underlying. Because they force the two parties to transact in the future at a previously agreed-on price, these instruments are called **forward commitments**. The various types of forward commitments are called forward contracts, futures contracts, and swaps. Another class of derivatives provides *the right but not the obligation* to buy or sell the underlying at a pre-determined price. Because the choice of buying or selling versus doing nothing depends on a particular random outcome, these derivatives are called **contingent claims**. The primary contingent claim is called an **option**. The types of derivatives will be covered in more detail later in this reading and in considerably more depth later in the curriculum.

The existence of derivatives begs the obvious question of what purpose they serve. If one can participate in the success of a company by holding its equity, what reason can possibly explain why another instrument is required that takes its value from the performance of the equity? Although equity and other fundamental markets exist and usually perform reasonably well without derivative markets, it is possible that derivative markets can *improve* the performance of the markets for the underlyings. As you will see later in this reading, that is indeed true in practice.

Derivative markets create beneficial opportunities that do not exist in their absence. Derivatives can be used to create strategies that cannot be implemented with the underlyings alone. For example, derivatives make it easier to go short, thereby benefiting from a decline in the value of the underlying. In addition, derivatives, in and of themselves, are characterized by a relatively high degree of leverage, meaning that participants in derivatives transactions usually have to invest only a small amount of their own capital relative to the value of the underlying. As such, small movements in the underlying can lead to fairly large movements in the amount of money made or lost on the derivative. Derivatives generally trade at lower transaction costs than

---

1 Unfortunately, English financial language often evolves without regard to the rules of proper usage. *Underlying* is typically an adjective and, therefore, a modifier, but the financial world has turned it into a noun.
2 In the financial world, the *long* always benefits from an increase in the value of the instrument he owns, and the *short* always benefits from a decrease in the value of the instrument he has sold. Think of the long as having possession of something and the short as having incurred an obligation to deliver that something.

comparable spot market transactions, are often more liquid than their underlyings, and offer a simple, effective, and low-cost way to transfer risk. For example, a shareholder of a company can reduce or even completely eliminate the market exposure by trading a derivative on the equity. Holders of fixed-income securities can use derivatives to reduce or completely eliminate interest rate risk, allowing them to focus on the credit risk. Alternatively, holders of fixed-income securities can reduce or eliminate the credit risk, focusing more on the interest rate risk. Derivatives permit such adjustments easily and quickly. These features of derivatives are covered in more detail later in this reading.

The types of performance transformations facilitated by derivatives allow market participants to practice more effective risk management. Indeed, the entire field of derivatives, which at one time was focused mostly on the instruments themselves, is now more concerned with the *uses* of the instruments. Just as a carpenter uses a hammer, nails, screws, a screwdriver, and a saw to build something useful or beautiful, a financial expert uses derivatives to manage risk. And just as it is critically important that a carpenter understand how to use these tools, an investment practitioner must understand how to properly use derivatives. In the case of the carpenter, the result is building something useful; in the case of the financial expert, the result is managing financial risk. Thus, like tools, derivatives serve a valuable purpose but like tools, they must be used carefully.

The practice of risk management has taken a prominent role in financial markets. Indeed, whenever companies announce large losses from trading, lending, or operations, stories abound about how poorly these companies managed risk. Such stories are great attention grabbers and a real boon for the media, but they often miss the point that risk management does not guarantee that large losses will not occur. Rather, **risk management** *is the process by which an organization or individual defines the level of risk it wishes to take, measures the level of risk it is taking, and adjusts the latter to equal the former*. Risk management never offers a guarantee that large losses will not occur, and it does not eliminate the possibility of total failure. To do so would typically require that the amount of risk taken be so small that the organization would be effectively constrained from pursuing its primary objectives. Risk taking is inherent in all forms of economic activity and life in general. The possibility of failure is never eliminated.

EXAMPLE 1

Characteristics of Derivatives

1 Which of the following is the best example of a derivative?
   A A global equity mutual fund
   B A non-callable government bond
   C A contract to purchase Apple Computer at a fixed price

2 Which of the following is **not** a characteristic of a derivative?
   A An underlying
   B A low degree of leverage
   C Two parties—a buyer and a seller

3 Which of the following statements about derivatives is **not** true?
   A They are created in the spot market.
   B They are used in the practice of risk management.
   C They take their values from the value of something else.

Solution to 1:

C is correct. Mutual funds and government bonds are not derivatives. A government bond is a fundamental asset on which derivatives might be created, but it is not a derivative itself. A mutual fund can technically meet the definition of a derivative, but as noted in the reading, derivatives transform the value of a payoff of an underlying asset. Mutual funds merely pass those payoffs through to their holders.

Solution to 2:

B is correct. All derivatives have an underlying and must have a buyer and a seller. More importantly, derivatives have high degrees of leverage, not low degrees of leverage.

Solution to 3:

A is correct. Derivatives are used to practice risk management and they take (derive) their values from the value of something else, the underlying. They are not created in the spot market, which is where the underlying trades.

Note also that risk management is a dynamic and ongoing process, reflecting the fact that the risk assumed can be difficult to measure and is constantly changing. As noted, derivatives are tools, indeed *the* tools that make it easier to manage risk. Although one can trade stocks and bonds (the underlyings) to adjust the level of risk, it is almost always more effective to trade derivatives.

Risk management is addressed more directly elsewhere in the CFA curriculum, but the study of derivatives necessarily entails the concept of risk management. In an explanation of derivatives, the focus is usually on the instruments and it is easy to forget the overriding objective of managing risk. Unfortunately, that would be like a carpenter obsessed with his hammer and nails, forgetting that he is building a piece of furniture. It is important to always try to keep an eye on the objective of managing risk.

THE STRUCTURE OF DERIVATIVE MARKETS

Having an understanding of equity, fixed-income, and currency markets is extremely beneficial—indeed, quite necessary—in understanding derivatives. One could hardly consider the wisdom of using derivatives on a share of stock if one did not understand the equity markets reasonably well. As you likely know, equities trade on organized exchanges as well as in over-the-counter (OTC) markets. These exchange-traded equity markets—such as the Deutsche Börse, the Tokyo Stock Exchange, and the New York Stock Exchange and its Eurex affiliate—are formal organizational structures that bring buyers and sellers together through market makers, or dealers, to facilitate transactions. Exchanges have formal rule structures and are required to comply with all securities laws.

OTC securities markets operate in much the same manner, with similar rules, regulations, and organizational structures. At one time, the major difference between OTC and exchange markets for securities was that the latter brought buyers and sellers together in a physical location, whereas the former facilitated trading strictly in an electronic manner. Today, these distinctions are blurred because many organized securities exchanges have gone completely to electronic systems. Moreover, OTC securities markets can be formally organized structures, such as NASDAQ, or can merely refer to informal networks of parties who buy and sell with each other, such as the corporate and government bond markets in the United States.

The derivatives world also comprises organized exchanges and OTC markets. Although the derivatives world is also moving toward less distinction between these markets, there are clear differences that are important to understand.

3.1 Exchange-Traded Derivatives Markets

Derivative instruments are created and traded either on an exchange or on the OTC market. Exchange-traded derivatives are standardized, whereas OTC derivatives are customized. To standardize a derivative contract means that its terms and conditions are precisely specified by the exchange and there is very limited ability to alter those terms. For example, an exchange might offer trading in certain types of derivatives that expire only on the third Friday of March, June, September, and December. If a party wanted the derivative to expire on any other day, it would not be able to trade such a derivative on that exchange, nor would it be able to persuade the exchange to create it, at least not in the short run. If a party wanted a derivative on a particular entity, such as a specific stock, that party could trade it on that exchange only if the exchange had specified that such a derivative could trade. Even the magnitudes of the contracts are specified. If a party wanted a derivative to cover €150,000 and the exchange specified that contracts could trade only in increments of €100,000, the party could do nothing about it if it wanted to trade that derivative on that exchange.

This standardization of contract terms facilitates the creation of a more liquid market for derivatives. If all market participants know that derivatives on the euro trade in 100,000-unit lots and that they all expire only on certain days, the market functions more effectively than it would if there were derivatives with many different unit sizes and expiration days competing in the same market at the same time. This standardization makes it easier to provide liquidity. Through designated market makers, derivatives exchanges guarantee that derivatives can be bought and sold.[3]

The cornerstones of the exchange-traded derivatives market are the market makers (or dealers) and the speculators, both of whom typically own memberships on the exchange.[4] The market makers stand ready to buy at one price and sell at a higher price. With standardization of terms and an active market, market makers are often able to buy and sell almost simultaneously at different prices, locking in small, short-term profits—a process commonly known as scalping. In some cases, however, they are unable to do so, thereby forcing them to either hold exposed positions or find other parties with whom they can trade and thus lay off (get rid of) the risk. This is when speculators come in. Although speculators are market participants who are willing to take risks, it is important to understand that being a speculator does not mean the reckless assumption of risk. Although speculators will take large losses at times, good speculators manage those risks by watching their exposures, absorbing market information, and observing the flow of orders in such a manner that they are able to survive and profit. Often, speculators will hedge their risks when they become uncomfortable.

---

3 It is important to understand that merely being able to buy and sell a derivative, or even a security, does not mean that liquidity is high and that the cost of liquidity is low. Derivatives exchanges guarantee that a derivative can be bought and sold, but they do not guarantee the price. The ask price (the price at which the market maker will sell) and the bid price (the price at which the market maker will buy) can be far apart, which they will be in a market with low liquidity. Hence, such a market can have liquidity, loosely defined, but the cost of liquidity can be quite high. The factors that can lead to low liquidity for derivatives are similar to those for securities: little trading interest and a high level of uncertainty.

4 Exchanges are owned by their *members*, whose memberships convey the right to trade. In addition, some exchanges are themselves publicly traded corporations whose members are shareholders, and there are also non-member shareholders.

Standardization also facilitates the creation of a clearing and settlement operation. **Clearing** refers to the process by which the exchange verifies the execution of a transaction and records the participants' identities. **Settlement** refers to the related process in which the exchange transfers money from one participant to the other or from a participant to the exchange or vice versa. This flow of money is a critical element of derivatives trading. Clearly, there would be no confidence in markets in which money is not efficiently collected and disbursed. Derivatives exchanges have done an excellent job of clearing and settlement, especially in comparison to securities exchanges. Derivatives exchanges clear and settle all contracts overnight, whereas most securities exchanges require two business days.

The clearing and settlement process of derivative transactions also provides a credit guarantee. If two parties engage in a derivative contract on an exchange, one party will ultimately make money and the other will lose money. Derivatives exchanges use their clearinghouses to provide a guarantee to the winning party that if the loser does not pay, the clearinghouse will pay the winning party. The clearinghouse is able to provide this credit guarantee by requiring a cash deposit, usually called the **margin bond** or **performance bond**, from the participants to the contract. Derivatives clearinghouses manage these deposits, occasionally requiring additional deposits, so effectively that they have never failed to pay in the nearly 100 years they have existed. We will say more about this process later and illustrate how it works.

Exchange markets are said to have **transparency**, which means that full information on all transactions is disclosed to exchanges and regulatory bodies. All transactions are centrally reported within the exchanges and their clearinghouses, and specific laws require that these markets be overseen by national regulators. Although this would seem a strong feature of exchange markets, there is a definite cost. Transparency means a loss of privacy: National regulators can see what transactions have been done. Standardization means a loss of flexibility: A participant can do only the transactions that are permitted on the exchange. Regulation means a loss of both privacy and flexibility. It is not that transparency or regulation is good and the other is bad. It is simply a trade-off.

Derivatives exchanges exist in virtually every developed (and some emerging market) countries around the world. Some exchanges specialize in derivatives and others are integrated with securities exchanges.

Although there have been attempts to create somewhat non-standardized derivatives for trading on an exchange, such attempts have not been particularly successful. Standardization is a critical element by which derivatives exchanges are able to provide their services. We will look at this point again when discussing the alternative to standardization: customized OTC derivatives.

3.2 Over-the-Counter Derivatives Markets

The OTC derivatives markets comprise an informal network of market participants that are willing to create and trade virtually any type of derivative that can legally exist. The backbone of these markets is the set of dealers, which are typically banks. Most of these banks are members of a group called the International Swaps and Derivatives Association (ISDA), a worldwide organization of financial institutions that engage in derivative transactions, primarily as dealers. As such, these markets are sometimes called *dealer markets*. Acting as principals, these dealers informally agree to buy and sell various derivatives. It is *informal* because the dealers are not obligated to do so. Their participation is based on a desire to profit, which they do by purchasing at one price and selling at a higher price. Although it might seem that a dealer who can "buy low, sell high" could make money easily, the process in practice is not that simple.

Because OTC instruments are not standardized, a dealer cannot expect to buy a derivative at one price and simultaneously sell it to a different party who happens to want to buy the same derivative at the same time and at a higher price.

To manage the risk they assume by buying and selling customized derivatives, OTC derivatives dealers typically hedge their risks by engaging in alternative but similar transactions that pass the risk on to other parties. For example, if a company comes to a dealer to buy a derivative on the euro, the company would effectively be transferring the risk of the euro to the dealer. The dealer would then attempt to lay off (get rid of) that risk by engaging in an alternative but similar transaction that would transfer the risk to another party. This hedge might involve another derivative on the euro or it might simply be a transaction in the euro itself. Of course, that begs the question of why the company could not have laid off the risk itself and avoided the dealer. Indeed, some can and do, but laying off risk is not simple. Unable to find identical offsetting transactions, dealers usually have to find *similar* transactions with which they can lay off the risk. Hedging one derivative with a different kind of derivative on the same underlying is a similar but not identical transaction. It takes specialized knowledge and complex models to be able to do such transactions effectively, and dealers are more capable of doing so than are ordinary companies. Thus, one might think of a dealer as a middleman, a sort of financial wholesaler using its specialized knowledge and resources to facilitate the transfer of risk. In the same manner that one could theoretically purchase a consumer product from a manufacturer, a network of specialized middlemen and retailers is often a more effective method.

Because of the customization of OTC derivatives, there is a tendency to think that the OTC market is less liquid than the exchange market. That is not necessarily true. Many OTC instruments can easily be created and then essentially offset by doing the exact opposite transaction, often with the same party. For example, suppose Corporation A buys an OTC derivative from Dealer B. Before the expiration date, Corporation A wants to terminate the position. It can return to Dealer B and ask to sell a derivative with identical terms. Market conditions will have changed, of course, and the value of the derivative will not be the same, but the transaction can be conducted quite easily with either Corporation A or Dealer B netting a gain at the expense of the other. Alternatively, Corporation A could do this transaction with a different dealer, the result of which would remove exposure to the underlying risk but would leave two transactions open and some risk that one party would default to the other. In contrast to this type of OTC liquidity, some exchange-traded derivatives have very little trading interest and thus relatively low liquidity. Liquidity is always driven by trading interest, which can be strong or weak in both types of markets.

OTC derivative markets operate at a lower degree of regulation and oversight than do exchange-traded derivative markets. In fact, until around 2010, it could largely be said that the OTC market was essentially unregulated. OTC transactions could be executed with only the minimal oversight provided through laws that regulated the parties themselves, not the specific instruments. Following the financial crisis that began in 2007, new regulations began to blur the distinction between OTC and exchange-listed markets. In both the United States (the Wall Street Reform and Consumer Protection Act of 2010, commonly known as the Dodd–Frank Act) and Europe (the Regulation of the European Parliament and of the Council on OTC Derivatives, Central Counterparties, and Trade Repositories), regulations are changing the characteristics of OTC markets.

When the full implementation of these new laws takes place, a number of OTC transactions will have to be cleared through central clearing agencies, information on most OTC transactions will need to be reported to regulators, and entities that operate in the OTC market will be more closely monitored. There are, however, quite a few exemptions that cover a significant percentage of derivative transactions. Clearly, the degree of OTC regulation, although increasing in recent years, is still lighter than that of exchange-listed market regulation. Many transactions in OTC markets will retain a degree of privacy with lower transparency, and most importantly, the OTC markets will remain considerably more flexible than the exchange-listed markets.

EXAMPLE 2

Exchange-Traded versus Over-the-Counter Derivatives

1 Which of the following characteristics is **not** associated with exchange-traded derivatives?

   A Margin or performance bonds are required.

   B The exchange guarantees all payments in the event of default.

   C All terms except the price are customized to the parties' individual needs.

2 Which of the following characteristics is associated with over-the-counter derivatives?

   A Trading occurs in a central location.

   B They are more regulated than exchange-listed derivatives.

   C They are less transparent than exchange-listed derivatives.

3 Market makers earn a profit in both exchange and over-the-counter derivatives markets by:

   A charging a commission on each trade.

   B a combination of commissions and markups.

   C buying at one price, selling at a higher price, and hedging any risk.

4 Which of the following statements *most* accurately describes exchange-traded derivatives relative to over-the-counter derivatives? Exchange-traded derivatives are more likely to have:

   A greater credit risk.

   B standardized contract terms.

   C greater risk management uses.

Solution to 1:

C is correct. Exchange-traded contracts are standardized, meaning that the exchange determines the terms of the contract except the price. The exchange guarantees against default and requires margins or performance bonds.

Solution to 2:

C is correct. OTC derivatives have a lower degree of transparency than exchange-listed derivatives. Trading does not occur in a central location but, rather, is quite dispersed. Although new national securities laws are tightening the regulation of OTC derivatives, the degree of regulation is less than that of exchange-listed derivatives.

Solution to 3:

C is correct. Market makers buy at one price (the bid), sell at a higher price (the ask), and hedge whatever risk they otherwise assume. Market makers do not charge a commission. Hence, A and B are both incorrect.

TYPES OF DERIVATIVES

As previously stated, derivatives fall into two general classifications: forward commitments and contingent claims. The factor that distinguishes forward commitments from contingent claims is that the former *obligate* the parties to engage in a transaction at a future date on terms agreed upon in advance, whereas the latter provide one party the *right but not the obligation* to engage in a future transaction on terms agreed upon in advance.

4.1 Forward Commitments

Forward commitments are contracts entered into at one point in time that require both parties to engage in a transaction at a later point in time (the expiration) on terms agreed upon at the start. The parties establish the identity and quantity of the underlying, the manner in which the contract will be executed or settled when it expires, and the fixed price at which the underlying will be exchanged. This fixed price is called the **forward price**.

As a hypothetical example of a forward contract, suppose that today Markus and Johannes enter into an agreement that Markus will sell his BMW to Johannes for a price of €30,000. The transaction will take place on a specified date, say, 180 days from today. At that time, Markus will deliver the vehicle to Johannes's home and Johannes will give Markus a bank-certified check for €30,000. There will be no recourse, so if the vehicle has problems later, Johannes cannot go back to Markus for compensation. It should be clear that both Markus and Johannes must do their due diligence and carefully consider the reliability of each other. The car could have serious quality issues and Johannes could have financial problems and be unable to pay the €30,000. Obviously, the transaction is essentially unregulated. Either party could renege on his obligation, in response to which the other party could go to court, provided a formal contract exists and is carefully written. Note finally that one of the two parties is likely to end up gaining and the other losing, depending on the secondary market price of this type of vehicle at expiration of the contract.

This example is quite simple but illustrates the essential elements of a forward contract. In the financial world, such contracts are very carefully written, with legal provisions that guard against fraud and require extensive credit checks. Now let us take a deeper look at the characteristics of forward contracts.

4.1.1 *Forward Contracts*

The following is the formal definition of a forward contract:

> *A forward contract is an over-the-counter derivative contract in which two parties agree that one party, the buyer, will purchase an underlying asset from the other party, the seller, at a later date at a fixed price they agree on when the contract is signed.*

In addition to agreeing on the price at which the underlying asset will be sold at a later date, the two parties also agree on several other matters, such as the specific identity of the underlying, the number of units of the underlying that will be delivered, and where the future delivery will occur. These are important points but relatively minor in this discussion, so they can be left out of the definition to keep it uncluttered.

As noted earlier, a forward contract is a commitment. Each party agrees that it will fulfill its responsibility at the designated future date. Failure to do so constitutes a default and the non-defaulting party can institute legal proceedings to enforce performance. It is important to recognize that although either party could default to the other, only one party at a time can default. The party owing the greater amount could default to the other, but the party owing the lesser amount cannot default because its claim on the other party is greater. The amount owed is always based on the net owed by one party to the other.

To gain a better understanding of forward contracts, it is necessary to examine their payoffs. As noted, forward contracts—and indeed all derivatives—take (derive) their payoffs from the performance of the underlying asset. To illustrate the payoff of a forward contract, start with the assumption that we are at time $t = 0$ and that the forward contract expires at a later date, time $t = T$.[5] The spot price of the underlying asset at time 0 is S_0 and at time T is S_T. Of course, when we initiate the contract at time 0, we do not know what S_T will ultimately be. Remember that the two parties, the buyer and the seller, are going long and short, respectively.

At time $t = 0$, the long and the short agree that the short will deliver the asset to the long at time T for a price of $F_0(T)$. The notation $F_0(T)$ denotes that this value is established at time 0 and applies to a contract expiring at time T. $F_0(T)$ is the forward price. Later, you will learn how the forward price is determined. It turns out that it is quite easy to do, but we do not need to know right now.[6]

So, let us assume that the buyer enters into the forward contract with the seller for a price of $F_0(T)$, with delivery of one unit of the underlying asset to occur at time T. Now, let us roll forward to time T, when the price of the underlying is S_T. The long is obligated to pay $F_0(T)$, for which he receives an asset worth S_T. If $S_T > F_0(T)$, it is clear that the transaction has worked out well for the long. He paid $F_0(T)$ and receives something of greater value. Thus, the contract effectively pays off $S_T - F_0(T)$ to the long, which is the value of the contract at expiration. The short has the mirror image of the long. He is required to deliver the asset worth S_T and accept a smaller amount, $F_0(T)$. The contract has a payoff for him of $F_0(T) - S_T$, which is negative. Even if the asset's value, S_T, is less than the forward price, $F_0(T)$, the payoffs are still $S_T - F_0(T)$ for the long and $F_0(T) - S_T$ for the short. We can consolidate these results by writing the short's payoff as the negative of the long's, $-[S_T - F_0(T)]$, which serves as a useful reminder that the long and the short are engaged in a zero-sum game, which is a type of competition in which one participant's gains are the other's losses. Although both lose a modest amount in the sense of both having some costs to engage in the transaction, these costs are relatively small and worth ignoring for our purposes at this time. In addition, it is worthwhile to note how derivatives transform the performance of the underlying. The gain from owning the underlying would be $S_T - S_0$, whereas the gain from owning the forward contract would be $S_T - F_0(T)$. Both figures are driven by S_T, the price of the underlying at expiration, but they are not the same.

---

5 Such notations as $t = 0$ and $t = T$ are commonly used in explaining derivatives. To indicate that $t = 0$ simply means that we initiate a contract at an imaginary time designated like a counter starting at zero. To indicate that the contract expires at $t = T$ simply means that at some future time, designated as T, the contract expires. Time T could be a certain number of days from now or a fraction of a year later or T years later. We will be more specific in later readings that involve calculations. For now, just assume that $t = 0$ and $t = T$ are two dates—the initiation and the expiration—of the contract.

6 This point is covered more fully elsewhere in the readings on derivatives, but we will see it briefly later in this reading.

Exhibit 1 illustrates the payoffs from both buying and selling a forward contract.

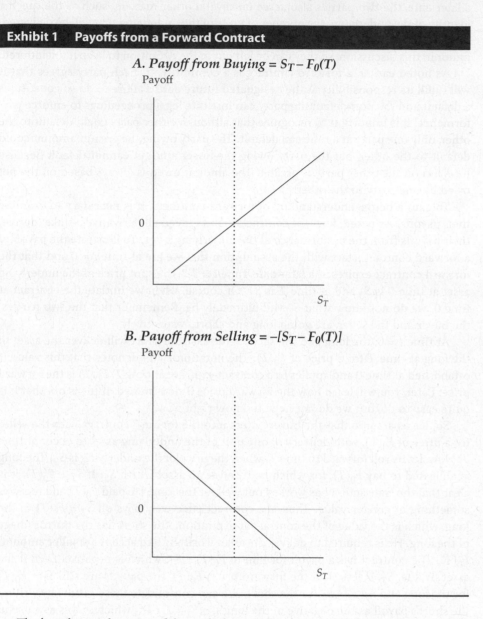

Exhibit 1   Payoffs from a Forward Contract

A. Payoff from Buying = $S_T - F_0(T)$

Payoff

S_T

B. Payoff from Selling = $-[S_T - F_0(T)]$

Payoff

S_T

The long hopes the price of the underlying will rise above the forward price, $F_0(T)$, whereas the short hopes the price of the underlying will fall below the forward price. Except in the extremely rare event that the underlying price at T equals the forward price, there will ultimately be a winner and a loser.

An important element of forward contracts is that no money changes hands between parties when the contract is initiated. Unlike in the purchase and sale of an asset, there is no value exchanged at the start. The buyer does not pay the seller some money and obtain something. In fact, forward contracts have zero value at the start. They are neither assets nor liabilities. As you will learn in later readings, their values will deviate from zero later as prices move. Forward contracts will almost always have non-zero values at expiration.

As noted previously, the primary purpose of derivatives is for risk management. Although the uses of forward contracts are covered in depth later in the curriculum, there are a few things to note here about the purposes of forward contracts. It should be apparent that locking in the future buying or selling price of an underlying asset can be extremely attractive for some parties. For example, an airline anticipating the purchase of jet fuel at a later date can enter into a forward contract to buy the fuel at a price agreed upon when the contract is initiated. In so doing, the airline has hedged its cost of fuel. Thus, forward contracts can be structured to create a perfect hedge, providing an assurance that the underlying asset can be bought or sold at a price known when the contract is initiated. Likewise, speculators, who ultimately assume the risk laid off by hedgers, can make bets on the direction of the underlying asset without having to invest the money to purchase the asset itself.

Finally, forward contracts need not specifically settle by delivery of the underlying asset. They can settle by an exchange of cash. These contracts—called **non-deliverable forwards** (NDFs), **cash-settled forwards**, or **contracts for differences**—have the same economic effect as do their delivery-based counterparts. For example, for a physical delivery contract, if the long pays $F_0(T)$ and receives an asset worth S_T, the contract is worth $S_T - F_0(T)$ to the long at expiration. A non-deliverable forward contract would have the short simply pay cash to the long in the amount of $S_T - F_0(T)$. The long would not take possession of the underlying asset, but if he wanted the asset, he could purchase it in the market for its current price of S_T. Because he received a cash settlement in the amount of $S_T - F_0(T)$, in buying the asset the long would have to pay out only $S_T - [S_T - F_0(T)]$, which equals $F_0(T)$. Thus, the long could acquire the asset, effectively paying $F_0(T)$, exactly as the contract promised. Transaction costs do make cash settlement different from physical delivery, but this point is relatively minor and can be disregarded for our purposes here.

As previously mentioned, forward contracts are OTC contracts. There is no formal forward contract exchange. Nonetheless, there are exchange-traded variants of forward contracts, which are called futures contracts or just futures.

4.1.2 *Futures*

Futures contracts are specialized versions of forward contracts that have been standardized and that trade on a futures exchange. By standardizing these contracts and creating an organized market with rules, regulations, and a central clearing facility, the futures markets offer an element of liquidity and protection against loss by default.

Formally, a futures contract is defined as follows:

> *A futures contract is a standardized derivative contract created and traded on a futures exchange in which two parties agree that one party, the buyer, will purchase an underlying asset from the other party, the seller, at a later date and at a price agreed on by the two parties when the contract is initiated and in which there is a daily settling of gains and losses and a credit guarantee by the futures exchange through its clearinghouse.*

First, let us review what standardization means. Recall that in forward contracts, the parties customize the contract by specifying the underlying asset, the time to expiration, the delivery and settlement conditions, and the quantity of the underlying, all according to whatever terms they agree on. These contracts are not traded on an exchange. As noted, the regulation of OTC derivatives markets is increasing, but these contracts are not subject to the traditionally high degree of regulation that applies to securities and futures markets. Futures contracts first require the existence of a futures exchange, a legally recognized entity that provides a market for trading these contracts. Futures exchanges are highly regulated at the national level in all countries. These exchanges specify that only certain contracts are authorized for trading. These contracts have specific underlying assets, times to expiration, delivery and settlement conditions, and quantities. The exchange offers a facility in the form of a physical location and/or an electronic system as well as liquidity provided by authorized market makers.

Probably the most important distinctive characteristic of futures contracts is the daily settlement of gains and losses and the associated credit guarantee provided by the exchange through its clearinghouse. When a party buys a futures contract, it commits to purchase the underlying asset at a later date and at a price agreed upon when the contract is initiated. The counterparty (the seller) makes the opposite commitment, an agreement to sell the underlying asset at a later date and at a price agreed upon when the contract is initiated. The agreed-upon price is called the **futures price**. Identical contracts trade on an ongoing basis at different prices, reflecting the passage of time and the arrival of new information to the market. Thus, as the futures price changes, the parties make and lose money. Rising (falling) prices, of course, benefit (hurt) the long and hurt (benefit) the short. At the end of each day, the clearinghouse engages in a practice called **mark to market**, also known as the **daily settlement**. The clearinghouse determines an average of the final futures trades of the day and designates that price as the **settlement price**. All contracts are then said to be *marked to the settlement price*. For example, if the long purchases the contract during the day at a futures price of £120 and the settlement price at the end of the day is £122, the long's account would be marked for a gain of £2. In other words, the long has made a profit of £2 and that amount is credited to his account, with the money coming from the account of the short, who has lost £2. Naturally, if the futures price decreases, the long loses money and is charged with that loss, and the money is transferred to the account of the short.[7]

The account is specifically referred to as a **margin** account. Of course, in equity markets, margin accounts are commonly used, but there are significant differences between futures margin accounts and equity margin accounts. Equity margin accounts involve the extension of credit. An investor deposits part of the cost of the stock and borrows the remainder at a rate of interest. With futures margin accounts, both parties deposit a required minimum sum of money, but the remainder of the price is not borrowed. This required margin is typically less than 10% of the futures price, which is considerably less than in equity margin trading. In the example above, let us assume that the required margin is £10, which is referred to as the **initial margin**. Both the long and the short put that amount into their respective margin accounts. This money is deposited there to support the trade, not as a form of equity, with the remaining amount borrowed. There is no formal loan created as in equity markets. A futures margin is more of a performance bond or good faith deposit, terms that were previously mentioned. It is simply an amount of money put into an account that covers possible future losses.

Associated with each initial margin is another figure called the **maintenance margin**. The maintenance margin is the amount of money that each participant must maintain in the account after the trade is initiated, and it is always significantly lower than the initial margin. Let us assume that the maintenance margin in this example is £6. If the buyer's account is marked to market with a credit of £2, his margin balance moves to £12, while the seller's account is charged £2 and his balance moves to £8. The clearinghouse then compares each participant's balance with the maintenance margin. At this point, both participants more than meet the maintenance margin.

Let us say, however, that the price continues to move in the long's favor and, therefore, against the short. A few days later, assume that the short's balance falls to £4, which is below the maintenance margin requirement of £6. The short will then get a **margin call**, which is a request to deposit additional funds. The amount that

---

7 The actual amount of money charged and credited depends on the contract size and the number of contracts. A price of £120 might actually refer to a contract that has a standard size of £100,000. Thus, £120 might actually mean 120% of the standard size, or £120,000. In addition, the parties are likely to hold more than one contract. Hence, the gain of £2 referred to in the text might really mean £2,000 (122% minus 120% times the £100,000 standard size) times the number of contracts held by the party.

the short has to deposit, however, is *not* the £2 that would bring his balance up to the maintenance margin. Instead, the short must deposit enough funds to bring the balance up to the initial margin. So, the short must come up with £6. The purpose of this rule is to get the party's position significantly above the minimum level and provide some breathing room. If the balance were brought up only to the maintenance level, there would likely be another margin call soon. A party can choose not to deposit additional funds, in which case the party would be required to close out the contract as soon as possible and would be responsible for any additional losses until the position is closed.

As with forward contracts, neither party pays any money to the other when the contract is initiated. Value accrues as the futures price changes, but at the end of each day, the mark-to-market process settles the gains and losses, effectively resetting the value for each party to zero.

The clearinghouse moves money between the participants, crediting gains to the winners and charging losses to the losers. By doing this on a daily basis, the gains and losses are typically quite small, and the margin balances help ensure that the clearinghouse will collect from the party losing money. As an extra precaution, in fast-moving markets, the clearinghouse can make margin calls during the day, not just at the end of the day. Yet there still remains the possibility that a party could default. A large loss could occur quickly and consume the entire margin balance, with additional money owed.[8] If the losing party cannot pay, the clearinghouse provides a guarantee that it will make up the loss, which it does by maintaining an insurance fund. If that fund were depleted, the clearinghouse could levy a tax on the other market participants, though that has never happened.

Some futures contracts contain a provision limiting price changes. These rules, called **price limits**, establish a band relative to the previous day's settlement price, within which all trades must occur. If market participants wish to trade at a price above the upper band, trading stops, which is called **limit up**, until two parties agree on a trade at a price lower than the upper limit. Likewise, if market participants wish to trade at a price below the lower band, which is called **limit down**, no trade can take place until two parties agree to trade at a price above the lower limit. When the market hits these limits and trading stops, it is called **locked limit**. Typically, the exchange rules provide for an expansion of the limits the next day. These price limits, which may be somewhat objectionable to proponents of free markets, are important in helping the clearinghouse manage its credit exposure. Just because two parties wish to trade a futures contract at a price beyond the limits does not mean they should be allowed to do so. The clearinghouse is a third participant in the contract, guaranteeing to each party that it ensures against the other party defaulting. Therefore, the clearinghouse has a vested interest in the price and considerable exposure. Sharply moving prices make it more difficult for the clearinghouse to collect from the parties losing money.

Most participants in futures markets buy and sell contracts, collecting their profits and incurring their losses, with no ultimate intent to make or take delivery of the underlying asset. For example, the long may ultimately sell her position before expiration. When a party re-enters the market at a later date but before expiration and engages in the opposite transaction—a long selling her previously opened contract or a short buying her previously opened contract—the transaction is referred to as an offset. The clearinghouse marks the contract to the current price relative to the previous settlement price and closes out the participant's position.

---

8 For example, let us go back to when the short had a balance of £4, which is £2 below the maintenance margin and £6 below the initial margin. The short will get a margin call, but suppose he elects not to deposit additional funds and requests that his position be terminated. In a fast-moving market, the price might increase more than £4 before his broker can close his position. The remaining balance of £4 would then be depleted, and the short would be responsible for any additional losses.

At any given time, the number of outstanding contracts is called the **open interest**. Each contract counted in the open interest has a long and a corresponding short. The open interest figure changes daily as some parties open up new positions, while other parties offset their old positions. It is theoretically possible that all longs and shorts offset their positions before expiration, leaving no open interest when the contract expires, but in practice there is nearly always some open interest at expiration, at which time there is a final delivery or settlement.

When discussing forward contracts, we noted that a contract could be written such that the parties engage in physical delivery or cash settlement at expiration. In the futures markets, the exchange specifies whether physical delivery or cash settlement applies. In physical delivery contracts, the short is required to deliver the underlying asset at a designated location and the long is required to pay for it. Delivery replaces the mark-to-market process on the final day. It also ensures an important principle that you will use later: *The futures price converges to the spot price at expiration.* Because the short delivers the actual asset and the long pays the current spot price for it, the futures price at expiration has to be the spot price at that time. Alternatively, a futures contract initiated right at the instant of expiration is effectively a spot transaction and, therefore, the futures price at expiration must equal the spot price. Following this logic, in cash settlement contracts, there is a final mark to market, with the futures price formally set to the spot price, thereby ensuring automatic convergence.

In discussing forward contracts, we described the process by which they pay off as the spot price at expiration minus the forward price, $S_T - F_0(T)$, the former determined at expiration and the latter agreed upon when the contract is initiated. Futures contracts basically pay off the same way, but there is a slight difference. Let us say the contract is initiated on Day 0 and expires on Day T. The intervening days are designated Days 1, 2, ..., T. The initial futures price is designated $f_0(T)$ and the daily settlement prices on Days 1, 2, ..., T are designated $f_1(T), f_2(T), ... f_T(T)$. There are, of course, futures prices within each trading day, but let us focus only on the settlement prices for now. For simplicity, let us assume that the long buys at the settlement price on Day 0 and holds the position all the way to expiration. Through the mark-to-market process, the cash flows to the account of the long will be

$$f_1(T) - f_0(T) \text{ on Day 1}$$
$$f_2(T) - f_1(T) \text{ on Day 2}$$
$$f_3(T) - f_2(T) \text{ on Day 3}$$
$$...$$
$$f_T(T) - f_{T-1}(T) \text{ on Day } T$$

These add up to

$f_T(T) - f_0(T)$ on Day T.

And because of the convergence of the final futures price to the spot price,

$f_T(T) - f_0(T) = S_T - f_0(T)$,

which is the same as with forward contracts.[9] Note, however, that the timing of these profits is different from that of forwards. Forward contracts realize the full amount, $S_T - f_0(T)$, at expiration, whereas futures contracts realize this amount in parts on a day-to-day basis. Naturally, the time value of money principle says that these are not equivalent amounts of money. But the differences tend to be small, particularly in low-interest-rate environments, some of these amounts are gains and some are losses, and most futures contracts have maturities of less than a year.

---

9 Because of this equivalence, we will not specifically illustrate the profit graphs of futures contracts. You can generally treat them the same as those of forwards, which were shown in Exhibit 1.

But the near equivalence of the profits from a futures and a forward contract disguises an important distinction between these types of contracts. In a forward contact, with the entire payoff made at expiration, a loss by one party can be large enough to trigger a default. Hence, forward contracts are subject to default and require careful consideration of the credit quality of the counterparties. Because futures contracts settle gains and collect losses daily, the amounts that could be lost upon default are much smaller and naturally give the clearinghouse much greater flexibility to manage the credit risk it assumes.

Unlike forward markets, futures markets are highly regulated at the national level. National regulators are required to approve new futures exchanges and even new contracts proposed by existing exchanges as well as changes in margin requirements, price limits, and any significant changes in trading procedures. Violations of futures regulations can be subject to governmental prosecution. In addition, futures markets are far more transparent than forward markets. Futures prices, volume, and open interest are widely reported and easily obtained. Futures prices of nearby expiring contracts are often used as proxies for spot prices, particularly in decentralized spot markets, such as gold, which trades in spot markets all over the world.

In spite of the advantages of futures markets over forward markets, forward markets also have advantages over futures markets. Transparency is not always a good thing. Forward markets offer more privacy and fewer regulatory encumbrances. In addition, forward markets offer more flexibility. With the ability to tailor contracts to the specific needs of participants, forward contracts can be written exactly the way the parties want. In contrast, the standardization of futures contracts makes it more difficult for participants to get exactly what they want, even though they may get close substitutes. Yet, futures markets offer a valuable credit guarantee.

Like forward markets, futures markets can be used for hedging or speculation. For example, a jewelry manufacturer can buy gold futures, thereby hedging the price it will have to pay for one of its key inputs. Although it is more difficult to construct a futures strategy that hedges perfectly than to construct a forward strategy that does so, futures offer the benefit of the credit guarantee. It is not possible to argue that futures are better than forwards or vice versa. Market participants always trade off advantages against disadvantages. Some participants prefer futures, and some prefer forwards. Some prefer one over the other for certain risks and the other for other risks. Some might use one for a particular risk at a point in time and a different instrument for the same risk at another point in time. The choice is a matter of taste and constraints.

The third and final type of forward commitment we will cover is swaps. They go a step further in committing the parties to buy and sell something at a later date: They obligate the parties to a sequence of multiple purchases and sales.

4.1.3 *Swaps*

The concept of a swap is that two parties exchange (swap) a series of cash flows. One set of cash flows is variable or floating and will be determined by the movement of an underlying asset or rate. The other set of cash flows can be variable and determined by a different underlying asset or rate, or it can be fixed. Formally, a swap is defined as follows:

> A swap is an over-the-counter derivative contract in which two parties agree to exchange a series of cash flows whereby one party pays a variable series that will be determined by an underlying asset or rate and the other party pays either (1) a variable series determined by a different underlying asset or rate or (2) a fixed series.

As with forward contracts, swap contracts also contain other terms—such as the identity of the underlying, the relevant payment dates, and the payment procedure—that are negotiated between the parties and written into the contract. A swap is a bit more like a forward contract than a futures contract in that it is an OTC contract, so it is privately negotiated and subject to default. Nonetheless, the similarities between futures and forwards apply to futures and swaps and, indeed, combinations of futures contracts expiring at different dates are often compared to swaps.

As with forward contracts, either party can default but only one party can default at a particular time. The money owed is always based on the net owed by one party to the other. Hence, the party owing the lesser amount cannot default to the party owing the greater amount. Only the latter can default, and the amount it owes is the net of what it owes and what is owed to it, which is also true with forwards.

Swaps are relatively young financial instruments, having been created only in the early 1980s. Thus, it may be somewhat surprising to learn that the swap is the most widely used derivative, a likely result of its simplicity and embracement by the corporate world. The most common swap is the **fixed-for-floating interest rate swap**. In fact, this type of swap is so common that it is often called a "plain vanilla swap" or just a "vanilla swap," owing to the notion that vanilla ice cream is considered plain (albeit tasty).

Let us examine a scenario in which the vanilla interest rate swap is frequently used. Suppose a corporation borrows from a bank at a floating rate. It would prefer a fixed rate, which would enable it to better anticipate its cash flow needs in making its interest payments.[10] The corporation can effectively convert its floating-rate loan to a fixed-rate loan by adding a swap, as shown in Exhibit 2.

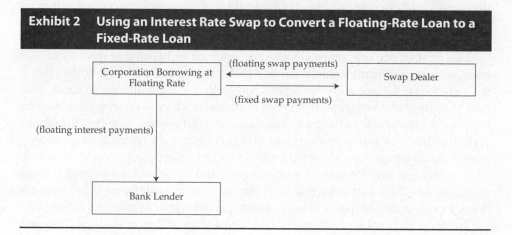

Exhibit 2   Using an Interest Rate Swap to Convert a Floating-Rate Loan to a Fixed-Rate Loan

The interest payments on the loan are tied to a specific floating rate. For a dollar-based loan, that rate has typically been US dollar Libor.[11] The payments would be based on the rate from the Libor market on a specified reset date times the loan balance times a factor reflecting the number of days in the current interest calculation period. The actual payment is made at a later date. Thus, for a loan balance of, say, $10 million with monthly payments, the rate might be based on Libor on the first business day of the month, with interest payable on the first business day of the next month, which is the next reset date, and calculated as $10 million times the rate times 30/360. The

---

10 Banks prefer to make floating-rate loans because their own funding is typically short term and at floating rates. Thus, their borrowing rates reset frequently, giving them a strong incentive to pass that risk on to their customers through floating-rate loans.

11 Recall that US dollar Libor (London Interbank Offered Rate) is the estimated rate on a dollar-based loan made by one London bank to another. Such a loan takes the form of a time deposit known as a Eurodollar because it represents a dollar deposited in a European bank account. In fact, Libor is the same as the so-called Eurodollar rate. The banks involved can be British banks or British branches of non-British banks. The banks estimate their borrowing rates, and a single average rate is assembled and reported each day. That rate is then commonly used to set the rate on many derivative contracts.

30/360 convention, an implicit assumption of 30 days in a month, is common but only one of many interest calculation conventions used in the financial world. Often, "30" is replaced by the exact number of days since the last interest payment. The use of a 360-day year is a common assumption in the financial world, which originated in the pre-calculator days when an interest rate could be multiplied by a number like 30/360, 60/360, 90/360, etc., more easily than if 365 were used.

Whatever the terms of the loan are, the terms of the swap are typically set to match those of the loan. Thus, a Libor-based loan with monthly payments based on the 30/360 convention would be matched with a swap with monthly payments based on Libor and the 30/360 convention and the same reset and payment dates. Although the loan has an actual balance (the amount owed by borrower to creditor), the swap does not have such a balance owed by one party to the other. Thus, it has no principal, but it does have a balance of sorts, called the **notional principal**, which ordinarily matches the loan balance. A loan with only one principal payment, the final one, will be matched with a swap with a fixed notional principal. An amortizing loan, which has a declining principal balance, will be matched with a swap with a pre-specified declining notional principal that matches the loan balance.

As with futures and forwards, no money changes hands at the start; thus, the value of a swap when initiated must be zero. The fixed rate on the swap is determined by a process that forces the value to zero, a procedure that will be covered later in the curriculum. As market conditions change, the value of a swap will deviate from zero, being positive to one party and negative to the other.

As with forward contracts, swaps are subject to default, but because the notional amount of a swap is not typically exchanged, the credit risk of a swap is much less than that of a loan.[12] The only money passing from one party to the other is the net difference between the fixed and floating interest payments. In fact, the parties do not even pay each other. Only one party pays the other, as determined by the net of the greater amount owed minus the lesser amount. This does not mean that swaps are not subject to a potentially large amount of credit risk. At a given point in time, one party could default, effectively owing the value of all remaining payments, which could substantially exceed the value that the non-defaulting party owes to the defaulting party. Thus, there is indeed credit risk in a swap. This risk must be managed by careful analysis before the transaction and by the potential use of such risk-mitigating measures as collateral.

There are also interest rate swaps in which one party pays on the basis of one interest rate and the other party pays on the basis of a different interest rate. For example, one party might make payments at Libor, whereas the other might make payments on the basis of the U. S. Treasury bill rate. The difference between Libor and the T-bill rate, often called the TED spread (T-bills versus Eurodollar), is a measure of the credit risk premium of London banks, which have historically borrowed short term at Libor, versus that of the U. S. government, which borrows short term at the T-bill rate. This transaction is called a basis swap. There are also swaps in which the floating rate is set as an average rate over the period, in accordance with the convention for many loans. Some swaps, called overnight indexed swaps, are tied to a Fed funds–type rate, reflecting the rate at which banks borrow overnight. As we will cover later, there are many other different types of swaps that are used for a variety of purposes. The plain vanilla swap is merely the simplest and most widely used.

---

12 It is possible that the notional principal will be exchanged in a currency swap, whereby each party makes a series of payments to the other in different currencies. Whether the notional principal is exchanged depends on the purpose of the swap. This point will be covered later in the curriculum. At this time, you should see that it would be fruitless to exchange notional principals in an interest rate swap because that would mean each party would give the other the same amount of money when the transaction is initiated and re-exchange the same amount of money when the contract terminates.

Because swaps, forwards, and futures are forward commitments, they can all accomplish the same thing. One could create a series of forwards or futures expiring at a set of dates that would serve the same purpose as a swap. Although swaps are better suited for risks that involve multiple payments, at its most fundamental level, a swap is more or less just a series of forwards and, acknowledging the slight differences discussed above, more or less just a series of futures.

EXAMPLE 3

Forward Contracts, Futures Contracts, and Swaps

1   Which of the following characterizes forward contracts and swaps but **not** futures?
    A   They are customized.
    B   They are subject to daily price limits.
    C   Their payoffs are received on a daily basis.
2   Which of the following distinguishes forwards from swaps?
    A   Forwards are OTC instruments, whereas swaps are exchange traded.
    B   Forwards are regulated as futures, whereas swaps are regulated as securities.
    C   Swaps have multiple payments, whereas forwards have only a single payment.
3   Which of the following occurs in the daily settlement of futures contracts?
    A   Initial margin deposits are refunded to the two parties.
    B   Gains and losses are reported to other market participants.
    C   Losses are charged to one party and gains credited to the other.

Solution to 1:

A is correct. Forwards and swaps are OTC contracts and, therefore, are customized. Futures are exchange traded and, therefore, are standardized. Some futures contracts are subject to daily price limits and their payoffs are received daily, but these characteristics are not true for forwards and swaps.

Solution to 2:

C is correct. Forwards and swaps are OTC instruments and both are regulated as such. Neither is regulated as a futures contract or a security. A swap is a series of multiple payments at scheduled dates, whereas a forward has only one payment, made at its expiration date.

Solution to 3:

C is correct. Losses and gains are collected and distributed to the respective parties. There is no specific reporting of these gains and losses to anyone else. Initial margin deposits are not refunded and, in fact, additional deposits may be required.

This material completes our introduction to forward commitments. All forward commitments are firm contracts. The parties are required to fulfill the obligations they agreed to. The benefit of this rigidity is that neither party pays anything to the other when the contract is initiated. If one party needs some flexibility, however, it can get it by agreeing to pay the other party some money when the contract is initiated. When the contract expires, the party who paid at the start has some flexibility in deciding whether to buy the underlying asset at the fixed price. Thus, that party did not actually agree to do anything. It had a choice. This is the nature of contingent claims.

4.2 Contingent Claims

A **contingent claim** is a derivative in which the outcome or payoff is dependent on the outcome or payoff of an underlying asset. Although this characteristic is also associated with forward commitments, a contingent claim has come to be associated with a *right*, but not an *obligation*, to make a final payment contingent on the performance of the underlying. Given that the holder of the contingent claim has a choice, the term *contingent claim* has become synonymous with the term *option*. The holder has a choice of whether or not to exercise the option. This choice creates a payoff that transforms the underlying payoff in a more pronounced manner than does a forward, futures, or swap. Those instruments provide linear payoffs: As the underlying goes up (down), the derivative gains (loses). The further up (down) the underlying goes, the more the derivative gains (loses). Options are different in that they limit losses in one direction. In addition, options can pay off as the underlying goes down. Hence, they transform the payoffs of the underlying into something quite different.

4.2.1 *Options*

We might say that an option, as a contingent claim, grants the right but not the obligation to buy an asset at a later date and at a price agreed on when the option is initiated. But there are so many variations of options that we cannot settle on this statement as a good formal definition. For one thing, options can also grant the right to sell instead of the right to buy. Moreover, they can grant the right to buy or sell earlier than at expiration. So, let us see whether we can combine these points into an all-encompassing definition of an option.

> *An option is a derivative contract in which one party, the buyer, pays a sum of money to the other party, the seller or writer, and receives the right to either buy or sell an underlying asset at a fixed price either on a specific expiration date or at any time prior to the expiration date.*

Unfortunately, even that definition does not cover every unique aspect of options. For example, options can be created in the OTC market and customized to the terms of each party, or they can be created and traded on options exchanges and standardized. As with forward contracts and swaps, customized options are subject to default but are less regulated and relatively transparent. Exchange-traded options are protected against default by the clearinghouse of the options exchange and are relatively transparent and regulated at the national level. As noted in the definition above, options can be terminated early or at their expirations. When an option is terminated, either early or at expiration, the holder of the option chooses whether to exercise it. If he exercises it, he either buys or sells the underlying asset, but he does not have both rights. The right to buy is one type of option, referred to as a **call** or **call option**, whereas the right to sell is another type of option, referred to as a **put** or **put option**. With one very unusual and advanced exception that we do not cover, an option is either a call or a put, and that point is made clear in the contract.

An option is also designated as exercisable early (before expiration) or only at expiration. Options that can be exercised early are referred to as **American-style**. Options that can be exercised only at expiration are referred to as **European-style**. *It is extremely important that you do not associate these terms with where these options are traded.* Both types of options trade on all continents.[13]

As with forwards and futures, an option can be exercised by physical delivery or cash settlement, as written in the contract. For a call option with physical delivery, upon exercise the underlying asset is delivered to the call buyer, who pays the call seller the exercise price. For a put option with physical delivery, upon exercise the put buyer delivers the underlying asset to the put seller and receives the strike price. For a cash settlement option, exercise results in the seller paying the buyer the cash equivalent value as if the asset were delivered and paid for.

The fixed price at which the underlying asset can be purchased is called the **exercise price** (also called the "strike price," the "strike," or the "striking price"). This price is somewhat analogous to the forward price because it represents the price at which the underlying will be purchased or sold if the option is exercised. The forward price, however, is set in the pricing of the contract such that the contract value at the start is zero. The strike price of the option is chosen by the participants. The actual price or value of the option is an altogether different concept.

As noted, the buyer pays the writer a sum of money called the **option premium**, or just the "premium." It represents a fair price of the option, and in a well-functioning market, it would be the value of the option. Consistent with everything we know about finance, it is the present value of the cash flows that are expected to be received by the holder of the option during the life of the option. At this point, we will not get into how this price is determined, but you will learn that later. For now, there are some fundamental concepts you need to understand, which form a basis for understanding how options are priced and why anyone would use an option.

Because the option buyer (the long) does not have to exercise the option, beyond the initial payment of the premium, there is no obligation of the long to the short. Thus, only the short can default, which would occur if the long exercises the option and the short fails to do what it is supposed to do. Thus, in contrast to forwards and swaps, in which either party could default to the other, default in options is possible only from the short to the long.

Ruling out the possibility of default for now, let us examine what happens when an option expires. Using the same notation used previously, let S_T be the price of the underlying at the expiration date, T, and X be the exercise price of the option. Remember that a call option allows the holder, or long, to pay X and receive the underlying. It should be obvious that the long would exercise the option at expiration if S_T is greater than X, meaning that the underlying value is greater than what he would pay to obtain the underlying. Otherwise, he would simply let the option expire. Thus, on the expiration date, the option is described as having a payoff of $Max(0, S_T - X)$. Because the holder of the option would be entitled to exercise it and claim this amount, it also represents the value of the option at expiration. Let us denote that value as c_T. Thus,

$$c_T = Max(0, S_T - X) \qquad \text{(payoff to the call buyer)},$$

which is read as "take the maximum of either zero or $S_T - X$." Thus, if the underlying value exceeds the exercise price ($S_T > X$), then the option value is positive and equal to $S_T - X$. The call option is then said to be **in the money**. If the underlying value is less than the exercise price ($S_T < X$), then $S_T - X$ is negative; zero is greater than a

---

13 For example, you do not associate French dressing with France. It is widely available and enjoyed worldwide. If you dig deeper into the world of options, you will find Asian options and Bermuda options. Geography is a common source of names for options as well as foods and in no way implies that the option or the food is available only in that geographical location.

negative number, so the option value would be zero. When the underlying value is less than the exercise price, the call option is said to be **out of the money**. When $S_T = X$, the call option is said to be **at the money**, although at the money is, for all practical purposes, out of the money because the value is still zero.

This payoff amount is also the value of the option at expiration. It represents value because it is what the option is worth at that point. If the holder of the option sells it to someone else an instant before expiration, it should sell for that amount because the new owner would exercise it and capture that amount. To the seller, the value of the option at that point is $-Max(0, S_T - X)$, which is negative to the seller if the option is in the money and zero otherwise.

Using the payoff value and the price paid for the option, we can determine the profit from the strategy, which is denoted with the Greek symbol Π. Let us say the buyer paid c_0 for the option at time 0. Then the profit is

$$\Pi = Max(0, S_T - X) - c_0 \qquad \text{(profit to the call buyer).}$$

To the seller, who received the premium at the start, the payoff is

$$-c_T = -Max(0, S_T - X) \qquad \text{(payoff to the call seller).}$$

The profit is

$$\Pi = -Max(0, S_T - X) + c_0 \qquad \text{(profit to the call seller).}$$

Exhibit 3 illustrates the payoffs and profits to the call buyer and seller as graphical representations of these equations, with the payoff or value at expiration indicated by the dark line and the profit indicated by the light line. Note in Panel A that the buyer has no upper limit on the profit and has a fixed downside loss limit equal to the premium paid for the option. Such a condition, with limited loss and unlimited gain, is a temptation to many unsuspecting investors, but keep in mind that the graph does not indicate the frequency with which gains and losses will occur. Panel B is the mirror image of Panel A and shows that the seller has unlimited losses and limited gains. One might suspect that selling a call is, therefore, the worst investment strategy possible. Indeed, it is a risky strategy, but at this point these are only simple strategies. Other strategies can be added to mitigate the seller's risk to a substantial degree.

Exhibit 3   Payoff and Profit from a Call Option

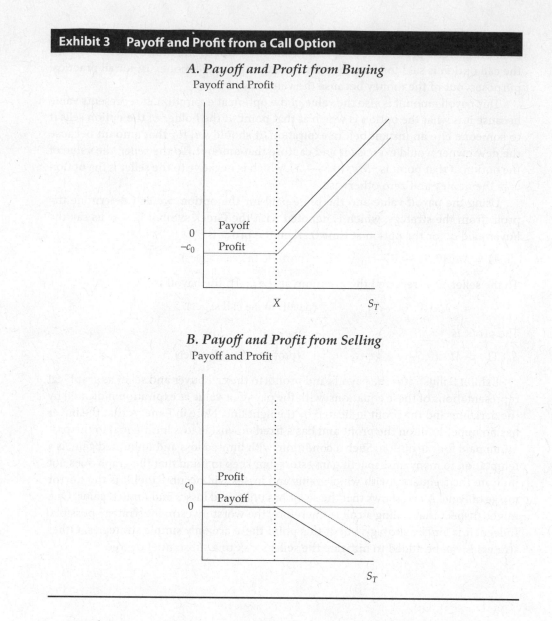

A. Payoff and Profit from Buying

B. Payoff and Profit from Selling

Now let us consider put options. Recall that a put option allows its holder to sell the underlying asset at the exercise price. Thus, the holder should exercise the put at expiration if the underlying asset is worth less than the exercise price ($S_T < X$). In that case, the put is said to be in the money. If the underlying asset is worth the same as the exercise price ($S_T = X$), meaning the put is at the money, or more than the exercise price ($S_T > X$), meaning the put is out of the money, the option holder would not exercise it and it would expire with zero value. Thus, the payoff to the put holder is

$$p_T = Max(0, X - S_T) \qquad \text{(payoff to the put buyer)}.$$

If the put buyer paid p_0 for the put at time 0, the profit is

$$\Pi = Max(0, X - S_T) - p_0 \qquad \text{(profit to the put buyer)}.$$

And for the seller, the payoff is

$$-p_T = -Max(0, X - S_T) \qquad \text{(payoff to the put seller)}.$$

And the profit is

$$\Pi = -Max(0, X - S_T) + p_0 \qquad \text{(profit to the put seller)}.$$

Exhibit 4 illustrates the payoffs and profits to the buyer and seller of a put.

Exhibit 4   Payoff and Profit from a Put Option

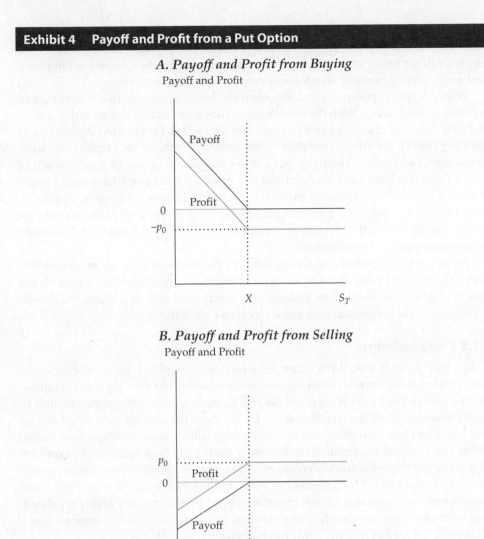

A. Payoff and Profit from Buying
Payoff and Profit

B. Payoff and Profit from Selling
Payoff and Profit

The put buyer has a limited loss, and although the gain is limited by the fact that the underlying value cannot go below zero, the put buyer does gain more the lower the value of the underlying. In this manner, we see how a put option is like insurance. Bad outcomes for the underlying trigger a payoff for both the insurance policy and the put, whereas good outcomes result only in loss of the premium. The put seller, like the insurer, has a limited gain and a loss that is larger the lower the value of the underlying. As with call options, these graphs must be considered carefully because they do not indicate the frequency with which gains and losses will occur. At this point, it should be apparent that buying a call option is consistent with a bullish point of view and buying a put option is consistent with a bearish point of view. Moreover, in contrast to forward commitments, which have payoffs that are linearly related to the payoffs of the underlying (note the straight lines in Exhibit 1), contingent claims have payoffs that are non-linear in relation to the underlying. There is linearity over a range—say, from 0 to X or from X upward or downward—but over the entire range of values for the underlying, the payoffs of contingent claims cannot be depicted with a single straight line.

We have seen only a snapshot of the payoff and profit graphs that can be created with options. Calls can be combined with puts, the underlying asset, and other calls or puts with different expirations and exercise prices to create a diverse set of payoff and profit graphs, some of which are covered later in the curriculum.

Before leaving options, let us again contrast the differences between options and forward commitments. With the former, the parties agree to trade an underlying asset at a later date and at a price agreed upon when the contract is initiated. Neither party pays any cash to the other at the start. With options, the buyer pays cash to the seller at the start and receives the right, but not the obligation, to buy (if a call) or sell (if a put) the underlying asset at expiration at a price agreed upon (the exercise price) when the contract is initiated. In contrast to forwards, futures, and swaps, options do have value at the start: the premium paid by buyer to seller. That premium pays for the *right*, eliminating the *obligation*, to trade the underlying at a later date, as would be the case with a forward commitment.

Although there are numerous variations of options, most have the same essential features described here. There is, however, a distinctive family of contingent claims that emerged in the early 1990s and became widely used and, in some cases, heavily criticized. These instruments are known as credit derivatives.

4.2.2 *Credit Derivatives*

Credit risk is surely one of the oldest risks known to mankind. Human beings have been lending things to each other for thousands of years, and even the most primitive human beings must have recognized the risk of lending some of their possessions to their comrades. Until the last 20 years or so, however, the management of credit risk was restricted to simply doing the best analysis possible before making a loan, monitoring the financial condition of the borrower during the loan, limiting the exposure to a given party, and requiring collateral. Some modest forms of insurance against credit risk have existed for a number of years, but insurance can be a slow and cumbersome way of protecting against credit loss. Insurance is typically highly regulated, and insurance laws are usually very consumer oriented. Thus, credit insurance as a financial product has met with only modest success.

In the early 1990s, however, the development of the swaps market led to the creation of derivatives that would hedge credit risk. These instruments came to be known as **credit derivatives**, and they avoided many of the regulatory constraints of the traditional insurance industry. Here is a formal definition:

> *A credit derivative is a class of derivative contracts between two parties, a credit protection buyer and a credit protection seller, in which the latter provides protection to the former against a specific credit loss.*

One of the first credit derivatives was a **total return swap**, in which the underlying is typically a bond or loan, in contrast to, say, a stock or stock index. The credit protection buyer offers to pay the credit protection seller the total return on the underlying bond. This total return consists of all interest and principal paid by the borrower plus any changes in the bond's market value. In return, the credit protection seller typically pays the credit protection buyer either a fixed or a floating rate of interest. Thus, if the bond defaults, the credit protection seller must continue to make its promised payments, while receiving a very small return or virtually no return from the credit protection buyer. If the bond incurs a loss, as it surely will if it defaults, the credit protection seller effectively pays the credit protection buyer.

Another type of credit derivative is the **credit spread option**, in which the underlying is the credit (yield) spread on a bond, which is the difference between the bond's yield and the yield on a benchmark default-free bond. As you will learn in the fixed-income material, the credit spread is a reflection of investors' perception of credit risk. Because a credit spread option requires a credit spread as the underlying, this type of derivative works only with a traded bond that has a quoted price. The credit protection buyer selects the strike spread it desires and pays the option premium to the credit protection seller. At expiration, the parties determine whether the option is in the money by comparing the bond's yield spread with the strike chosen, and if it is, the credit protection seller pays the credit protection buyer the established payoff. Thus, this instrument is essentially a call option in which the underlying is the credit spread.

A third type of credit derivative is the **credit-linked note**. With this derivative, the credit protection buyer holds a bond or loan that is subject to default risk (the underlying reference security) and issues its own security (the credit-linked note) with the condition that if the bond or loan it holds defaults, the principal payoff on the credit-linked note is reduced accordingly. Thus, the buyer of the credit-linked note effectively insures the credit risk of the underlying reference security.

These three types of credit derivatives have had limited success compared with the fourth type of credit derivative, the **credit default swap (CDS)**. The credit default swap, in particular, has achieved much success by capturing many of the essential features of insurance while avoiding the high degree of consumer regulations that are typically associated with traditional insurance products.

In a CDS, one party—the credit protection buyer, who is seeking credit protection against a third party—makes a series of regularly scheduled payments to the other party, the credit protection seller. The seller makes no payments until a credit event occurs. A declaration of bankruptcy is clearly a credit event, but there are other types of credit events, such as a failure to make a scheduled payment or an involuntary restructuring. The CDS contract specifies what constitutes a credit event, and the industry has a procedure for declaring credit events, though that does not guarantee the parties will not end up in court arguing over whether something was or was not a credit event.

Formally, a credit default swap is defined as follows:

> *A credit default swap is a derivative contract between two parties, a credit protection buyer and a credit protection seller, in which the buyer makes a series of cash payments to the seller and receives a promise of compensation for credit losses resulting from the default of a third party.*

A CDS is conceptually a form of insurance. Sellers of CDSs, oftentimes banks or insurance companies, collect periodic payments and are required to pay out if a loss occurs from the default of a third party. These payouts could take the form of restitution of the defaulted amount or the party holding the defaulting asset could turn it over to the CDS seller and receive a fixed amount. The most common approach is for the payout to be determined by an auction to estimate the market value of the defaulting debt. Thus, CDSs effectively provide coverage against a loss in return for the protection buyer paying a premium to the protection seller, thereby taking the form of insurance against credit loss. Although insurance contracts have certain legal characteristics that are not found in credit default swaps, the two instruments serve similar purposes and operate in virtually the same way: payments made by one party in return for a promise to cover losses incurred by the other.

Exhibit 5 illustrates the typical use of a CDS by a lender. The lender is exposed to the risk of non-payment of principal and interest. The lender lays off this risk by purchasing a CDS from a CDS seller. The lender—now the CDS buyer—promises to make a series of periodic payments to the CDS seller, who then stands ready to compensate the CDS buyer for credit losses.

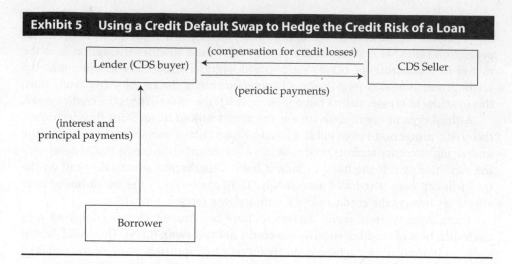

Exhibit 5   Using a Credit Default Swap to Hedge the Credit Risk of a Loan

Clearly, the CDS seller is betting on the borrower's not defaulting or—more generally, as insurance companies operate—that the total payouts it is responsible for are less than the total payments collected. Of course, most insurance companies are able to do this by having reliable actuarial statistics, diversifying their risk, and selling some of the risk to other insurance companies. Actuarial statistics are typically quite solid. Average claims for life, health, and casualty insurance are well documented, and insurers can normally set premiums to cover losses and operate at a reasonable profit. Although insurance companies try to manage some of their risks at the micro level (e.g., charging smokers more for life and health insurance), most of their risk management is at the macro level, wherein they attempt to make sure their risks are not concentrated. Thus, they avoid selling too much homeowners insurance to individuals in tornado-prone areas. If they have such an exposure, they can use the reinsurance market to sell some of the risk to other companies that are not overexposed to that risk. Insurance companies attempt to diversify their risks and rely on the principle of uncorrelated risks, which plays such an important role in portfolio management. A well-diversified insurance company, like a well-diversified portfolio, should be able to earn a return commensurate with its assumed risk in the long run.

Credit default swaps should operate the same way. Sellers of CDSs should recognize when their credit risk is too concentrated. When that happens, they become buyers of CDSs from other parties or find other ways to lay off the risk. Unfortunately, during the financial crisis that began in 2007, many sellers of CDSs failed to recognize the high correlations among borrowers whose debt they had guaranteed. One well-known CDS seller, AIG, is a large and highly successful traditional insurance company that got into the business of selling CDSs. Many of these CDSs insured against mortgages. With the growth of the subprime mortgage market, many of these CDS-insured mortgages had a substantial amount of credit risk and were often poorly documented. AIG and many other CDS sellers were thus highly exposed to systemic credit contagion, a situation in which defaults in one area of an economy ripple into another, accompanied by bank weaknesses and failures, rapidly falling equity markets, rising credit risk premiums, and a general loss of confidence in the financial system and the economy. These presumably well-diversified risks guaranteed by CDS sellers, operating as though they were insurance companies, ultimately proved to be poorly diversified. Systemic financial risks can spread more rapidly than fire, health, and casualty risks. Virtually no other risks, except those originating from wars or epidemics, spread in the manner of systemic financial risks.

Thus, to understand and appreciate the importance of the CDS market, it is necessary to recognize how that market can fail. The ability to separate and trade risks is a valuable one. Banks can continue to make loans to their customers, thereby satisfying the customers' needs, while laying off the risk elsewhere. In short, parties not wanting to bear certain risks can sell them to parties wanting to assume certain risks. If all parties do their jobs correctly, the markets and the economy work more efficiently. If, as in the case of certain CDS sellers, not everyone does a good job of managing risk, there can be serious repercussions. In the case of AIG and some other companies, taxpayer bailouts were the ultimate price paid to keep these large institutions afloat so that they could continue to provide their other critical services to consumers. The rules proposed in the new OTC derivatives market regulations—which call for greater regulation and transparency of OTC derivatives and, in particular, CDSs—have important implications for the future of this market and these instruments.

EXAMPLE 4

Options and Credit Derivatives

1 An option provides which of the following?

   A Either the right to buy or the right to sell an underlying

   B The right to buy and sell, with the choice made at expiration

   C The obligation to buy or sell, which can be converted into the right to buy or sell

2 Which of the following is **not** a characteristic of a call option on a stock?

   A A guarantee that the stock will increase

   B A specified date on which the right to buy expires

   C A fixed price at which the call holder can buy the stock

3 A credit derivative is which of the following?

   A A derivative in which the premium is obtained on credit

   B A derivative in which the payoff is borrowed by the seller

   C A derivative in which the seller provides protection to the buyer against credit loss from a third party

Solution to 1:

A is correct. An option is strictly the right to buy (a call) or the right to sell (a put). It does not provide both choices or the right to convert an obligation into a right.

Solution to 2:

A is correct. A call option on a stock provides no guarantee of any change in the stock price. It has an expiration date, and it provides for a fixed price at which the holder can exercise the option, thereby purchasing the stock.

Solution to 3:

C is correct. Credit derivatives provide a guarantee against loss caused by a third party's default. They do not involve borrowing the premium or the payoff.

4.2.3 Asset-Backed Securities

Although these instruments are covered in more detail in the fixed-income material, we would be remiss if we failed to include them with derivatives. But we will give them only light coverage here.

As discussed earlier, derivatives take (derive) their value from the value of the underlying, as do mutual funds and exchange-traded funds (ETFs). A mutual fund or an ETF holding bonds is virtually identical to the investor holding the bonds directly. Asset-backed securities (ABSs) take this concept a step further by altering the payment streams. ABSs typically divide the payments into slices, called tranches, in which the priority of claims has been changed from equivalent to preferential. For example, in a bond mutual fund or an ETF, all investors in the fund have equal claims, and so the rate of return earned by each investor is exactly the same. If a portfolio of the same bonds were assembled into an ABS, some investors in the ABS would have claims that would supersede those of other investors. The differential nature of these claims becomes relevant when either prepayments or defaults occur.

Prepayments mostly affect only mortgages. When a portfolio of mortgages is assembled into an ABS, the resulting instrument is called a **collateralized mortgage obligation (CMO)**. Commonly but not always, the credit risk has been reduced or eliminated, perhaps by a CDS, as discussed earlier. When homeowners pay off their mortgages early due to refinancing at lower rates, the holders of the mortgages suffer losses. They expected to receive a stream of returns that is now terminated. The funds that were previously earning a particular rate will now have to be invested to earn a lower rate. These losses are the mirror images of the gains homeowners make when they proudly proclaim that they refinanced their mortgages and substantially lowered their payments.

CMOs partition the claims against these mortgages into different tranches, which are typically called A, B, and C. Class C tranches bear the first wave of prepayments until that tranche has been completely repaid its full principal investment. At that point, the Class B tranche holders bear the next prepayments until they have been fully repaid. The Class A tranche holders then bear the next wave of prepayments.[14] Thus, the risk faced by the various tranche holders is different from that of a mutual fund or ETF, which would pass the returns directly through such that investors would all receive the same rates of return. Therefore, the expected returns of CMO tranches vary and are commensurate with the prepayment risk they assume. Some CMOs are also characterized by credit risk, perhaps a substantial amount, from subprime mortgages.

When bonds or loans are assembled into ABSs, they are typically called **collateralized bond obligations** (CBOs) or **collateralized loan obligations** (CLOs). These instruments (known collectively as **collateralized debt obligations**, or CDOs) do not traditionally have much prepayment risk but they do have credit risk and oftentimes a great deal of it. The CDO structure allocates this risk to tranches that are called senior, mezzanine, or junior tranches (the last sometimes called equity tranches). When defaults occur, the junior tranches bear the risk first, followed by the mezzanine tranches, and then the senior tranches. The expected returns of the tranches vary according to the perceived credit risk, with the senior tranches having the highest credit quality and the junior the lowest. Thus, the senior tranches have the lowest expected returns and the junior tranches have the highest.

An asset-backed security is formally defined as follows:

> *An asset-backed security is a derivative contract in which a portfolio of debt instruments is assembled and claims are issued on the portfolio in the form of tranches, which have different priorities of claims on the payments made by the debt securities such that prepayments or credit losses are allocated to the most-junior tranches first and the most-senior tranches last.*

---

14 The reference to only three tranches is just a general statement. There are many more types of tranches. Our discussion of the three classes is for illustrative purposes only and serves to emphasize that there are high-priority claims, low-priority claims, and other claims somewhere in the middle.

ABSs seem to have only an indirect and subtle resemblance to options, but they are indeed options. They promise to make a series of returns that are typically steady. These returns can be lowered if prepayments or defaults occur. Thus, they are contingent on prepayments and defaults. Take a look again at Exhibit 4, Panel B (the profit and payoff of a short put option). If all goes well, there is a fixed return. If something goes badly, the return can be lowered, and the worse the outcome, the lower the return. Thus, holders of ABSs have effectively written put options.

This completes the discussion of contingent claims. Having now covered forward commitments and contingent claims, the final category of derivative instruments is more or less just a catch-all category in case something was missed.

4.3 Hybrids

The instruments just covered encompass all the fundamental instruments that exist in the derivatives world. Yet, the derivatives world is truly much larger than implied by what has been covered here. We have not covered and will touch only lightly on the many hybrid instruments that combine derivatives, fixed-income securities, currencies, equities, and commodities. For example, options can be combined with bonds to form either callable bonds or convertible bonds. Swaps can be combined with options to form swap payments that have upper and lower limits. Options can be combined with futures to obtain options on futures. Options can be created with swaps as the underlying to form swaptions. Some of these instruments will be covered later. For now, you should just recognize that the possibilities are almost endless.

We will not address these hybrids directly, but some are covered elsewhere in the curriculum. The purpose of discussing them here is for you to realize that derivatives create possibilities not otherwise available in their absence. This point will lead to a better understanding of why derivatives exist, a topic we will get to very shortly.

EXAMPLE 5

Forward Commitments versus Contingent Claims

1 Which of the following is **not** a forward commitment?

   A An agreement to take out a loan at a future date at a specific rate

   B An offer of employment that must be accepted or rejected in two weeks

   C An agreement to lease a piece of machinery for one year with a series of fixed monthly payments

2 Which of the following statements is true about contingent claims?

   A Either party can default to the other.

   B The payoffs are linearly related to the performance of the underlying.

   C The most the long can lose is the amount paid for the contingent claim.

Solution to 1:

B is correct. Both A and C are commitments to engage in transactions at future dates. In fact, C is like a swap because the party agrees to make a series of future payments and in return receives temporary use of an asset whose value could vary. B is a contingent claim. The party receiving the employment offer can accept it or reject it if there is a better alternative.

Solution to 2:

C is correct. The maximum loss to the long is the premium. The payoffs of contingent claims are not linearly related to the underlying, and only one party, the short, can default.

4.4 Derivatives Underlyings

Before discussing the purposes and benefits of derivatives, we need to clarify some points that have been implied so far. We have alluded to certain underlying assets, this section will briefly discuss the underlyings more directly.

4.4.1 *Equities*

Equities are one of the most popular categories of underlyings on which derivatives are created. There are two types of equities on which derivatives exist: individual stocks and stock indices. Derivatives on individual stocks are primarily options. Forwards, futures, and swaps on individual stocks are not widely used. Index derivatives in the form of options, forwards, futures, and swaps are very popular. Index swaps, more often called equity swaps, are quite popular and permit investors to pay the return on one stock index and receive the return on another index or a fixed rate. They can be very useful in asset allocation strategies by allowing an equity manager to increase or reduce exposure to an equity market or sector without trading the individual securities.

In addition, options on stocks are frequently used by companies as compensation and incentives for their executives and employees. These options are granted to provide incentives to work toward driving the stock price up and can result in companies paying lower cash compensation.[15] Some companies also issue warrants, which are options sold to the public that allow the holders to exercise them and buy shares directly from the companies.[16]

4.4.2 *Fixed-Income Instruments and Interest Rates*

Options, forwards, futures, and swaps on bonds are widely used. The problem with creating derivatives on bonds, however, is that there are almost always many issues of bonds. A single issuer, whether it is a government or a private borrower, often has more than one bond issue outstanding. For futures contracts, with their standardization requirements, this problem is particularly challenging. What does it mean to say that a futures contract is on a German bund, a US Treasury note, or a UK gilt? The most common solution to this problem is to allow multiple issues to be delivered on a single futures contract. This feature adds some interesting twists to the pricing and trading strategies of these instruments.

Until now, we have referred to the underlying as an *asset*. Yet, one of the largest derivative underlyings is not an asset. It is simply an interest rate. An interest rate is not an asset. One cannot hold an interest rate or place it on a balance sheet as an asset. Although one can hold an instrument that pays an interest rate, the rate itself is not

---

15 Unfortunately, the industry has created some confusion with the terminology of these instruments. They are often referred to as *stock options*, and yet ordinary publicly traded options not granted to employees are sometimes referred to as stock options. The latter are also sometimes called *equity options*, whereas employee-granted options are almost never referred to as equity options. If the terms *executive stock options* and *employee stock options* were always used, there would be no problem. You should be aware of and careful about this confusion.

16 A warrant is a type of option, similar to the employee stock option, written by the company on its own stock, in contrast to exchange-traded and OTC options, in which the company is not a party to the option contract. Also note that, unfortunately, the financial world uses the term *warrant* to refer to a number of other option-like instruments. Like a lot of words that have multiple meanings, one must understand the context to avoid confusion.

an asset. But there are derivatives in which the rate, not the instrument that pays the rate, is the underlying. In fact, we have already covered one of these derivatives: The plain vanilla interest rate swap in which Libor is the underlying.[17] Instead of a swap, an interest rate derivative could be an option. For example, a call option on 90-day Libor with a strike of 5% would pay off if at expiration Libor exceeds 5%. If Libor is below 5%, the option simply expires unexercised.

Interest rate derivatives are the most widely used derivatives. With that in mind, we will be careful in using the expression *underlying asset* and will use the more generic *underlying*.

4.4.3 *Currencies*

Currency risk is a major factor in global financial markets, and the currency derivatives market is extremely large. Options, forwards, futures, and swaps are widely used. Currency derivatives can be complex, sometimes combining elements of other underlyings. For example, a currency swap involves two parties making a series of interest rate payments to each other in different currencies. Because interest rates and currencies are both subject to change, a currency swap has two sources of risk. Although this instrument may sound extremely complicated, it merely reflects the fact that companies operating across borders are subject to both interest rate risk and currency risk and currency swaps are commonly used to manage those risks.

4.4.4 *Commodities*

Commodities are resources, such as food, oil, and metals, that humans use to sustain life and support economic activity. Because of the economic principle of comparative advantage, countries often specialize in the production of certain resources. Thus, the commodities market is extremely large and subject to an almost unimaginable array of risks. One need only observe how the price of oil moves up as tension builds in the Middle East or how the price of orange juice rises on a forecast of cold weather in Florida.

Commodity derivatives are widely used to speculate in and manage the risk associated with commodity price movements. The primary commodity derivatives are futures, but forwards, swaps, and options are also used. The reason that futures are in the lead in the world of commodities is simply history. The first futures markets were futures on commodities. The first futures exchange, the Chicago Board of Trade, was created in 1848, and until the creation of currency futures in 1972, there were no futures on any underlying except commodities.

There has been a tendency to think of the commodities world as somewhat separate from the financial world. Commodity traders and financial traders were quite different groups. Since the creation of financial futures, however, commodity and financial traders have become relatively homogeneous. Moreover, commodities are increasingly viewed as an important asset class that should be included in investment strategies because of their ability to help diversify portfolios.

4.4.5 *Credit*

As we previously discussed, credit is another underlying and quite obviously not an asset. Credit default swaps (CDSs) and collateralized debt obligations (CDOs) were discussed extensively in an earlier section. These instruments have clearly established that credit is a distinct underlying that has widespread interest from a trading and risk management perspective. In addition, to the credit of a single entity, credit derivatives

---

17 As you will see later, there are also futures in which the underlying is an interest rate (Eurodollar futures) and forwards in which the underlying is an interest rate (forward rate agreements, or FRAs).

are created on multiple entities. CDOs themselves are credit derivatives on portfolios of credit risks. In recent years, indices of CDOs have been created, and instruments based on the payoffs of these CDO indices are widely traded.

4.4.6 *Other*

This category is included here to capture some of the really unusual underlyings. One in particular is weather. Although weather is hardly an asset, it is certainly a major force in how some entities perform. For example, a ski resort needs snow, farmers need an adequate but not excessive amount of rain, and public utilities experience strains on their capacity during temperature extremes. Derivatives exist in which the payoffs are measured as snowfall, rainfall, and temperature. Although these derivatives have not been widely used—because of some complexities in pricing, among other things—they continue to exist and may still have a future. In addition, there are derivatives on electricity, which is also not an asset. It cannot be held in the traditional sense because it is created and consumed almost instantaneously. Another unusual type of derivative is based on disasters in the form of insurance claims.

Financial institutions will continue to create derivatives on all types of risks and exposures. Most of these derivatives will fail because of little trading interest, but a few will succeed. If that speaks badly of derivatives, it must be remembered that most small businesses fail, most creative ideas fail, and most people who try to become professional entertainers or athletes fail. It is the sign of a healthy and competitive system that only the very best survive.

THE SIZE OF THE DERIVATIVES MARKET

In case anyone thinks that the derivatives market is not large enough to justify studying, we should consider how big the market is. Unfortunately, gauging the size of the derivatives market is not a simple task. OTC derivatives contracts are private transactions. No reporting agency gathers data, and market size is not measured in traditional volume-based metrics, such as shares traded in the stock market. Complicating things further is the fact that derivatives underlyings include equities, fixed-income securities, interest rates, currencies, commodities, and a variety of other underlyings. All these underlyings have their own units of measurement. Hence, measuring how "big" the underlying derivatives markets are is like trying to measure how much fruit consumers purchase; the proverbial mixing of apples, oranges, bananas, and all other fruits.

The exchange-listed derivatives market reports its size in terms of volume, meaning the number of contracts traded. Exchange-listed volume, however, is an inconsistent number. For example, US Treasury bond futures contracts trade in units covering $100,000 face value. Eurodollar futures contracts trade in units covering $1,000,000 face value. Crude oil trades in 1,000-barrel (42 gallons each) units. Yet, one traded contract of each gets equal weighting in volume totals.

The March–April issue of the magazine *Futures Industry* (available to subscribers) reports the annual volume of the entire global futures and options industry. For 2011, that volume was more than 25 billion contracts.

OTC volume is even more difficult to measure. There is no count of the number of contracts that trade. In fact, *volume* is an almost meaningless concept in OTC markets because any notion of volume requires a standardized size. If a customer goes to a swaps dealer and enters into a swap to hedge a $50 million loan, there is no measure of how much volume that transaction generated. The $50 million swap's notional principal, however, does provide a measure to some extent. Forwards, swaps, and OTC options all have notional principals, so they can be measured in that manner. Another measure of the size of the derivatives market is the market value of these contracts. As noted, forwards and swaps start with zero market value, but their market value changes as market conditions change. Options do not start with zero market value and almost always have a positive market value until expiration, when some options expire out of the money.

The OTC industry has taken both of these concepts—notional principal and market value—as measures of the size of the market. Notional principal is probably a more accurate measure. The amount of a contract's notional principal is unambiguous: It is written into the contract and the two parties cannot disagree over it. Yet, notional principal terribly overstates the amount of money actually at risk. For example, a $50 million notional principal swap will have nowhere near $50 million at risk. The payments on such a swap are merely the net of two opposite series of interest payments on $50 million. The market value of such a swap is the present value of one stream of payments minus the present value of the other. This market value figure will always be well below the notional principal. Thus, market value seems like a better measure except that, unlike notional principal, it is not unambiguous. Market value requires measurement, and two parties can disagree on the market value of the same transaction.

Notional principal and market value estimates for the global OTC derivatives market are collected semi-annually by the Bank for International Settlements of Basel, Switzerland, and published on its website (http://www.bis.org/statistics/derstats.htm). At the end of 2011, notional principal was more than $600 trillion and market value was about $27 trillion. A figure of $600 trillion is an almost unfathomable number and, as noted, is a misleading measure of the amount of money at risk.[18] The market value figure of $27 trillion is a much more realistic measure, but as noted, it is less accurate, relying on estimates provided by banks.

Hence, the exchange-listed and OTC markets use different measures and each of those measures is subject to severe limitations. About all we can truly say for sure about the derivatives market is, "It is big."

THE PURPOSES AND BENEFITS OF DERIVATIVES

5

Economic historians know that derivatives markets have existed since at least the Middle Ages. It is unclear whether derivatives originated in the Asian rice markets or possibly in medieval trade fairs in Europe. We do know that the origin of modern futures markets is the creation of the Chicago Board of Trade in 1848. To understand why derivatives markets exist, it is useful to take a brief look at why the Chicago Board of Trade was formed.

In the middle of the 19th century, midwestern America was rapidly becoming the center of agricultural production in the United States. At the same time, Chicago was evolving into a major American city, a hub of transportation and commerce. Grain markets in Chicago were the central location to which midwestern farmers brought their wheat, corn, and soybeans to sell. Unfortunately, most of these products arrived at approximately the same time of the year, September through November. The storage facilities in Chicago were strained beyond capacity. As a result, prices would fall tremendously and some farmers reportedly found it more economical to dump their grains in the Chicago River rather than transport them back to the farm. At other times of the year, prices would rise steeply. A group of businessmen saw this situation as unnecessary volatility and a waste of valuable produce. To deal with this problem, they created the Chicago Board of Trade and a financial instrument called the "to-arrive" contract. A farmer could sell a to-arrive contract at any time during the year. This contract fixed the price of the farmer's grain on the basis of delivery in Chicago at a specified later date. Grain is highly storable, so farmers can hold on to the grain and deliver it at almost any later time. This plan substantially reduced seasonal market volatility and made the markets work much better for all parties.

---

18 To put it in perspective, it would take 19 million years for a clock to tick off 600 trillion seconds!

The traders in Chicago began to trade these contracts, speculating on movements in grain prices. Soon, it became apparent that an important and fascinating market had developed. Widespread hedging and speculative interest resulted in substantial market growth, and about 80 years later, a clearinghouse and a performance guarantee were added, thus completing the evolution of the to-arrive contract into today's modern futures contract.

Many commodities and all financial assets that underlie derivatives contracts are not seasonally produced. Hence, this initial motivation for futures markets is only a minor advantage of derivatives markets today. But there are many reasons why derivative markets serve an important and useful purpose in contemporary finance.

5.1 Risk Allocation, Transfer, and Management

Until the advent of derivatives markets, risk management was quite cumbersome. Setting the actual level of risk to the desired level of risk required engaging in transactions in the underlyings. Such transactions typically had high transaction costs and were disruptive of portfolios. In many cases, it is quite difficult to fine-tune the level of risk to the desired level. From the perspective of a risk taker, it was quite costly to buy risk because a large amount of capital would be required.

Derivatives solve these problems in a very effective way: They allow trading the risk without trading the instrument itself. For example, consider a stockholder who wants to reduce exposure to a stock. In the pre-derivatives era, the only way to do so was to sell the stock. Now, the stockholder can sell futures, forwards, calls, or swaps, or buy put options, all while retaining the stock. For a company founder, these types of strategies can be particularly useful because the founder can retain ownership and probably board membership. Many other excellent examples of the use of derivatives to transfer risk are covered elsewhere in the curriculum. The objective at this point is to establish that derivatives provide an effective method of transferring risk from parties who do not want the risk to parties who do. In this sense, risk allocation is improved within markets and, indeed, the entire global economy.

The overall purpose of derivatives is to obtain more effective risk management within companies and the entire economy. Although some argue that derivatives do not serve this purpose very well (we will discuss this point in Section 6), for now you should understand that derivatives can improve the allocation of risk and facilitate more effective risk management for both companies and economies.

5.2 Information Discovery

One of the advantages of futures markets has been described as *price discovery*. A futures price has been characterized by some experts as a revelation of some information about the future. Thus, a futures price is sometimes thought of as predictive. This statement is not strictly correct because futures prices are not really forecasts of future spot prices. They provide only a little more information than do spot prices, but they do so in a very efficient manner. The markets for some underlyings are highly decentralized and not very efficient. For example, what is gold worth? It trades in markets around the world, but probably the best place to look is at the gold futures contract expiring soonest. What is the value of the S&P 500 Index when the US markets are not open? As it turns out, US futures markets open before the US stock market opens. The S&P 500 futures price is frequently viewed as an indication of where the stock market will open.

Derivative markets can, however, convey information not impounded in spot markets. By virtue of the fact that derivative markets require less capital, information can flow into the derivative markets before it gets into the spot market. The difference may well be only a matter of minutes or possibly seconds, but it can provide the edge to astute traders.

Finally, we should note that futures markets convey another simple piece of information: What price would one accept to avoid uncertainty? If you hold a stock worth $40 and could hedge the next 12 months' uncertainty, what locked-in price should you expect to earn? As it turns out, it should be the price that guarantees the risk-free rate minus whatever dividends would be paid on the stock. Derivatives—specifically, futures, forwards, and swaps—reveal the price that the holder of an asset could take and avoid the risk.

What we have said until now applies to futures, forwards, and swaps. What about options? As you will learn later, given the underlying and the type of option (call or put), an option price reflects two characteristics of the option (exercise price and time to expiration), three characteristics of the underlying (price, volatility, and cash flows it might pay), and one general macroeconomic factor (risk-free rate). Only one of these factors, volatility, is not relatively easy to identify. But with the available models to price the option, we can infer what volatility people are using from the actual market prices at which they execute trades. That volatility, called **implied volatility**, measures the risk of the underlying. It reflects the volatility that investors use to determine the market price of the option. Knowing the risk of the underlying asset is an extremely useful piece of information. In fact, for options on broad-based market indices, such as the S&P 500, the implied volatility is a good measure of the general level of uncertainty in the market. Some experts have even called it a measure of fear. Thus, options provide information about what investors think of the uncertainty in the market, if not their fear of it.[19]

In addition, options allow the creation of trading strategies that cannot be done by using the underlying. As the exhibits on options explained, these strategies provide asymmetrical performance: limited movement in one direction and movement in the other direction that changes with movements in the underlying.

5.3 Operational Advantages

We noted earlier that derivatives have lower transaction costs than the underlying. The transaction costs of derivatives can be high relative to the value of the derivatives, but these costs are typically low relative to the value of the underlying. Thus, an investor who wants to take a position in, say, an equity market index would likely find it less costly to use the futures to get a given degree of exposure than to invest directly in the index to get that same exposure.

Derivative markets also typically have greater liquidity than the underlying spot markets, a result of the smaller amount of capital required to trade derivatives than to get the equivalent exposure directly in the underlying. Futures margin requirements and option premiums are quite low relative to the cost of the underlying.

One other extremely valuable operational advantage of derivative markets is the ease with which one can go short. With derivatives, it is nearly as easy to take a short position as to take a long position, whereas for the underlying asset, it is almost always much more difficult to go short than to go long. In fact, for many commodities, short selling is nearly impossible.

---

19 The Chicago Board Options Exchange publishes a measure of the implied volatility of the S&P 500 Index option, which is called the VIX (volatility index). The VIX is widely followed and is cited as a measure of investor uncertainty and sometimes fear.

5.4 Market Efficiency

In the study of portfolio management, you learn that an efficient market is one in which no single investor can consistently earn returns in the long run in excess of those commensurate with the risk assumed. Of course, endless debates occur over whether equity markets are efficient. No need to resurrect that issue here, but let us proceed with the assumption that equity markets—and, in fact, most free and competitive financial markets—are reasonably efficient. This assumption does not mean that abnormal returns can never be earned, and indeed prices do get out of line with fundamental values. But competition, the relatively free flow of information, and ease of trading tend to bring prices back in line with fundamental values. Derivatives can make this process work even more rapidly.

When prices deviate from fundamental values, derivative markets offer less costly ways to exploit the mispricing. As noted earlier, less capital is required, transaction costs are lower, and short selling is easier. We also noted that as a result of these features, it is possible, indeed likely, that fundamental value will be reflected in the derivatives markets before it is restored in the underlying market. Although this time difference could be only a matter of minutes, for a trader seeking abnormal returns, a few minutes can be a valuable opportunity.

All these advantages of derivatives markets make the financial markets in general function more effectively. Investors are far more willing to trade if they can more easily manage their risk, trade at lower cost and with less capital, and go short more easily. This increased willingness to trade increases the number of market participants, which makes the market more liquid. A very liquid market may not automatically be an efficient market, but it certainly has a better chance of being one.

Even if one does not accept the concept that financial markets are efficient, it is difficult to say that markets are not more effective and competitive with derivatives. Yet, many blame derivatives for problems in the market. Let us take a look at these arguments.

6   CRITICISMS AND MISUSES OF DERIVATIVES

The history of financial markets is filled with extreme ups and downs, which are often called bubbles and crashes. Bubbles occur when prices rise for a long time and appear to exceed fundamental values. Crashes occur when prices fall rapidly. Although bubbles, if they truly exist, are troublesome, crashes are even more so because nearly everyone loses substantial wealth in a crash. A crash is then typically followed by a government study commissioned to find the causes of the crash. In the last 30 years, almost all such studies have implicated derivatives as having some role in causing the crash. Of course, because derivatives are widely used and involve a high degree of leverage, it is a given that they would be seen in a crash. It is unclear whether derivatives are the real culprit or just the proverbial smoking gun used by someone to do something wrong.

The two principal arguments against derivatives are that they are such speculative devices that they effectively permit legalized gambling and that they destabilize the financial system. Let us look at these points more closely.

6.1 Speculation and Gambling

As noted earlier, derivatives are frequently used to manage risk. In many contexts, this use involves hedging or laying off risk. Naturally, for hedging to work, there must be speculators. Someone must accept the risk. Derivatives markets are unquestionably attractive to speculators. All the benefits of derivatives draw speculators in large numbers, and indeed they should. The more speculators that participate in the market, the cheaper it is for hedgers to lay off risk. These speculators take the form of hedge funds and other professional traders who willingly accept risk that others need to shed. In recent years, the rapid growth of these types of investors has been alarming to some but almost surely has been beneficial for all investors.

Unfortunately, the general image of speculators is not a good one. Speculators are often thought to be short-term traders who attempt to exploit temporary inefficiencies, caring little about long-term fundamental values. The profits from short-term trading are almost always taxed more heavily than the profits from long-term trading, clearly targeting and in some sense punishing speculators. Speculators are thought to engage in price manipulation and to trade at extreme prices.[20] All of this type of trading is viewed more or less as just a form of legalized gambling.

In most countries, gambling is a heavily regulated industry. In the United States, only certain states permit private industry to offer gambling. Many states operate gambling only through the public sector in the form of state-run lotteries. Many people view derivatives trading as merely a form of legalized and uncontrolled gambling.

Yet, there are notable differences between gambling and speculation. Gambling typically benefits only a limited number of participants and does not generally help society as a whole. But derivatives trading brings extensive benefits to financial markets, as explained earlier, and thus does benefit society as a whole. In short, the benefits of derivatives are broad, whereas the benefits of gambling are narrow.

Nonetheless, the argument that derivatives are a form of legalized gambling will continue to be made. Speculation and gambling are certainly both forms of financial risk taking, so these arguments are not completely off base. But insurance companies speculate on loss claims, mutual funds that invest in stocks speculate on the performance of companies, and entrepreneurs go up against tremendous odds to speculate on their own ability to create successful businesses. These so-called speculators are rarely criticized for engaging in a form of legalized gambling, and indeed entrepreneurs are praised as the backbone of the economy. Really, all investment is speculative. So, why is speculation viewed as such a bad thing by so many? The answer is unclear.

6.2 Destabilization and Systemic Risk

The arguments against speculation through derivatives often go a step further, claiming that it is not merely speculation or gambling per se but rather that it has destabilizing consequences. Opponents of derivatives claim that the very benefits of derivatives (low cost, low capital requirements, ease of going short) result in an excessive amount of speculative trading that brings instability to the market. They argue that speculators use large amounts of leverage, thereby subjecting themselves and their creditors to substantial risk if markets do not move in their hoped-for direction. Defaults by speculators can then lead to defaults by their creditors, their creditors' creditors, and so on. These effects can, therefore, be systemic and reflect an epidemic contagion whereby instability can spread throughout markets and an economy, if not the entire world. Given that governments often end up bailing out some banks and insurance companies, society has expressed concern that the risk managed with derivatives must be controlled.

This argument is not without merit. Such effects occurred in the Long-Term Capital Management fiasco of 1998 and again in the financial crisis of 2008, in which derivatives, particularly credit default swaps, were widely used by many of the problem

---

20 Politicians and regulators have been especially critical of energy market speculators. Politicians, in particular, almost always blame rising oil prices on speculators, although credit is conspicuously absent for falling oil prices.

entities. Responses to such events typically take the course of calling for more rules and regulations restricting the use of derivatives, requiring more collateral and credit mitigation measures, backing up banks with more capital, and encouraging, if not requiring, OTC derivatives to be centrally cleared like exchange-traded derivatives.

In response, however, we should note that financial crises—including the South Sea and Mississippi bubbles and the stock market crash of 1929, as well as a handful of economic calamities of the 19th and 20th centuries—have existed since the dawn of capitalism. Some of these events preceded the era of modern derivatives markets, and others were completely unrelated to the use of derivatives. Some organizations, such as Orange County, California, in 1994–1995, have proved that derivatives are not required to take on excessive leverage and nearly bring the entity to ruin. Proponents of derivatives argue that derivatives are but one of many mechanisms through which excessive risk can be taken. Derivatives may seem dangerous, and they can be if misused, but there are many ways to take on leverage that look far less harmful but can be just as risky.

Another criticism of derivatives is simply their complexity. Many derivatives are extremely complex and require a high-level understanding of mathematics. The financial industry employs many mathematicians, physicists, and computer scientists. This single fact has made many distrust derivatives and the people who work on them. It is unclear why this reason has tarnished the reputation of the derivatives industry. Scientists work on complex problems in medicine and engineering without public distrust. One explanation probably lies in the fact that scientists create models of markets by using scientific principles that often fail. To a physicist modeling the movements of celestial bodies, the science is reliable and the physicist is unlikely to misapply the science. The same science applied to financial markets is far less reliable. Financial markets are driven by the actions of people who are not as consistent as the movements of celestial bodies. When financial models fail to work as they should, the scientists are often blamed for either building models that are too complex and unable to accurately capture financial reality or misusing those models, such as using poor estimates of inputs. And derivatives, being so widely used and heavily leveraged, are frequently in the center of it all.

EXAMPLE 6

Purposes and Controversies of Derivative Markets

1　Which of the following is **not** an advantage of derivative markets?

　A　They are less volatile than spot markets.

　B　They facilitate the allocation of risk in the market.

　C　They incur lower transaction costs than spot markets.

2　Which of the following pieces of information is **not** conveyed by at least one type of derivative?

　A　The volatility of the underlying

　B　The most widely used strategy of the underlying

　C　The price at which uncertainty in the underlying can be eliminated

3　Which of the following responds to the criticism that derivatives can be destabilizing to the underlying market?

　A　Market crashes and panics have occurred since long before derivatives existed.

B Derivatives are sufficiently regulated that they cannot destabilize the spot market.

C The transaction costs of derivatives are high enough to keep their use at a minimum level.

Solution to 1:

A is correct. Derivative markets are not by nature more or less volatile than spot markets. They facilitate risk allocation by making it easier and less costly to transfer risk, and their transaction costs are lower than those of spot markets.

Solution to 2:

B is correct. Options do convey the volatility of the underlying, and futures, forwards, and swaps convey the price at which uncertainty in the underlying can be eliminated. Derivatives do not convey any information about the use of the underlying in strategies.

Solution to 3:

A is correct. Derivatives regulation is not more and is arguably less than spot market regulation, and the transaction costs of derivatives are not a deterrent to their use; in fact, derivatives are widely used. Market crashes and panics have a very long history, much longer than that of derivatives.

An important element of understanding and using derivatives is having a healthy respect for their power. Every day, we use chemicals, electricity, and fire without thinking about their dangers. We consume water and drive automobiles, both of which are statistically quite dangerous. Perhaps these risks are underappreciated, but it is more likely the case that most adults learn how to safely use chemicals, electricity, fire, water, and automobiles. Of course, there are exceptions, many of which are foolish, and foolishness is no stranger to the derivatives industry. The lesson here is that derivatives can make our financial lives better, but like chemicals, electricity, and all the rest, we need to know how to use them safely, which is why they are an important part of the CFA curriculum.

Later in the curriculum, you will learn a great deal about how derivatives are priced. At this point, we introduce the pricing of derivatives. This material not only paves the way for a deeper understanding of derivatives but also complements earlier material by helping you understand how derivatives work.

ELEMENTARY PRINCIPLES OF DERIVATIVE PRICING

Pricing and valuation are fundamental elements of the CFA Program. The study of fixed-income and equity securities, as well as their application in portfolio management, is solidly grounded on the principle of valuation. In valuation, the question is simple: What is something worth? Without an answer to that question, one can hardly proceed to use that *something* wisely.

Determining what a derivative is worth is similar to determining what an asset is worth. As you learn in the fixed-income and equity readings, value is the present value of future cash flows, with discounting done at a rate that reflects both the opportunity cost of money and the risk. Derivatives valuation applies that same principle but in a somewhat different way.

Think of a derivative as *attached* to an underlying. We know that the derivative *derives* its value from the value of the underlying. If the underlying's value changes, so should the value of the derivative. The underlying takes its value from the discounted present value of the expected future cash flows it offers, with discounting done at a rate reflecting the investor's risk tolerance. But if the value of the underlying is embedded in the value of the derivative, it would be double counting to discount the derivative's expected future cash flows at a risky discount rate. That effect has already been incorporated into the value of the underlying, which goes into the value of the derivative.

Derivatives usually take their values from the underlying by constructing a hypothetical combination of the derivatives and the underlyings that eliminates risk. This combination is typically called a **hedge portfolio**. With the risk eliminated, it follows that the hedge portfolio should earn the risk-free rate. A derivative's value is the price of the derivative that forces the hedge portfolio to earn the risk-free rate.

This principle of derivative valuation relies completely on the ability of an investor to hold or store the underlying asset. Let us take a look at what that means.

7.1 Storage

As noted previously, the first derivatives were agricultural commodities. Most of these commodities can be stored (i.e., held) for a period of time. Some extreme cases, such as oil and gold, which are storable for millions of years, are excellent examples of fully storable commodities. Grains, such as wheat and corn, can be stored for long but not infinite periods of time. Some commodities, such as bananas, are storable for relatively short periods of time. In the CFA Program, we are more interested in financial assets. Equities and currencies have perpetual storability, whereas bonds are storable until they mature.

Storage incurs costs. Commodity storage costs can be quite expensive. Imagine storing 1,000 kilograms of gold or a million barrels of oil. Financial assets, however, have relatively low storage costs. Some assets pay returns during storage. Stocks pay dividends and bonds pay interest. The net of payments offered minus storage costs plays a role in the valuation of derivatives.

An example earlier in this reading illustrates this point. Suppose an investor holds a dividend-paying stock and wants to eliminate the uncertainty of its selling price over a future period of time. Suppose further that the investor enters into a forward contract that commits him to deliver the stock at a later date, for which he will receive a fixed price. With uncertainty eliminated, the investor should earn the risk-free rate, but in fact, he does not. He earns more because while holding the stock, he collects dividends. Therefore, he should earn the risk-free rate *minus* the dividend yield, a concept known as the cost of carry, which will be covered in great detail in later readings. The cost of carry *plus* the dividends he earns effectively means that he makes the risk-free rate. Now, no one is claiming that this is a good way to earn the risk-free rate. There are many better ways to do that, but this strategy could be executed. There is one and only one forward price that guarantees that this strategy earns a return of the risk-free rate minus the dividend yield, or the risk-free rate after accounting for the dividends collected. If the forward price at which contracts are created does not equal this price, investors can take advantage of this discrepancy by engaging in arbitrage, which is discussed in the next section.

Forwards, futures, swaps, and options are all priced in this manner. Hence, they rely critically on the ability to store or hold the asset. Some underlyings are not storable. We previously mentioned electricity. It is produced and consumed almost instantaneously. Weather is also not storable. Fresh fish have very limited storability. Although this absence of storability may not be the reason, derivative markets in these types of underlyings have not been particularly successful, whereas those in underlyings that are more easily storable have often been successful.

The opposite of storability is the ability to go short—that is, to borrow the underlying, sell it, and buy it back later. We discussed earlier that short selling of some assets can be difficult. It is not easy to borrow oil or soybeans. There are ways around this constraint, but derivatives valuation is generally much easier when the underlying can be shorted. This point is discussed in more depth later in the curriculum.

7.2 Arbitrage

What we have been describing is the foundation of the principle of **arbitrage**. In well-functioning markets with low transaction costs and a free flow of information, the same asset cannot sell for more than one price. If it did, someone would buy it in the cheaper market and sell it in the more expensive market, earning a riskless profit. The combined actions of all parties doing this would push up the lower price and push down the higher price until they converged. For this reason, arbitrage is often referred to as the **law of one price**. Of course, for arbitrage to be feasible, the ability to purchase and sell short the asset is important.

Obviously, this rule does not apply to all markets. The same consumer good can easily sell for different prices, which is one reason why people spend so much time shopping on the internet. The costs associated with purchasing the good in the cheaper market and selling it in the more expensive market can make the arbitrage not worthwhile. The absence of information on the very fact that different prices exist would also prevent the arbitrage from occurring. Although the internet and various price-comparing websites reduce these frictions and encourage all sellers to offer competitive prices, consumer goods are never likely to be arbitragable.[21]

Financial markets, of course, are a different matter. Information on securities prices around the world is quite accessible and relatively inexpensive. Most financial markets are fairly competitive because dealers, speculators, and brokers attempt to execute trades at the best prices. Arbitrage is considered a dependable rule in the financial markets. Nonetheless, there are people who purport to make a living as arbitrageurs. How could they exist? To figure that out, first consider some examples of arbitrage.

The simplest case of an arbitrage might be for the same stock to sell at different prices in two markets. If the stock were selling at $52 in one market and $50 in another, an arbitrageur would buy the stock at $50 in the one market and sell it at $52 in the other. This trade would net an immediate $2 profit at no risk and would not require the commitment of any of the investor's capital. This outcome would be a strong motivation for all arbitrageurs, and their combined actions would force the lower price up and the higher price down until the prices converged.

But what would be the final price? It is entirely possible that $50 is the true fundamental value and $52 is too high. Or $52 could be the true fundamental value and $50 is too low. Or the true fundamental value could lie somewhere between the two. Arbitrage does not tell us the true fundamental value. It is not an *absolute* valuation methodology, such as the discounted cash flow equity valuation model. It is a *relative* valuation methodology. It tells us the correct price of one asset or derivative *relative to* another asset or derivative.

Now, consider another situation, illustrated in Exhibit 6. Observe that we have one stock, AXE Electronics, that today is worth $50 and one period later will be worth either $75 or $40. We will denote these prices as AXE = $50, AXE$^+$ = $75, and AXE$^-$ = $40. Another stock, BYF Technology, is today worth $38 and one period later will

---

21 If the same consumer good sells for different prices in markets with a relatively free flow of information (e.g., via price-comparing websites), it still may not be possible to truly arbitrage. Buying the good at a lower price and selling it at a higher price but less than the price of the most expensive seller may not be practical, but the most expensive seller may be driven out of business. When everyone knows what everyone else is charging, the same effect of arbitrage can still occur.

be worth $60 or $32. Thus, BYF = $38, BYF⁺ = $60, and BYF⁻ = $32. Assume that the risk-free borrowing and lending rate is 4%. Also assume no dividends are paid on either stock during the period covered by this example.

Exhibit 6   Arbitrage Opportunity with Stock AXE, Stock BYF, and a Risk-Free Bond

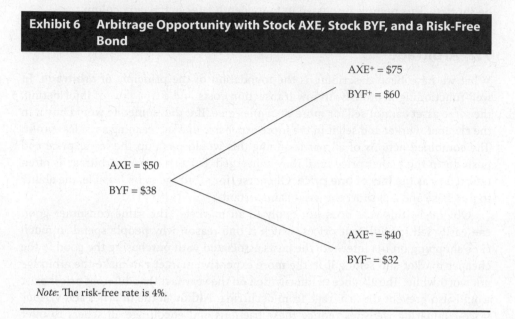

Note: The risk-free rate is 4%.

The opportunity exists to make a profit at no risk without committing any of our funds, as demonstrated in Exhibit 7. Suppose we borrow 100 shares of stock AXE, which is selling for $50, and sell them short, thereby receiving $5,000. We take $4,750 and purchase 125 shares of stock BYF (125 × $38 = $4,750). We invest the remaining $250 in risk-free bonds at 4%. This transaction will not require us to use any funds of our own: The short sale will be sufficient to fund the investment in BYF and leave money to invest in risk-free bonds.

Exhibit 7   Execution of Arbitrage Transaction with Stock AXE, Stock BYF, and a Risk-Free Bond

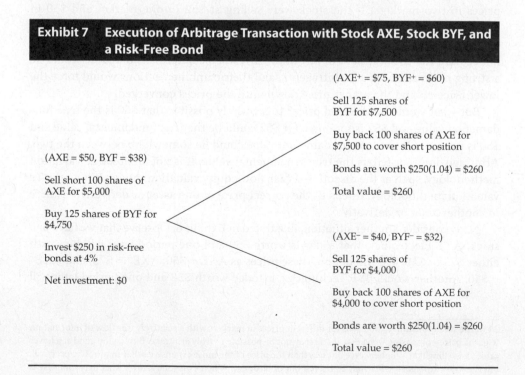

If the top outcome in Exhibit 7 occurs, we sell the 125 shares of BYF for 125 × $60 = $7,500. This amount is sufficient to buy back the 100 shares of AXE, which is selling for $75. But we will also have the bonds, which are worth $250 × 1.04 = $260. If the bottom outcome occurs, we sell the 125 shares of BYF for 125 × $32 = $4,000—enough money to buy back the 100 shares of AXE, which is selling for $40. Again, we will have the risk-free bonds, worth $260. Regardless of the outcome, we end up with $260.

Recall that we invested no money of our own and end up with a sure $260. It should be apparent that this transaction is extremely attractive, so everyone would do it. The combined actions of multiple investors would drive down the price of AXE and/or drive up the price of BYF until an equilibrium is reached, at which point this transaction would no longer be profitable. As noted earlier, we cannot be sure of the correct fundamental price, but let us assume that BYF's price remains constant. Then AXE would fall to $47.50. Alternatively, if we assume that AXE's price remains constant, then the price of BYF would rise to $40. These values are obtained by noting that the prices for both outcomes occur according to the ratio 1.25 ($75/$60 = 1.25; $40/$32 = 1.25). Thus, their initial prices should be consistent with that ratio. If BYF is $38, AXE should be $38 × 1.25 = $47.50. If AXE is $50, BYF should be $40.00 because $40.00 × 1.25 = $50. Of course, the two prices could settle in between. Arbitrage is only a relative pricing method. It prices the two stocks in relation to each other but does not price either on the basis of its own fundamentals.

Of course, this example is extremely simplified. Clearly, a stock price can change to more than two other prices. Also, if a given stock is at one price, another stock may be at any other price. We have created a simple case here to illustrate a point. But as you will learn later in the curriculum, when derivatives are involved, the simplification here is relatively safe. As we know, the price of a derivative is determined by the price of the underlying. Hence, when the underlying is at one particular price, the derivative's price will be determined by that price. The two assets need not be two stocks; one can be a stock and the other can be a derivative on the stock.

To see that point, consider another type of arbitrage opportunity that involves a forward contract. Recall from the previous example that at the start, AXE sells for $50. Suppose we borrow $50 at 4% interest by issuing a risk-free bond, use the money to buy one share of stock AXE, and simultaneously enter into a forward contract to sell this share at a price of $54 one period later. The stock will then move to either $75 or $40 in the next period. The forward contract requires that we deliver the stock and accept $54 for it. And of course, we will owe $50 × 1.04 = $52 on the loan.

Now consider the two outcomes. Regardless of the outcome, the end result is the same. The forward contract fixes the delivery price of the stock at $54:

AXE goes to $75

Deliver stock to settle forward contract	+ $54
Pay back loan	− $52
Net	+ $2

AXE goes to $40

Deliver stock to settle forward contract	+ $54
Pay back loan	− $52
Net	+ $2

In either case, we made $2, free and clear. In fact, we can even accommodate the possibility of more than two future prices for AXE and we will always make $2.[22] The key point is that we faced no risk and did not have to invest any of our own money, but ended up with $2, which is clearly a good trade. The $2 is an arbitrage profit. But where did it originate?

It turns out that the forward price, $54, was an inappropriate price given current market conditions. In fact, it was just an arbitrary price made up to illustrate the point. To eliminate the opportunity to earn the $2 profit, the forward price should be $52, which is equal, not coincidentally, to the amount owed on the loan. It is also no coincidence that $52 is the price of the asset increased by the rate of interest. We will cover this point later in the curriculum, but for now consider that you have just seen your first derivative pricing model.[23]

Of course, many market participants would do this transaction as long as it generated an arbitrage profit. These forces of arbitrage would either push the forward price down or the stock price up, or both, until an equilibrium is reached that eliminates the opportunity to profit at no risk with no commitment of one's own funds.

To summarize, the forces of arbitrage in financial markets assure us that the same asset cannot sell for different prices, nor can two equivalent combinations of assets that produce the same results sell for different prices. Realistically, some arbitrage opportunities can exist on a temporary basis, but they will be quickly exploited, bringing relative prices back in line with each other. Other apparent arbitrage opportunities will be too small to warrant exploiting.

Not to be naive, however, we must acknowledge that there is a large industry of people who call themselves arbitrageurs. So, how can such an industry exist if there are no opportunities for riskless profit? One explanation is that most of the arbitrage transactions are more complex than the simple examples used here. Many involve estimating information, which can result in differing opinions. Arbitrage involving options, for example, usually requires an estimate of a stock's volatility. Different participants have different opinions about the volatility. It is quite possible that the two counterparties trading with each other believe that each is arbitraging against the other.[24]

But more importantly, the absence of arbitrage opportunities is upheld, ironically, only if participants believe that arbitrage opportunities do exist. If traders believe that no opportunities exist to earn arbitrage profits, then traders will not follow market prices and compare those prices with what they ought to be. Thus, eliminating arbitrage opportunities requires that participants be alert in watching for arbitrage opportunities. In other words, strange as it may sound, disbelief and skepticism concerning the absence of arbitrage opportunities are required for the no-arbitrage rule to be upheld.

Markets in which arbitrage opportunities are either nonexistent or quickly eliminated are relatively efficient markets. Recall that efficient markets are those in which it is not possible to consistently earn returns in excess of those that would be fair compensation for the risk assumed. Although abnormal returns can be earned in a variety of ways, arbitrage profits are definitely examples of abnormal returns. Thus, they are the most egregious violations of the principle of market efficiency.

---

22 A good study suggestion is to try this example with any future stock price. You should get the same result, a $2 risk-free profit.
23 This illustration is the quick look at forward pricing alluded to in Section 3.1.1.
24 In reality, many of the transactions that arbitrageurs do are not really arbitrage. They are quite speculative. For example, many people call themselves arbitrageurs because they buy companies that are potential takeover targets and sell the companies they think will be the buyers. This transaction is not arbitrage by any stretch of the definition. Some transactions are called "risk arbitrage," but this term is an oxymoron. As an investment professional, you should simply be prepared for such misuses of words, which simply reflect the flexibility of language.

Throughout the derivatives component of the CFA curriculum, we will use the principle of arbitrage as a dominant theme and assume that arbitrage opportunities cannot exist for any significant length of time nor can any one investor consistently capture them. Thus, prices must conform to models that assume no arbitrage. But we do not want to take the absence of arbitrage opportunities so seriously that we give up and believe that arbitrage opportunities never exist. Otherwise, they will arise and someone else will take them. Consider the rule of arbitrage a law that will be broken from time to time but one that holds far more often than not and one that should be understood and respected.

EXAMPLE 7

Arbitrage

1 Which of the following is a result of arbitrage?

   A The law of one price

   B The law of similar prices

   C The law of limited profitability

2 When an arbitrage opportunity exists, what happens in the market?

   A The combined actions of all arbitrageurs force the prices to converge.

   B The combined actions of arbitrageurs result in a locked-limit situation.

   C The combined actions of all arbitrageurs result in sustained profits to all.

3 Which of the following accurately defines arbitrage?

   A An opportunity to make a profit at no risk

   B An opportunity to make a profit at no risk and with the investment of no capital

   C An opportunity to earn a return in excess of the return appropriate for the risk assumed

4 Which of the following ways best describes how arbitrage contributes to market efficiency?

   A Arbitrage penalizes those who trade too rapidly.

   B Arbitrage equalizes the risks taken by all market participants.

   C Arbitrage improves the rate at which prices converge to their relative fair values.

Solution to 1:

A is correct. Arbitrage forces equivalent assets to have a single price. There is nothing called the law of similar prices or the law of limited profitability.

Solution to 2:

A is correct. Prices converge because of the heavy demand for the cheaper asset and the heavy supply of the more expensive asset. Profits are not sustained, and, in fact, they are eradicated as prices converge. Locked-limit is a condition in the futures market and has nothing to do with arbitrage.

Solution to 3:

B is correct. An opportunity to profit at no risk could merely describe the purchase of a risk-free asset. An opportunity to earn a return in excess of the return appropriate for the risk assumed is a concept studied in portfolio management and is often referred to as an abnormal return. It is certainly desirable but is hardly an arbitrage because it requires the assumption of risk and the investment of capital. Arbitrage is risk free and requires no capital because selling the overpriced asset produces the funds to buy the underpriced asset.

Solution to 4:

C is correct. Arbitrage imposes no penalties on rapid trading; in fact, it tends to reward those who trade rapidly to take advantage of arbitrage opportunities. Arbitrage has no effect of equalizing risk among market participants. Arbitrage does result in an acceleration of price convergence to fair values relative to instruments with equivalent payoffs.

SUMMARY

This first reading on derivatives introduces you to the basic characteristics of derivatives, including the following points:

■ A derivative is a financial instrument that derives its performance from the performance of an underlying asset.

■ The underlying asset, called the underlying, trades in the cash or spot markets and its price is called the cash or spot price.

■ Derivatives consist of two general classes: forward commitments and contingent claims.

■ Derivatives can be created as standardized instruments on derivatives exchanges or as customized instruments in the over-the-counter market.

■ Exchange-traded derivatives are standardized, highly regulated, and transparent transactions that are guaranteed against default through the clearinghouse of the derivatives exchange.

■ Over-the-counter derivatives are customized, flexible, and more private and less regulated than exchange-traded derivatives, but are subject to a greater risk of default.

■ A forward contract is an over-the-counter derivative contract in which two parties agree that one party, the buyer, will purchase an underlying asset from the other party, the seller, at a later date and at a fixed price they agree upon when the contract is signed.

■ A futures contract is similar to a forward contract but is a standardized derivative contract created and traded on a futures exchange. In the contract, two parties agree that one party, the buyer, will purchase an underlying asset from the other party, the seller, at a later date and at a price agreed on by the two parties when the contract is initiated. In addition, there is a daily settling of gains and losses and a credit guarantee by the futures exchange through its clearinghouse.

■ A swap is an over-the-counter derivative contract in which two parties agree to exchange a series of cash flows whereby one party pays a variable series that will be determined by an underlying asset or rate and the other party pays either a variable series determined by a different underlying asset or rate or a fixed series.

- An option is a derivative contract in which one party, the buyer, pays a sum of money to the other party, the seller or writer, and receives the right to either buy or sell an underlying asset at a fixed price either on a specific expiration date or at any time prior to the expiration date.

- A call is an option that provides the right to buy the underlying.

- A put is an option that provides the right to sell the underlying.

- Credit derivatives are a class of derivative contracts between two parties, the credit protection buyer and the credit protection seller, in which the latter provides protection to the former against a specific credit loss.

- A credit default swap is the most widely used credit derivative. It is a derivative contract between two parties, a credit protection buyer and a credit protection seller, in which the buyer makes a series of payments to the seller and receives a promise of compensation for credit losses resulting from the default of a third party.

- An asset-backed security is a derivative contract in which a portfolio of debt instruments is assembled and claims are issued on the portfolio in the form of tranches, which have different priorities of claims on the payments made by the debt securities such that prepayments or credit losses are allocated to the most-junior tranches first and the most-senior tranches last.

- Derivatives can be combined with other derivatives or underlying assets to form hybrids.

- Derivatives are issued on equities, fixed-income securities, interest rates, currencies, commodities, credit, and a variety of such diverse underlyings as weather, electricity, and disaster claims.

- Derivatives facilitate the transfer of risk, enable the creation of strategies and payoffs not otherwise possible with spot assets, provide information about the spot market, offer lower transaction costs, reduce the amount of capital required, are easier than the underlyings to go short, and improve the efficiency of spot markets.

- Derivatives are sometimes criticized for being a form of legalized gambling and for leading to destabilizing speculation, although these points can generally be refuted.

- Derivatives are typically priced by forming a hedge involving the underlying asset and a derivative such that the combination must pay the risk-free rate and do so for only one derivative price.

- Derivatives pricing relies heavily on the principle of storage, meaning the ability to hold or store the underlying asset. Storage can incur costs but can also generate cash, such as dividends and interest.

- Arbitrage is the condition that two equivalent assets or derivatives or combinations of assets and derivatives sell for different prices, leading to an opportunity to buy at the low price and sell at the high price, thereby earning a risk-free profit without committing any capital.

- The combined actions of arbitrageurs bring about a convergence of prices. Hence, arbitrage leads to the law of one price: Transactions that produce equivalent results must sell for equivalent prices.

PRACTICE PROBLEMS

1   A derivative is *best* described as a financial instrument that derives its performance by:

    A   passing through the returns of the underlying.

    B   replicating the performance of the underlying.

    C   transforming the performance of the underlying.

2   Compared with exchange-traded derivatives, over-the-counter derivatives would *most likely* be described as:

    A   standardized.

    B   less transparent.

    C   more transparent.

3   Exchange-traded derivatives are:

    A   largely unregulated.

    B   traded through an informal network.

    C   guaranteed by a clearinghouse against default.

4   Which of the following derivatives is classified as a contingent claim?

    A   Futures contracts

    B   Interest rate swaps

    C   Credit default swaps

5   In contrast to contingent claims, forward commitments provide the:

    A   right to buy or sell the underlying asset in the future.

    B   obligation to buy or sell the underlying asset in the future.

    C   promise to provide credit protection in the event of default.

6   Which of the following derivatives provide payoffs that are non-linearly related to the payoffs of the underlying?

    A   Options

    B   Forwards

    C   Interest-rate swaps

7   An interest rate swap is a derivative contract in which:

    A   two parties agree to exchange a series of cash flows.

    B   the credit seller provides protection to the credit buyer.

    C   the buyer has the right to purchase the underlying from the seller.

8   Forward commitments subject to default are:

    A   forwards and futures.

    B   futures and interest rate swaps.

    C   interest rate swaps and forwards.

9   Which of the following derivatives is *least likely* to have a value of zero at initiation of the contract?

    A   Futures

    B   Options

    C   Forwards

10 A credit derivative is a derivative contract in which the:

   A clearinghouse provides a credit guarantee to both the buyer and the seller.

   B seller provides protection to the buyer against the credit risk of a third party.

   C the buyer and seller provide a performance bond at initiation of the contract.

11 Compared with the underlying spot market, derivative markets are *more likely* to have:

   A greater liquidity.

   B higher transaction costs.

   C higher capital requirements.

12 Which of the following characteristics is *least likely* to be a benefit associated with using derivatives?

   A More effective management of risk

   B Payoffs similar to those associated with the underlying

   C Greater opportunities to go short compared with the spot market

13 Which of the following is *most likely* to be a destabilizing consequence of speculation using derivatives?

   A Increased defaults by speculators and creditors

   B Market price swings resulting from arbitrage activities

   C The creation of trading strategies that result in asymmetric performance

14 The law of one price is *best* described as:

   A the true fundamental value of an asset.

   B earning a risk-free profit without committing any capital.

   C two assets that will produce the same cash flows in the future must sell for equivalent prices.

15 Arbitrage opportunities exist when:

   A two identical assets or derivatives sell for different prices.

   B combinations of the underlying asset and a derivative earn the risk-free rate.

   C arbitrageurs simultaneously buy takeover targets and sell takeover acquirers.

SOLUTIONS

1 C is correct. A derivative is a financial instrument that transforms the performance of the underlying. The transformation of performance function of derivatives is what distinguishes it from mutual funds and exchange traded funds that pass through the returns of the underlying.

   A is incorrect because derivatives, in contrast to mutual funds and exchange traded funds, do not simply pass through the returns of the underlying at payout. B is incorrect because a derivative transforms rather than replicates the performance of the underlying.

2 B is correct. Over-the counter-derivatives markets are customized and mostly unregulated. As a result, over-the-counter markets are less transparent in comparison with the high degree of transparency and standardization associated with exchange-traded derivative markets.

   A is incorrect because exchange-traded derivatives are standardized, whereas over-the counter derivatives are customized. C is incorrect because exchange-traded derivatives are characterized by a high degree of transparency because all transactions are disclosed to exchanges and regulatory agencies, whereas over-the-counter derivatives are relatively opaque.

3 C is correct. Exchanged-traded derivatives are guaranteed by a clearinghouse against default.

   A is incorrect because traded derivatives are characterized by a relatively high degree of regulation. B is incorrect because the terms of exchange-traded derivatives terms are specified by the exchange.

4 C is correct. A credit default swap (CDS) is a derivative in which the credit protection seller provides protection to the credit protection buyer against the credit risk of a separate party. CDS are classified as a contingent claim.

   A is incorrect because futures contracts are classified as forward commitments. B is incorrect because interest rate swaps are classified as forward commitments.

5 B is correct. Forward commitments represent an obligation to buy or sell the underlying asset at an agreed upon price at a future date.

   A is incorrect because the right to buy or sell the underlying asset is a characteristic of contingent claims, not forward commitments. C is incorrect because a credit default swap provides a promise to provide credit protection to the credit protection buyer in the event of a credit event such as a default or credit downgrade and is classified as a contingent claim.

6 A is correct. Options are classified as a contingent claim which provides payoffs that are non-linearly related to the performance of the underlying.

   B is incorrect because forwards are classified as a forward commitment, which provides payoffs that are linearly related to the performance of the underlying. C is incorrect because interest-rate swaps are classified as a forward commitment, which provides payoffs that are linearly related to the performance of the underlying.

7 A is correct. An interest rate swap is defined as a derivative in which two parties agree to exchange a series of cash flows: One set of cash flows is variable, and the other set can be variable or fixed.

B is incorrect because a credit derivative is a derivative contract in which the credit protection seller provides protection to the credit protection buyer. C is incorrect because a call option gives the buyer the right to purchase the underlying from the seller.

8   C is correct. Interest rate swaps and forwards are over-the-counter contracts that are privately negotiated and are both subject to default. Futures contracts are traded on an exchange, which provides a credit guarantee and protection against default.

A is incorrect because futures are exchange-traded contracts which provide daily settlement of gains and losses and a credit guarantee by the exchange through its clearinghouse. B is incorrect because futures are exchange-traded contracts which provide daily settlement of gains and losses and a credit guarantee by the exchange through its clearinghouse.

9   B is correct. The buyer of the option pays the option premium to the seller of the option at the initiation of the contract. The option premium represents the value of the option, whereas futures and forwards have a value of zero at the initiation of the contract.

A is incorrect because no money changes hands between parties at the initiation of the futures contract, thus the value of the futures contract is zero at initiation. C is incorrect because no money changes hands between parties at the initiation of the forward contract, thus the value of the forward contract is zero at initiation.

10   B is correct. A credit derivative is a derivative contract in which the credit protection seller provides protection to the credit protection buyer against the credit risk of a third party.

A is incorrect because the clearinghouse provides a credit guarantee to both the buyer and the seller of a futures contract, whereas a credit derivative is between two parties, in which the credit protection seller provides a credit guarantee to the credit protection buyer. C is incorrect because futures contracts require that both the buyer and the seller of the futures contract provide a cash deposit for a portion of the futures transaction into a margin account, often referred to as a performance bond or good faith deposit.

11   A is correct. Derivative markets typically have greater liquidity than the underlying spot market as a result of the lower capital required to trade derivatives compared with the underlying. Derivatives also have lower transaction costs and lower capital requirements than the underlying.

B is incorrect because transaction costs for derivatives are lower than the underlying spot market. C is incorrect because derivatives markets have lower capital requirements than the underlying spot market.

12   B is correct. One of the benefits of derivative markets is that derivatives create trading strategies not otherwise possible in the underlying spot market, thus providing opportunities for more effective risk management than simply replicating the payoff of the underlying.

A is incorrect because effective risk management is one of the primary purposes associated with derivative markets. C is incorrect because one of the operational advantages associated with derivatives is that it is easier to go short compared to the underlying spot market.

13   A is correct. The benefits of derivatives, such as low transaction costs, low capital requirements, use of leverage, and the ease in which participants can go short, also can result in excessive speculative trading. These activities can lead to defaults on the part of speculators and creditors.

B is incorrect because arbitrage activities tend to bring about a convergence of prices to intrinsic value. C is incorrect because asymmetric performance is not itself destabilizing.

14 C is correct. The law of one price occurs when market participants engage in arbitrage activities so that identical assets sell for the same price in different markets.

A is incorrect because the law of one price refers to identical assets. B is incorrect because it refer to arbitrage not the law of one price.

15 A is correct. Arbitrage opportunities exist when the same asset or two equivalent combinations of assets that produce the same results sell for different prices. When this situation occurs, market participants would buy the asset in the cheaper market and simultaneously sell it in the more expensive market, thus earning a riskless arbitrage profit without committing any capital.

B is incorrect because it is not the definition of an arbitrage opportunity. C is incorrect because it is not the definition of an arbitrage opportunity.

READING

58

Basics of Derivative Pricing and Valuation

by Don M. Chance, CFA

LEARNING OUTCOMES

Mastery	The candidate should be able to:
☐	a. explain how the concepts of arbitrage, replication, and risk neutrality are used in pricing derivatives;
☐	b. distinguish between value and price of forward and futures contracts;
☐	c. explain how the value and price of a forward contract are determined at expiration, during the life of the contract, and at initiation;
☐	d. describe monetary and nonmonetary benefits and costs associated with holding the underlying asset, and explain how they affect the value and price of a forward contract;
☐	e. define a forward rate agreement and describe its uses;
☐	f. explain why forward and futures prices differ;
☐	g. explain how swap contracts are similar to but different from a series of forward contracts;
☐	h. distinguish between the value and price of swaps;
☐	i. explain how the value of a European option is determined at expiration;
☐	j. explain the exercise value, time value, and moneyness of an option;
☐	k. identify the factors that determine the value of an option, and explain how each factor affects the value of an option;
☐	l. explain put–call parity for European options;
☐	m. explain put–call–forward parity for European options;
☐	n. explain how the value of an option is determined using a one-period binomial model;
☐	o. explain under which circumstances the values of European and American options differ.

INTRODUCTION

It is important to understand how prices of derivatives are determined. Whether one is on the buy side or the sell side, a solid understanding of pricing financial products is critical to effective investment decision making. After all, one can hardly determine what to offer or bid for a financial product, or any product for that matter, if one has no idea how its characteristics combine to create value.

Understanding the pricing of financial assets is important. Discounted cash flow methods and models, such as the capital asset pricing model and its variations, are useful for determining the prices of financial assets. The unique characteristics of derivatives, however, pose some complexities not associated with assets, such as equities and fixed-income instruments. Somewhat surprisingly, however, derivatives also have some simplifying characteristics. For example, as we will see in this reading, in well-functioning derivatives markets the need to determine risk premiums is obviated by the ability to construct a risk-free hedge. Correspondingly, the need to determine an investor's risk aversion is irrelevant for derivative pricing, although it is certainly relevant for pricing the underlying.

The purpose of this reading is to establish the foundations of derivative pricing on a basic conceptual level. The following topics are covered:

- How does the pricing of the underlying asset affect the pricing of derivatives?
- How are derivatives priced using the principle of arbitrage?
- How are the prices and values of forward contracts determined?
- How are futures contracts priced differently from forward contracts?
- How are the prices and values of swaps determined?
- How are the prices and values of European options determined?
- How does American option pricing differ from European option pricing?

This reading is organized as follows. Section 2 explores two related topics, the pricing of the underlying assets on which derivatives are created and the principle of arbitrage. Section 3 describes the pricing and valuation of forwards, futures, and swaps. Section 4 introduces the pricing and valuation of options. Section 5 provides a summary.

FUNDAMENTAL CONCEPTS OF DERIVATIVE PRICING

In this section, we will briefly review the concepts associated with derivatives, the types of derivatives, and the pricing principles of the underlying assets. We will also look at arbitrage, a critical concept that links derivative pricing to the price of the underlying.

2.1 Basic Derivative Concepts

The definition of a derivative is as follows:

> *A derivative is a financial instrument that derives its performance from the performance of an underlying asset.*

A derivative is created as a contract between two parties, the buyer and the seller. Derivatives trade in markets around the world, which include organized exchanges, where highly standardized and regulated versions exist, and over-the-counter markets, where customized and more lightly regulated versions trade. The basic characteristics of derivatives that influence pricing are not particularly related to where the derivatives trade, but are critically dependent on the types of derivatives.

The two principal types of derivatives are forward commitments and contingent claims. A forward commitment is an obligation to engage in a transaction in the spot market at a future date at terms agreed upon today.[1] By entering into a forward commitment, a party locks in the terms of a transaction that he or she will conduct later. The word "commitment" is critical here. A forward contract is a firm obligation.

There are three types of forward commitments: forward contracts, futures contracts, and swap contracts. These contracts can be referred to more simply as forwards, futures, and swaps.

> A **forward contract** is an over-the-counter derivative contract in which two parties agree that one party, the buyer, will purchase an underlying asset from the other party, the seller, at a later date at a fixed price they agree upon when the contract is signed.

> A **futures contract** is a standardized derivative contract created and traded on a futures exchange in which two parties agree that one party, the buyer, will purchase an underlying asset from the other party, the seller, at a later date at a price agreed upon by the two parties when the contract is initiated and in which there is a daily settling of gains and losses and a credit guarantee by the futures exchange through its clearinghouse.

> A **swap contract** is an over-the-counter derivative contract in which two parties agree to exchange a series of cash flows whereby one party pays a variable series that will be determined by an underlying asset or rate and the other party pays either 1) a variable series determined by a different underlying asset or rate or 2) a fixed series.

As these definitions illustrate, forwards and futures are similar. They both establish the terms of a spot transaction that will occur at a later date. Forwards are customized, less transparent, less regulated, and subject to higher counterparty default risk. Futures are standardized, more transparent, more regulated, and generally immune to counterparty default. A swap is equivalent to a series of forward contracts, a point that will be illustrated later.

A contingent claim is a derivative in which the outcome or payoff is determined by the outcome or payoff of an underlying asset, conditional on some event occurring. Contingent claims include options, credit derivatives, and asset-backed securities. Because credit derivatives and asset-backed securities are highly specialized, this reading will focus only on options.

Recall the definition of an option:

> An **option** is a derivative contract in which one party, the buyer, pays a sum of money to the other party, the seller or writer, and receives the right to either buy or sell an underlying asset at a fixed price either on a specific expiration date or at any time prior to the expiration date.

Options can be either customized over-the-counter contracts or standardized and traded on exchanges.

---

1 Remember that the term "spot market" refers to the market in which the underlying trades. A transaction in the spot market involves a buyer paying for an asset and receiving it right away or at least within a few days, given the normal time required to settle a financial transaction.

Because derivatives take their prices from the price of the underlying, it is important to first understand how the underlying is priced. We will approach the underlying from a slightly different angle, one that emphasizes the often-subtle costs of holding the underlying, which turn out to play a major role in derivative pricing.

2.2 Pricing the Underlying

The four main types of underlying on which derivatives are based are equities, fixed-income securities/interest rates, currencies, and commodities. Equities, fixed-income securities (but not interest rates), currencies, and commodities are all assets. An interest rate is not an asset, but it can be structured as the underlying of a derivative.[2]

Consider a generic underlying asset. This asset is something of value that you can own. Some assets are financial assets, such as equities, bonds, and currencies, and some are real assets, such as commodities (e.g., gold, oil, and agricultural products) and certain physical objects (e.g., houses, automobiles, and computers).

The price of a financial asset is often determined using a present value of future cash flows approach. The value of the financial asset is the expected future price plus any interim payments such as dividends or coupon interest discounted at a rate appropriate for the risk assumed. Such a definition presumes a period of time over which an investor anticipates holding an asset, known as the holding period. The investor forecasts the price expected to prevail at the end of the holding period as well as any cash flows that are expected to be earned over the holding period. He then takes that predicted future price and expected cash flows and finds their current value by discounting them to the present. Thereby, the investor arrives at a fundamental value for the asset and will compare that value with its current market price. Based on any differential relative to the cost of trading and his confidence in his valuation model, he will make a decision about whether to trade.

2.2.1 *The Formation of Expectations*

Let us first assume that the underlying does not pay interest or dividends, nor does it have any other cash flows attributable to holding the asset. Exhibit 1 illustrates the basic idea behind the valuation process. Using a probability distribution, the investor forecasts the future over a holding period spanning time 0 to time T. The center of the distribution is the expected price of the asset at time T, which we denote as $E(S_T)$, and represents the investor's prediction of the spot price at T. The investor knows there is risk, so this prediction is imperfect—hence the reason for the probability distribution. Nonetheless, at time 0 the investor makes her best prediction of the spot price at time T, which becomes the foundation for determining what she perceives to be the value of the asset.[3]

---

2 This is a good example of why it is best not to use the term "underlying *asset*" when speaking of derivatives. Not all derivatives have underlying assets, but all have underlyings, some of which are not assets. Some other examples of non-asset underlyings used in derivatives are weather, insurance claims, and shipping rates. There are also some derivatives in which the underlying is another derivative.

3 The distribution shown here is symmetrical and relatively similar to a normal distribution, but this characterization is for illustrative purposes only. We are making no assumptions about symmetry or normality at this point.

Exhibit 1   The Formation of Expectations for an Asset

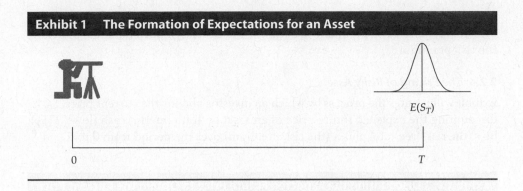

$E(S_T)$

0   T

2.2.2 *The Required Rate of Return on the Underlying Asset*

To determine the value of the asset, this prediction must be converted into its price or present value. The specific procedure is to discount this expected future price, but that is the easy part. Determining the rate at which to discount the expected future price is the hard part. We use the symbol k to denote this currently unknown discount rate, which is often referred to as the required rate of return and sometimes the expected rate of return or just the expected return. At a minimum, that rate will include the risk-free rate of interest, which we denote as r. This rate represents the opportunity cost, or so-called time value of money, and reflects the price of giving up your money today in return for receiving more money later.

2.2.3 *The Risk Aversion of the Investor*

At this point, we must briefly discuss an important characteristic of investors: their degree of risk aversion. We can generally characterize three potential types of investors by how they feel about risk: risk averse, risk neutral, or risk seeking.

Risk-neutral investors are willing to engage in risky investments for which they expect to earn only the risk-free rate. Thus, they do not expect to earn a premium for bearing risk. For risk-averse investors, however, risk is undesirable, so they do not consider the risk-free rate an adequate return to compensate them for the risk. Thus, risk-averse investors require a risk premium, which is an increase in the expected return that is sufficient to justify the acceptance of risk. All things being equal, an investment with a higher risk premium will have a lower price. It is very important to understand, however, that risk premiums are not automatically earned. They are merely expectations. Actual outcomes can differ. Clearly stocks that decline in value did not earn risk premiums, even though someone obviously bought them with the expectation that they would. Nonetheless, risk premiums must exist in the long run or risk-averse investors would not accept the risk.

The third type of investor is one we must mention but do not treat as realistic. Risk seekers are those who prefer risk over certainty and will pay more to invest when there is risk, implying a negative risk premium. We almost always assume that investors prefer certainty over uncertainty, so we generally treat a risk-seeking investor as just a theoretical possibility and not a practical reality.[4]

---

4 People who gamble in casinos or play lotteries appear to be risk-seekers, given the advantage of the casino or the lottery organizer, but they are merely earning utility from the game itself, not necessarily from the expected financial outcome.

We will assume that investors are risk averse. To justify taking risk, risk-averse investors require a risk premium. We will use the Greek symbol λ (lambda) to denote the risk premium.[5]

2.2.4 *The Pricing of Risky Assets*

Exhibit 2 illustrates the process by which an investor obtains the current price, S_0, by discounting the expected future price of an asset with no interim cash flows, $E(S_T)$, by r (the risk-free rate) plus λ (the risk premium) over the period from 0 to T.

Exhibit 2   Discounting the Expected Future Price to Obtain the Current Price

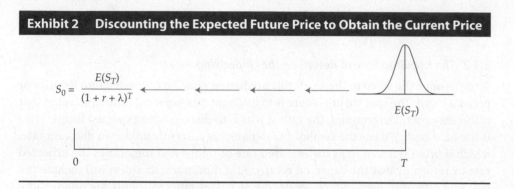

$$S_0 = \frac{E(S_T)}{(1 + r + \lambda)^T}$$

2.2.5 *Other Benefits and Costs of Holding an Asset*

Many assets generate benefits and some incur costs to their owners. Some of these costs are monetary and others are nonmonetary. The dividends paid by companies and coupon interest paid by borrowers on their bonds represent obvious benefits to the holders of these securities. With currencies representing investments that earn the risk-free rate in a foreign country, they too generate benefits in the form of interest. Barring default, interest payments on bonds and currencies are relatively certain, so we will treat them as such. Dividend payments are not certain, but dividends do tend to be fairly predictable. As such, we will make an assumption common to most derivative models that dividends are certain.[6]

There is substantial evidence that some commodities generate a benefit that is somewhat opaque and difficult to measure. This benefit is called the **convenience yield**. It represents a nonmonetary advantage of holding the asset. For most financial assets, convenience yields are either nonexistent or extremely limited. Financial assets do not possess beauty that might make a person enjoy owning them just to look at them. Convenience yields are primarily associated with commodities and generally exist as a result of difficulty in either shorting the commodity or unusually tight supplies. For example, if a commodity cannot be sold short without great difficulty or cost, the holder of the commodity has an advantage if market conditions suggest that the commodity should be sold. Also, if a commodity is in short supply, the holders of the commodity can sometimes extract a price premium that is believed by some to be higher than what would be justified in well-functioning markets. The spot price of the commodity could even be above the market's expectation of its future price, a condition that would seem to imply a negative expected return. This scenario raises the question of why anyone would want to hold the commodity if its expected return is negative. The convenience yield provides a possible explanation that attributes an

---

5 Although the risk-free rate is invariant with a country's economy, the risk premium varies with the amount of risk taken. Thus, while the risk-free rate is the same when applied to every investment, the risk premium is not the same for every investment.

6 Some derivative models incorporate uncertain dividends and interest, but those are beyond the scope of this introductory reading.

implied but non-financial expected return to the advantage of holding a commodity in short supply. The holder of the commodity has the ability to sell it when market conditions suggest that selling is advisable and short selling is difficult.

One cost incurred in owning commodities is the cost of storage. One could hardly own gold, oil, or wheat without incurring some costs in storing these assets. There are also costs incurred in protecting and insuring some commodities against theft or destruction. Depending on the commodity, these costs can be quite significant. For financial assets, however, the storage costs are so low that we can safely ignore them.

Finally, there is the opportunity cost of the money invested. If a person buys an asset, he forgoes interest on his money. The effect on this interest is reflected by compounding the price paid for the asset to a future value at the risk-free rate of interest. Thus, an investor who buys a stock that costs £50 in a market in which the risk-free rate is 4% will effectively have paid £50 × 1.04 = £52 a year later. Of course, the stock could be worth any value at that time, and any gain or loss should be determined in comparison to the effective price paid of £52.

As we described earlier, we determine the current price of an asset by discounting the expected future price by the sum of the risk-free rate (r) plus the risk premium (λ). When we introduce costs and benefits of holding the asset, we have to make an adjustment. With the exception of this opportunity cost of money, we will incorporate the effect of these costs and benefits by determining their value at the end of the holding period. Under the assumption that these costs and benefits are certain, we can then discount them at the risk-free rate to obtain their present value. There is a logic to doing it this way (i.e., finding their future value and discounting back to the present, as opposed to finding their present value directly). By finding their future value, we are effectively saying that the costs and benefits adjust the expected payoff at the end of the holding period. But because they are certain, we can discount their effects at the risk-free rate. So we have effectively just found their present value. The net effect is that the costs reduce the current price and the benefits increase the current price. We use the symbol θ (theta) to denote the present value of the costs and γ (gamma) as the present value of any benefits.

The net of the costs and benefits is often referred to by the term **carry**, or sometimes **cost of carry**. The holding, storing, or "carrying" of an asset is said to incur a net cost that is essentially what it takes to "carry" an asset. Exhibit 3 illustrates the effect in which the carry adjusts the price of an asset in the valuation process.

Exhibit 3   Pricing an Asset That Incurs Costs and Generates Benefits

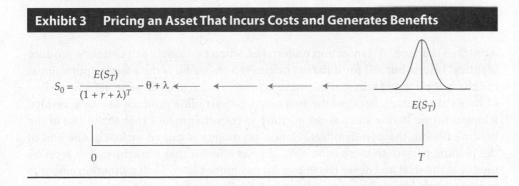

$$S_0 = \frac{E(S_T)}{(1 + r + \lambda)^T} - \theta + \lambda$$

$E(S_T)$

0   T

EXAMPLE 1

Pricing the Spot Asset

1 Which of the following factors does **not** affect the spot price of an asset that has no interim costs or benefits?

   A The time value of money

   B The risk aversion of investors

   C The price recently paid by other investors

2 Which of the following does **not** represent a benefit of holding an asset?

   A The convenience yield

   B An optimistic expected outlook for the asset

   C Dividends if the asset is a stock or interest if the asset is a bond

Solution to 1:

C is correct. The price recently paid by other investors is past information and does not affect the spot price. The time value of money and the risk aversion of investors determine the discount rate. Only current information is relevant as investors look ahead, not back.

Solution to 2:

B is correct. An optimistic forecast for the asset is not a benefit of holding the asset, but it does appear in the valuation of the asset as a high expected price at the horizon date. Convenience yields and dividends and interest are benefits of holding the asset.

To recap, although the various underlyings differ with respect to the specifics of pricing, all of them are based on expectations, risk, and the costs and benefits of holding a specific underlying. Understanding how assets are priced in the spot market is critical to understanding how derivatives are priced. To understand derivative pricing, it is necessary to establish a linkage between the derivative market and the spot market. That linkage occurs through arbitrage.

2.3 The Principle of Arbitrage

Arbitrage is a type of transaction undertaken when two assets or portfolios produce identical results but sell for different prices. If a trader buys the asset or portfolio at the cheaper price and sells it at the more expensive price, she will generate a net inflow of funds at the start. Because the two assets or portfolios produce identical results, a long position in one and a short position in the other means that at the end of the holding period, the payoffs offset. Hence, no money is gained or lost at the end of the holding period, so there is no risk. The net effect is that the arbitrageur receives money at the start and never has to pay out any money later. Such a situation amounts to free money, like walking down the street, finding money on the ground, and never having to give it up. Exhibit 4 illustrates this process for assets A and B, which have no dividends or other benefits or costs and pay off identically but sell for different prices, with $S_0^A < S_0^B$.

Exhibit 4   Executing an Arbitrage

Given: Assets A and B produce the same values at time T but at time 0, A is selling for less than B.

$S_0^A < S_0^B$:
Buy A at S_0^A
Sell B at S_0^B
Cash flow = $S_0^B - S_0^A (> 0)$

$S_T^A = S_T^B$:
Sell A for S_T^A
Buy B for S_T^B
Cash flow = $S_T^A - S_T^B (= 0)$

0   T

2.3.1 *The (In)Frequency of Arbitrage Opportunities*

When arbitrage opportunities exist, traders exploit them very quickly. The combined actions of many traders engaging in the same transaction of buying the low-priced asset or portfolio and selling the high-priced asset or portfolio results in increased demand and an increasing price for the former and decreased demand and a decreasing price for the latter. This market activity will continue until the prices converge. Assets that produce identical results can thus have only one true market price. This rule is called the "law of one price." With virtually all market participants alert for the possibility of earning such profits at no risk, it should not be surprising that arbitrage opportunities are rare.

In practice, prices need not converge precisely, or even all that quickly, because the transaction cost of exploiting an opportunity could exceed the benefit. For example, say you are walking down the sidewalk of the Champs-Élysées in Paris and notice a €1 coin on the sidewalk. You have a bad back, and it would take some effort to bend over. The transaction cost of exploiting this opportunity without any risk could exceed the benefit of the money. Some arbitrage opportunities represent such small discrepancies that they are not worth exploiting because of transaction costs.

Significant arbitrage opportunities, however, will be exploited. A significant opportunity arises from a price differential large enough to overcome the transaction costs. Any such price differential will continue to be exploited until the opportunity disappears. Thus, if you find a €10 note on the Champs-Élysées sidewalk, there is a good chance you will find it worth picking up (even with your bad back), and even if you do not pick it up, it will probably not be there for long. With enough people alert for such opportunities, only a few will arise, and the ones that do will be quickly exploited and disappear. In this manner, arbitrage makes markets work much more efficiently.

2.3.2 *Arbitrage and Derivatives*

It may be difficult to conceive of many investments that would produce identical payoffs. Even similar companies such as McDonalds and Burger King, which are in the same line of business, do not perform identically. Their performance may be correlated, but each has its own unique characteristics. For equity securities and with no derivatives involved, about the only such situation that could exist in reality is a stock that trades simultaneously in two different markets, such as Royal Dutch Shell, which trades in Amsterdam and London but is a single company. Clearly there can be only one price. If those two markets operate in different currencies, the currency-adjusted prices should be the same. Bonds issued by the same borrower are also potentially arbitrageable. All bonds of an issuer will be priced off of the term structure of interest rates. Because of this common factor, bonds of different maturities can be arbitraged against each other. But in general, two securities are unlikely to perform identically.

The picture changes, however, if we introduce derivatives. For most derivatives, the payoffs come (derive) directly from the value of the underlying at the expiration of the derivative. Although no one can predict with certainty the value of the underlying at expiration, as soon as that value is determined, the value of the derivative at expiration becomes certain. So, while the performance of McDonalds' stock may have a strong correlation to the performance of Burger King's stock, neither completely determines the other. But derivatives on McDonalds' stock and derivatives on Burger King's stock are completely determined by their respective stocks. All of the uncertainty in a derivative comes from the uncertainty in the underlying. As a result, the price of the derivative is tied to the price of the underlying. That being the case, the derivative can be used to hedge the underlying, or vice versa.

Exhibit 5 illustrates this point. When the underlying is combined with the derivative to produce a perfect hedge, all of the risk is eliminated and the position should earn the risk-free rate. If not, arbitrageurs begin to trade. If the position generates a return in excess of the risk-free rate, the arbitrageurs see an opportunity because the hedged position of the underlying and derivative earns more than the risk-free rate and a risk-free loan undertaken as a borrower incurs a cost equal to the risk-free rate. Therefore, going long the hedged position and borrowing at the risk-free rate earns a return in excess of the risk-free rate, incurs a cost of the risk-free rate, and has no risk. As a result, an investor can earn excess return at no risk without committing any capital. Arbitrageurs will execute this transaction in large volumes, continuing to exploit the pricing discrepancy until market forces push prices back in line such that both risk-free transactions earn the risk-free rate.

Exhibit 5   Hedging the Underlying with a Derivative (or Vice Versa)

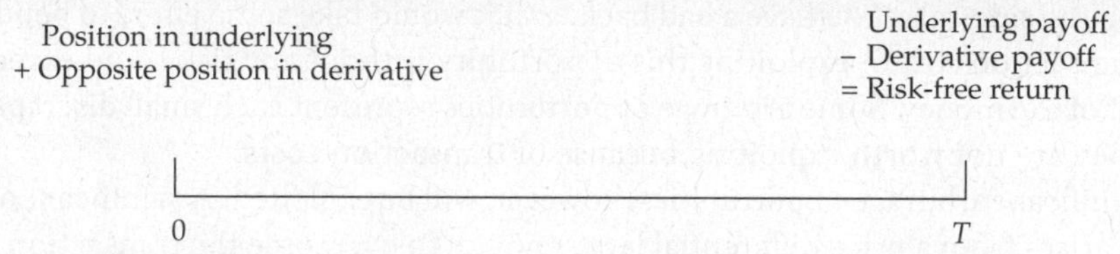

Position in underlying
+ Opposite position in derivative

Underlying payoff
– Derivative payoff
= Risk-free return

0   T

Out of this process, one and only one price can exist for the derivative. Otherwise, there will be an arbitrage opportunity. We typically take the underlying price as given and infer the unique derivative price that prohibits any arbitrage opportunities. Most derivatives pricing models are established on this foundation. We simply assume that no arbitrage opportunities can exist and infer the derivative price that guarantees there are no arbitrage opportunities.

2.3.3 *Arbitrage and Replication*

Because an asset and a derivative on the asset can be combined to produce a position equivalent to a risk-free bond, it follows that the asset and the risk-free asset can be combined to produce the derivative. Alternatively, the derivative and the risk-free asset can be combined to produce the asset. Exhibit 6 shows this process, referred to as **replication**. Replication is the creation of an asset or portfolio from another asset, portfolio, and/or derivative. Exhibit 6 shows first that an asset plus the derivative can replicate the risk-free asset. Second, an asset minus the risk-free asset (meaning to borrow at the risk-free rate) is equivalent to the opposite position in the derivative, and third, a derivative minus the risk-free asset is equivalent to the opposite position in the asset.

Exhibit 6   Arbitrage, Replication, and Derivatives

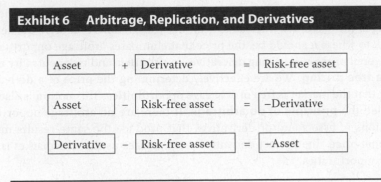

If all assets are correctly priced to prohibit arbitrage, however, the ability to replicate seems useless. Why would one replicate an asset or derivative if there is no cost advantage? Buying a government security to earn the risk-free rate is easier than buying the asset and selling a derivative to produce a risk-free position. At this point, that is certainly a reasonable question. As we progress through this material, however, we will relax the assumption that everything is always correctly priced and we will admit the possibility of occasional arbitrage opportunities. For example, it may be more profitable to hedge a portfolio with a derivative to produce a risk-free rate than to invest in the risk-free asset. In addition, we might find that replication can have lower transaction costs. For example, a derivative on a stock index combined with the risk-free asset can potentially replicate an index fund at lower transaction costs than buying all the securities in the index. Replication is the essence of arbitrage. The ability to replicate something with something else can be valuable to investors, either through pricing differentials, however temporary, or lower transaction costs.

2.3.4 *Risk Aversion, Risk Neutrality, and Arbitrage-Free Pricing*

Most investors are risk averse. They do not accept risk without the expectation of a return commensurate with that risk. Thus, they require risk premiums to justify the risk. One might think that this point implies a method for pricing derivatives based on the application of a risk premium to the expected payoff of the derivative and its risk. As we will describe later, this methodology is not appropriate in the pricing of derivatives.

As previously described, a derivative can be combined with an asset to produce a risk-free position. This fact does not mean that one *should* create such a combination. It merely means that one *can* do so. The derivative price is the price that guarantees the risk-free combination of the derivative and the underlying produces a risk-free return. The derivative price can then be inferred from the characteristics of the underlying, the characteristics of the derivative, and the risk-free rate. The investor's risk aversion is not a factor in determining the derivative price. Because the risk aversion of the investor is not relevant to pricing the derivative, one can just as easily obtain the derivative price by assuming that the investor is risk neutral. That means that the expected payoff of the derivative can be discounted at the risk-free rate rather than the risk-free rate plus a risk premium. Virtually all derivative pricing models ultimately take this form: discounting the expected payoff of the derivative at the risk-free rate.

The entire process of pricing derivatives is not exactly as we have described it at this point. There is an intermediate step, which entails altering the probabilities of the outcomes from the true probabilities to something called risk-neutral probabilities. We will illustrate this process later in this reading. The important point to understand is that while the risk aversion of investors is relevant to pricing assets, it is not relevant to pricing derivatives. As such, derivatives pricing is sometimes called **risk-neutral pricing**. Risk-neutral pricing uses the fact that arbitrage opportunities guarantee that a risk-free portfolio consisting of the underlying and the derivative must earn the risk-free rate. There is only one derivative price that meets that condition. Any mispricing of the derivative will lead to arbitrage transactions that drive the derivative price back to where it should be, the price that eliminates arbitrage opportunities.

The overall process of pricing derivatives by arbitrage and risk neutrality is called **arbitrage-free pricing**. We are effectively determining the price of a derivative by assuming that the market is free of arbitrage opportunities. This notion is also sometimes called the **principle of no arbitrage**. If there are no arbitrage opportunities, combinations of assets and/or derivatives that produce the same results must sell for the same price. The correct derivative price assures us that the market is free of arbitrage opportunities.

2.3.5 Limits to Arbitrage

As we previously described, there may be reasons to not pick up a coin lying on the ground. Likewise, some small arbitrage profits are never exploited. A bond selling for €1,000 might offer an arbitrage profit by trading a derivative on the bond and a risk-free asset at a total cost of €999, but the profit of €1 might be exceeded by the transaction costs. Such small differentials can easily remain essentially trapped within the bounds of transaction costs. In addition, arbitrage can require capital. Not everyone can borrow virtually unlimited amounts of money at what amounts to a risk-free rate. Moreover, some transactions can require additional capital to maintain positions. The corresponding gains from an offsetting position might not be liquid. Hence, on paper the position is hedged, but in practice, one position has a cash outflow while the other generates gains on paper that are realized only later. Borrowing against those future gains is not always easy.

Moreover, some apparent arbitrage transactions are not completely risk free. As you will learn later, option pricing requires knowledge of the volatility of the underlying asset, which is information that is not easy to obtain and subject to different opinions. Executing an arbitrage can entail risk if one lacks accurate information on the model inputs.

Some arbitrage positions require short-selling assets that can be difficult to short. Some securities are held only by investors who are unwilling to lend the securities and who, by policy, are not arbitrageurs themselves. Some commodities, in particular, can be difficult and costly to sell short. Hence, the arbitrage might exist in only one direction, which keeps the price from becoming seemingly too high or seemingly too low but permitting it to move virtually without limit in the opposite direction.

Arbitrage positions rely on the ultimate realization by other investors of the existence of the mispricing. For some investors, bearing these costs and risks until other investors drive the price back to its appropriate level can be nearly impossible.

The arbitrage principle is the essence of derivative pricing models. Yet, clearly there are limits to the ability of all investors to execute arbitrage transactions. In studying derivative pricing, it is important to accept the no-arbitrage rule as a paradigm, meaning a framework for analysis and understanding. Although no market experts think that arbitrage opportunities never occur, it is a common belief that finding and exploiting them is a challenging and highly competitive process that will not yield frequent success. But it is important that market participants stay alert for and exploit whatever arbitrage opportunities arise. In response, the market functions more efficiently.

EXAMPLE 2

Arbitrage

1 Which of the following *best* describes an arbitrage opportunity? It is an opportunity to:

   A earn a risk premium in the short run.

   B buy an asset at less than its fundamental value.

   C make a profit at no risk with no capital invested.

2 What *most likely* happens when an arbitrage opportunity exists?

   A Investors trade quickly and prices adjust to eliminate the opportunity.

   B Risk premiums increase to compensate traders for the additional risk.

   C Markets cease operations to eliminate the possibility of profit at no risk.

3 Which of the following *best* describes how derivatives are priced?

   A A hedge portfolio is used that eliminates arbitrage opportunities.

   B The payoff of the underlying is adjusted downward by the derivative value.

   C The expected future payoff of the derivative is discounted at the risk-free rate plus a risk premium.

4 An investor who requires no premium to compensate for the assumption of risk is said to be which of the following?

   A Risk seeking

   B Risk averse

   C Risk neutral

5 Which of the following is a limit to arbitrage?

   A Clearinghouses restrict the transactions that can be arbitraged.

   B Pricing models do not show whether to buy or sell the derivative.

   C It may not always be possible to raise sufficient capital to engage in arbitrage.

Solution to 1:

C is correct because it is the only answer that is based on the notion of when an arbitrage opportunity exists: when two identical assets or portfolios sell for different prices. A risk premium earned in the short run can easily have occurred through luck. Buying an asset at less than fair value might not even produce a profit.

Solution to 2:

A is correct. The combined actions of traders push prices back in line to a level at which no arbitrage opportunities exist. Markets certainly do not shut down, and risk premiums do not adjust and, in fact, have no relevance to arbitrage profits.

Solution to 3:

A is correct. A hedge portfolio is formed that eliminates arbitrage opportunities and implies a unique price for the derivative. The other answers are incorrect because the underlying payoff is not adjusted by the derivative value and the discount rate of the derivative does not include a risk premium.

Solution to 4:

C is correct. Risk-seeking investors give away a risk premium because they enjoy taking risk. Risk-averse investors expect a risk premium to compensate for the risk. Risk-neutral investors neither give nor receive a risk premium because they have no feelings about risk.

Solution to 5:

C is correct. It may not always be possible to raise sufficient capital to engage in arbitrage. Clearinghouses do not restrict arbitrage. Pricing models show what the price of the derivative should be.

Thus, comparison with the market price will indicate if the derivative is overpriced and should be sold or if it is underpriced and should be purchased.

2.4 The Concept of Pricing vs. Valuation

In equity markets, analysis is undertaken with the objective of determining the value, sometimes called the fundamental value, of a stock. When a stock trades in the market for a price that differs from its fundamental value, investors will often buy or sell the stock based on the perceived mispricing. The fundamental value of a stock is typically determined by analyzing the company's financial statements, projecting its earnings and dividends, determining a discount rate based on the risk, and finding the present value of the future dividends. These steps make up the essence of dividend discount models. Other approaches include comparing the book value of a company to its market value, thereby using book value as a proxy for fundamental value, or by application of a price/earnings ratio to projected next-period earnings, or by discounting free cash flow. Each of these approaches purports to estimate the company's fundamental value, leading to the notion that a company is worth something that may or may not correspond to its price in the market.

In derivative markets, the notion of valuation as a representation of fundamental value is still a valid concept, but the terminology can be somewhat different and can lead to some confusion. Options are not a problem in this regard. They can be analyzed to determine their fundamental value, and the market price can be compared with the fundamental value. Any difference can then presumably be exploited via arbitrage. The combined actions of numerous investors should ultimately lead to the market price converging to its fundamental value, subject to the above limits to arbitrage.

The world of forwards, futures, and swaps, however, uses different terminology with respect to price and value. These contracts do not require the outlay of cash at the start the way an option, stock, or bond does. Forwards, futures, and swaps start off with values of zero. Then as the underlying moves, their values become either positive or negative. The forward, futures, or swap price is a concept that represents the fixed price or rate at which the underlying will be purchased at a later date. It is not an amount to be paid at the start. This fixed price or rate is embedded into the contract while the value will fluctuate as market conditions change. But more importantly, the value and price are not at all comparable with each other.

Consider a simple example. Suppose you own a stock priced at $102. You have a short forward contract to sell the stock at a price of $100 one year from now. The risk-free rate is 4%. Your position is riskless because you know that one year from now, you will sell the stock for $100. Thus, you know you will get $100 one year from now, which has a present value of $100/(1.04) = $96.15. Notice the discounting at the risk-free rate, which is appropriate because the position is riskless. Your overall position is that you own an asset worth $102 and are short a contract worth something, and the two positions combine to have a value of $96.15. Therefore, the forward contract must have a value of $96.15 − $102 = −$5.85. Your forward contract is thus worth −$5.85. To the party on the opposite side, it is worth +$5.85.[7] The price of the forward contract is still $100, which was set when you created the contract at an earlier date. As you can see, the $100 forward price is not comparable to the $5.85 value of the contract.

Although the forward price is fixed, any new forward contract calling for delivery of the same asset at the same time will have a different price. We will cover that point in more detail later. For now, it is important to see that your contract has a price of $100 but a value of –$5.85, which are two entirely different orders of magnitude. This information does not imply that the forward contract is mispriced. The value is the amount of wealth represented by owning the forward contract. The price is one of the terms the parties agreed on when they created the contract.[8] This idea applies in the same manner for futures and swaps.

PRICING AND VALUATION OF FORWARD COMMITMENTS

In this section, we will go into pricing forward commitments in a little more detail. Let us start by establishing that today, at time 0, we create a forward commitment that expires at time T. The value of the underlying today is S_0. At expiration the underlying value is S_T, which is not known at the initiation of the contract.

3.1 Pricing and Valuation of Forward Contracts

Previously, we noted that price and value are entirely different concepts for forward commitments. We gave an example of a forward contract with a price of $100 but a value of –$5.85 to the seller and +$5.85 to the buyer. In the next subsection, we will delve more deeply into understanding these concepts of pricing and valuation for forward contracts.

3.1.1 Pricing and Valuation of Forward Contracts at Expiration

Recall that a forward contract specifies that one party agrees to buy the underlying from the other at the expiration date at a price agreed on at the start of the contract. Suppose that you enter into a contract with another party in which you will buy a used car from that party in one year at a price of $10,000. Then $10,000 is the forward price. One year later, when the contract expires, you are committed to paying $10,000 and accepting delivery of the car. Let us say that at that time, you check the used car market and find that an identical car is worth $10,800. How much is your forward contract worth to you at that time? It obligates you to pay $10,000 for a car that you would otherwise have to pay $10,800. Thus, the contract benefits you by $800, so its value is $800. If you were on the opposite side of the transaction, its value would be –$800. If the market price of the car were below $10,000, the contract would have negative value to you and the mirror image positive value to the seller.

---

7 This concept of the value of the forward contract as it evolves toward expiration is sometimes referred to as its mark-to-market value. The same notion is applicable to swaps. In futures, of course, contracts are automatically marked to market by the clearinghouse, and gains and losses are converted into actual cash flows from one party to the other.

8 The forward price is more like the exercise price of the option. It is the price the two parties agree will be paid at a future date for the underlying. Of course, the option has the feature that the holder need not ever pay that price, which is the case if the holder chooses not to exercise the option.

This example leads us to our first important derivative pricing result. The forward price, established at the initiation date of contract is $F_0(T)$. Let us denote the value at expiration of the forward contract as $V_T(T)$. This value is formally stated as

$$V_T(T) = S_T - F_0(T) \tag{1}$$

In words,

> *The value of a forward contract at expiration is the spot price of the underlying minus the forward price agreed to in the contract.*

In the financial world, we generally define value as the value to the long position, so the above definition is generally correct but would be adjusted if we look at the transaction from the point of view of the short party. In that case, we would multiply the value to the long party by –1 to calculate the value to the short party. Alternatively, the value to the short party is the forward price minus the spot price at expiration.

If a forward contract could be initiated right at the instant of expiration, the forward price would clearly be the spot price. Such a contract would essentially be a spot transaction.

3.1.2 *Pricing and Valuation at Initiation Date*

In Exhibit 7, we see the nature of the problem of pricing a forward contract. We are situated at time 0, facing an uncertain future. At the horizon date, time T, the underlying price will be S_T. Of course, at time 0 we do not know what S_T will turn out to be. Yet at time 0, we need to establish the forward price, $F_0(T)$, which is the price we agree to pay at time T to purchase the asset.

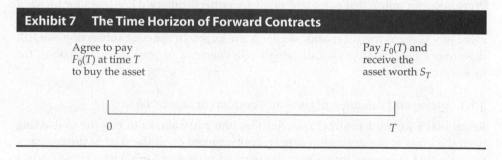

Exhibit 7   The Time Horizon of Forward Contracts

Agree to pay $F_0(T)$ at time T to buy the asset

Pay $F_0(T)$ and receive the asset worth S_T

0 T

When a forward contract is initiated, neither party pays anything to the other. It is a valueless contract, neither an asset nor a liability. Therefore, its value at initiation is zero:

$$V_0(T) = 0 \tag{2}$$

The forward price that the parties agree to at the initiation date of the contract is a special price that results in the contract having zero value and prohibiting arbitrage. This is our first important result:

> *Because neither the long nor the short pays anything to the other at the initiation date of a forward contract, the value of a forward contract when initiated is zero.*

If this statement were not true and one party paid a sum of money to the other, the party receiving the money could find another party and engage in the opposite transaction, with no money paid to the other on this second contract. The two transactions would completely offset, thereby eliminating the risk. Yet, the first party would have captured some cash from the second and consequently earned an arbitrage profit because his position is completely hedged. He would walk away with money and never have to worry about paying it back. The forward price is the price the two parties agree on that generates a value of zero at the initiation date. Finding that price is actually quite easy.

Consider a very simple asset price at S_0 today that pays no dividends or interest, nor does it yield any nonfinancial benefits or incur any carrying costs. As described earlier, we can peer into the future, but at best we can make only a forecast of the price of this asset at our horizon date of time T. That forecast was previously referred to as the expected spot price at expiration, $E(S_T)$. On the surface, it might seem that pricing a forward contract would somehow involve a discounting of the expected spot price. As we said earlier, however, that is not how derivatives are priced—they are priced using arbitrage.

Suppose we hold the asset and enter into a forward contract to sell the asset at the price $F_0(T)$. It should be easy to see that we have constructed a risk-free position. We know that the asset, currently worth S_0, will be sold later at $F_0(T)$ and that this price should guarantee a risk-free return. Thus, we should find the following relationship,

$$\frac{F_0(T)}{S_0} = (1 + r)^T \tag{3}$$

We can easily solve for the forward price to obtain

$$F_0(T) = S_0(1 + r)^T \tag{4}$$

Or, in words,

> *The forward price is the spot price compounded at the risk-free rate over the life of the contract.*

There is a nice logic to this relationship. While the spot price is what someone would have to pay today to buy the asset, a forward contract locks in the purchase price at the horizon date. When that date arrives, the investor will own the asset. Instead of buying the asset today, suppose the investor uses the forward contract to guarantee that she will own the asset at the horizon date. By using the forward contract, the investor will not have committed the money, S_0, that would have forgone interest at the rate r for the period 0 to T. Notice how the risk premium on the asset does not directly appear in the pricing relationship. It does appear implicitly, because it determines the spot price paid to buy the asset. Knowing the spot price, however, eliminates the necessity of determining the risk premium. The derivatives market can simply let the spot market derive the risk premium.

As a simple example, let us say the underlying price, S_0, is £50, the risk-free rate, r, is 3%, and the contract expires in three months, meaning that $T = 3/12 = 0.25$. Then the forward price is £50$(1.03)^{0.25}$ = £50.37. Thus, the two parties would agree that the buyer will pay £50.37 to the seller in three months, and the seller will deliver the underlying to the buyer at expiration.

Now suppose the asset generates cash payments and/or benefits and incurs storage costs. As we discussed, the net cost of carry consists of the benefits, denoted as γ (dividends or interest plus convenience yield), minus the costs, denoted as θ, both of which are in present value form. To put these concepts in future value form, we simply compound them at the risk-free rate, $(\gamma - \theta)(1 + r)^T$. Because this is their value at the expiration date of the contract, we can add them to $F_0(T)$ in Equation 3, thereby restating that equation as

$$(1 + r)^T = \frac{F_0(T) + (\gamma - \theta)(1 + r)^T}{S_0}$$

The numerator is how much money we end up with at T. Rearranging, we obtain the forward price as

$$F_0(T) = (S_0 - \gamma + \theta)(1 + r)^T$$

or

(5)

$$F_0(T) = S_0(1 + r)^T - (\gamma - \theta)(1 + r)^T$$

We see that the forward price determined using Equation 4 is reduced by the future value of any benefits and increased by the future value of any costs. In other words,

> *The forward price of an asset with benefits and/or costs is the spot price compounded at the risk-free rate over the life of the contract minus the future value of those benefits and costs.*

Again, the logic is straightforward. To acquire a position in the asset at time T, an investor could buy the asset today and hold it until time T. Alternatively, he could enter into a forward contract, committing him to buying the asset at T at the price $F_0(T)$. He would end up at T holding the asset, but the spot transaction would yield benefits and incur costs, whereas the forward transaction would forgo the benefits but avoid the costs.

Assume the benefits exceed the costs. Then the forward transaction would return less than the spot transaction. The formula adjusts the forward price downward by the expression $-(\gamma - \theta)(1 + r)^T$ to reflect this net loss over the spot transaction. In other words, acquiring the asset in the forward market would be cheaper because it forgoes benefits that exceed the costs. That does not mean the forward strategy is better. It costs less but also produces less. Alternatively, if the costs exceeded the benefits, the forward price would be higher because the forward contract avoids the costs at the expense of the lesser benefits.

Returning to our simple example, suppose the present value of the benefits is $\gamma = £3$ and the present value of the costs is $\theta = £4$. The forward price would be $£50(1.03)^{0.25} - (£3 - £4)(1.03)^{0.25} = £51.38$. The forward price, which was £50.37 without these costs and benefits, is now higher because the carrying costs exceed the benefits.

The value of the contract when initiated is zero provided the forward price conforms to the appropriate pricing formula. To keep the analysis as simple as possible, consider the case in which the asset yields no benefits and incurs no costs. Going long the forward contract or going long the asset produces the same position at T: ownership of the asset. Nonetheless, the strategies are not equivalent. Going long the forward contract enables the investor to avoid having to pay the price of the asset, S_0, so she would collect interest on the money. Thus, the forward strategy would have a value of S_0, reflecting the investment of that much cash invested in risk-free bonds, plus the value of the forward contract. The spot strategy would have a value of S_0, reflecting the investment in the asset. These two strategies must have equal values. Hence, the value of the forward contract must be zero.

Although a forward contract has zero value at the start, it will not have zero value during its life. We now take a look at what happens during the life of the contract.

3.1.3 *Pricing and Valuation during the Life of the Contract*

We previously worked an example in which a forward contract established with a price of $100 later has a value of –$5.85 to the seller and +$5.85 to the buyer. Generally we would say the value is $5.85. We explained that with the spot price at $102, a party that is long the asset and short the forward contract would guarantee the sale of the asset priced at $102 at a price of $100 in one year. The present value of $100 in one year at 4% is $96.15. Thus, the party guarantees that his $102 asset will be effectively sold at a present value of $96.15, for a present value loss of $5.85.

In general, we can say that

> *The value of a forward contract is the spot price of the underlying asset*
> *minus the present value of the forward price.*

Again, the logic is simple. A forward contract provides a type of synthetic position in the asset, for which we promise to pay the forward price at expiration. Thus, the value of the forward contract is the value of the asset minus the present value of the forward price. Let us write out this relationship using $V_t(T)$ as the value of the forward contract at time t, which is some point in time after the contract is initiated and before it expires:

$$V_t(T) = S_t - F_0(T)(1 + r)^{-(T-t)} \qquad (6)$$

Note that we are working with the spot price at t, but the forward price was fixed when the contract was initiated.[9]

Now, recall the problem we worked in which the underlying had a price of £50 and the contract was initiated with a three-month life at a price of £50.37. Move one month later, so that the remaining time is two months: $T - t = 2/12 = 0.167$. Let the underlying price be £52. The value of the contract would be £52 – £50.37$(1.03)^{-0.167}$ = £1.88.

If the asset has a cost of carry, we must make only a small adjustment:

$$V_t(T) = S_t - (\gamma - \theta)(1 + r)^t - F_0(T)(1 + r)^{-(T-t)} \qquad (7)$$

Note how we adjust the formula by the net of benefits minus costs. The forward contract forgoes the benefits and avoids the costs of holding the asset. Consequently, we adjust the value downward to reflect the forgone benefits and upward to reflect the avoided costs. Remember that the costs (θ) and benefits (γ) are expressed on a present value basis as of time 0. We need their value at time t. We could compound them from 0 to T and then discount them back to t by the period $T - t$, but a shorter route is to simply compound them from 0 to t. In the problem we previously worked, in which we priced the forward contract when the asset has costs and benefits, the benefits (γ) were £3 and the costs (θ) were £4, giving us a forward price of £51.38. We have now moved one month ahead, so $t = 1/12 = 0.0833$ and $T - t = 2/12 = 0.167$. Hence the value of the forward contract would be £52 – (£3 – £4)$(1.03)^{0.0833}$ – £51.38$(1.03)^{-0.167}$ = £1.88. In this case, the effect of the compounding of the net of costs and benefits (£1) over one month has no appreciable effect on the value, but that result is not a general rule.

It is important to note that although we say that Equation 7 holds during the life of the contract at some arbitrary time t, it also holds at the initiation date and at expiration. For the initiation date, we simply change t to 0 in Equation 7. Then we substitute Equation 5 for $F_0(T)$ in Equation 7, obtaining $V_0(T) = 0$, confirming that the value of a forward contract at initiation is zero. At expiration, we let $t = T$ in Equation 7 and obtain the spot price minus the forward price, as presented in Equation 1.[10]

3.1.4 *A Word about Forward Contracts on Interest Rates*

Forward contracts in which the underlying is an interest rate are called **forward rate agreements**, or FRAs. These instruments differ slightly from most other forward contracts in that the underlying is not an asset. Changes in interest rates, such as the value of an asset, are unpredictable. Moreover, virtually every company and organization is affected by the uncertainty of interest rates. Hence, FRAs are very useful

---

9 An alternative approach to valuing a forward contract during its life is to determine the price of a new forward contract that would offset the old one. The discounted difference between the new forward price and the original forward price will lead to the same value.

10 You might be wondering whether the cost and benefit terms disappear when $t = T$. With the costs and benefits defined as those incurred over the period t to T, at expiration their value is zero by definition.

devices for many companies. FRAs are forward contracts that allow participants to make a known interest payment at a later date and receive in return an unknown interest payment. In that way, a participant whose business will involve borrowing at a future date can lock in a fixed payment and receive a random payment that offsets the unknown interest payment it will make on its loan. Turning that argument around, a lender can also lock in a fixed rate on a loan it will make at a future date.

Even though FRAs do not involve an underlying asset, they can still be combined with an underlying asset to produce a hedged position, thereby leading to fairly straightforward pricing and valuation equations. The math is a little more complex than the math for forwards on assets, but the basic ideas are the same.

FRAs are often based on Libor, the London Interbank Offered Rate, which represents the rate on a Eurodollar time deposit, a loan in dollars from one London bank to another.[11] As an example, assume we are interested in going long a 30-day FRA in which the underlying is 90-day Libor. A long position means that in 30 days, we will make a known interest payment and receive an interest payment corresponding to 90-day Libor on that day. We can either enter into a 30-day FRA on 90-day Libor or create a synthetic FRA. To do the latter, we would go long a 120-day Eurodollar time deposit and short a 30-day Eurodollar time deposit. Exhibit 8 shows the structure of this strategy. We omit some of the details here, such as how much face value we should take on the two Eurodollar transactions as well as the size of the FRA. Those technical issues are covered in more advanced material. At this time, we focus on the fact that going long over the 120-day period and short over the 30-day period leaves an investor with no exposure over the 30-day period and then converts to a position that starts 30 days from now and matures 90 days later. This synthetic position corresponds to a 30-day FRA on 90-day Libor. Exhibit 8 illustrates this point.[12]

Exhibit 8   Real FRA and Synthetic FRA (30-Day FRA on 90-Day Libor)

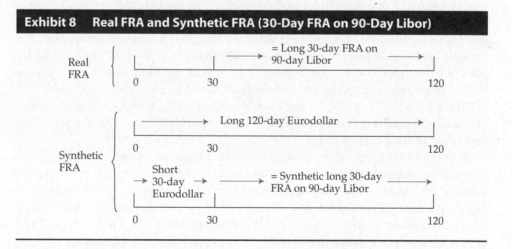

FRAs, and indeed all forward contracts relating to bonds and interest rates, are closely tied to the term structure of interest rates, a concept covered in virtually all treatments of fixed-income securities. Buying a 120-day zero-coupon bond and selling a 30-day zero-coupon bond produces a forward position in a 90-day zero-coupon bond

---

11 Other rates such as Euribor (Euro Interbank Offered Rate) and Tibor (Tokyo Interbank Offered Rate) are also used.
12 The real FRA we show appears to imply that an investor enters into a Eurodollar transaction in 30 days that matures 90 days later. This is not technically true. The investor does, however, engage in a cash settlement in 30 days that has the same value and economic form as such a transaction.

that begins in 30 days. From that forward position, one can infer the forward rate. It would then be seen that the FRA rate *is* the forward rate, even though the derivative itself is not a forward contract on a bond.

EXAMPLE 3

Forward Contract Pricing and Valuation

1 Which of the following *best* describes the difference between the price of a forward contract and its value?

   A The forward price is fixed at the start, and the value starts at zero and then changes.

   B The price determines the profit to the buyer, and the value determines the profit to the seller.

   C The forward contract value is a benchmark against which the price is compared for the purposes of determining whether a trade is advisable.

2 Which of the following *best* describes the value of the forward contract at expiration? The value is the price of the underlying:

   A minus the forward price.

   B divided by the forward price.

   C minus the compounded forward price.

3 Which of the following factors does *not* affect the forward price?

   A The costs of holding the underlying

   B Dividends or interest paid by the underlying

   C Whether the investor is risk averse, risk seeking, or risk neutral

4 Which of the following *best* describes the forward rate of an FRA?

   A The spot rate implied by the term structure

   B The forward rate implied by the term structure

   C The rate on a zero-coupon bond of maturity equal to that of the forward contract

Solution to 1:

A is correct. The forward price is fixed at the start, whereas the value starts at zero and then changes. Both price and value are relevant in determining the profit for both parties. The forward contract value is not a benchmark for comparison with the price.

Solution to 2:

A is correct because the holder of the contract gains the difference between the price of the underlying and the forward price. That value can, of course, be negative, which will occur if the holder is forced to buy the underlying at a price higher than the market price.

Solution to 3:

C is correct. The costs of holding the underlying, known as carrying costs, and the dividends and interest paid by the underlying are extremely relevant to the forward price. How the investor feels about risk is irrelevant, because the forward price is determined by arbitrage.

Solution to 4:

B is correct. FRAs are based on Libor, and they represent forward rates, not spot rates. Spot rates are needed to determine forward rates, but they are not equal to forward rates. The rate on a zero-coupon bond of maturity equal to that of the forward contract describes a spot rate.

As noted, we are not covering the details of derivative pricing but rather are focusing on the intuition. At this point, we have covered the intuition of pricing forward contracts. We now move to futures contracts.

3.2 Pricing and Valuation of Futures Contracts

Futures contracts differ from forward contracts in that they have standard terms, are traded on a futures exchange, and are more heavily regulated, whereas forward contracts are typically private, customized transactions. Perhaps the most important distinction is that they are marked to market on a daily basis, meaning that the accumulated gains and losses from the previous day's trading session are deducted from the accounts of those holding losing positions and transferred to the accounts of those holding winning positions. This daily settling of gains and losses enables the futures exchange to guarantee that a party that earns a profit from a futures transaction will not have to worry about collecting the money. Thus, futures exchanges provide a credit guarantee, which is facilitated through the use of a clearinghouse. The clearinghouse collects and disburses cash flows from the parties on a daily basis, thereby settling obligations quickly before they accumulate to much larger amounts. There is no absolute assurance that a clearinghouse will not fail, but none has ever done so since the first one was created in the 1920s.

The pattern of cash flows in a futures contract is quite similar to that in a forward contract. Suppose you enter into a forward contract two days before expiration in which you agree to buy an asset at €100, the forward price. Two days later, the asset is selling for €103, and the contract expires. You therefore pay €100 and receive an asset worth €103, for a gain of €3. If the contract were cash settled, instead of involving physical delivery, you would receive €3 in cash, which you could use to defer a portion of the cost of the asset. The net effect is that you are buying the asset for €103, paying €100 plus the €3 profit on the forward contract.

Had you chosen a futures contract, the futures price at expiration would still converge to the spot price of €103. But now it would matter what the futures settlement price was on the next to last day. Let us assume that price was €99. That means on the next to last day, your account would be marked to market for a loss of €1, the price of €100 having fallen to €99. That is, you would be charged €1, with the money passed on to the opposite party. But then on the last day, your position would be marked from €99 to €103, a gain of €4. Your net would be €1 lost on the first day and €4 gained on the second for a total of €3. In both situations you gain €3, but with the forward contract, you gain it all at expiration, whereas with the futures contract, you gain it over two days. With this two-day example, the interest on the interim cash flow would be virtually irrelevant, but over longer periods and with sufficiently high interest rates, the difference in the amount of money you end up with could be noticeable.

The value of a futures contract is the accumulated gain or loss on a futures contract since its previous day's settlement. When that value is paid out in the daily settlement, the futures price is effectively reset to the settlement price and the value goes to zero. The different patterns of cash flows for forwards and futures can lead to differences in the pricing of forwards versus futures. But there are some conditions under which the pricing is the same. It turns out that if interest rates were constant, forwards and futures would have the same prices. The differential will vary with the volatility of interest rates. In addition, if futures prices and interest rates are uncorrelated, forwards and futures prices will be the same. If futures prices are positively correlated with interest rates, futures contracts are more desirable to holders of long positions than are forwards. The reason is because rising prices lead to futures profits that are reinvested in periods of rising interest rates, and falling prices leads to losses that occur in periods of falling interest rates. It is far better to receive cash flows in the interim than all at expiration under such conditions. This condition makes futures more attractive than forwards, and therefore their prices will be higher than forward prices. A negative correlation between futures prices and interest rates leads to the opposite interpretation, with forwards being more desirable than futures to the long position. The more desirable contract will tend to have the higher price.

The practical realities, however, are that the derivatives industry makes virtually no distinction between futures and forward prices.[13] Thus, we will make no distinction between futures and forward pricing, except possibly in noting some subtle issues that may arise from time to time.

EXAMPLE 4

Futures Pricing and Valuation

1 Which of the following *best* describes how futures contract payoffs differ from forward contract payoffs?

   A Forward contract payoffs are larger.

   B They are equal, ignoring the time value of money.

   C Futures contract payoffs are larger if the underlying is a commodity.

2 Which of the following conditions will not make futures and forward prices equivalent?

   A Interest rates are known.

   B Futures prices are uncorrelated with interest rates.

   C The volatility of the forward price is different from the volatility of the futures price.

3 With respect to the value of a futures contract, which of the following statements is *most* accurate? The value is the:

   A futures price minus the spot price.

   B present value of the expected payoff at expiration.

   C accumulated gain since the previous settlement, which resets to zero upon settlement.

Solution to 1:

B is correct. Forward payoffs occur all at expiration, whereas futures payoffs occur on a day-to-day basis but would equal forward payoffs ignoring interest. Payoffs could differ, so forward payoffs are not always larger. The type of underlying is not relevant to the point of which payoff is larger.

---

13 At the time of this writing, many forwards (and swaps) are being processed through clearinghouses, a response to changes brought about by key legislation in several countries that was adopted following the financial crises of 2008. These OTC instruments are thus being effectively marked to market in a similar manner to the futures contracts described here. The full extent of this evolution of OTC trading through clearinghouses is not yet clear.

Solution to 2:

C is correct. Known interest rates and the condition that futures prices are uncorrelated with forward prices will make forward and futures prices equivalent. The volatility of forward and futures prices has no relationship to any difference.

Solution to 3:

C is correct. Value accumulates from the previous settlement and goes to zero when distributed.

3.3 Pricing and Valuation of Swap Contracts

Recall the structure of a forward contract, as depicted in Exhibit 7. The investor is at time 0 and needs to determine the price, $F_0(T)$, that she will agree to pay at time T to purchase the asset. This price is set such that there is no value to the contract at that time. Value can arise later as prices change, but when initiated, the contract has zero value. Neither party pays anything to the other at the start.

Now consider a swap starting at time 0 and ending at time T. We will let this swap be the type that involves a fixed payment exchanged for a floating payment. The contract specifies that the two parties will make a series of n payments at times that we will designate as 1, 2, ..., n, with the last payment occurring at time T. On each of these payment dates, the owner of the swap makes a payment of $FS_0(n, T)$ and receives a payment based on the value of the underlying at the time of each respective payment, $S_1, S_2, ..., S_n$. So from the point of view of the buyer, the sequence of cash flows from the swap is $S_1 - FS_0(n, T)$, $S_2 - FS_0(n, T)$, ..., $S_n - FS_0(n, T)$. The notation $FS_0(n, T)$ denotes the fixed payment established at time 0 for a swap consisting of n payments with the last payment at time T. We denote the time to each payment as $t_1, t_2, ..., t_n$, where $t_n = T$. This structure is shown in Exhibit 9.

Exhibit 9   Structure of Cash Flows in a Swap

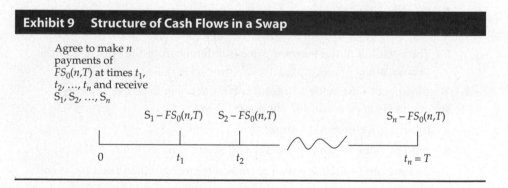

Comparing Exhibit 7 with Exhibit 9 reveals some similarities. A swap is in some sense a series of forward contracts, specifically a set of contracts expiring at various times in which one party agrees to make a fixed payment and receive a variable payment. Now consider Exhibit 10, which breaks down a swap into a series of implicit forward contracts, with the expiration of each forward contract corresponding to a swap payment date.

Exhibit 10   A Swap as a Series of Forward Contracts

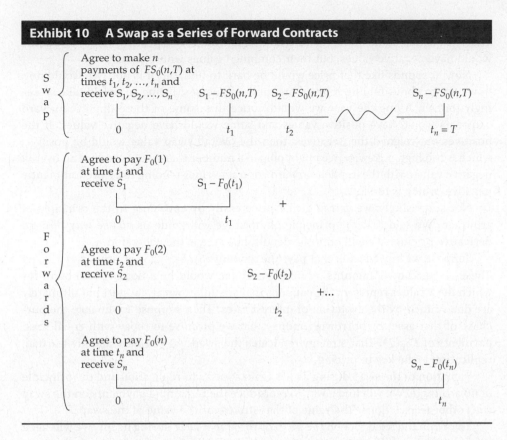

Recall from the material on forward contracts that the forward price is determined by the spot price and the net cost of carry (Equation 5), the latter being partially determined by the length of time of the contract. It should be obvious that a forward contract expiring at time t_1 will not have the same price, $F_0(t_1)$, as a forward contract expiring at time t_2, $F_0(t_2)$, and likewise for all of the implicit remaining forward contracts expiring up through time t_n. The cost of carrying an asset over different time periods will vary by the length of the time periods. In other words, the prices of the implicit forward contracts imbedded in a swap will not be equal:

$$F_0(t_1) \neq F_0(t_2) \neq \ldots \neq F_0(t_n)$$

But for a swap, all the fixed payments are equal. So, how can we equate a swap to a series of forward contracts? It turns out that we can, and in doing so, we recall a valuable point about forward pricing.

Recall that the forward price is the price that produces a zero value of the contract at the start. Zero value is essential if there is no exchange of cash flows from one party to the other. And although no exchange of cash flows is customary, it is not mandatory. The parties could agree on any forward price at the start. If the zero-value forward price were $30 and the parties agreed on a price of $28, it should be apparent that the buyer would be getting a great price. The seller, being rational, would require that the buyer compensate him at the start. The seller should be getting $30 at expiration and instead will get $28. So the buyer should compensate the seller to the amount of the present value of $2 at expiration. If the parties agree on a price greater than $30, similar compensation would have to be paid from seller to buyer.

A forward transaction that starts with a nonzero value is called an off-market forward. There is generally no prohibition on the use of off-market forward contracts, so two parties can engage in a series of forward contracts at whatever fixed price they so desire. Assume they agree on the price $FS_0(T)$. That is, each forward contract will be created at the fixed price that corresponds to the fixed price of a swap of the same maturity with payments made at the same dates as the series of forward contracts. That means that some of the forward contracts would have positive values and some would have negative values, but their combined values would equal zero.

Now, it sounds like that price would be hard to find, but it is not. We would not, however, go about finding it by taking random guesses. Doing so would take seemingly forever. Along the way, we would notice that some of these implicit forward contracts would have positive values and some would have negative values. If the positives outweighed the negatives, then the overall swap value would be positive, which is too high. Likewise, we might plug in a number that would produce an overall negative value, with the implicit forward contract values tending to be predominantly negative, which is too low.

Not surprisingly, we can find that price easily by appealing to the principle of arbitrage. We said that the principle of arbitrage will guide us *all the way through* derivative pricing. We will omit the details, but here is the general idea.

Suppose we buy an asset that pays the amounts $S_1, S_2, ..., S_n$ at times $t_1, t_2, ..., t_n$. These are unknown amounts. A simple example would be a floating-rate bond for which the S values represent the coupons that are unknown at the start but ultimately are determined by the evolution of interest rates. Then suppose we finance the purchase of that asset by borrowing money that we promise to repay with equal fixed payments of $FS_0(T)$. That strategy replicates the swap. As you have already learned, replication is the key to pricing.

Valuation of the swap during its life again appeals to replication and the principle of no arbitrage. We will find a way to reproduce the remaining payments on the swap with other transactions. The value of that strategy is the value of the swap.

To obtain the fixed rate on the swap or to value it later during its life, we will need information from the market for the underlying. As we previously noted, there are derivatives on bonds and interest rates, equities, currencies, and commodities. It is not possible to provide a general and simple statement of how to price swaps that covers all of these cases, but that topic is covered in advanced material.

EXAMPLE 5

Swap Pricing and Valuation

1   A swap is equivalent to a series of:

   A   forward contracts, each created at the swap price.

   B   long forward contracts, matched with short futures contracts.

   C   forward contracts, each created at their appropriate forward prices.

2   If the present value of the payments in a forward contract or swap is not zero, which of the following is most likely to be true?

   A   The contract cannot legally be created.

   B   The contract must be replicated by another contract with zero value.

   C   The party whose stream of payments to be received is greater has to pay the other party the present value difference.

Solution to 1:

A is correct. Each implicit forward contract is said to be off-market, because it is created at the swap price, not the appropriate forward price, which would be the price created in the forward market.

PRICING AND VALUATION OF OPTIONS

Unlike a forward, futures, or swap contract, an option is clearly an asset to the holder and a liability to the seller. The buyer of an option pays a sum of money, called the premium, and receives the right to buy (a call) or sell (a put) the underlying. The seller receives the premium and undertakes a potential obligation because the buyer has the right, but not the obligation, to exercise the option. Options are, therefore, contingent claims. Pricing the option is the same as assigning its value. Some confusion from that terminology may still arise, in that an option could trade in the market for an amount that differs from its value.

As mentioned, there are two general types of options. Calls represent the right to buy, and puts represent the right to sell. There are also two important exercise characteristics of options. American options allow exercise at any time up to the expiration, while European options allow exercise only at expiration. It is important to understand that the terms "American" and "European" have no relationship to where the options are traded. Because the right to exercise can be a complex feature of an option, European options are easier to understand, and we will focus on them first.

We will use the same notation used with forwards. We start by assuming that today is time 0, and the option expires at time T. The underlying is an asset currently priced at S_0, and at time T, its price is S_T. Of course, we do not know S_T until we get to the expiration. The option has an exercise or strike price of X. The symbols we use are as follows:

For calls,

c_0 = value (price) of European call today
c_T = value (price) of European call at expiration
C_0 = value (price) of American call today
C_T = value (price) of American call at expiration

For puts,

p_0 = value (price) of European put today
p_T = value (price) of European put at expiration
P_0 = value (price) of American put today
P_T = value (price) of American put at expiration

4.1 European Option Pricing

Recall that in studying forward contracts earlier in this reading, the first thing we learned is how a forward contract pays off at expiration. Then we backed up and determined how forward contracts are priced and valued prior to expiration. We follow that same approach for options.

4.1.1 *Value of a European Option at Expiration*

Recall that a European call option allows the holder to buy the underlying at expiration by paying the exercise price. Therefore, exercise is justified only if the value of the underlying exceeds the exercise price. Otherwise, the holder would simply let the call expire. So if the call is worth exercising ($S_T > X$), the holder pays X and receives an asset worth S_T. Thus, the option is worth $S_T - X$. If the call is not worth exercising ($S_T \leq X$), the option simply expires and is worth nothing at expiration.[14] Thus, the value of the option at expiration is the greater of either zero or the underlying price at expiration minus the exercise price, which is typically written as

$$c_T = \text{Max}\big(0, S_T - X\big) \tag{8}$$

This formula is also sometimes referred to as the **exercise value** or **intrinsic value**. In this reading, we will use the term exercise value.

Taking a simple example, if the exercise price is €40 and the underlying price is at expiration €43, the call is worth c_T = Max(€0, €43 − €40) = Max(€0, €3) = €3. If the underlying price at expiration is €39, the call is worth c_T = Max(0, €39 − €40) = Max(€0, −€1) = €0.

For puts, the holder has the right to sell the underlying at X. If the underlying is worth less than X at expiration ($X > S_T$), the put will be exercised and worth $X - S_T$ because it allowed the holder to avoid the loss in value of the asset of that amount. If the underlying is equal to or worth more than the exercise price at expiration ($S_T \geq X$), the put will simply expire with no value. So, the put is worth the greater of either zero or the exercise price minus the price of the underlying at expiration.

$$p_T = \text{Max}\big(0, X - S_T\big) \tag{9}$$

As discussed above, this formula is referred to as the exercise value or intrinsic value, and as noted, we will use the term exercise value.

Using the same example as with the call, if the underlying is €43 at expiration, the put is worth p_T = Max(€0, €40 − €43) = Max(0, −€3) = €0. If the underlying is €39 at expiration, the put is worth p_T = Max(€0, €40 − €39) = Max(€0, €1) = €1.

Thus, the holder of an option looks out into the future and sees these relationships as the payoff possibilities. That does not mean the holder knows what S_T will be, but the holder knows that all of the uncertainty of the option payoff is determined by the behavior of the underlying.

The results of this section can be restated as follows:

> *The value of a European call at expiration is the exercise value, which is the greater of zero or the value of the underlying minus the exercise price.*

> *The value of a European put at expiration is the exercise value, which is the greater of zero or the exercise price minus the value of the underlying.*

To understand option pricing, we have to work our way forward in a gradual manner. The next valuable steps involve using our intuition to identify some characteristics that will influence the value of the option. We might not be able to quantify their effects just yet, but we can rationalize why these factors affect the value of an option.

---

14 In all the remaining material, we identify conditions at expiration, such as $S_T > X$ and $S_T \leq X$. Here we merged the equality case ($S_T = X$) with the less-than case ($<$). We could have done it the other way around ($S_T < X$ and $S_T \geq X$), which would have had no effect on our interpretations or any calculations of option value. For convenience, in some situations we will use one specification and in some the other.

4.1.2 *Effect of the Value of the Underlying*

The value of the underlying is obviously a critical element in determining the value of an option. It is the uncertainty of the underlying that provides the motivation for using options. It is easy to rationalize the direction of the effect of the underlying.

A call option can be viewed as a mean of acquiring the underlying, whereas a put option can be viewed as a means of selling the underlying. Thus, a call option is logically worth more if the underlying is worth more, and a put option is logically worth more if the underlying is worth less.

The value of the underlying also forms one of the boundaries for calls. The value of a call option cannot exceed the value of the underlying. After all, a call option is only a means of acquiring the underlying. It can never give the holder more benefit than the underlying. Hence, the value of the underlying forms an upper boundary on what a call is worth. The underlying does not provide an upper or lower boundary for puts. That role is played by the exercise price, as we will see in the next section.

To recap what we learned here,

> The value of a European call option is directly related to the value of the underlying.

> The value of a European put option is inversely related to the value of the underlying.

4.1.3 *Effect of the Exercise Price*

The exercise price is a critical factor in determining the value of an option. The exercise price is the hurdle beyond which the underlying must go to justify exercise. For a call, the underlying must rise above the exercise price, and for a put, the underlying must fall below the exercise price, to justify exercise. When the underlying is beyond the exercise price in the appropriate direction (higher for a call, lower for a put), the option is said to be **in-the-money**. When the underlying is precisely at the exercise price, the option is said to be **at-the-money**. When the underlying has not reached the exercise price (currently lower for a call, higher for a put), the option is said to be **out-of-the-money**. This characterization of whether the option is in-, at-, or out-of-the-money is referred to as the option's **moneyness**.

For a call option, a lower exercise price has two benefits. One is that there are more values of the underlying at expiration that are above the exercise price, meaning that there are more outcomes in which the call expires in-the-money. The other benefit is that assuming the call expires in-the-money, for any value of the underlying, the option value is greater the lower the exercise price. In other words, at expiration the underlying value S_T will be above the exercise price far more often, the lower is X. And if S_T is indeed higher than X, the payoff of $S_T - X$ is greater, the lower is X.

For puts, the effect is just the opposite. To expire in-the-money, the value of the underlying must fall below the exercise price. The higher the exercise price, the better chance the underlying has of getting below it. Likewise, if the value of the underlying does fall below the exercise price, the higher the exercise price, the greater the payoff. So, if X is higher, S_T will be below it more often, and if S_T is less than X, the payoff of $X - S_T$ is greater, the higher is X for whatever value of S_T occurs.

The exercise price also helps form an upper bound for the value of a European put. If you were holding a European put, the best outcome you could hope for is a zero value of the underlying. For equities, that would mean complete failure and dissolution of the company with shareholders receiving no final payment.[15] In that case, the put would pay $X - S_T$, but with S_T at zero, the put would pay X. If the underlying value goes to zero during the life of the European put, however, the holder cannot collect that payoff until expiration. Nonetheless, the holder would have a risk-free claim on a payoff of X at expiration. Thus, the most the put would be worth is the present value of X, meaning X discounted from expiration to the current day at the risk-free rate.[16] Although the holder cannot collect the payoff by exercising the option, he could sell it for the present value of X.

To recap these results,

The value of a European call option is inversely related to the exercise price.

The value of a European put option is directly related to the exercise price.

4.1.4 *Effect of Time to Expiration*

Logic suggests that longer-term options should be worth more than shorter-term options. That statement is usually true but not always. A call option unquestionably benefits from additional time. For example, the right to buy an asset for $50 is worth a lot more if that right is available for two years instead of one. The additional time provides further opportunity for the underlying to rise above the exercise price. Although that means there is also additional time for the underlying to fall below the exercise price, it hardly matters to the holder of the call because the loss on the downside is limited to the premium paid.

For a European put option, the additional time still provides more opportunity for the underlying price to fall below the exercise price, but with the additional risk of it rising above the exercise price mitigated by the limited loss of the premium if the put expires out-of-the-money. Thus, it sounds as if puts benefit from longer time, but that is not necessarily true. There is a subtle penalty for this additional time. Put option holders are awaiting the sale of the underlying, for which they will receive the exercise price. The longer they have to wait, the lower the present value of the payoff. For some puts, this negative effect can dwarf the positive effect. This situation occurs with a put the longer the time to expiration, the higher the risk-free rate of interest, and the deeper it is in-the-money. The positive effect of time, however, is somewhat more dominant.

Note that we did not mention this effect for calls. For calls, the holder is waiting to pay out money at expiration. More time lowers the value of this possible outlay. Hence, a longer time period helps call option buyers in this regard.

To recap these results,

The value of a European call option is directly related to the time to expiration.

---

15 You might think this point means that people who buy puts are hoping the company goes bankrupt, a seemingly morbid motivation. Yet, put buyers are often people who own the stock and buy the put for protection. This motivation is no different from owning a house and buying fire insurance. You do not want the house to burn down. If your sole motivation in buying the insurance were to make a profit on the insurance, you would want the house to burn down. This moral hazard problem illustrates why it is difficult, if not impossible, to buy insurance on a house you do not own. Likewise, executives are prohibited from owning puts on their companies' stock. Individual investors can own puts on stocks they do not own, because they cannot drive the stock price down.

16 For the put holder to truly have a risk-free claim on X at expiration, given zero value of the underlying today, the underlying value must go to zero and have no possibility of any recovery. If there is any possibility of recovery, the underlying value would not go to zero, as is often observed when a legal filing for bankruptcy is undertaken. Many equities do recover. If there were some chance of recovery but the equity value was zero, demand for the stock would be infinite, which would push the price up.

The value of a European put option can be either directly or inversely related to the time to expiration. The direct effect is more common, but the inverse effect can prevail with a put the longer the time to expiration, the higher the risk-free rate, and the deeper it is in-the-money.

4.1.5 *Effect of the Risk-Free Rate of Interest*

We have already alluded to the effect of the risk-free rate. For call options, a longer time to expiration means that the present value of the outlay of the exercise price is lower. In other words, with a longer time to expiration, the call option holder continues to earn interest on the money that could be expended later in paying the exercise price upon exercise of the option. If the option is ultimately never exercised, this factor is irrelevant, but it remains at best a benefit and at worst has no effect. For puts, the opposite argument prevails. A longer time to expiration with a higher interest rate lowers the present value of the receipt of the exercise price upon exercise. Thus, the value today of what the put holder might receive at expiration is lower. If the put is ultimately never exercised, the risk-free rate has no effect. Thus, at best, a higher risk-free rate has no effect on the value of a put. At worst, it decreases the value of the put.

These results are summarized as follows:

The value of a European call is directly related to the risk-free interest rate.

The value of a European put is inversely related to the risk-free interest rate.

4.1.6 *Effect of Volatility of the Underlying*

In studying the pricing of equities, we are conditioned to believe that volatility has a negative effect. After all, investors like return and dislike risk. Volatility is certainly an element of risk. Therefore, volatility is bad for investors, right? Well, partially right.

First, not all volatility is bad for investors. Unsystematic volatility should be irrelevant. Investors can hold diversified portfolios. Systematic volatility is clearly undesirable, but do not think that this means that volatility should be completely avoided where possible. If volatility were universally undesirable, no one would take risks. Clearly risks have to be taken to provide opportunity for reward.

With options, volatility of the underlying is, however, universally desirable. The greater the volatility of the underlying, the more an option is worth. This seemingly counterintuitive result is easy to understand with a little explanation.

First, let us make sure we know what volatility really means. In studying asset returns, we typically represent volatility with the standard deviation of the return, which measures the variation from the average return. The S&P 500 Index has an approximate long-run volatility of around 20%. Under the assumption of a normal distribution, a standard deviation of 20% implies that about 68% of the time, the returns will be within plus or minus one standard deviation of the average. About 95% of the time, they will be within plus or minus two standard deviations of the average. About 99% of the time, they will be within plus or minus three standard deviations of the average. When the distribution is non-normal, different interpretations apply, and in some extreme cases, the standard deviation can be nearly impossible to interpret.

Standard deviation is not the only notion of volatility, however, and it is not even needed at this point. You can proceed fairly safely with a measure as simple as the highest possible value minus the lowest, known as the range. The only requirement we need right now is that the concept of volatility reflects dispersion—how high and how low the underlying can go.

So, regardless of how we measure volatility, the following conditions will hold:

1   A call option will have a higher payoff the higher the underlying is at expiration.

2   A call option will have a zero payoff if it expires with the underlying below the exercise price.

If we could impose greater volatility on the underlying, we should be able to see that in Condition 1, the payoff has a better chance of being greater because the underlying has a greater possibility of large positive returns. In Condition 2, however, the zero payoff is unaffected if we impose greater volatility. Expiring more out-of-the-money is not worse than expiring less out-of-the-money, but expiring more in-the-money is better than expiring less-in-the-money.[17]

For puts, we have

1   A put option will have a higher payoff the lower the underlying is at expiration.

2   A put option will have a zero payoff if it expires with the underlying above the exercise price.

If we could impose greater volatility, we would find that it would have a beneficial effect in (1) because a larger positive payoff would have a greater chance of occurring. In (2), the zero payoff is unaffected. The greater of the option expiring more out-of-the-money is irrelevant. Expiring more out-of-the-money is not worse than expiring less out-of-the-money.

Thus, we summarize our results in this section as

> *The value of a European call is directly related to the volatility of the underlying.*

> *The value of a European put is directly related to the volatility of the underlying.*

The combined effects of time and volatility give rise to the concept of the **time value** of an option. Time value of an option is not to be confused with the time value of money, which is the notion of money later being worth less than money today as a result of the combined effects of time and interest. The time value of an option reflects the value of the uncertainty that arises from the volatility of the underlying. Time value results in an option price being greater with volatility and time but declining as expiration approaches. At expiration, no time value remains and the option is worth only its exercise value. As such, an option price is said to decay over time, a process characterized as **time value decay**, which is covered in more advanced material.

4.1.7 *Effect of Payments on the Underlying and the Cost of Carry*

We previously discussed how payments on the underlying and carrying costs enter into the determination of forward prices. They also affect option prices. Payments on the underlying refer to dividends on stocks and interest on bonds. In addition, some commodities offer a convenience yield benefit. Carrying costs include the actual physical costs of maintaining and/or storing an asset.

Let us first consider the effect of benefits. Payments of dividends and interest reduce the value of the underlying. Stocks and bonds fall in value as dividends and interest are paid. These benefits to holders of these securities do not flow to holders of options. For call option holders, this reduction is a negative factor. The price of

---

17 Think of an option expiring out-of-the-money as like it being dead. (Indeed, the option is dead.) Being "more dead" is not worse than being "less dead."

the underlying is hurt by such payments, and call holders do not get to collect these payments. For put holders, the effect is the opposite. When the value of the underlying is reduced, put holders are helped.

Carrying costs have the opposite effect. They raise the effective cost of holding or shorting the asset. Holding call options enables an investor to participate in movements of the underlying without incurring these costs. Holding put options makes it more expensive to participate in movements in the underlying than by short selling because short sellers benefit from carrying costs, which are borne by owners of the asset.

To summarize the results from this section,

> *A European call option is worth less the more benefits that are paid by the underlying and worth more the more costs that are incurred in holding the underlying.*
>
> *A European put option is worth more the more benefits that are paid by the underlying and worth less the more costs that are incurred in holding the underlying.*

4.1.8 *Lowest Prices of Calls and Puts*

What we have learned so far forms a framework for understanding how European options are priced. Let us now go a step further and establish a minimum price for these options.

First, we need to look at a call option as similar to the purchase of the underlying with a portion of the purchase price financed by borrowing. If the underlying is a stock, this transaction is usually called a margin transaction. Assume that the underlying is worth S_0. Also assume that you borrow cash in the amount of the present value of X, promising to pay X back T periods later at an interest rate of r. Thus, $X/(1 + r)^T$ is the amount borrowed, and X is the amount to be paid back. Now move forward to time T and observe the price of the underlying, S_T. Upon paying back the loan, the overall strategy will be worth $S_T - X$, which can be positive or negative.

Next, consider an alternative strategy of buying a call option expiring at T with an exercise price of X, the same value as the face value of the loan. We know that the option payoffs will be $S_T - X$ if it expires in-the- money ($S_T > X$) and zero if not ($S_T \le X$). Exhibit 11 compares these two strategies.[18]

	Exhibit 11 Call Option vs. Leveraged (Margin) Transaction	
	Outcome at T	
	Call Expires Out-of-the-Money ($S_T \le X$)	**Call Expires In-the-Money** ($S_T > X$)
Call	0	$S_T - X$
Leveraged transaction		
Asset	S_T	S_T

(continued)

---

18 Note in Exhibit 11, and in others to come, that the inequality ≤ is referred to as out-of-the-money. The case of equality is technically referred to as at-the-money but the verbiage is simplified if we continue to call it out-of-the-money. It is certainly not in-the-money and at-the-money is arguably the same as out-of-the-money. Regardless of one's preference, the equality case can be attached to either of the two outcomes with no effect on our conclusions.

Exhibit 11   (Continued)

	Outcome at T	
	Call Expires Out-of-the-Money $(S_T \leq X)$	Call Expires In-the-Money $(S_T > X)$
Loan	$-X$	$-X$
Total	$S_T - X$	$S_T - X$

When the call expires in-the-money, both transactions produce identical payoffs. When the call expires out-of-the-money, the call value is zero, but the leveraged transaction is almost surely a loss. Its value $S_T - X$ is negative or zero at best (if S_T is exactly equal to X).

If two strategies are found to produce equivalent results in some outcomes but one produces a better result in all other outcomes, then one strategy dominates the former. Here we see that the call strategy dominates the leveraged strategy. Any strategy that dominates the other can never have a lower value at any time. Why would anyone pay more for one strategy than for another if the former will never produce a better result than the latter? Thus, the value of the call strategy, c_0, has to be worth at least the value of the leveraged transaction, S_0 (the value of the asset), minus $X/(1 + r)^T$ (the value of the loan). Hence, $c_0 \geq S_0 - X/(1 + r)^T$.

The inequality means that this statement provides the lowest price of the call, but there is one more thing we need to do. It can easily be true that $X/(1 + r)^T > S_0$. In that case, we are saying that the lowest value is a negative number, but that statement is meaningless. A call can never be worth less than zero, because its holder cannot be forced to exercise it. Thus, we tend to express this relationship as

$$c_0 \geq \text{Max}\left[0, S_0 - X/(1 + r)^T\right] \tag{10}$$

which represents the greater of the value of zero or the underlying price minus the present value of the exercise price. This value becomes the lower limit of the call price.

Now consider an analogous result for puts. Suppose we want to profit from a declining price of the underlying. One way to do this is to sell the underlying short. Suppose we do that and invest cash equal to the present value of X into risk-free bonds that pay X at time T. At time T, given a price of the underlying of S_T, the short sale pays off $-S_T$, a reflection of the payment of S_T to cover the short sale. The bonds pay X. Hence, the total payoff is $X - S_T$.

Now, compare that result with the purchase of a put expiring at T with exercise price of X. If the put expires in–the-money ($S_T < X$), it is worth $X - S_T$. If it expires out-of-the-money ($S_T \geq X$), it is worth zero. Exhibit 12 illustrates the comparison of the put with the short sale and bond strategy. We see that for the in-the-money case, the put and short sale and bond strategies match each other. For the out-of-the-money case, however, the put performs better because the short sale and bond strategy pays $X - S_T$. With $S_T \geq X$, this payment amount is negative. With the put dominating the short sale and bond strategy, the put value cannot be less than the value of the short sale and bond strategy, meaning $p_0 \geq X/(1 + r)^T - S_0$. But as with calls, the right-hand side can be negative, and it hardly helps us to say that a put must sell for more than a negative number. A put can never be worth less than zero, because its owner cannot be forced to exercise it. Thus, the overall result is expressed succinctly as

$$p_0 \geq \text{Max}\left[0, X/(1 + r)^T - S_0\right] \tag{11}$$

Exhibit 12	Put vs. Short Sale and Bond Purchase	
	Outcome at T	
	Put Expires in-the-Money $(S_T < X)$	**Put Expires Out-of-the-Money** $(S_T \geq X)$
Put	$X - S_T$	0
Short sale and bond purchase		
Short sale	$-S_T$	$-S_T$
Bond	X	X
Total	$X - S_T$	$X - S_T$

Let us look at some basic examples. Assume the exercise price is €60, the risk-free rate is 4%, and the expiration is nine months, so $T = 9/12 = 0.75$. Consider two cases: Underlying: $S_0 = $ €70

Minimum call price = Max[0, €70 − €60/(1.04)$^{0.75}$] = Max(0, €11.74) = €11.74

Minimum put price = Max[0, €60/(1.04)$^{0.75}$ − €70] = Max(0, −€11.74) = €0.00

Underlying: $S_0 = $ €50

Minimum call price = Max[0, €50 − €60/(1.04)$^{0.75}$] = Max(0, −€8.26) = €0.00

Minimum put price = Max[0, €60/(1.04)$^{0.75}$ − €50] = Max(0, €8.26) = €8.26

To recap, in this section we have established lower limits for call and put option values. Formally restating these results in words,

> *The lowest value of a European call is the greater of zero or the value of the underlying minus the present value of the exercise price.*

> *The lowest value of a European put is the greater of zero or the present value of the exercise price minus the value of the underlying.*

EXAMPLE 6

Basic Principles of European Option Pricing

1   Which of the following factors does *not* affect the value of a European option?

A   The volatility of the underlying

B   Dividends or interest paid by the underlying

C   The percentage of the investor's assets invested in the option

2   Which of the following statements imply that a European call on a stock is worth more?

A   Less time to expiration

B   A higher stock price relative to the exercise price

C   Larger dividends paid by the stock during the life of the option

3   Why might a European put be worth less the longer the time to expiration?

    A　The cost of waiting to receive the exercise price is higher.

    B　The risk of the underlying is lower over a longer period of time.

    C　The longer time to expiration means that the put is more likely to expire out-of-the-money.

4　The loss in value of an option as it moves closer to expiration is called what?

    A　Time value decay

    B　Volatility diminution

    C　Time value of money

5　How does the minimum value of a call or put option differ from its exercise value?

    A　The exercise price is adjusted for the time value of money.

    B　The minimum value reflects the volatility of the underlying.

    C　The underlying price is adjusted for the time value of money.

Solution to 1:

C is correct. The investor's exposure to the option is not relevant to the price one should pay to buy or ask to sell the option. Volatility and dividends or interest paid by the underlying are highly relevant to the value of the option.

Solution to 2:

B is correct. The higher the stock price and the lower the exercise price, the more valuable is the call. Less time to expiration and larger dividends reduce the value of the call.

Solution to 3:

A is correct. Although the longer time benefits the holder of the option, it also has a cost in that exercise of a longer-term put comes much later. Therefore, the receipt of the exercise price is delayed. Longer time to expiration does not lower the risk of the underlying. The longer time also does not increase the likelihood of the option expiring out-of-the-money.

Solution to 4:

A is correct. An option has time value that decays as the expiration approaches. There is no such concept as volatility diminution. Time value of money relates only to the value of money at one point in time versus another.

Solution to 5:

A is correct. The minimum value formula is the greater of zero or the difference between the underlying price and the present value of the exercise price, whereas the exercise value is the maximum of zero and the appropriate difference between the underlying price and the exercise price. Volatility does not affect the minimum price. It does not make sense to adjust the underlying price for the time value of money for the simple reason that it is already adjusted for the time value of money.

4.1.9　Put–Call Parity

One of the first concepts that a trader learns in options is the parity relationship between puts and calls. Even though the word "parity" means "equivalence," puts and calls are not equivalent. There is, however, a relationship between the call price and the price of its corresponding put, which we refer to as put–call parity.

Suppose Investor A owns an asset that has a current price of S_0. Assume the asset makes no cash payments and has no carrying costs. The end of the holding period is time T, at which point the asset will be worth S_T. Fearing the possibility that S_T will decline, Investor A buys a put option with an exercise price of X, which can be used to sell the asset for X at time T. This put option has a premium of p_0. Combined with the value of the asset, the investor's current position is worth $S_0 + p_0$, which is the investor's money at risk. This strategy of holding the asset and a put is sometimes called a **protective put**.

At expiration, the value of the asset is S_T. The value of the put will be either zero or $X - S_T$. If the asset increases in value such that $S_T \geq X$, then the overall position is worth S_T. The asset has performed well, and the investor will let the put expire. If the asset value declines to the point at which $S_T < X$, the asset is worth S_T, and the put is worth $X - S_T$, for a total of X. In other words, the investor would exercise the put, selling the asset for X, which exceeds the asset's current value of S_T.

This strategy seems like a reasonable and possibly quite attractive investment. Investor A receives the benefit of unlimited upside potential, with the downside performance truncated at X. Exhibit 13 shows the performance of the protective put. The graph on the left illustrates the underlying asset and the put. The graph on the right shows their combined effects.

Exhibit 13   Protective Put (Asset Plus Long Put)

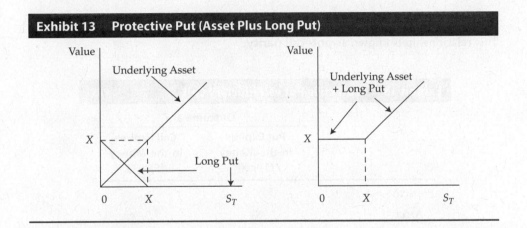

Consider Investor B, an options trader. At time 0, this investor buys a call option on this asset with an exercise price of X that expires at T and a risk-free zero-coupon bond with a face value of X that matures at T. The call costs c_0, and the bond costs the present value of X, which is $X/(1 + r)^T$. Thus, Investor B has invested funds of $c_0 + X/(1 + r)^T$. This strategy is sometimes known as a **fiduciary call**. If the underlying price exceeds the exercise price at expiration, the call will be worth $S_T - X$, and the bond will mature and pay a value of X. These values combine to equal S_T. If the underlying price does not exceed the exercise price at expiration, the call expires worthless and the bond is worth X for a combined value of X.

Exhibit 14 shows the performance of the fiduciary call. The graph on the left shows the call and bond, and the graph on the right shows the combined effects of the two strategies.

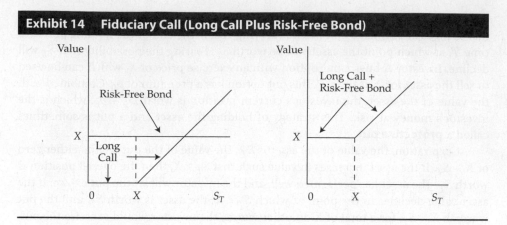

Exhibit 14   Fiduciary Call (Long Call Plus Risk-Free Bond)

Comparing Exhibit 13 with Exhibit 14 shows that a protective put and a fiduciary call produce the same result. Exhibit 15 shows this result more directly by identifying the payoffs in the various outcomes. Recall that Investor A committed funds of $S_0 + p_0$, while Investor B committed funds of $c_0 + X/(1 + r)^T$. If both investors receive the same payoffs at time T regardless of the asset price at T, the amounts they invest at time 0 have to be the same. Thus, we require

$$S_0 + p_0 = c_0 + X\big/(1 + r)^T \tag{12}$$

This relationship is known as **put–call parity**.

Exhibit 15   Protective Put vs. Fiduciary Call

	Outcome at T	
	Put Expires In-the-Money $(S_T < X)$	**Call Expires In-the-Money** $(S_T \geq X)$
Protective put		
Asset	S_T	S_T
Long put	$X - S_T$	0
Total	X	S_T
Fiduciary call		
Long call	0	$S_T - X$
Risk-free bond	X	X
Total	X	S_T

For a simple example, assume call and put options with an exercise price of ¥100,000 in which the underlying is at ¥90,000 at time 0. The risk-free rate is 2% and the options expire in two months, so $T = 2/12 = 0.167$. To completely fill in the puzzle, we would need to know the put or call price, from which we could obtain the other. For now, let us write this relationship as

$$p_0 - c_0 = X\big/(1 + r)^T - S_0$$

The right side would be ¥100,000/(1.02)$^{0.167}$ − ¥90,000 = ¥9,670. Thus, the put price should exceed the call price by ¥9,670. Thus, if the call were priced at ¥5,000, the put price would be ¥14,670. If we knew the put price, we could obtain the call price. Put–call parity does not tell us which price is correct, and it requires knowledge of one price to get the other. Alternatively, it can tell us the difference in the put and call prices.

Put–call parity must hold, at least within transaction costs, or arbitrage opportunities would arise. For example, suppose Investor C observes market prices and finds that the left- hand side of put–call parity, $S_0 + p_0$, is less than the right-hand side, $c_0 + X/(1 + r)^T$. Thus, the put and the stock cost less than the call and the bond. Knowing that there should be equality (parity), Investor C executes an arbitrage transaction, selling the overpriced transactions (the call and the bond) and buying the underpriced transactions (the asset and the put).[19] By selling the higher priced side and buying the lower priced side, Investor C will take in more money than she will pay out, a net inflow of $c_0 + X/(1 + r)^T − (S_0 + p_0)$. At expiration, the long put and long asset will offset the short call and bond, as shown in Exhibit 16.

Exhibit 16   Put–Call Parity Arbitrage

| | | Outcome at T | |
| | | Put Expires In-the- Money $(S_T < X)$ | Call Expires In-the-Money $(S_T \geq X)$ |
Transaction	Cash Flow at Time 0		
Buy asset	$−S_0$	S_T	S_T
Buy put	$−p_0$	$X − S_T$	0
Sell call	$+c_0$	0	$−(S_T − X)$
Borrow	$+X/(1 + r)^T$	$−X$	$−X$
Total	$−S_0 − p_0 + c_0 + X/(1 + r)^T > 0$	0	0

In simple terms, if $S_T < X$, the short call expires out-of-the-money and the put is exercised to sell the asset for X. This cash, X, is then used to pay off the loan. The net effect is that no money flows in or out at T. If $S_T \geq X$, the put expires out-of-the money, and the short call is exercised, meaning that Investor C must sell the asset for X. This cash, X, is then used to pay off the loan. Again, no money flows in or out. The net effect is a perfect hedge in which no money is paid out or received at T. But there was money taken in at time 0. Taking in money today and never having to pay it out is an arbitrage profit. Arbitrage opportunities like this, however, will be noticed by many investors who will engage in the same transactions. Prices will adjust until parity is restored, whereby $S_0 + p_0 = c_0 + X/(1 + r)^T$.

Put–call parity provides tremendous insights into option pricing. Recall that we proved that going long the asset and long a put is equivalent to going long a call and long a risk-free bond. We can rearrange the put–call parity equation in the following ways:

---

19 Selling the bond is equivalent to borrowing, meaning to issue a loan.

$$S_0 + p_0 = c_0 + X/(1+r)^T$$
$$\Rightarrow$$
$$p_0 = c_0 - S_0 + X/(1+r)^T$$
$$c_0 = p_0 + S_0 - X/(1+r)^T$$
$$S_0 = c_0 - p_0 + X/(1+r)^T$$
$$X/(1+r)^T = S_0 + p_0 - c_0$$

By using the symbols and the signs in these versions of put–call parity, we can see several important interpretations. In the equations below, plus signs mean long and minus signs mean short:

$$p_0 = c_0 - S_0 + X/(1+r)^T \quad \Rightarrow \quad \text{long put = long call, short asset, long bond}$$

$$c_0 = p_0 + S_0 - X/(1+r)^T \quad \Rightarrow \quad \text{long call = long put, long asset, short bond}$$

$$S_0 = c_0 - p_0 + X/(1+r)^T \quad \Rightarrow \quad \text{long asset = long call, short put, long bond}$$

$$X/(1+r)^T = S_0 + p_0 - c_0 \quad \Rightarrow \quad \text{long bond = long asset, long put, short call}$$

You should be able to convince yourself of any of these points by constructing a table similar to Exhibit 15.[20]

4.1.10 *Put–Call–Forward Parity*

Recall that we demonstrated that one could create a risk-free position by going long the asset and selling a forward contract.[21] It follows that one can synthetically create a position in the asset by going long a forward contract and long a risk-free bond. Recall our put–call parity discussion and assume that Investor A creates his protective put in a slightly different manner. Instead of buying the asset, he buys a forward contract and a risk-free bond in which the face value is the forward price. Exhibit 17 shows that this strategy is a synthetic protective put. Because we showed that the fiduciary call is equivalent to the protective put, a fiduciary call has to be equivalent to a protective put with a forward contract. Exhibit 18 demonstrates this point.

Exhibit 17	Protective Put with Forward Contract vs. Protective Put with Asset	

| | Outcome at T | |
	Put Expires In-the-Money $(S_T < X)$	Put Expires Out-of-the-Money $(S_T \geq X)$
Protective put with asset		
Asset	S_T	S_T
Long put	$X - S_T$	0
Total	X	S_T
Protective put with forward contract		
Risk-free bond	$F_0(T)$	$F_0(T)$

---

[20] As a further exercise, you might change the signs of each term in the above and provide the appropriate interpretations.
[21] You might wish to review Exhibit 6.

Exhibit 17	(Continued)

	Outcome at T	
	Put Expires In-the-Money $(S_T < X)$	**Put Expires Out-of-the-Money** $(S_T \geq X)$
Forward contract	$S_T - F_0(T)$	$S_T - F_0(T)$
Long put	$X - S_T$	0
Total	X	S_T

Exhibit 18	Protective Put with Forward Contract vs. Fiduciary Call

	Outcome at T	
	Put Expires In-the-Money $(S_T < X)$	**Call Expires In-the-Money** $(S_T \geq X)$
Protective Put with Forward Contract		
Risk-free bond	$F_0(T)$	$F_0(T)$
Forward contract	$S_T - F_0(T)$	$S_T - F_0(T)$
Long put	$X - S_T$	0
Total	X	S_T
Fiduciary Call		
Call	0	$S_T - X$
Risk-free bond	X	X
Total	X	S_T

It follows that the cost of the fiduciary call must equal the cost of the synthetic protective put, giving us what is referred to as **put–call–forward parity**,

$$F_0(T)\big/(1+r)^T + p_0 = c_0 + X\big/(1+r)^T \tag{13}$$

Returning to our put–call parity example, a forward contract on ¥90,000 expiring in two months with a 2% interest rate would have a price of ¥90,000(1.02)$^{0.167}$ = ¥90,298. Rearranging Equation 13, we have

$$p_0 - c_0 = \left[X - F_0(T)\right]\big/(1+r)^T$$

The right-hand side is (¥100,000 – ¥90,298)/(1.02)$^{0.167}$ = ¥9,670, which is the same answer we obtained using the underlying asset rather than the forward contract. Naturally these two models give us the same answer. They are both based on the assumption that no arbitrage is possible within the spot, forward, and options markets.

So far we have learned only how to price options in relation to other options, such as a call versus a put or a call or a put versus a forward. We need a way to price options versus their underlying.

EXAMPLE 7

Put–Call Parity

1 Which of the following statements *best* describes put–call parity?

   A The put price always equals the call price.

   B The put price equals the call price if the volatility is known.

   C The put price plus the underlying price equals the call price plus the present value of the exercise price.

2 From put–call parity, which of the following transactions is risk-free?

   A Long asset, long put, short call

   B Long call, long put, short asset

   C Long asset, long call, short bond

Solution to 1:

C is correct. The put and underlying make up a protective put, while the call and present value of the exercise price make up a fiduciary call. The put price equals the call price for certain combinations of interest rates, times to expiration, and option moneyness, but these are special cases. Volatility has no effect on put–call parity.

Solution to 2:

A is correct. The combination of a long asset, long put, and short call is risk free because its payoffs produce a known cash flow of the value of the exercise price. The other two combinations do not produce risk-free positions. You should work through the payoffs of these three combinations in the form of Exhibit 12.

4.2 Binomial Valuation of Options

Because the option payoff is determined by the underlying, if we know the outcome of the underlying, we know the payoff of the option. That means that the price of the underlying is the only element of uncertainty. Moreover, the uncertainty is not so much the value of the underlying at expiration as it is whether the underlying is above or below the exercise price. If the underlying is above the exercise price at expiration, the payoff is $S_T - X$ for calls and zero for puts. If the underlying is below the exercise price at expiration, the payoff is zero for calls and $X - S_T$ for puts. In other words, the payoff of the option is straightforward and known, as soon as we know whether the option expires in- or out-of-the-money. Note that for forwards, futures, and swaps, there is no such added complexity. The payoff formula is the same regardless of whether the underlying is above or below the hurdle.

As a result of this characteristic of options, derivation of an option pricing model requires the specification of a model of a random process that describes movements in the underlying. Given the entirely different nature of the payoffs above and below the exercise price, it might seem difficult to derive the option price, even if we could model movements in the underlying. Fortunately, the process is less difficult than it first appears.

At this level of treatment, we will start with a very simple model that allows only two possible movements in the underlying—one going up and one going down from where it is now. This model with two possible outcomes is called the **binomial model**. Start with the underlying at S_0, and let it go up to S_1^+ or down to S_1^-. We cannot arbitrarily set these values at just anything. We will be required to know the values of S_1^+ and S_1^-. That does not mean we know which outcome will occur. It means that we know only what the possibilities are. In doing so, we effectively know the volatility. Assume the probability of the move to S_1^+ is q and the probability of the move to S_1^- is $1 - q$. We specify the returns implied by these moves as up and down factors, u and d, where

$$u = \frac{S_1^+}{S_0}, \quad d = \frac{S_1^-}{S_0} \tag{14}$$

Now, consider a European call option that expires at time 1 and has an exercise price of X. Let the call prices be c_0 today and c_1^+ and c_1^- at expiration. Exhibit 19 illustrates the model. Our objective is to determine the price of the option today, meaning to determine a formula for c_0. Knowing what we know about arbitrage and the pricing of forward contracts, it would seem we could construct a risk-free portfolio involving this option.

Exhibit 19   The Binomial Option Pricing Model

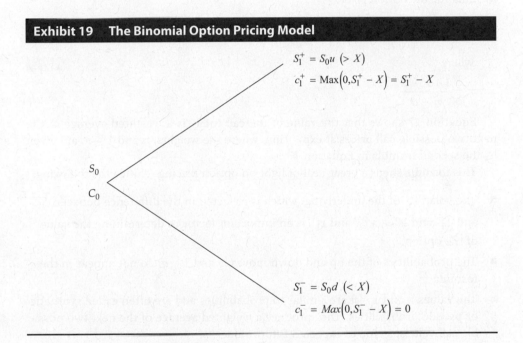

$$S_1^+ = S_0 u \; (> X)$$
$$c_1^+ = \text{Max}\left(0, S_1^+ - X\right) = S_1^+ - X$$

$$S_0$$
$$C_0$$

$$S_1^- = S_0 d \; (< X)$$
$$c_1^- = Max\left(0, S_1^- - X\right) = 0$$

Because call options and the underlying move together, one possibility is that buying the underlying and selling a call could create a hedge. Indeed it does, but one unit of each is not the appropriate balance. Let us sell one call and hold h units of the underlying. The value h is unknown at the moment, but we will be able to determine its value. The value today of a combination of h units of the underlying and one short call is

$$V_0 = hS_0 - c_0$$

Think of V_0 as the amount of money invested. Depending on which of the two paths is taken by the underlying, the value of this portfolio at time 1 will be

$$V_1^+ = hS_1^+ - c_1^+$$

or $\tag{15}$

$$V_1^- = hS_1^- - c_1^-$$

If the portfolio were hedged, then V_1^+ would equal V_1^-. We can set V_1^+ and V_1^- equal to each other and solve for the value of h that assures us that the portfolio is hedged:

$$V_1^+ = V_1^-$$

$$\Rightarrow hS_1^+ - c_1^+ = hS_1^- - c_1^-$$

$$\Rightarrow h = \frac{c_1^+ - c_1^-}{S_1^+ - S_1^-}$$

(16)

The values on the right-hand side are known, so we can easily calculate h. Thus, we can derive the number of units of the underlying that will perfectly hedge one unit of the short call.

We know that a perfectly hedged investment should earn the risk-free rate, r. Thus, the following statement must be true:

$$V_1^+ (\text{or } V_1^-) = V_0(1 + r)$$

We can substitute the value of V_1^+ or V_1^- from Equation 15 into the above equation. Then we do a little algebra, which is not important to this discussion, and obtain the formula for the option price,

$$c_0 = \frac{\pi c_1^+ + (1 - \pi)c_1^-}{1 + r}$$

where

(17)

$$\pi = \frac{1 + r - d}{u - d}$$

Equation 17 shows that the value of the call today is a weighted average of the next two possible call prices at expiration, where the weights, π and $1 - \pi$, are given by the second formula in Equation 17.

This formula sheds a great deal of light on option pricing. Notice the following:

- The volatility of the underlying, which is reflected in the difference between S_1^+ and S_1^- and affects c_1^+ and c_1^-, is an important factor in determining the value of the option.

- The probabilities of the up and down moves, q and $1 - q$, do not appear in the formula.[22]

- The values π and $1 - \pi$ are similar to probabilities and are often called synthetic or pseudo probabilities. They produce a weighted average of the next two possible call values, a type of expected future value.

- The formula takes the form of an expected future value, the numerator, discounted at the risk-free rate.

On the first point, if volatility increases, the difference between S_1^+ and S_1^- increases, which widens the range between c_1^+ and c_1^-, leading to a higher option value. The upper payoff, c_1^+, will be larger and the lower payoff, c_1^-, will still be zero.[23] On the second point, the actual probabilities of the up and down moves do not matter. This result is because of our ability to construct a hedge and the rule of arbitrage. On the third point, the irrelevance of the actual probabilities is replaced by the relevance of a set of synthetic or pseudo probabilities, π and $1 - \pi$, which are called **risk-neutral probabilities**. On the fourth point, these risk-neutral probabilities are used to find a

---

22 We introduced them earlier to help make this point, but ultimately they serve no purpose.
23 Although the lower payoff is zero in this example, that will not always be the case.

synthetic expected value, which is then discounted at the risk-free rate. Thus, the option is valued as though investors are risk neutral. As we discussed extensively earlier, that is not the same as assuming that investors are risk neutral.

If the option does not trade at the specified formula, Equation 17, investors can engage in arbitrage transactions. If the option is trading too high relative to the formula, investors can sell the call, buy h shares of the underlying, and earn a return in excess of the risk-free rate, while funding the transaction by borrowing at the risk-free rate. The combined actions of arbitrageurs will result in downward pressure on the option price until it converges to the model price. If the option price is too low, buying the call, selling short h units of the asset, and investing the proceeds in risk-free bonds will generate risk-free cash that will earn more than the risk-free rate. The combined actions of arbitrageurs doing this will pressure the call price to rise until it reaches the price given by the model.

We will omit the details, but the hedge portfolio can also be constructed with puts.[24] Changing the c's to p's leads to the binomial put option pricing formula,

$$p_0 = \frac{\pi p_1^+ + (1 - \pi)p_1^-}{1 + r} \qquad \text{(18)}$$

with the risk-neutral probability π determined by the same formula as for calls, as shown in Equation 17.

Let us construct a simple example. Let S_0 be £40 and the risk-free rate be 5%. The up and down factors are $u = 1.20$ and $d = 0.75$. Thus, the next two possible prices of the asset are $S_1^+ = £40(1.20) = £48$ and $S_1^- = £40(0.75) = £30$. Consider a call and a put that have exercise prices of £38. Then the next two possible values of the call and put are

$$c_1^+ = \text{Max}(0, £48 - £38) = £10$$

$$c_1^- = \text{Max}(0, £30 - £38) = £0$$

$$p_1^+ = \text{Max}(0, £38 - £48) = £0$$

$$p_1^- = \text{Max}(0, £38 - £30) = £8$$

Next we compute the risk-neutral probability,

$$\pi = \frac{1 + 0.05 - 0.75}{1.20 - 0.75} = 0.667$$

The values of the call and put are

$$c_0 = \frac{0.667(£10) + (1 - 0.667)£0}{1.05} = £6.35$$

and

$$p_0 = \frac{0.667(£0) + (1 - 0.667)£8}{1.05} = £2.54$$

The binomial model, as we see it here, is extremely simple. In reality, of course, there are more than two possible next-period prices for the underlying. As it turns out, we can extend the number of periods and subdivide an option's life into an increasing number of smaller time periods. In that case, we can obtain a more accurate and realistic model for option pricing, one that is widely used in practice. Given our objective in this reading of understanding the basic ideas behind derivative pricing, the one-period model is sufficient for the time being.

---

24 A long position in h units of the underlying would be hedged with one long put. The formula for h is the same as the one given here for calls, with call prices in the numerator instead of put prices.

EXAMPLE 8

Binomial Valuation of Options

1 Which of the following terms directly represents the volatility of the underlying in the binomial model?

   A The standard deviation of the underlying

   B The difference between the up and down factors

   C The ratio of the underlying value to the exercise price.

2 Which of the following is *not* a factor in pricing a call option in the binomial model?

   A The risk-free rate

   B The exercise price

   C The probability that the underlying will go up

3 Which of the following *best* describes the binomial option pricing formula?

   A The expected payoff is discounted at the risk-free rate plus a risk premium.

   B The spot price is compounded at the risk-free rate minus the volatility premium.

   C The expected payoff based on risk-neutral probabilities is discounted at the risk-free rate.

Solution to 1:

B is correct. The up and down factors express how high and how low the underlying can go. Standard deviation does not appear directly in the binomial model, although it is implicit. The ratio of the underlying value to the exercise price expresses the moneyness of the option.

Solution to 2:

C is correct. The actual probabilities of the up and down moves are irrelevant to pricing options. The risk-free and exercise price are, of course, highly relevant.

Solution to 3:

C is correct. Risk-neutral probabilities are used, and discounting is at the risk-free rate. There is no risk premium incorporated into option pricing because of the use of arbitrage.

We have now seen how to obtain the price of a European option. Let us now consider what happens if the options are American, meaning they have the right to be exercised early.

4.3 American Option Pricing

First, we will use upper case letters for American call and put prices: C_0 and P_0. Second, we know that American options possess every characteristic of European options and one additional trait: They can be exercised at any time prior to expiration. Early exercise cannot be required, so the right to exercise early cannot have negative value. Thus, American options cannot sell for less than European options. Thus, we can state the following:

$$C_0 \geq c_0$$
$$P_0 \geq p_0 \tag{19}$$

Given the price of the underlying at S_0, the early-exercise feature means that we can exercise the option at any time. So, we can claim the value $Max(0, S_0 - X)$ for calls and $Max(0, X - S_0)$ for puts. These values establish new minimum prices for American calls and puts,

$$C_0 = Max(0, S_0 - X)$$
$$P_0 = Max(0, X - S_0) \tag{20}$$

For call options, we previously learned that a European call has a minimum value given by Equation 10, which is restated here:

$$c_0 \geq Max\left[0, S_0 - X/(1 + r)^T\right]$$

Comparing $Max(0, S_0 - X)$ (the minimum for American calls) with $Max[0, S_0 - X/(1 + r)^T]$ (the minimum for European calls) reveals that the latter is either the same or higher. There are some circumstances in which both minima are zero, some in which the American minimum is zero and the European minimum is positive, and some in which both are positive, in which case $S_0 - X/(1 + r)^T$ is unquestionably more than $S_0 - X$. Given that an American call price cannot be less than a European call price, we have to reestablish the American call minimum as $Max[0, S_0 - X/(1 + r)^T]$.

For put options, we previously learned that a European put has a minimum value given by Equation 11, which is restated here:

$$p_0 \geq Max\left[0, X/(1 + r)^T - S_0\right]$$

Comparing $Max(0, X - S_0)$ (the minimum for American puts) with $Max[0, X/(1 + r)^T - S_0]$ (the minimum for European puts) reveals that the former is never less. In some circumstances, they are both zero. In some, $X - S_0$ is positive and $X/(1 + r)^T - S_0$ is negative, and in some cases both are positive but $X - S_0$ is unquestionably more than $X/(1 + r)^T - S_0$. Thus, the American put minimum value is the exercise value, which is $Max(0, X - S_0)$.

So, now we have new minimum prices for American calls and puts:

$$C_0 \geq Max\left[0, S_0 - X/(1 + r)^T\right]$$
$$P_0 \geq Max(0, X - S_0) \tag{21}$$

Thus, in the market these options will trade for at least these values.

Let us return to the previous examples for the minimum values. The exercise price is €60, the risk-free rate is 4%, and the expiration is $T = 0.75$. Consider the two cases below:

Underlying: $S_0 = €70$

- The minimum European call price was previously calculated as €11.74. The exercise value of the American call is $Max(0, €70 - €60) = €10$. The American call has to sell for at least as much as the European call, so the minimum price of the American call is €11.74.

- The minimum European put price was €0.00. This is also the exercise value of the American put [$Max(0, €60 - €70) = €0.00$], so the minimum price of the American put is still €0.00

Underlying: $S_0 = €50$

- The minimum European call price was previously calculated as €0.00. The exercise value of the American call is Max(0, €50 − €60) = €0.00, so €0.00 is still the minimum price of the American call.

- The minimum European put price was previously calculated as €8.26. The exercise value of the American put is Max(0, €60 − €50) = €10. So, €10 is the minimum price of the American put.

The call result leads us to a somewhat surprising conclusion. With the exception of what happens at expiration when American and European calls are effectively the same and both worth the exercise value, an American call is always worth more in the market than exercised. That means that an American call will never be exercised early. This result is probably not intuitive.

Consider a deep in-the-money call. One might think that if the holder expected the underlying to not increase any further, exercise might be justified. Yet, we said the call would sell for more in the market than its exercise value. What is the rationale? If the investor thinks the underlying will not go up any further and thus expects no further gains from the option, why would she prefer the underlying? Would the investor be happier holding the underlying, which she believes is not expected to increase? Moreover, she would tie up more funds exercising to acquire the underlying than if she just held on to the option or, better yet, sold it to another investor.

So far, however, we have left out a possible factor that can affect early exercise. Suppose the underlying is a stock and pays dividends. When a stock goes ex-dividend, its price instantaneously falls. Although we will omit the details, an investor holding a call option may find it worthwhile to exercise the call just before the stock goes ex-dividend. The capture of the dividend, thereby avoiding the ex-dividend drop in the price of the underlying, can make early exercise worthwhile. If the underlying is a bond, coupon interest can also motivate early exercise. But if there are significant carrying costs, the motivation for early exercise is weakened. Storage costs lend a preference for owning the option over owning the underlying.

Because the minimum value of an American put exceeds the minimum value of the European put, there is a much stronger motivation for early exercise. Suppose you owned an American put on a stock that is completely bankrupt, with a zero stock price and no possibility of recovery. You can either wait until expiration and capture its exercise value of Max(0, $X − S_T$) = Max(0, $X − 0$) = Max(0, X) = X, or you can capture that value by exercising now. Obviously now is better. As it turns out, however, the underlying does not need to go all the way to zero. There is a critical point at which a put is so deep in-the-money that early exercise is justified. This rationale works differently for a call. A deep in-the-money put has a limit to its ultimate value. It can get no deeper than when the underlying goes to zero. For a call, there is no limit to its moneyness because the underlying has no upper limit to its price.

Although dividends and coupon interest encourage early exercise for calls, they discourage early exercise for puts. The loss from the decline in the price of the underlying that is avoided by exercising a call just before the decline works to the benefit of a put holder. Therefore, if a put holder were considering exercising early, he would be better off waiting until right after the dividend or interest were paid. Carrying costs on the underlying, which discourage exercise for calls, encourage exercise for puts.

At this point, we cannot determine the critical prices at which American options are best exercised early. We require more knowledge and experience with option pricing models, which is covered in more advanced material.

EXAMPLE 9

American Option Pricing

1 With respect to American calls, which of the following statements is *most* accurate?

   A American calls should be exercised early if the underlying has reached its expected maximum price.

   B American calls should be exercised early if the underlying has a lower expected return than the risk-free rate.

   C American calls should be exercised early only if there is a dividend or other cash payment on the underlying.

2 The effect of dividends on a stock on early exercise of a put is to:

   A make early exercise less likely.

   B have no effect on early exercise.

   C make early exercise more likely.

Solution to 1:

C is correct. Cash payments on the underlying are the only reason to exercise American calls early. Interest rates, the expected return on the underlying, and any notion of a maximum price is irrelevant. But note that a dividend does not mean that early exercise should automatically be conducted. A dividend is only a necessary condition to justify early exercise for calls.

Solution to 2:

A is correct. Dividends drive down the stock price when the dividend is paid. Thus, all else being equal, a stock paying dividends has a built-in force that drives down the stock price. This characteristic discourages early exercise, because stock price declines are beneficial to holders of puts.

SUMMARY

This reading on derivative pricing provides a foundation for understanding how derivatives are valued and traded. Key points include the following:

■ The price of the underlying asset is equal to the expected future price discounted at the risk-free rate, plus a risk premium, plus the present value of any benefits, minus the present value of any costs associated with holding the asset.

■ An arbitrage opportunity occurs when two identical assets or combinations of assets sell at different prices, leading to the possibility of buying the cheaper asset and selling the more expensive asset to produce a risk-free return without investing any capital.

■ In well-functioning markets, arbitrage opportunities are quickly exploited, and the resulting increased buying of underpriced assets and increased selling of overpriced assets returns prices to equivalence.

- Derivatives are priced by creating a risk-free combination of the underlying and a derivative, leading to a unique derivative price that eliminates any possibility of arbitrage.

- Derivative pricing through arbitrage precludes any need for determining risk premiums or the risk aversion of the party trading the option and is referred to as risk-neutral pricing.

- The value of a forward contract at expiration is the value of the asset minus the forward price.

- The value of a forward contract prior to expiration is the value of the asset minus the present value of the forward price.

- The forward price, established when the contract is initiated, is the price agreed to by the two parties that produces a zero value at the start.

- Costs incurred and benefits received by holding the underlying affect the forward price by raising and lowering it, respectively.

- Futures prices can differ from forward prices because of the effect of interest rates on the interim cash flows from the daily settlement.

- Swaps can be priced as an implicit series of off-market forward contracts, whereby each contract is priced the same, resulting in some contracts being positively valued and some negatively valued but with their combined value equaling zero.

- At expiration, a European call or put is worth its exercise value, which for calls is the greater of zero or the underlying price minus the exercise price and for puts is the greater of zero and the exercise price minus the underlying price.

- European calls and puts are affected by the value of the underlying, the exercise price, the risk-free rate, the time to expiration, the volatility of the underlying, and any costs incurred or benefits received while holding the underlying.

- Option values experience time value decay, which is the loss in value due to the passage of time and the approach of expiration, plus the moneyness and the volatility.

- The minimum value of a European call is the maximum of zero and the underlying price minus the present value of the exercise price.

- The minimum value of a European put is the maximum of zero and the present value of the exercise price minus the price of the underlying.

- European put and call prices are related through put–call parity, which specifies that the put price plus the price of the underlying equals the call price plus the present value of the exercise price.

- European put and call prices are related through put–call–forward parity, which shows that the put price plus the value of a risk-free bond with face value equal to the forward price equals the call price plus the value of a risk-free bond with face value equal to the exercise price.

- The values of European options can be obtained using the binomial model, which specifies two possible prices of the asset one period later and enables the construction of a risk-free hedge consisting of the option and the underlying.

- American call prices can differ from European call prices only if there are cash flows on the underlying, such as dividends or interest; these cash flows are the only reason for early exercise of a call.

- American put prices can differ from European put prices, because the right to exercise early always has value for a put, which is because of a lower limit on the value of the underlying.

PRACTICE PROBLEMS

1 An arbitrage opportunity is *least likely* to be exploited when:

A one position is illiquid.

B the price differential between assets is large.

C the investor can execute a transaction in large volumes.

2 An arbitrageur will *most likely* execute a trade when:

A transaction costs are low.

B costs of short-selling are high.

C prices are consistent with the law of one price.

3 An arbitrage transaction generates a net inflow of funds:

A throughout the holding period.

B at the end of the holding period.

C at the start of the holding period.

4 The price of a forward contract:

A is the amount paid at initiation.

B is the amount paid at expiration.

C fluctuates over the term of the contract.

5 Assume an asset pays no dividends or interest, and also assume that the asset does not yield any non-financial benefits or incur any carrying cost. At initiation, the price of a forward contract on that asset is:

A lower than the value of the contract.

B equal to the value of the contract.

C greater than the value of the contract.

6 With respect to a forward contract, as market conditions change:

A only the price fluctuates.

B only the value fluctuates.

C both the price and the value fluctuate.

7 The value of a forward contract at expiration is:

A positive to the long party if the spot price is higher than the forward price.

B negative to the short party if the forward price is higher than the spot price.

C positive to the short party if the spot price is higher than the forward price.

8 At the initiation of a forward contract on an asset that neither receives benefits nor incurs carrying costs during the term of the contract, the forward price is equal to the:

A spot price.

B future value of the spot price.

C present value of the spot price.

9 Stocks BWQ and ZER are each currently priced at $100 per share. Over the next year, stock BWQ is expected to generate significant benefits whereas stock ZER is not expected to generate any benefits. There are no carrying costs associated with holding either stock over the next year. Compared with ZER, the one-year forward price of BWQ is *most likely*:

   A lower.

   B the same.

   C higher.

10 If the net cost of carry of an asset is positive, then the price of a forward contract on that asset is *most likely*:

   A lower than if the net cost of carry was zero.

   B the same as if the net cost of carry was zero.

   C higher than if the net cost of carry was zero.

11 If the present value of storage costs exceeds the present value of its convenience yield, then the commodity's forward price is *most likely*:

   A less than the spot price compounded at the risk-free rate.

   B the same as the spot price compounded at the risk-free rate.

   C higher than the spot price compounded at the risk-free rate.

12 Which of the following factors *most likely* explains why the spot price of a commodity in short supply can be greater than its forward price?

   A Opportunity cost

   B Lack of dividends

   C Convenience yield

13 When interest rates are constant, futures prices are *most likely*:

   A less than forward prices.

   B equal to forward prices.

   C greater than forward prices.

14 In contrast to a forward contract, a futures contract:

   A trades over-the-counter.

   B is initiated at a zero value.

   C is marked-to-market daily.

15 To the holder of a long position, it is more desirable to own a forward contract than a futures contract when interest rates and futures prices are:

   A negatively correlated.

   B uncorrelated.

   C positively correlated.

16 The value of a swap typically:

   A is non-zero at initiation.

   B is obtained through replication.

   C does not fluctuate over the life of the contract.

17 The price of a swap typically:

   A is zero at initiation.

   B fluctuates over the life of the contract.

   C is obtained through a process of replication.

18 The value of a swap is equal to the present value of the:

   A fixed payments from the swap.

   B net cash flow payments from the swap.

   C underlying at the end of the contract.

19 A European call option and a European put option are written on the same underlying, and both options have the same expiration date and exercise price. At expiration, it is possible that both options will have:

A negative values.

B the same value.

C positive values.

20 At expiration, a European put option will be valuable if the exercise price is:

A less than the underlying price.

B equal to the underlying price.

C greater than the underlying price.

21 The value of a European call option at expiration is the greater of zero or the:

A value of the underlying.

B value of the underlying minus the exercise price.

C exercise price minus the value of the underlying.

22 For a European call option with two months until expiration, if the spot price is below the exercise price, the call option will *most likely* have:

A zero time value.

B positive time value.

C positive exercise value.

23 When the price of the underlying is below the exercise price, a put option is:

A in-the-money.

B at-the-money.

C out-of-the-money.

24 If the risk-free rate increases, the value of an in-the-money European put option will *most likely*:

A decrease.

B remain the same.

C increase.

25 The value of a European call option is inversely related to the:

A exercise price.

B time to expiration.

C volatility of the underlying.

26 The table below shows three European call options on the same underlying:

	Time to Expiration	Exercise Price
Option 1	3 months	$100
Option 2	6 months	$100
Option 3	6 months	$105

The option with the highest value is *most likely*:

A Option 1.

B Option 2.

C Option 3.

27 The value of a European put option can be either directly or inversely related to the:

A exercise price.

   B time to expiration.

   C volatility of the underlying.

28 Prior to expiration, the lowest value of a European put option is the greater of zero or the:

   A exercise price minus the value of the underlying.

   B present value of the exercise price minus the value of the underlying.

   C value of the underlying minus the present value of the exercise price.

29 A European put option on a dividend-paying stock is *most likely* to increase if there is an increase in:

   A carrying costs.

   B the risk-free rate.

   C dividend payments.

30 Based on put-call parity, a trader who combines a long asset, a long put, and a short call will create a synthetic:

   A long bond.

   B fiduciary call.

   C protective put.

31 Which of the following transactions is the equivalent of a synthetic long call position?

   A Long asset, long put, short call

   B Long asset, long put, short bond

   C Short asset, long call, long bond

32 Which of the following is *least likely* to be required by the binomial option pricing model?

   A Spot price

   B Two possible prices one period later

   C Actual probabilities of the up and down moves

33 An at-the-money American call option on a stock that pays no dividends has three months remaining until expiration. The market value of the option will *most likely* be:

   A less than its exercise value.

   B equal to its exercise value.

   C greater than its exercise value.

34 At expiration, American call options are worth:

   A less than European call options.

   B the same as European call options.

   C more than European call options.

35 Which of the following circumstances will *most likely* affect the value of an American call option relative to a European call option?

   A Dividends are declared

   B Expiration date occurs

   C The risk-free rate changes

36 Combining a protective put with a forward contract generates equivalent outcomes at expiration to those of a:

   A fiduciary call.

    B long call combined with a short asset.

    C forward contract combined with a risk-free bond.

SOLUTIONS

1 A is correct. An illiquid position is a limit to arbitrage because it may be difficult to realize gains of an illiquid offsetting position. A significant opportunity arises from a sufficiently large price differential or a small price differential that can be employed on a very large scale.

2 A is correct. Some arbitrage opportunities represent such small price discrepancies that they are only worth exploiting if the transaction costs are low. An arbitrage opportunity may require short-selling assets at costs that eliminate any profit potential. If the law of one price holds, there is no arbitrage opportunity.

3 C is correct. Arbitrage is a type of transaction undertaken when two assets or portfolios produce identical results but sell for different prices. A trader buys the asset or portfolio with the lower price and sells the asset or portfolio with the higher price, generating a net inflow of funds at the start of the holding period. Because the two assets or portfolios produce identical results, a long position in one and short position in the other means that at the end of the holding period, the payoffs offset. Therefore, there is no money gained or lost at the end of the holding period, so there is no risk.

4 B is correct. The forward price is agreed upon at the start of the contract and is the fixed price at which the underlying will be purchased (or sold) at expiration. Payment is made at expiration. The value of the forward contract may change over time, but the forward price does not change.

5 C is correct. The price of a forward contract is a contractually fixed price, established at initiation, at which the underlying will be purchased (or sold) at expiration. The value of a forward contract at initiation is zero; therefore, the forward price is greater than the value of the forward contract at initiation.

6 B is correct. The value of the forward contract, unlike its price, will adjust as market conditions change. The forward price is fixed at initiation.

7 A is correct. When a forward contract expires, if the spot price is higher than the forward price, the long party profits from paying the lower forward price for the underlying. Therefore, the forward contract has a positive value to the long party and a negative value to the short party. However, if the forward price is higher than the spot price, the short party profits from receiving the higher forward price (the contract value is positive to the short party and negative to the long party).

8 B is correct. At initiation, the forward price is the future value of the spot price (spot price compounded at the risk-free rate over the life of the contract). If the forward price were set to the spot price or the present value of the spot price, it would be possible for one side to earn an arbitrage profit by selling the asset and investing the proceeds until contract expiration.

9 A is correct. The forward price of each stock is found by compounding the spot price by the risk-free rate for the period and then subtracting the future value of any benefits and adding the future value of any costs. In the absence of any benefits or costs, the one-year forward prices of BWQ and ZER should be equal. After subtracting the benefits related to BWQ, the one-year forward price of BWQ is lower than the one-year forward price of ZER.

10 A is correct. An asset's forward price is increased by the future value of any costs and decreased by the future value of any benefits: $F_0(T) = S_0(1 + r)^T - (\gamma - \theta)(1 + r)^T$ If the net cost of carry (benefits less costs) is positive, the forward price is lower than if the net cost of carry was zero.

11 C is correct. When a commodity's storage costs exceed its convenience yield benefits, the net cost of carry (benefits less costs) is negative. Subtracting this negative amount from the spot price compounded at the risk-free rate results in an addition to the compounded spot price. The result is a commodity forward price which is higher than the spot price compounded. The commodity's forward price is less than the spot price compounded when the convenience yield benefits exceed the storage costs and the commodity's forward price is the same as the spot price compounded when the costs equal the benefits.

12 C is correct. The convenience yield is a benefit of holding the asset and generally exists when a commodity is in short supply. The future value of the convenience yield is subtracted from the compounded spot price and reduces the commodity's forward price relative to it spot price. The opportunity cost is the risk-free rate. In the absence of carry costs, the forward price is the spot price compounded at the risk-free rate and will exceed the spot price. Dividends are benefits that reduce the forward price but the lack of dividends has no effect on the spot price relative to the forward price of a commodity in short supply.

13 B is correct. When interest rates are constant, forwards and futures will likely have the same prices. The price differential will vary with the volatility of interest rates. In addition, if futures prices and interest rates are uncorrelated, forward and futures prices will be the same. If futures prices are positively correlated with interest rates, futures contracts are more desirable to holders of long positions than are forwards. This is because rising prices lead to future profits that are reinvested in periods of rising interest rates, and falling prices lead to losses that occur in periods of falling interest rates. If futures prices are negatively correlated with interest rates, futures contracts are less desirable to holders of long positions than are forwards. The more desirable contract will tend to have the higher price.

14 C is correct. Futures contracts are marked-to-market on a daily basis. The accumulated gains and losses from the previous day's trading session are deducted from the accounts of those holding losing positions and transferred to the accounts of those holding winning positions. Futures contracts trade on an exchange, forward contracts are over-the-counter transactions. Typically both forward and futures contracts are initiated at a zero value.

15 A is correct. If futures prices and interest rates are negatively correlated, forwards are more desirable to holders of long positions than are futures. This is because rising prices lead to futures profits that are reinvested in periods of falling interest rates. It is better to receive all of the cash at expiration under such conditions. If futures prices and interest rates are uncorrelated, forward and futures prices will be the same. If futures prices are positively correlated with interest rates, futures contracts are more desirable to holders of long positions than are forwards.

16 B is correct. Valuation of the swap during its life appeals to replication and the principle of arbitrage. Valuation consists of reproducing the remaining payments on the swap with other transactions. The value of that replication strategy is the value of the swap. The swap price is typically set such that the swap contract has a value of zero at initiation. The value of a swap contract will change during the life of the contract as the value of the underlying changes in value.

17 C is correct. Replication is the key to pricing a swap. The swap price is determined at initiation by replication. The value (not the price) of the swap is typically zero at initiation and the fixed swap price is typically determined such that the value of the swap will be zero at initiation.

18 B is correct. The principal of replication articulates that the valuation of a swap is the present value of all the net cash flow payments from the swap, not simply the present value of the fixed payments of the swap or the present value of the underlying at the end of the contract.

19 B is correct. If the underlying has a value equal to the exercise price at expiration, both options will have zero value since they both have the same exercise price. For example, if the exercise price is $25 and at expiration the underlying price is $25, both the call option and the put option will have a value of zero. The value of an option cannot fall below zero. The holder of an option is not obligated to exercise the option; therefore, the options each have a minimum value of zero. If the call has a positive value, the put, by definition, must have a zero value and vice versa. Both cannot have a positive value.

20 C is correct. A European put option will be valuable at expiration if the exercise price is greater than the underlying price. The holder can put (deliver) the underlying and receive the exercise price which is higher than the spot price. A European put option would be worthless if the exercise price was equal to or less than the underlying price.

21 B is correct. The value of a European call option at expiration is the greater of zero or the value of the underlying minus the exercise price.

22 B is correct. A European call option with two months until expiration will typically have positive time value, where time value reflects the value of the uncertainty that arises from the volatility in the underlying. The call option has a zero exercise value if the spot price is below the exercise price. The exercise value of a European call option is $Max(0, S_t - X)$, where S_t is the current spot price at time t and X is the exercise price.

23 A is correct. When the price of the underlying is below the exercise price for a put, the option is said to be in-the-money. If the price of the underlying is the same as the exercise price, the put is at-the-money and if it is above the exercise price, the put is out-of-the-money.

24 A is correct. An in-the-money European put option decreases in value with an increase in the risk-free rate. A higher risk-free rate reduces the present value of any proceeds received on exercise.

25 A is correct. The value of a European call option is inversely related to the exercise price. A lower exercise price means there are more potential outcomes at which the call expires in-the-money. The option value will be greater the lower the exercise price. For a higher exercise price, the opposite is true. Both the time to expiration and the volatility of the underlying are directly (positively) related to the value of a European call option.

26 B is correct. The value of a European call option is inversely related to the exercise price and directly related to the time to expiration. Option 1 and Option 2 have the same exercise price; however, Option 2 has a longer time to expiration. Consequently, Option 2 would likely have a higher value than Option 1. Option 2 and Option 3 have the same time to expiration; however, Option 2 has a lower exercise price. Thus, Option 2 would likely have a higher value than Option 3.

27 B is correct. The value of a European put option can be either directly or indirectly related to time to expiration. The direct effect is more common, but the inverse effect can prevail the longer the time to expiration, the higher the risk-free rate, and the deeper in-the-money is the put. The value of a European put option is directly related to the exercise price and the volatility of the underlying.

28 B is correct. Prior to expiration, the lowest value of a European put is the greater of zero or the present value of the exercise price minus the value of the underlying.

29 C is correct. Payments, such as dividends, reduce the value of the underlying which increases the value of a European put option. Carrying costs reduce the value of a European put option. An increase in the risk-free interest rate may decrease the value of a European put option.

30 A is correct. A long bond can be synthetically created by combining a long asset, a long put, and a short call. A fiduciary call is created by combining a long call with a risk free bond. A protective put is created by combining a long asset with a long put.

31 B is correct. According to put–call parity, a synthetic call can be constructed by combining a long asset, long put, and short bond positions.

32 C is correct. The actual probabilities of the up and down moves in the underlying do not appear in the binomial option pricing model, only the pseudo or "risk-neutral" probabilities. Both the spot price of the underlying and two possible prices one period later are required by the binomial option pricing model.

33 C is correct. Prior to expiration, an American call option will typically have a value in the market that is greater than its exercise value. Although the American option is at-the-money and therefore has an exercise value of zero, the time value of the call option would likely lead to the option having a positive market value.

34 B is correct. At expiration, the values of American and European call options are effectively the same; both are worth the greater of zero and the exercise value.

35 A is correct. When a dividend is declared, an American call option will have a higher value than a European call option because an American call option holder can exercise early to capture the value of the dividend. At expiration, both types of call options are worth the greater of zero and the exercise value. A change in the risk-free rate does not affect the relative values of American and European call options.

36 A is correct. Put–call forward parity demonstrates that the outcome of a protective put with a forward contract (long put, long risk-free bond, long forward contract) equals the outcome of a fiduciary call (long call, long risk-free bond). The outcome of a protective put with a forward contract is also equal to the outcome of a protective put with asset (long put, long asset).

Risk Management Applications of Option Strategies

by Don M. Chance, CFA

LEARNING OUTCOMES

Mastery	The candidate should be able to:
☐	**a.** determine the value at expiration, the profit, maximum profit, maximum loss, breakeven underlying price at expiration, and payoff graph of the strategies of buying and selling calls and puts and determine the potential outcomes for investors using these strategies;
☐	**b.** determine the value at expiration, profit, maximum profit, maximum loss, breakeven underlying price at expiration, and payoff graph of a covered call strategy and a protective put strategy, and explain the risk management application of each strategy.

INTRODUCTION

1

In a previous reading we examined strategies that employ forward and futures contracts. Recall that forward and futures contracts have linear payoffs and do not require an initial outlay. Options, on the other hand, have nonlinear payoffs and require the payment of cash up front. By having nonlinear payoffs, options permit their users to benefit from movements in the underlying in one direction and to not be harmed by movements in the other direction. In many respects, they offer the best of all worlds, a chance to profit if expectations are realized with minimal harm if expectations turn out to be wrong. The price for this opportunity is the cash outlay required to establish the position. From the standpoint of the holder of the short position, options can lead to extremely large losses. Hence, sellers of options must be well compensated in the form of an adequate up-front premium and must skillfully manage the risk they assume.

In this reading, we look at option strategies that are typically used in equity investing, which include standard strategies involving single options and strategies that combine options with the underlying.

Analysis of Derivatives for the Chartered Financial Analyst® Program, by Don M. Chance, CFA. Copyright © 2003 by CFA Institute.

Let us begin by reviewing the necessary notation. These symbols are the same ones we have previously used. First recall that time 0 is the time at which the strategy is initiated and time T is the time the option expires, stated as a fraction of a year. Accordingly, the amount of time until expiration is simply $T - 0 = T$, which is (Days to expiration)/365. The other symbols are

c_0, c_T = price of the call option at time 0 and time T

p_0, p_T = price of the put option at time 0 and time T[1]

X = exercise price

S_0, S_T = price of the underlying at time 0 and time T

V_0, V_T = value of the position at time 0 and time T

Π = profit from the transaction: V_0, V_T

r = risk free rate

Some additional notation will be introduced when necessary.

Note that we are going to measure the profit from an option transaction, which is simply the final value of the transaction minus the initial value of the transaction. Profit does not take into account the time value of money or the risk. Although a focus on profit is not completely satisfactory from a theoretical point of view, it is nonetheless instructive, simple, and a common approach to examining options. Our primary objective here is to obtain a general picture of the manner in which option strategies perform. With that in mind, discussing profit offers probably the best trade-off in terms of gaining the necessary knowledge with a minimum of complexity.

In this reading, we assume that the option user has a view regarding potential movements of the underlying. In most cases that view is a prediction of the direction of the underlying, but in some cases it is a prediction of the volatility of the underlying. In all cases, we assume this view is specified over a horizon that corresponds to the option's life or that the option expiration can be tailored to the horizon date. Hence, for the most part, these options should be considered customized, over-the-counter options.[2] Every interest rate option is a customized option.

Because the option expiration corresponds to the horizon date for which a particular view is held, there is no reason to use American options. Accordingly, all options in this reading are European options. Moreover, we shall not consider terminating the strategy early. Putting an option in place and closing the position prior to expiration is certainly a legitimate strategy. It could reflect the arrival of new information over the holding period, but it requires an understanding of more complex issues, such as valuation of the option and the rate at which the option loses its time value. Thus, we shall examine the outcome of a particular strategy over a range of possible values of the underlying only on the expiration day.

2   OPTION STRATEGIES FOR EQUITY PORTFOLIOS

Many typical illustrations of option strategies use individual stocks, but we shall use options on a stock index, the NASDAQ 100, referred to simply as the NASDAQ. We shall assume that in addition to buying and selling options on the NASDAQ, we can

---

1 As in the reading on option markets and contracts, lower case indicates European options, and upper case indicates American options. In this reading, all options are European.

2 If the options discussed were exchange-listed options, it would not significantly alter the material in this reading.

also buy the index, either through construction of the portfolio itself, through an index mutual fund, or an exchange-traded fund.[3] We shall simply refer to this instrument as a stock. We are given the following numerical data:

S_0 = 2000, value of the NASDAQ 100 when the strategy is initiated

T = 0.0833, the time to expiration (one month = 1/12)

The options available will be the following:[4]

Exercise Price	Call Price	Put Price
1950	108.43	56.01
2000	81.75	79.25
2050	59.98	107.39

Let us start by examining an initial strategy that is the simplest of all: to buy or sell short the underlying. Panel A of Exhibit 1 illustrates the profit from the transaction of buying a share of stock. We see the obvious result that if you buy the stock and it goes up, you make a profit; if it goes down, you incur a loss. Panel B shows the case of selling short the stock. Recall that this strategy involves borrowing the shares from a broker, selling them at the current price, and then buying them back at a later date. In this case, if you sell short the stock and it goes down, you make a profit. Conversely, if it goes up, you incur a loss. Now we shall move on to strategies involving options, but we shall use the stock strategies again when we combine options with stock.

In this section we examine option strategies in the context of their use in equity portfolios. Although these strategies are perfectly applicable for fixed-income portfolios, corporate borrowing scenarios, or even commodity risk management situations, they are generally more easily explained and understood in the context of investing in equities or equity indices.

---

3 Exchange-traded shares on the NASDAQ 100 are called NASDAQ 100 Trust Shares and QQQs, for their ticker symbol. They are commonly referred to as Qubes, trade on the AMEX, and are the most active exchange-traded fund and often the most actively traded of all securities. Options on the NASDAQ 100 are among the most actively traded as well.

4 These values were obtained using the Black–Scholes–Merton model. By using this model, we know we are working with reasonable values that do not permit arbitrage opportunities.

Exhibit 1   Simple Stock Strategies

A. Buy Stock

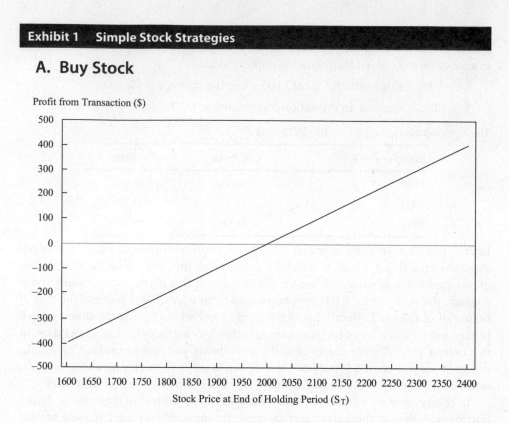

Profit from Transaction ($)

Stock Price at End of Holding Period (S_T)

B. Sell Short Stock

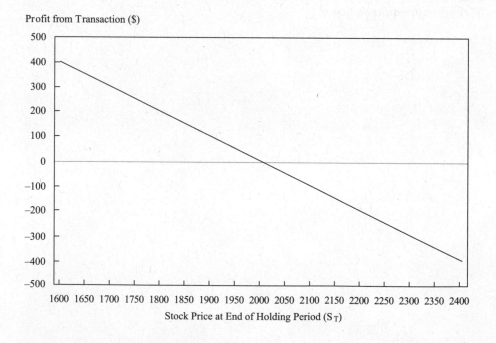

Profit from Transaction ($)

Stock Price at End of Holding Period (S_T)

To analyze an equity option strategy, we first assume that we establish the position at the current price. We then determine the value of the option at expiration for a specific value of the index at expiration. We calculate the profit as the value at expiration minus the current price. We then generate a graph to illustrate the value at expiration and profit for a range of index values at expiration. Although the underlying is a stock index, we shall just refer to it as the underlying to keep things as general as possible. We begin by examining the most fundamental option transactions, long and short positions in calls and puts.

2.1 Standard Long and Short Positions

2.1.1 *Calls*

Consider the purchase of a call option at the price c_0. The value at expiration, c_T, is $c_T = \max(0, S_T - X)$. Broken down into parts,

$$c_T = 0 \qquad \text{if } S_T \leq X$$
$$c_T = S_T - X \quad \text{if } S_T > X$$

The profit is obtained by subtracting the option premium, which is paid to purchase the option, from the option value at expiration, $\Pi = c_T - c_0$. Broken down into parts,

$$\Pi = -c_0 \qquad \text{if } S_T \leq X$$
$$\Pi = S_T - X - c_0 \quad \text{if } S_T > X$$

Now consider this example. We buy the call with the exercise price of 2000 for 81.75. Consider values of the index at expiration of 1900 and 2100. For $S_T = 1900$,

$$c_T = \max(0, 1900 - 2000) = 0$$
$$\Pi = 0 - 81.75 = -81.75$$

For $S_T = 2100$,

$$c_T = \max(0, 2100 - 2000) = 100$$
$$\Pi = 100 - 81.75 = 18.25$$

Exhibit 2 illustrates the value at expiration and profit when S_T, the underlying price at expiration, ranges from 1600 to 2400. We see that buying a call results in a limited loss of the premium, 81.75. For an index value at expiration greater than the exercise price of 2000, the value and profit move up one-for-one with the index value, and there is no upper limit.

It is important to identify the breakeven index value at expiration. Recall that the formula for the profit is $\Pi = \max(0, S_T - X) - c_0$. We would like to know the value of S_T for which $\Pi = 0$. We shall call that value S_T^*. It would be nice to be able to solve $\Pi = \max(0, S_T^* - X) - c_0 = 0$ for S_T^*, but that is not directly possible. Instead, we observe that there are two ranges of outcomes, one in which $\Pi = S_T^* - X - c_0$ for $S_T^* > X$, the case of the option expiring in-the-money, and the other in which $\Pi = -c_0$ for $S_T \leq X$, the case of the option expiring out-of-the-money. It is obvious from the equation and by observing Exhibit 2 that in the latter case, there is no possibility of breaking even. In the former case, we see that we can solve for S_T^*. Setting $\Pi = S_T^* - X - c_0 = 0$, we obtain $S_T^* = X + c_0$.

Thus, the breakeven is the exercise price plus the option premium. This result should be intuitive: The value of the underlying at expiration must exceed the exercise price by the amount of the premium to recover the cost of the premium. In this problem, the breakeven is $S_T^* = 2000 + 81.75 = 2081.75$. Observe in Exhibit 2 that the profit line crosses the axis at this value.

In summarizing the strategy, we have the following results for the option buyer:

$c_T = \max(0, S_T - X)$

Value at expiration $= c_T$

Profit: $\Pi = c_T - c_0$

Maximum profit $= \infty$

Maximum loss $= c_0$

Breakeven: $S_T^* = X + c_0$

Exhibit 2   Buy Call

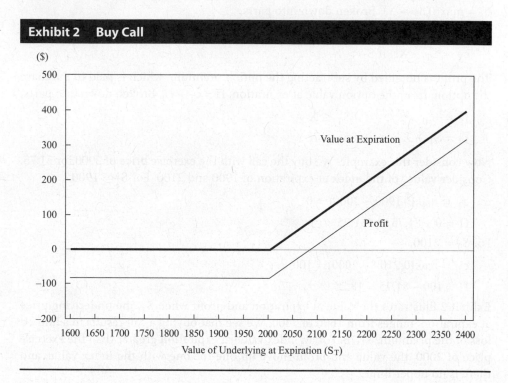

Call options entice naive speculators, but it is important to consider the *likely* gains and losses more than the *potential* gains and losses. For example, in this case, the underlying must go up by about 4.1 percent in one month to cover the cost of the call. This increase equates to an annual rate of almost 50 percent and is an unreasonable expectation by almost any standard. If the underlying does not move at all, the loss is 100 percent of the premium.

For the seller of the call, the results are just the opposite. The sum of the positions of the seller and buyer is zero. Hence, we can take the value and profit results for the buyer and change the signs. The results for the maximum profit and maximum loss are changed accordingly, and the breakeven is the same. Hence, for the option seller,

$c_T = \max(0, S_T - X)$

Value at expiration $= -c_T$

Profit: $\Pi = -c_T + c_0$

Maximum profit $= c_0$

Maximum loss $= \infty$

Breakeven: $S_T^* = X + c_0$

Exhibit 3 shows the results for the seller of the call. Note that the value and profit have a fixed maximum. The worst case is an infinite loss. Just as there is no upper limit to the buyer's potential gain, there is no upper limit to how much the seller can lose.

Call options are purchased by investors who are bullish. We now turn to put options, which are purchased by investors who are bearish.

Exhibit 3   Sell Call

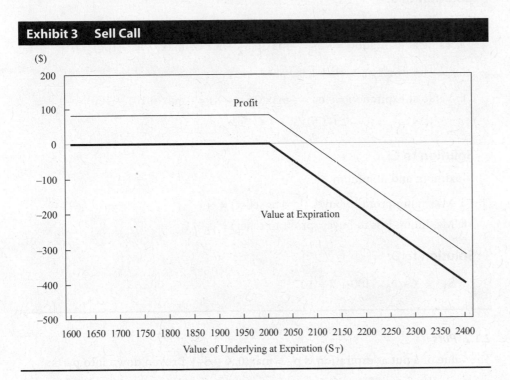

EXAMPLE 1

Consider a call option selling for $7 in which the exercise price is $100 and the price of the underlying is $98.

A Determine the value at expiration and the profit for a buyer under the following outcomes:

   i. The price of the underlying at expiration is $102.

   ii. The price of the underlying at expiration is $94.

B Determine the value at expiration and the profit for a seller under the following outcomes:

   i. The price of the underlying at expiration is $91.

   ii. The price of the underlying at expiration is $101.

C Determine the following:

   i. The maximum profit to the buyer (maximum loss to the seller).

   ii. The maximum loss to the buyer (maximum profit to the seller).

D Determine the breakeven price of the underlying at expiration.

Solution to A:

Call buyer

   i. Value at expiration $= c_T = \max(0, S_T - X) = \max(0, 102 - 100) = 2$

$$\Pi = c_T - c_0 = 2 - 7 = -5$$

   ii. Value at expiration $= c_T = \max(0, S_T - X) = \max(0, 94 - 100) = 0$

$$\Pi = c_T - c_0 = 0 - 7 = -7$$

Solution to B:

Call seller

   i. Value at expiration $= -c_T = -\max(0, S_T - X) = -\max(0, 91 - 100) = 0$

        $\Pi = -c_T + c_0 = -0 + 7 = 7$

   ii. Value at expiration $= -c_T = -\max(0, S_T - X) = -\max(0, 101 - 100) = -1$

        $\Pi = -c_T + c_0 = -1 + 7 = 6$

Solution to C:

Maximum and minimum

   i. Maximum profit to buyer (loss to seller) $= \infty$

   ii. Maximum loss to buyer (profit to seller) $= c_0 = 7$

Solution to D:

$$S_T^* = X + c_0 = 100 + 7 = 107$$

2.1.2 *Puts*

The value of a put at expiration is $p_T = \max(0, X - S_T)$. Broken down into parts,

   $p_T = X - S_T$ if $S_T < X$
   $p_T = 0$ if $S_T \geq X$

The profit is obtained by subtracting the premium on the put from the value at expiration:

   $\Pi = p_T - p_0$

Broken down into parts,

   $\Pi = X - S_T - p_0$ if $S_T < X$
   $\Pi = -p_0$ if $S_T \geq X$

For our example and outcomes of $S_T = 1900$ and 2100, the results are as follows:

   $S_T = 1900$:

        $p_T = \max(0, 2000 - 1900) = 100$
        $\Pi = 100 - 79.25 = 20.75$

   $S_T = 2100$:

        $p_T = \max(0, 2000 - 2100) = 0$
        $\Pi = 0 - 79.25 = -79.25$

These results are shown in Exhibit 4. We see that the put has a maximum value and profit and a limited loss, the latter of which is the premium. The maximum value is obtained when the underlying goes to zero.[5] In that case, $p_T = X$. So the maximum profit is $X - p_0$. Here that will be $2000 - 79.25 = 1920.75$.

---

[5] The maximum value and profit are not visible on the graph because we do not show S_T all the way down to zero.

The breakeven is found by breaking up the profit equation into its parts, $\Pi = X - S_T - p_0$ for $S_T < X$ and $\Pi = -p_0$ for $S_T \geq X$. In the latter case, there is no possibility of breaking even. It refers to the range over which the entire premium is lost. In the former case, we denote the breakeven index value as S_T^*, set the equation to zero, and solve for S_T^* to obtain $S_T^* = X - p_0$. In our example, the breakeven is $S_T^* = 2000 - 79.25 = 1920.75$.

Exhibit 4   Buy Put

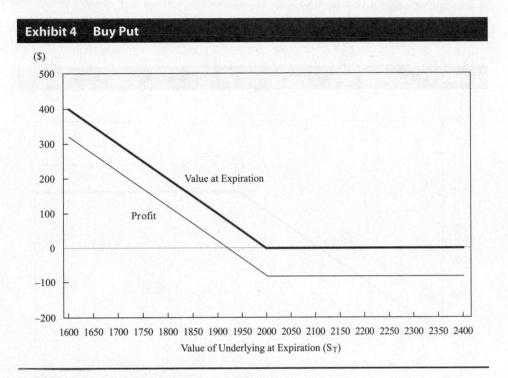

($)

Value at Expiration

Profit

Value of Underlying at Expiration (S_T)

In summary, for the strategy of buying a put we have

$p_T = \max(0, X - S_T)$

Value at expiration $= p_T$

Profit: $\Pi = p_T - p_0$

Maximum profit $= X - p_0$

Maximum loss $= p_0$

Breakeven: $S_T^* = X - p_0$

Now consider the *likely* outcomes for the holder of the put. In this case, the underlying must move down by almost 4 percent in one month to cover the premium. One would hardly ever expect the underlying to move down at an annual rate of almost 50 percent. Moreover, if the underlying does not move downward at all (a likely outcome given the positive expected return on most assets), the loss is 100 percent of the premium.

For the sale of a put, we simply change the sign on the value at expiration and profit. The maximum profit for the buyer becomes the maximum loss for the seller and the maximum loss for the buyer becomes the maximum profit for the seller. The breakeven for the seller is the same as for the buyer. So, for the seller,

$$p_T = \max(0, X - S_T)$$

Value at expiration $= -p_T$

Profit: $\Pi = -p_T + p_0$

Maximum profit $= p_0$

Maximum loss $= X - p_0$

Breakeven: $S_T^* = X - p_0$

Exhibit 5 graphs the value at expiration and the profit for this transaction.

Exhibit 5   Sell Put

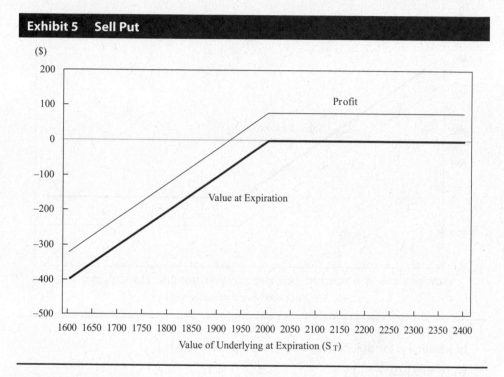

EXAMPLE 2

Consider a put option selling for $4 in which the exercise price is $60 and the price of the underlying is $62.

A Determine the value at expiration and the profit for a buyer under the following outcomes:

   i. The price of the underlying at expiration is $62.

   ii. The price of the underlying at expiration is $55.

B Determine the value at expiration and the profit for a seller under the following outcomes:

   i. The price of the underlying at expiration is $51.

   ii. The price of the underlying at expiration is $68.

C Determine the following:

   i. The maximum profit to the buyer (maximum loss to the seller).

   ii. The maximum loss to the buyer (maximum profit to the seller).

D Determine the breakeven price of the underlying at expiration.

Solution to A:

Put buyer

$$\text{Value at expiration} = p_T = \max(0, X - S_T) = \max(0, 60 - 62) = 0$$

$$\Pi = p_T - p_0 = 0 - 4 = -4$$

$$\text{Value at expiration} = p_T = \max(0, X - S_T) = \max(0, 60 - 55) = 5$$

$$\Pi = p_T - p_0 = 5 - 4 = 1$$

Solution to B:

Put seller

i. $\text{Value at expiration} = -p_T = -\max(0, X - S_T) = -\max(0, 60 - 51) = -9$

$$\Pi = -p_T + p_0 = -9 + 4 = -5$$

ii. $\text{Value at expiration} = -p_T = -\max(0, X - S_T) = -\max(0, 60 - 68) = 0$

$$\Pi = -p_T + p_0 = 0 + 4 = 4$$

Solution to C:

Maximum and minimum

i. Maximum profit to buyer (loss to seller) $= X - p_0 = 60 - 4 = 56$
ii. Maximum loss to buyer (profit to seller) $= p_0 = 4$

Solution to D:

$$S_T^* = X - p_0 = 60 - 4 = 56$$

It may be surprising to find that we have now covered all of the information we need to examine all of the other option strategies. We need to learn only a few basic facts. We must know the formula for the value at expiration of a call and a put. Then we need to know how to calculate the profit for the purchase of a call and a put, but that calculation is simple: the value at expiration minus the initial value. If we know these results, we can calculate the value at expiration of the option and the profit for any value of the underlying at expiration. If we can do that, we can graph the results for a range of possible values of the underlying at expiration. Because graphing can take a long time, however, it is probably helpful to learn the basic shapes of the value and profit graphs for calls and puts. Knowing the profit equation and the shapes of the graphs, it is easy to determine the maximum profit and maximum loss. The breakeven can be determined by setting the profit equation to zero for the case in which the profit equation contains S_T. Once we have these results for the long call and put, it is an easy matter to turn them around and obtain the results for the short call and put. Therefore, little if any memorization is required. From there, we can go on to strategies that combine an option with another option and combine options with the underlying.

2.2 Risk Management Strategies with Options and the Underlying

In this section, we examine two of the most widely used option strategies, particularly for holders of the underlying. One way to reduce exposure without selling the underlying is to sell a call on the underlying; the other way is to buy a put.

2.2.1 Covered Calls

A **covered call** is a relatively conservative strategy, but it is also one of the most mis-understood strategies. A covered call is a position in which you own the underlying and sell a call. The value of the position at expiration is easily found as the value of the underlying plus the value of the short call:

$$V_T = S_T - \max(0, S_T - X)$$

Therefore,

$$V_T = S_T \qquad\qquad\qquad \text{if } S_T \leq X$$
$$V_T = S_T - (S_T - X) = X \quad \text{if } S_T > X$$

We obtain the profit for the covered call by computing the change in the value of the position, $V_T - V_0$. First recognize that V_0, the value of the position at the start of the contract, is the initial value of the underlying minus the call premium. We are long the underlying and short the call, so we must subtract the call premium that was received from the sale of the call. The initial investment in the position is what we pay for the underlying less what we receive for the call. Hence, $V_0 = S_0 - c_0$. The profit is thus

$$\Pi = S_T - \max(0, S_T - X) - (S_0 - c_0)$$
$$= S_T - S_0 - \max(0, S_T - X) + c_0$$

With the equation written in this manner, we see that the profit for the covered call is simply the profit from buying the underlying, $S_T - S_0$, plus the profit from selling the call, $-\max(0, S_T - X) + c_0$. Breaking it down into ranges,

$$\Pi = S_T - S_0 + c_0 \qquad\qquad\qquad\quad \text{if } S_T \leq X$$
$$\Pi = S_T - S_0 - (S_T - X) + c_0 = X - S_0 + c_0 \quad \text{if } S_T > X$$

In our example, $S_0 = 2000$. In this section we shall use a call option with the exercise price of 2050. Thus $X = 2050$, and the premium, c_0, is 59.98. Let us now examine two outcomes: $S_T = 2100$ and $S_T = 1900$. The value at expiration when $S_T = 2100$ is $V_T = 2100 - (2100 - 2050) = 2050$, and when $S_T = 1900$, the value of the position is $V_T = 1900$.

In the first case, we hold the underlying worth 2100 but are short a call worth 50. Thus, the net value is 2050. In the second case, we hold the underlying worth 1900 and the option expires out-of-the-money.

In the first case, $S_T = 2100$, the profit is $\Pi = 2050 - 2000 + 59.98 = 109.98$. In the second case, $S_T = 1900$, the profit is $\Pi = 1900 - 2000 + 59.98 = -40.02$. These results are graphed for a range of values of S_T in Exhibit 6. Note that for all values of S_T greater than 2050, the value and profit are maximized. Thus, 2050 is the maximum value and 109.98 is the maximum profit.[6]

As evident in Exhibit 6 and the profit equations, the maximum loss would occur when S_T is zero. Hence, the profit would be $S_T - S_0 + c_0$. The profit is $-S_0 + c_0$ when $S_T = 0$. This means that the maximum loss is $S_0 - c_0$. In this example, $-S_0 + c_0$ is $-2000 + 59.98 = -1940.02$. Intuitively, this would mean that you purchased the underlying for 2000 and sold the call for 59.98. The underlying value went to zero, resulting in a loss of 2000, but the call expired with no value, so the gain from the option is the option premium. The total loss is 1940.02.

---

6 Note in Exhibit 6 that there is a large gap between the value at expiration and profit, especially compared with the graphs of buying and selling calls and puts. This difference occurs because a covered call is mostly a position in the underlying asset. The initial value of the asset, S_0, accounts for most of the difference in the two lines. Note also that because of the put–call parity relationship we covered in the reading on option markets and contracts, a covered call looks very similar to a short put.

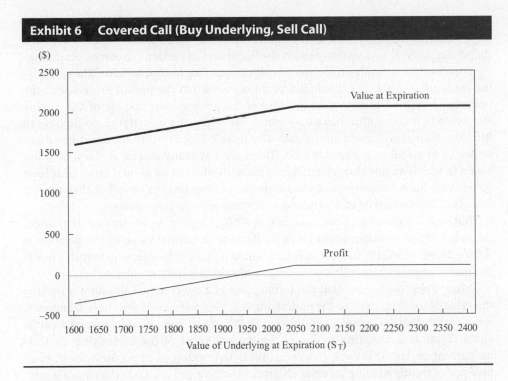

Exhibit 6 Covered Call (Buy Underlying, Sell Call)

The breakeven underlying price is found by examining the profit equations and focusing on the equation that contains S_T. In equation form, $\Pi = S_T - S_0 + c_0$ when $S_T \leq X$. We let S_T^* denote the breakeven value of S_T, set the equation to zero, and solve for S_T^* to obtain $S_T^* = S_0 - c_0$. The breakeven and the maximum loss are identical. In this example, the breakeven is $S_T^* = 2000 - 59.98 = 1940.02$, which is seen in Exhibit 6.

To summarize the covered call, we have the following:

Value at expiration: $V_T = S_T - \max(0, S_T - X)$

Profit: $\Pi = V_T - S_0 + c_0$

Maximum profit $= X - S_0 + c_0$

Maximum loss $= S_0 - c_0$

Breakeven: $S_T^* = S_0 - c_0$

Because of the importance and widespread use of covered calls, it is worthwhile to discuss this strategy briefly to dispel some misunderstandings. First of all, some investors who do not believe in using options fail to see that selling a call on a position in the underlying reduces the risk of that position. Options do not automatically increase risk. The option part of this strategy alone, viewed in isolation, seems an extremely risky strategy. We noted in Section 2.1.1 that selling a call without owning the stock exposes the investor to unlimited loss potential. But selling a covered call—adding a short call to a long position in a stock—reduces the overall risk. Thus, any investor who holds a stock cannot say he is too conservative to use options.

Following on that theme, however, one should also view selling a covered call as a strategy that reduces not only the risk but also the expected return compared with simply holding the underlying. Hence, one should not expect to make a lot of money writing calls on the underlying. It should be apparent that in fact the covered call writer could miss out on significant gains in a strong bull market. The compensation for this willingness to give up potential upside gains, however, is that in a bear market the losses on the underlying will be cushioned by the option premium.

It may be disconcerting to some investors to look at the profit profile of a covered call. The immediate response is to think that no one in their right mind would invest in a strategy that has significant downside risk but a limited upside. Just owning the underlying has significant downside risk, but at least there is an upside. But it is important to note that the visual depiction of the strategy, as in Exhibit 6, does not tell the whole story. It says nothing about the likelihood of certain outcomes occurring.

For example, consider the covered call example we looked at here. The underlying starts off at 2000. The maximum profit occurs when the option expires with the underlying at 2050 or above, an increase of 2.5 percent over the life of the option. We noted that this option has a one-month life. Thus, the underlying would have to increase at an approximate annual rate of at least 2.5%(12) = 30% for the covered call writer to forgo all of the upside gain. There are not many stocks, indices, or other assets in which an investor would expect the equivalent of an annual move of at least 30 percent. Such movements obviously do occur from time to time, but they are not common. Thus, covered call writers do not often give up large gains.

But suppose the underlying did move to 2050 or higher. As we previously showed, the value of the position would be 2050. Because the initial value of the position is 2000 − 59.98 = 1940.02, the rate of return would be 5.7 percent for one month. Hence, the maximum return is still outstanding by almost anyone's standards.[7]

Many investors believe that the initial value of a covered call should not include the value of the underlying if the underlying had been previously purchased. Suppose, for example, that this asset, currently worth 2000, had been bought several months ago at 1900. It is tempting to ignore the current value of the underlying; there is no current outlay. This view, however, misses the notion of opportunity cost. If an investor currently holding an asset chooses to write a call on it, she has made a conscious decision not to sell the asset. Hence, the current value of the asset should be viewed as an opportunity cost that is just as real as the cost to an investor buying the underlying at this time.

Sellers of covered calls must make a decision about the chosen exercise price. For example, one could sell the call with an exercise price of 1950 for 108.43, or sell the call with an exercise price of 2000 for 81.75, or sell the call with an exercise price of 2050 for 59.98. The higher the exercise price, the less one receives for the call but the more room for gain on the upside. There is no clear-cut solution to deciding which call is best; the choice depends on the risk preferences of the investor.

Finally, we should note that anecdotal evidence suggests that writers of call options make small amounts of money, but make it often. The reason for this phenomenon is generally thought to be that buyers of calls tend to be overly optimistic, but that argument is fallacious. The real reason is that the expected profits come from rare but large payoffs. For example, consider the call with exercise price of 2000 and a premium of 81.75. As we learned in Section 2.1, the breakeven underlying price is 2081.75—a gain of about 4.1 percent in a one-month period, which would be an exceptional return for almost any asset. These prices were obtained using the Black–Scholes–Merton model, so they are fair prices. Yet the required underlying price movement to profit on the call is exceptional. Obviously someone buys calls, and naturally, someone must be on the other side of the transaction. Sellers of calls tend to be holders of the underlying or other calls, which reduces the enormous risk they would assume if they sold calls without any other position.[8] Hence, it is reasonable to expect that sellers of calls would make money often, because large underlying price movements occur only rarely. Following this line of reasoning, however, it would appear that sellers of calls can consistently take advantage of buyers of calls. That cannot possibly be the case. What happens is that buyers of calls make money less often than sellers, but when

---

7 Of course, we are not saying that the performance reflects a positive alpha. We are saying only that the upside performance given up reflects improbably high returns, and therefore the limits on the upside potential are not too restrictive.

8 Sellers of calls who hold other calls are engaged in transactions called spreads.

they do make money, the leverage inherent in call options amplifies their returns. Therefore, when call writers lose money, they tend to lose big, but most call writers own the underlying or are long other calls to offset the risk.

EXAMPLE 3

Consider a bond selling for $98 per $100 face value. A call option selling for $8 has an exercise price of $105. Answer the following questions about a covered call.

A Determine the value of the position at expiration and the profit under the following outcomes:

  i. The price of the bond at expiration is $110.

  ii. The price of the bond at expiration is $88.

B Determine the following:

  i. The maximum profit.

  ii. The maximum loss.

C Determine the breakeven bond price at expiration.

Solution to A:

  i. $V_T = S_T - \max(0, S_T - X) = 110 - \max(0, 110 - 105) = 110 - 110 + 105 = 105$

  $\Pi = V_T - V_0 = 105 - (S_0 - c_0) = 105 - (98 - 8) = 15$

  ii. $V_T = S_T - \max(0, S_T - X) = 88 - \max(0, 88 - 105) = 88 - 0 = 88$

  $\Pi = V_T - V_0 = 88 - (S_0 - c_0) = 88 - (98 - 8) = -2$

Solution to B:

  i. Maximum profit $= X - S_0 + c_0 = 105 - 98 + 8 = 15$

  ii. Maximum loss $= S_0 - c_0 = 98 - 8 = 90$

Solution to C:

  $S_T^* = S_0 - c_0 = 98 - 8 = 90$

Covered calls represent one widely used way to protect a position in the underlying. Another popular means of providing protection is to buy a put.

2.2.2 *Protective Puts*

Because selling a call provides some protection to the holder of the underlying against a fall in the price of the underlying, buying a put should also provide protection. A put, after all, is designed to pay off when the price of the underlying moves down. In some ways, buying a put to add to a long stock position is much better than selling a call. As we shall see here, it provides downside protection while retaining the upside potential, but it does so at the expense of requiring the payment of cash up front. In contrast, a covered call generates cash up front but removes some of the upside potential.

Holding an asset and a put on the asset is a strategy known as a **protective put**. The value at expiration and the profit of this strategy are found by combining the value and profit of the two strategies of buying the asset and buying the put. The value is $V_T = S_T + \max(0, X - S_T)$. Thus, the results can be expressed as

$$V_T = S_T + (X - S_T) = X \quad \text{if } S_T \le X$$
$$V_T = S_T \qquad\qquad\qquad \text{if } S_T > X$$

When the underlying price at expiration exceeds the exercise price, the put expires with no value. The position is then worth only the value of the underlying. When the underlying price at expiration is less than the exercise price, the put expires in-the-money and is worth $X - S_T$, while the underlying is worth S_T. The combined value of the two instruments is X. When the underlying is worth less than the exercise price at expiration, the put can be used to sell the underlying for the exercise price.

The initial value of the position is the initial price of the underlying, S_0, plus the premium on the put, p_0. Hence, the profit is $\Pi = S_T + \max(0, X - S_T) - (S_0 + p_0)$. The profit can be broken down as follows:

$$\Pi = X - (S_0 + p_0) \quad \text{if } S_T \le X$$
$$\Pi = S_T - (S_0 + p_0) \quad \text{if } S_T > X$$

In this example, we are going to use the put with an exercise price of 1950. Its premium is 56.01. Recalling that the initial price of the underlying is 2000, the value at expiration and profit for the case of $S_T = 2100$ are

$$V_T = 2100$$
$$\Pi = 2100 - (2000 + 56.01) = 43.99$$

For the case of $S_T = 1900$, the value at expiration and profit are

$$V_T = 1950$$
$$\Pi = 1950 - (2000 + 56.01) = -106.01$$

The results for a range of outcomes are shown in Exhibit 7. Note how the protective put provides a limit on the downside with no limit on the upside.[9] Therefore, we can say that the upper limit is infinite. The lower limit is a loss of 106.01. In the worst possible case, we can sell the underlying for the exercise price, but the up-front cost of the underlying and put are 2056.01, for a maximum loss of 106.01.

Now let us find the breakeven price of the underlying at expiration. Note that the two profit equations are $\Pi = S_T - (S_0 + p_0)$ if $S_T > X$ and $\Pi = X - (S_0 + p_0)$ if $S_T \le X$. In the latter case, there is no value of the underlying that will allow us to break even. In the former case, $S_T > X$, we change the notation on S_T to S_T^* to denote the breakeven value, set this expression equal to zero, and solve for S_T^*:

$$S_T^* = S_0 + p_0$$

---

[9] Note that the graph for a protective put looks like the graph for a call. This result is due to put–call parity, as covered in the reading on option markets and contracts.

Exhibit 7   Protective Put (Buy Underlying, Buy Put)

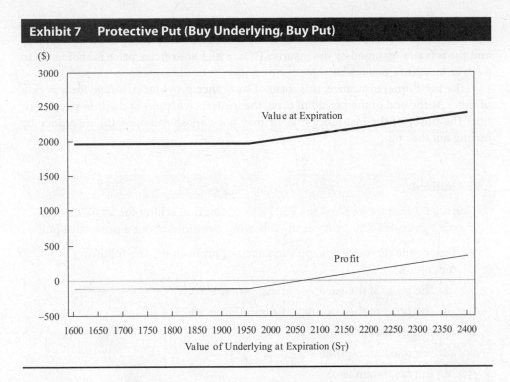

To break even, the underlying must be at least as high as the amount expended up front to establish the position. In this problem, this amount is 2000 + 56.01 = 2056.01.

To summarize the protective put, we have the following:

Value at expiration: $V_T = S_T + \max(0, X - S_T)$

Profit: $\Pi = V_T - S_0 - p_0$

Maximum profit $= \infty$

Maximum loss $= S_0 + p_0 - X$

Breakeven: $S_T^* = S_0 + p_0$

A protective put can appear to be a great transaction with no drawbacks. It provides downside protection with upside potential, but let us take a closer look. First recall that this is a one-month transaction and keep in mind that the option has been priced by the Black–Scholes–Merton model and is, therefore, a fair price. The maximum loss of 106.01 is a loss of 106.01/2056.01 = 5.2%. The breakeven of 2056.01 requires an upward move of 2.8 percent, which is an annual rate of about 34 percent. From this angle, the protective put strategy does not look quite as good, but in fact, these figures simply confirm that protection against downside loss is expensive. When the protective put is fairly priced, the protection buyer must give up considerable upside potential that may not be particularly evident from just looking at a graph.

The purchase of a protective put also presents the buyer with some choices. In this example, the buyer bought the put with exercise price of 1950 for 56.01. Had he bought the put with exercise price of 2000, he would have paid 79.25. The put with exercise price of 2050 would have cost 107.39. The higher the price for which the investor wants to be able to sell the underlying, the more expensive the put will be.

The protective put is often viewed as a classic example of insurance. The investor holds a risky asset and wants protection against a loss in value. He then buys insurance in the form of the put, paying a premium to the seller of the insurance, the put writer. The exercise price of the put is like the insurance deductible because the magnitude of the exercise price reflects the risk assumed by the party holding the underlying. The higher the exercise price, the less risk assumed by the holder of the underlying and the more risk assumed by the put seller. The lower the exercise price, the more risk assumed by the holder of the underlying and the less risk assumed by the put seller. In insurance, the higher the deductible, the more risk assumed by the insured party and the less risk assumed by the insurer. Thus, a higher exercise price is analogous to a lower insurance deductible.

Like traditional insurance, this form of insurance provides coverage for a period of time. At the end of the period of time, the insurance expires and either pays off or not. The buyer of the insurance may or may not choose to renew the insurance by buying another put.

EXAMPLE 4

Consider a currency selling for $0.875. A put option selling for $0.075 has an exercise price of $0.90. Answer the following questions about a protective put.

A   Determine the value at expiration and the profit under the following outcomes:

   i. The price of the currency at expiration is $0.96.

   ii. The price of the currency at expiration is $0.75.

B   Determine the following:

   i. The maximum profit.

   ii. The maximum loss.

C   Determine the breakeven price of the currency at expiration.

Solutions:

A   **i.** $V_T = S_T + \max(0, X - S_T) = 0.96 + \max(0, 0.90 - 0.96) = 0.96$

   $\Pi = V_T - V_0 = 0.96 - (S_0 + p_0) = 0.96 - (0.875 + 0.075) = 0.01$

   ii. $V_T = S_T + \max(0, X - S_T) = 0.75 + \max(0, 0.90 - 0.75) = 0.90$

   $\Pi = V_T - V_0 = 0.90 - (S_0 + p_0) = 0.90 - (0.875 + 0.075) = -0.05$

B   **i.** Maximum profit = ∞

   ii. Maximum loss = $S_0 + p_0 - X = 0.875 + 0.075 - 0.90 = 0.05$

C $S_T^* = S_0 + p_0 = 0.875 + 0.075 = 0.95$

Finally, we note that a protective put can be modified in a number of ways. One in particular is to sell a call to generate premium income to pay for the purchase of the put. This strategy is known as a collar.

SUMMARY

- The profit from buying a call is the value at expiration, $\max(0, S_T - X)$, minus c_0, the option premium. The maximum profit is infinite, and the maximum loss is the option premium. The breakeven underlying price at expiration is the exercise price plus the option premium. When one sells a call, these results are reversed.

- The profit from buying a put is the value at expiration, $\max(0, X - S_T)$, minus p_0, the option premium. The maximum profit is the exercise price minus the option premium, and the maximum loss is the option premium. The breakeven underlying price at expiration is the exercise price minus the option premium. When one sells a put, these results are reversed.

- The profit from a covered call—the purchase of the underlying and sale of a call—is the value at expiration, $S_T - \max(0, S_T - X)$, minus $S_0 - c_0$, the cost of the underlying minus the option premium. The maximum profit is the exercise price minus the original underlying price plus the option premium, and the maximum loss is the cost of the underlying less the option premium. The breakeven underlying price at expiration is the original price of the underlying minus the option premium.

- The profit from a protective put—the purchase of the underlying and a put—is the value at expiration, $S_T + \max(0, X - S_T)$, minus the cost of the underlying plus the option premium, $S_0 + p_0$. The maximum profit is infinite, and the maximum loss is the cost of the underlying plus the option premium minus the exercise price. The breakeven underlying price at expiration is the original price of the underlying plus the option premium.

PRACTICE PROBLEMS

1 Consider a call option selling for $4 in which the exercise price is $50.

  A Determine the value at expiration and the profit for a buyer under the following outcomes:

    i. The price of the underlying at expiration is $55.

    ii. The price of the underlying at expiration is $51.

    iii. The price of the underlying at expiration is $48.

  B Determine the value at expiration and the profit for a seller under the following outcomes:

    i. The price of the underlying at expiration is $49.

    ii. The price of the underlying at expiration is $52.

    iii. The price of the underlying at expiration is $55.

  C Determine the following:

    i. The maximum profit to the buyer (maximum loss to the seller).

    ii. The maximum loss to the buyer (maximum profit to the seller).

  D Determine the breakeven price of the underlying at expiration.

2 Suppose you believe that the price of a particular underlying, currently selling at $99, is going to increase substantially in the next six months. You decide to purchase a call option expiring in six months on this underlying. The call option has an exercise price of $105 and sells for $7.

  A Determine the profit under the following outcomes for the price of the underlying six months from now:

    i. $99.

    ii. $104.

    iii. $105.

    iv. $109.

    v. $112.

    vi. $115.

  B Determine the breakeven price of the underlying at expiration. Check that your answer is consistent with the solution to Part A of this problem.

3 Consider a put option on the NASDAQ 100 selling for $106.25 in which the exercise price is 2100.

  A Determine the value at expiration and the profit for a buyer under the following outcomes:

    i. The price of the underlying at expiration is 2125.

    ii. The price of the underlying at expiration is 2050.

    iii. The price of the underlying at expiration is 1950.

  B Determine the value at expiration and the profit for a seller under the following outcomes:

    i. The price of the underlying at expiration is 1975.

    ii. The price of the underlying at expiration is 2150.

C Determine the following:

   i. The maximum profit to the buyer (maximum loss to the seller).

   ii. The maximum loss to the buyer (maximum profit to the seller).

D Determine the breakeven price of the underlying at expiration.

4 Suppose you believe that the price of a particular underlying, currently selling at $99, will decrease considerably in the next six months. You decide to purchase a put option expiring in six months on this underlying. The put option has an exercise price of $95 and sells for $5.

   A Determine the profit for you under the following outcomes for the price of the underlying six months from now:

   i. $100.

   ii. $95.

   iii. $93.

   iv. $90.

   v. $85.

   B Determine the breakeven price of the underlying at expiration. Check that your answer is consistent with the solution to Part A of this problem.

   C **i.** What is the maximum profit that you can have?

   ii. At what expiration price of the underlying would this profit be realized?

5 You simultaneously purchase an underlying priced at $77 and write a call option on it with an exercise price of $80 and selling at $6.

   A What is the term commonly used for the position that you have taken?

   B Determine the value at expiration and the profit for your strategy under the following outcomes:

   i. The price of the underlying at expiration is $70.

   ii. The price of the underlying at expiration is $75.

   iii. The price of the underlying at expiration is $80.

   iv. The price of the underlying at expiration is $85.

   C Determine the following:

   i. The maximum profit.

   ii. The maximum loss.

   iii. The expiration price of the underlying at which you would realize the maximum profit.

   iv. The expiration price of the underlying at which you would incur the maximum loss.

   D Determine the breakeven price at expiration.

6 Suppose you simultaneously purchase an underlying priced at $77 and a put option on it, with an exercise price of $75 and selling at $3.

   A What is the term commonly used for the position that you have taken?

   B Determine the value at expiration and the profit for your strategy under the following outcomes:

   i. The price of the underlying at expiration is $70.

   ii. The price of the underlying at expiration is $75.

   iii. The price of the underlying at expiration is $80.

   iv. The price of the underlying at expiration is $85.

   v. The price of the underlying at expiration is $90.

C   Determine the following:

   i. The maximum profit.

   ii. The maximum loss.

   iii. The expiration price of the underlying at which you would incur the maximum loss.

D   Determine the breakeven price at expiration.

7   The recent price per share of Dragon Vacations, Inc. is $50 per share. Calls with exactly six months left to expiration are available on Dragon with strikes of $45, $50, and $55. The prices of the calls are $8.75, $6.00, and $4.00, respectively. Assume that each call contract is for 100 shares of stock and that at initiation of the strategy the investor purchases 100 shares of Dragon at the current market price. Further assume that the investor will close out the strategy in six months when the options expire, including the sale of any stock not delivered against exercise of a call, whether the stock price goes up or goes down. If the closing price of Dragon stock in six months is exactly $60, the profit to a covered call using the $50 strike call is *closest* to:

   A $400.

   B $600.

   C $1,600.

8   The recent price per share of Win Big, Inc. is €50 per share. Verna Hillsborough buys 100 shares at €50. To protect against a fall in price, Hillsborough buys one put, covering 100 shares of Win Big, with a strike price of €40. The put premium is €1 per share. If Win Big closes at €45 per share at the expiration of the put and Hillsborough sells her shares at €45, Hillsborough's profit from the stay/put is *closest* to:

   A   −€1,100.

   B   −€600.

   C   €900.

SOLUTIONS

1 A Call buyer

      i. $c_T = \max(0, S_T - X) = \max(0, 55 - 50) = 5$

          $\Pi = c_T - c_0 = 5 - 4 = 1$

      ii. $c_T = \max(0, S_T - X) = \max(0, 51 - 50) = 1$

          $\Pi = c_T - c_0 = 1 - 4 = -3$

      iii. $c_T = \max(0, S_T - X) = \max(0, 48 - 50) = 0$

          $\Pi = c_T - c_0 = 0 - 4 = -4$

B Call seller

      i. $\text{Value} = -c_T = -\max(0, S_T - X) = -\max(0, 49 - 50) = 0$

          $\Pi = -c_T + c_0 = -0 + 4 = 4$

      ii. $\text{Value} = -c_T = -\max(0, S_T - X) = -\max(0, 52 - 50) = -2$

          $\Pi = -c_T + c_0 = -2 + 4 = 2$

      iii. $\text{Value} = -c_T = -\max(0, S_T - X) = -\max(0, 55 - 50) = -5$

          $\Pi = -c_T + c_0 = -5 + 4 = -1$

C Maximum and minimum

      i. Maximum profit to buyer (loss to seller) $= \infty$

      ii. Maximum loss to buyer (profit to seller) $= c_0 = 4$

D $S_T^* = X + c_0 = 50 + 4 = 54$

2 A i. $c_T = \max(0, S_T - X) = \max(0, 99 - 105) = 0$

          $\Pi = c_T - c_0 = 0 - 7 = -7$

      ii. $c_T = \max(0, S_T - X) = \max(0, 104 - 105) = 0$

          $\Pi = c_T - c_0 = 0 - 7 = -7$

      iii. $c_T = \max(0, S_T - X) = \max(0, 105 - 105) = 0$

          $\Pi = c_T - c_0 = 0 - 7 = -7$

      iv. $c_T = \max(0, S_T - X) = \max(0, 109 - 105) = 4$

          $\Pi = c_T - c_0 = 4 - 7 = -3$

      v. $c_T = \max(0, S_T - X) = \max(0, 112 - 105) = 7$

          $\Pi = c_T - c_0 = 7 - 7 = 0$

      vi. $c_T = \max(0, S_T - X) = \max(0, 115 - 105) = 10$

          $\Pi = c_T - c_0 = 10 - 7 = 3$

B $S_T^* = X + c_0 = 105 + 7 = 112$

Clearly, this result is consistent with our solution above, where the profit is exactly zero in Part A(v), in which the price at expiration is 112.

3 A Put buyer

      i. $p_T = \max(0, X - S_T) = \max(0, 2100 - 2125) = 0$

          $\Pi = p_T - p_0 = 0 - 106.25 = -106.25$

      ii. $p_T = \max(0, X - S_T) = \max(0, 2100 - 2050) = 50$

          $\Pi = p_T - p_0 = 50 - 106.25 = -56.25$

      iii. $p_T = \max(0, X - S_T) = \max(0, 2100 - 1950) = 150$

          $\Pi = p_T - p_0 = 150 - 106.25 = 43.75$

B Put seller

      i. $\text{Value} = -p_T = -\max(0, X - S_T) = -\max(0, 2100 - 1975) = -125$

          $\Pi = -p_T + p_0 = -125 + 106.25 = -18.75$

    ii. Value $= -p_T = -\max(0, X - S_T) = -\max(0, 2100 - 2150) = 0$

$$\Pi = -p_T + p_0 = -0 + 106.25 = 106.25$$

C Maximum and minimum

    i. Maximum profit to buyer(loss to seller) $= X - p_0 = 2100 - 106.25$

$$= 1993.75$$

    ii. Maximum loss to buyer(profit to seller) $= p_0 = 106.25$

D $S_T^* = X - p_0 = 2100 - 106.25 = 1993.75$

4 **A**   **i.** $p_T = \max(0, X - S_T) = \max(0, 95 - 100) = 0$

$$\Pi = p_T - p_0 = 0 - 5 = -5$$

    ii. $p_T = \max(0, X - S_T) = \max(0, 95 - 95) = 0$

$$\Pi = p_T - p_0 = 0 - 5 = -5$$

    iii. $p_T = \max(0, X - S_T) = \max(0, 95 - 93) = 2$

$$\Pi = p_T - p_0 = 2 - 5 = -3$$

    iv. $p_T = \max(0, X - S_T) = \max(0, 95 - 90) = 5$

$$\Pi = p_T - p_0 = 5 - 5 = 0$$

    v. $p_T = \max(0, X - S_T) = \max(0, 95 - 85) = 10$

$$\Pi = p_T - p_0 = 10 - 5 = 5$$

B $S_T^* = X - p_0 = 95 - 5 = 90$

Clearly, this result is consistent with our solution above, where the profit is exactly zero in Part A(iv), in which the price at expiration is 90.

C   **i.** Maximum profit (to put buyer) $= X - p_0 = 95 - 5 = 90$.

    ii. This profit would be realized in the unlikely scenario of the price of the underlying falling all the way down to zero.

5 **A** This position is commonly called a covered call.

  B   **i.** $V_T = S_T - \max(0, S_T - X) = 70 - \max(0, 70 - 80) = 70 - 0 = 70$

$$\Pi = V_T - V_0 = 70 - (S_0 - c_0) = 70 - (77 - 6) = 70 - 71 = -1$$

    ii. $V_T = S_T - \max(0, S_T - X) = 75 - \max(0, 75 - 80) = 75 - 0 = 75$

$$\Pi = V_T - V_0 = 75 - (S_0 - c_0) = 75 - (77 - 6) = 4$$

    iii. $V_T = S_T - \max(0, S_T - X) = 80 - \max(0, 80 - 80) = 80 - 0 = 80$

$$\Pi = V_T - V_0 = 80 - (S_0 - c_0) = 80 - (77 - 6) = 9$$

    iv. $V_T = S_T - \max(0, S_T - X) = 85 - \max(0, 85 - 80) = 85 - 5 = 80$

$$\Pi = V_T - V_0 = 80 - (S_0 - c_0) = 80 - (77 - 6) = 9$$

  C   **i.** Maximum profit $= X - S_0 + c_0 = 80 - 77 + 6 = 9$

    ii. Maximum loss $= S_0 - c_0 = 77 - 6 = 71$

    iii. The maximum profit would be realized if the expiration price of the underlying is at or above the exercise price of \$80.

    iv. The maximum loss would be incurred if the underlying price drops to zero.

  D $S_T^* = S_0 - c_0 = 77 - 6 = 71$

6 **A** This position is commonly called a protective put.

  B   **i.** $V_T = S_T + \max(0, X - S_T) = 70 + \max(0, 75 - 70) = 70 + 5 = 75$

$$\Pi = V_T - V_0 = 75 - (S_0 + p_0) = 75 - (77 + 3) = 75 - 80 = -5$$

    ii. $V_T = S_T + \max(0, X - S_T) = 75 + \max(0, 75 - 75) = 75 + 0 = 75$

$$\Pi = V_T - V_0 = 75 - (S_0 + p_0) = 75 - (77 + 3) = 75 - 80 = -5$$

iii. $V_T = S_T + \max(0, X - S_T) = 80 + \max(0, 75 - 80) = 80 + 0 = 80$

$\Pi = V_T - V_0 = 80 - (S_0 + p_0) = 80 - (77 + 3) = 80 - 80 = 0$

iv. $V_T = S_T + \max(0, X - S_T) = 85 + \max(0, 75 - 85) = 85 + 0 = 85$

$\Pi = V_T - V_0 = 85 - (S_0 + p_0) = 85 - (77 + 3) = 85 - 80 = 5$

v. $V_T = S_T + \max(0, X - S_T) = 90 + \max(0, 75 - 90) = 90 + 0 = 90$

$\Pi = V_T - V_0 = 90 - (S_0 + p_0) = 90 - (77 + 3) = 90 - 80 = 10$

C **i.** Maximum profit = ∞

ii. Maximum loss = $-(X - S_0 - p_0) = -(75 - 77 - 3) = 5$

iii. The maximum loss would be incurred if the expiration price of the underlying were at or below the exercise price of $75.

D $S_T^* = S_0 + p_0 = 77 + 3 = 80$

7 B is correct. Buying the stock at $50 and delivering it against the $50 strike call generates a payoff of zero. The premium is retained by the writer. The net profit is $6.00 per share × 100 shares or $600.

8 B is correct. The loss on her stock is (€45 − €50) × 100 = −€500. She also paid €100 for the put. The put expires worthless, making her total loss €600.

Alternative Investments

TOPIC LEVEL LEARNING OUTCOME

The candidate should be able to demonstrate a working knowledge of alternative investments, including hedge funds, private equity, real estate, and commodities.

Alternative Investments

Investors are increasingly turning to alternative investments seeking diversification benefits and higher returns. This study session describes the common types of alternative investments, their valuation, their unique risks and opportunities, and their relation to traditional investments.

Although defining "alternative investments" is difficult, certain features (e.g., limited liquidity and specialized legal structures) are typically associated with alternative investments. This study session describes features of alternative investments and their effects on investment decisions. The study session provides an overview of major categories of alternative investments, including hedge funds, private equity, real estate, and commodities.

READING ASSIGNMENTS

Reading 60   Introduction to Alternative Investments
by Terri Duhon, George Spentzos, CFA, and Scott D. Stewart, CFA

60

Introduction to Alternative Investments

by Terri Duhon, George Spentzos, CFA, and Scott D. Stewart, CFA

LEARNING OUTCOMES

Mastery	The candidate should be able to:
☐	**a.** compare alternative investments with traditional investments;
☐	**b.** describe categories of alternative investments;
☐	**c.** describe potential benefits of alternative investments in the context of portfolio management;
☐	**d.** describe hedge funds, private equity, real estate, commodities, and other alternative investments, including, as applicable, strategies, sub-categories, potential benefits and risks, fee structures, and due diligence;
☐	**e.** describe issues in valuing, and calculating returns on, hedge funds, private equity, real estate, and commodities;
☐	**f.** describe, calculate, and interpret management and incentive fees and net-of-fees returns to hedge funds;
☐	**g.** describe risk management of alternative investments.

INTRODUCTION

1

Assets under management in vehicles classified as alternative investments have grown rapidly since the mid-1990s. This growth has largely been because of the interest in these investments by institutions, such as endowment and pension funds, and high net worth individuals seeking diversification and return opportunities. Alternative investments are perceived to behave differently from traditional investments. Many investors hope they will provide positive returns throughout the economic cycle; this goal is an absolute return objective. A relative return objective, which is often the objective of portfolios of traditional investments, seeks to achieve a return relative to an equity or fixed income benchmark. However, despite an absolute return objective, alternative investments are not free of risk and may be correlated with other investments, including traditional investments, especially in periods of financial crisis.

This reading is organized as follows. Section 2 describes alternative investments, their basic characteristics and categories; general strategies of alternative investment portfolio managers; the role of alternative investments in a diversified portfolio; and investment structures used to provide access to alternative investments. Sections 3, 4, 5, and 6 describe features of hedge funds, private equity, real estate, and commodities, respectively, along with issues in calculating returns to and valuation of each. Section 7 briefly describes other alternative investments. Section 8 provides an overview of risk management, including due diligence, of alternative investments. A summary and practice problems conclude the reading.

ALTERNATIVE INVESTMENTS

Alternative investments fall outside of the definition of long-only investments in stocks, bonds, and cash (often referred to as traditional investments). In other words, they are alternatives to long-only positions in stocks, bonds, and cash. The usage of the terms traditional and alternatives should not be construed to imply that alternatives are necessarily uncommon and/or relatively recent additions to the investment universe. Alternative investments include investments in assets such as real estate and commodities, which are arguably two of the oldest investment classes.

Alternative investments also include non-traditional approaches to investing within special vehicles, such as private equity funds, hedge funds, and some exchange traded funds (ETFs). These funds typically give the manager flexibility to use derivatives and leverage, make investments in illiquid assets, and take short positions. The assets invested in can include traditional assets (stocks, bonds, and cash) as well as other assets. Management of alternative investments is almost always active. Alternative investments, particularly investments through special vehicles, are often characterized by high fees, low diversification of managers and investments within the alternatives investment portfolio (because of the large size of investments), high use of leverage, and restrictions on fund redemptions.

There are several other characteristics common to many alternative investments. An alternative investment may not be expected to have all these characteristics but will typically be expected to have many of them. These characteristics include the following:

- Illiquidity of underlying investments
- Narrow manager specialization
- Low correlation with traditional investments
- Low level of regulation and less transparency
- Limited and potentially problematic historical risk and return data
- Unique legal and tax considerations

Although assets under management in alternative investments have grown rapidly, they remain a small part of total investable assets, as illustrated in Exhibit 1.

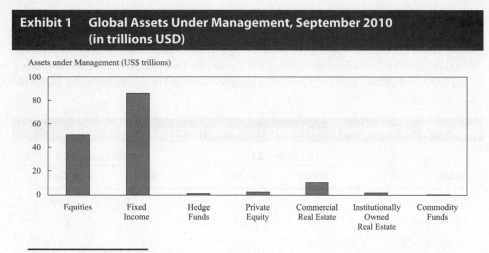

Exhibit 1 Global Assets Under Management, September 2010 (in trillions USD)

Assets under Management (US$ trillions)

Sources: Based on data from Asset Allocation Advisor, HFRI, Inc., Preqin, Prudential RE Advisors, and Barclays Capital.

Institutions and high net worth individuals have been at the forefront of those investing in alternative investments in the expectation of diversifying their portfolios and enhancing their risk/return profiles. Their hopes that alternative investments will behave differently from traditional investments and will provide positive absolute returns throughout the economic cycle may not be realistic. Alternative investments are not free of risk and may be correlated with other risky investments, especially in periods of financial crisis. Over a long historical time period, the average correlation with traditional investments may be low but, in any particular period, the correlation can differ from the average correlation.

Investors must be careful in evaluating the historical record of alternative investments because reported return data can be problematic. Further, reported returns and standard deviations are averages and may not be representative of sub-periods within the reported period or future periods. Many investments, such as direct real estate and private equity are often valued using estimated values (appraised values) rather than actual market prices for the subject investments; as a result, the volatility of returns, as well as the correlation of returns with the returns of traditional asset classes, will tend to be underestimated. Venture capital market returns may be estimated using the technique proposed by Woodward and Hall (2004) to address data problems with historical published indices, which reflect underlying investments held at cost.[1] The record of manager universes, such as hedge fund indices, may be subject to a variety of biases, including survivorship and backfill biases.[2] Thus, the indices may be inherently biased upwards. Commodity indices can be highly weighted in one particular sector, such as oil and gas. Different weightings and constituents in index construction can significantly affect the indices and their results and comparability.

Exhibit 2 shows the historical returns to various investment classes, as well as the standard deviations of the returns, based on selected indices. The indices were selected for their breadth and data quality but nevertheless may not be fully representative of returns to the investment class. For example, the return to the Global S&P REIT

---

1 This technique involves statistical estimation of quarterly market returns utilizing published Thomson Reuters VC index returns and NASDAQ market index returns.
2 Survivorship bias is a bias related to the inclusion of only "live" investment funds. The returns of funds that have been liquidated are excluded. Backfill bias is the bias that results from including previous return data for funds that enter the index. Both biases may result in returns that are artificially high because the survivorship bias most likely results in the index excluding poorly performing funds, and the backfill bias most likely results in the index including high-performing funds.

index may not be representative of returns to equity investment in real estate through private markets (direct ownership of real estate). For venture capital, the returns are modeled using the technique proposed by Woodward and Hall (2004). The average annual returns and standard deviations are shown for two periods: the 20-year period of 1Q1990 to 4Q2009 and the two and a quarter-year period of 4Q2007 to 4Q2009.

Exhibit 2	Alternative Investments Historical Returns and Volatilities			
	1Q1990–4Q2009		4Q2007–4Q2009	
Index	**Mean**	**St. Dev.**	**Mean**	**St. Dev.**
Global stocks	6.2%	16.8%	−10.8%	24.2%
Global bonds	7.2	6.0	6.7	9.0
Hedge funds	8.2	6.4	−4.9	8.0
Commodities	4.5	23.4	−15.9	32.1
Real estate	9.4	18.5	−17.6	33.8
Private equity	10.8	19.4	−10.0	27.8
Venture capital	12.4	25.9	−9.5	29.9
Libor	4.2	0.6	1.9	0.5

Note: Mean and standard deviation are based on annualized US dollar returns.
Sources: Global stocks = MSCI All Country World Index; Global bonds = Barclays Capital Global Aggregate Bond Index; Hedge funds = HFRI Fund of Funds Composite Index; Commodities = S&P GSCI Commodity Index; Real estate = S&P Global REIT Index; Private equity = S&P Listed Private Equity Index; Venture capital = Modeled using Thomson Reuters and NASDAQ indices.

Over the 20-year period, the mean returns to hedge funds, real estate, private equity, and venture capital exceeded the mean returns to global stocks and bonds. The average standard deviation of all but hedge funds also exceeded the average standard deviation of global stocks and bonds. Hedge funds appear to have had a higher average return and lower standard deviation than global stocks over the 20-year period but this may be due, at least partially, to hedge fund indices' reporting biases. Commodities had the lowest mean return over the 20-year period and higher standard deviation than all but venture capital. The higher mean returns of alternative investments, except for commodities, compared with stocks and bonds, may be because of active managers' exploitation of less efficiently priced assets, illiquidity premiums, and/or account leverage. The higher mean returns may also be the result of tax advantages. For example, REITs may not be subject to taxes at the fund level if they meet certain conditions. In a poorly performing economy, the use of leverage and investment in illiquid assets may be reasonably expected to lead to poor results. During 4Q2007 to 4Q2009, the mean returns to alternative investments, other than hedge funds, were similar to or even lower than those to global stocks, and the standard deviations exceeded those of global stocks. Alternative investments did not provide the desired protection during 4Q2007 to 4Q2009, a period categorized as a time of financial crisis. The average returns and standard deviations for the 20-year period of 1Q1990 to 4Q2009 are very different from the average returns and standard deviations for the shorter sub-period of 4Q2007 to 4Q2009. However, it is the long-term potential that attracts many investors.

The 2007 annual report for the Yale University Endowment provides one investor's reasoning behind the attractiveness of investing in alternatives:

"The heavy allocation [70% target allocation] in 2007 to nontraditional asset classes stems from their return potential and diversifying power. Today's actual and target portfolios have significantly higher expected returns and lower volatility than the 1987 portfolio. Alternative assets, by their very nature, tend to be less efficiently priced than traditional marketable securities, providing an opportunity to exploit market inefficiencies through active management. The Endowment's long time horizon is well suited to exploiting illiquid, less efficient markets such as venture capital, leveraged buyouts, oil and gas, timber, and real estate."[3]

The link between the quote above and the expected characteristics of alternative investments is clear: diversifying power (low correlation), higher expected returns (positive absolute return), and illiquid and potentially less efficient markets. This link also highlights the importance of having the ability and willingness to take a long-term prospective. Allocating a portion of an endowment portfolio to alternative investments is not unique to Yale. INSEAD, as of September 2007, had allocated its endowment heavily into alternative investments: 22 percent was in real assets, 24 percent was in hedge funds, and 10 percent was in private equity. The remaining 44 percent was invested evenly in traditional financial assets such as global stocks and bonds.[4] This example is not to imply that every university endowment fund is invested heavily in alternative investments. For example, the London School of Economics and Political Science endowment funds are split into three pools and only one, as of 2006, had a target asset allocation of 10 percent into alternative investments.[5]

High net worth investors have also embraced alternative investments. According to the Spectrem Group's 2010 study of American investors with assets greater than $25 million, more than half have allocations to hedge funds, private equity, and venture capital, with 20 percent of the total portfolio allocated to alternatives investments.[6] The increasing interest by institutions and high net worth individuals in alternative investments has resulted in significant growth in each category since the beginning of 2000. The following are examples of growth in the categories of private equity, real estate, and commodities in the period up to 2008.

- The Private Equity Council estimated that private equity **leveraged buyout** deals were approximately $720 billion in 2007 compared with $100 billion in 2000.[7]

- Ernst & Young reported a growth in global real estate investment trusts (REITs) from $608 billion as of 30 June 2006 to $764 billion as of 30 June 2007. In 1990, the market capitalization of the global REITs was less than $10 billion.[8]

- According to calculations published by the US Commodity Futures Trading Commission, assets allocated to commodity index trading strategies have risen from $13 billion in 2003 to $260 billion in March 2008.[9]

The enthusiasm for alternative investments was tested during 2008 when alternative investment assets under management declined as losses were incurred and funds were withdrawn. However, alternative investments continue to represent a significant proportion of the portfolios of pension funds, endowments, foundations, and high

---

3 www.yale.edu/investments/Yale_Endowment_07.pdf.
4 www.insead.com/campaign/how_contribute/documents/Endowment_FAQ's2007_10_15.doc.
5 www.lse.ac.uk/collections/financeDivision/pdf/2006AnnualAccounts.pdf.
6 See "Ultra-Wealthy Embracing Hedge Funds", *Financial Planning*, 12 November 2010.
7 Private Equity Council, *Public Value: A Primer on Private Equity*, 2007.
8 Ernst & Young, *Global Real Estate Investment Trust Report*, 2007.
9 CIT Supplemental Report, March 2008; CFTC Commitment of Traders Report.

net worth individuals. As of 2012, a resurgence of interest in alternative investments appears to have occurred. The alternative investments available vary in characteristics and performance, and suitability for an investor has to be carefully considered.

EXAMPLE 1

Characteristics of Alternative Investments

Compared with traditional investments, alternative investments are *most likely* to be characterized by high:

A   leverage.

B   liquidity.

C   regulation.

Solution:

A is correct. Alternative investments are likely to use more leverage than traditional investments. Alternative investments are likely to be more illiquid and subject to less regulation.

2.1 Categories of Alternative Investments

Considering the variety of characteristics common to many alternative investments, it is not surprising that no consensus exists on a definitive list of these investments. There is even considerable debate as to what represents a category versus a sub-category of alternative investments. For instance, some listings define distressed securities as a separate category whereas other listings consider distressed securities as a sub-category of the hedge funds and/or private equity categories, or even a subset of high yield bond investing. Similarly, managed futures are sometimes defined as a separate category and sometimes as a sub-category of hedge funds and/or commodities. The listing below is one approach to define broad categories of alternative investments. Each of the categories is described in detail later in this reading.

■ **Hedge Funds**: Hedge funds are private investment vehicles that manage portfolios of securities and derivative positions using a variety of strategies. They may employ long and short positions, are often highly leveraged, and aim to deliver positive total performance regardless of broad market performance.

■ **Private Equity Funds**: Private equity funds generally invest in companies (either start-up or established) that are not listed on a public exchange, or in public companies with the intent to take them private. The majority of private equity activity involves leveraged buyouts of established profitable and cash generative companies with solid customer bases, proven products, and high quality management. **Venture capital**, which typically involves investing in or providing financing to start-up or young companies with high growth potential, is a small portion of the private equity market.

■ **Real Estate**: Real estate investments may be in buildings and/or land, including timberland and farmland, either directly or indirectly. The growing popularity of securitization structures broadened the definition of real estate investing. It now includes private commercial real estate equity (e.g., ownership of an office building), private commercial real estate debt (e.g., directly issued loans or mortgages on commercial property), public real estate equity (e.g., REITs), and public commercial real estate debt (e.g., commercial mortgage-backed securities) investments.

- **Commodities**: Commodities investments may be in physical commodity products such as grains, metals, and crude oil, either through owning cash instruments, utilizing derivative products, or investing in businesses engaged in the production of physical commodities. The main vehicles used by investors to gain exposure to commodities are commodity futures contracts and funds benchmarked to commodity indices. Commodity indices are typically based on various underlying commodity futures.

- **Other**: Other alternative investments may include tangible assets (such as fine wine, art, antique furniture and automobiles, stamps, coins, and other collectibles) and intangible assets (such as patents).

2.2 Return: General Strategies

Managers of portfolios invest in one of two basic ways to achieve returns: passively or actively. Passive managers assume that markets are efficient and focus on beta drivers of return. Beta, a measure of sensitivity relative to a particular market index, is a measure of systematic risk.[10] Active managers, whether in alternative or traditional investments, assume that inefficiencies exist that may be exploited to earn positive return after adjusting for beta risk. This is defined as alpha return. The expected alpha return is zero for passive managers. There are many approaches to managing alternative investment funds, but typically these funds are actively managed and are expected to generate positive alpha return.

Total return = Alpha return + Beta return

Beta-driven portfolios are positioned to efficiently take on market risk. For example, an investment fund that closely tracks the S&P 500 index would be said to be entirely driven by beta. This type of fund seeks to replicate the return on the "market" and thus should be 100 percent correlated to the "market" as represented by the S&P 500 index.

Alpha returns are by definition uncorrelated with beta returns and are presumably the result of managers' special skills in capturing non-systematic opportunities in the market. The fact that these returns, at least in theory, cannot be explained by market risk makes them valuable and sought after. Alpha returns in theory are well suited as performance enhancers and diversifiers in an investment portfolio. In practice, managers' records of delivering unique alpha returns are mixed. Many purported active portfolio exposures, such as style biases and macro positions, are in fact correlated with the markets and as a result largely generate beta returns rather than alpha returns.

Portfolios of real estate investment trusts (REITs) and commodity and infrastructure exchange traded funds (ETFs) may provide beta exposure to a category of alternative investments. However, alternative investments generally claim to offer alpha return opportunities. Alpha-seeking alternative investment strategies reflect several characteristics that differentiate them from long-only passive investments in traditional assets. Basic alpha-seeking strategies (these are not mutually exclusive) can be categorized as follows:

- **Absolute return**: Absolute return strategies seek to generate returns that are independent of market returns; theoretically, betas of funds using absolute return strategies should be close to zero.[11] As a result, with an absolute return strategy, there is typically no market index specified to beat. Instead, the formal

---

10 Systematic risk should not be confused with the term "systemic" risk, which is used in the credit markets to mean highly correlated default risk.

11 In practice, most funds have some market exposure.

performance objective tends to be stated relative to either a cash rate such as Libor, a return over the rate of inflation (a real return target), or an absolute, nominal return target such as 10 percent.

■ **Market segmentation**: Market segmentation exists when capital cannot migrate effortlessly from lower expected return areas to higher ones. Segmentation typically results from institutional, contractual, or regulatory restrictions on traditional asset managers or from differences across investors in investment objectives or liabilities. Segmentation brought on by investment constraints includes portfolios managed relative to published market indices, limitations on the use of derivatives, and restrictions on the proportion of low quality or foreign securities. These restrictions provide an opportunity for more flexible managers to move into higher returning segments more quickly than more restricted or conservative investors.

■ **Concentrated portfolios**: This strategy entails concentrating assets among fewer securities, strategies, and/or managers, which results in less diversification but may enable an investor to achieve higher returns if these concentrated positions outperform the market. Concentrated portfolio strategies are attractive because of high-alpha potential.

Although much of the attraction of alternative investments seems to be based on returns, the risks associated with those returns must also be factored in. Risks can be considered both on a stand-alone basis and within the context of a portfolio (the modern portfolio theory approach). As mentioned earlier, risks for alternative investments include low liquidity, limited redemption availability and transparency, and the challenge of manager diversification.

Returns may be measured relative to stand-alone risk using risk ratios and exploring return distributions. A commonly reported risk ratio is the Sharpe Ratio, which equals an investment's return, net of a risk-free rate, divided by its return standard deviation; it is a common measure among the investment community because of the ease of calculation using historical results. Other risk measures, such as those that emphasize downside risk, are also frequently considered.[12]

Sharpe ratios for traditional and alternative investments, based on the same information used in Exhibit 2, are shown in Panel A of Exhibit 3. It should be noted that the reported or available historical return data used may not be reliable and/or representative of the return data for the investment class.

Many downside risk measures, such as the chance of losing a certain amount of money in a given period, are used in practice. Panel B of Exhibit 3 includes some measures indicative of downside risk: the frequencies of monthly returns less than −1 percent, −5 percent, and −10 percent during 1990–2009, and in the right column, the worst return reported in a month.

---

[12] The Sharpe ratio is discussed in greater detail in the CFA Program Level I Quantitative Methods reading "Statistical Concepts and Market Returns." Other risk measures include Treynor, Jensen, and Sortino ratios and value at risk (VaR), which are also discussed in Level I of the CFA Program.

Exhibit 3	Sharpe Ratios and Downside Risk Measures, Based on 1990–2009 Returns

Panel A: Sharpe Ratios (using annualized returns)

Index	
Global stocks	0.12
Global bonds	0.50
Hedge funds	0.62
Commodities	0.01
Real estate	0.28
Private equity	0.34
Venture capital	0.32

Panel B: Downside Frequencies

	Frequency of Monthly Return Less Than...			Worst Monthly Return
Index	–1%	–5%	–10%	
Global stocks	32.1%	10.0%	2.1%	–19.8%
Global bonds	15.0	0.0	0.0	–3.8
Hedge funds	12.5	1.3	0.0	–7.5
Commodities	37.1	16.3	4.6	–28.2
Real estate	28.8	5.8	2.5	–30.5
Private equity	29.6	10.8	2.5	–23.4
Venture capital	30.0	16.7	3.8	–24.5

Sharpe ratios (using Libor as a proxy for the risk-free rate) indicate that based on reported data, during 1990–2009, hedge funds offered the best risk–return trade-off and commodities the worst. Venture capital displayed a similar downside risk profile as commodities but its higher reported return (see Exhibit 2) results in a higher Sharpe ratio over the period. Hedge funds offered similar downside risk as bonds and a higher Sharpe ratio.

The Sharpe ratio and downside risk measures do not take into account the potentially low level of correlation of alternative investments with traditional investments. A less than perfect correlation between investments reduces the standard deviation of a diversified portfolio below the weighted average of the standard deviations of the investments. Risk in the portfolio context is discussed in the next section.

2.3 Portfolio Context: Integration of Alternative Investments with Traditional Investments

A key motivation cited for investing in alternative investments is their diversifying potential; there is a perceived opportunity to improve the risk/return relationship within the portfolio context. Given the historical return, volatility, and correlation profiles of alternative investments, combining a portfolio of alternative investments with a portfolio of traditional investments potentially improves the risk/return profile of the overall portfolio. The correlation between some categories of alternative investments and traditional investments has historically over long periods been low, or at least less than perfect, providing diversification opportunities. The historically higher returns to most categories of alternative investments compared with traditional investments result in potentially higher returns to a portfolio containing alternative investments, and the less than perfect correlation with traditional investments results in portfolio risk (standard deviation) being less than a weighting of the standard deviations. However, in identifying the appropriate allocation to alternative investments, an investment manager is likely to consider more than mean return and average standard deviation of returns. When considering potential portfolio combinations, historical downside frequencies and worst return in a month for potential portfolio combinations may be included in the analysis.

The purported diversification benefits and improved risk–return contributions of alternative investments to portfolios explains why institutional investors such as pension funds may allocate a portion of their portfolios to alternative investments. However, there are challenges; these include getting reliable measures of risk and return, identifying the appropriate allocation, and selecting portfolio managers.

2.4 Investment Structures

The most common structure for many alternative investments, such as hedge funds and private equity funds, is a partnership, where the fund is the **general partner** (GP) and investors are **limited partners** (LPs). Limited partnerships are restricted to investors who are expected to understand and to be able to assume the risks associated with the investments. Fund investments, because they are not offered to the general public, may not be regulated or be less regulated than offerings to the general public.[13] The GP runs the business and theoretically bears unlimited liability for anything that might go wrong. Because most individuals are unwilling to bear unlimited liability, the GP is usually a limited liability corporation. Limited partners own a fractional interest in the partnership based on their investment and as agreed to by the partners; an LP's fractional interest is often referred to as his or her share of the partnership. These partnerships are frequently located in tax-efficient locations, which benefit both the GP and the LPs. Funds set up as private investment partnerships typically have a limit on the number of LPs.[14]

Funds are generally structured with a **management fee** based on assets under management (sometimes called the base fee) plus an **incentive fee (or performance fee)** based on realized profits. Sometimes, the fee structure specifies that the incentive fee is only earned after the fund achieves a specified return known as a hurdle rate. Fee calculations also take into account **high water marks**, which reflect the highest cumulative return used to calculate an incentive fee. It is the highest value, net of fees, that the fund has reached. The use of high water marks protects clients from paying twice for the same performance. This basic partnership and fee structure is used by many alternative investment funds, including hedge funds. Fee structures are discussed in more detail later in the reading.

---

13 In the United States, the US Securities Act of 1933 regulates the process by which investment securities are offered. Most alternatives funds are structured as "private placements," which are defined within Regulation D of the Securities Act and sometimes called "Reg D Offerings."

14 Because of the inherent risk involved in alternative investments, investment is typically restricted to a specified number of investors meeting certain criteria. The number and the criteria can be specified by regulation or set by the fund. In the United States, the number depends on whether funds target "*Accredited Investors*" or "*Qualified Purchasers*" (as defined by the Investment Company Act of 1940, Sections 3(c) 1 and 7, respectively). A fund can have no more than 100 Accredited Investors (individuals with at least $1 million and institutions with at least $5 million in investable assets) or no more than 500 Qualified Purchasers (individuals with at least $5 million and institutions with at least $25 million in investable assets).

HEDGE FUNDS

In 1949 Alfred Winslow Jones, a sociologist investigating fundamental and technical research to forecast the stock market for *Fortune* magazine, set up an investment fund with himself as general partner. The fund followed three key tenets: (1) always maintain short positions, (2) always use leverage, and (3) only charge an incentive fee of 20 percent of profits with no fixed fees. Jones called his portfolio a "hedged" fund (eventually shortened to "hedge fund") because he had short positions to offset his long positions in the stock market. Theoretically, the overall portfolio was hedged against major market moves.

Although Jones' original three tenets still have some relevance to the hedge fund industry, not all hedge funds maintain short positions and/or use leverage, and most hedge funds have some non-incentive fees. The typical contemporary hedge fund can be characterized as follows:

- It is an aggressively managed portfolio of investments across asset classes and regions that is leveraged, takes long and short positions, and/or uses derivatives.

- It has a goal of generating high returns, either in an absolute sense or over a specified market benchmark and has few, if any, investment restrictions.

- It is set up as a private investment partnership open to a limited number of investors willing and able to make a large initial investment.

- It often imposes restrictions on **redemptions**. Investors may be required to keep their money in the hedge fund for a minimum period (referred to as a **lockup period**) before they are allowed to make withdrawals or redeem shares. Investors may be required to give notice of their intent to redeem; the **notice period** is typically 30 to 90 days in length. Also, investors may be charged a fee to redeem shares.

The willingness of investors to invest in hedge funds, despite the restrictions on redemptions, is largely because of the reported returns of some hedge funds and their perceived low correlation with traditional investments. The positive performance of many funds in the early 2000s when other investments had declined supported the diversification potential of hedge funds in a portfolio. The growth of interest in hedge funds as investments led to the emergence of funds of hedge funds.

Funds of hedge funds are funds that hold a portfolio of hedge funds. They make hedge funds accessible to smaller investors, while allowing them to be diversified to some extent among hedge funds. Also, funds of hedge funds presumably have some expertise in conducting due diligence on hedge funds and may be able to negotiate better redemption terms. Funds of hedge funds invest in numerous hedge funds, diversifying across fund strategies, investment regions, and management styles. The distinction between a single hedge fund and a fund of hedge funds is not necessarily clear-cut because many hedge funds invest in other hedge funds.

Hedge funds are less restricted than traditional investment managers and thus may have the flexibility to invest anywhere they see opportunity. Most hedge funds do have a broadly stated strategy but are allowed some deviation from the strategy. Hedge funds are often given the flexibility to invest a percentage of the assets under management, generally less than 20 percent, how and when they see fit. A hedge fund can also be structured as one "asset management" business that is "contracted" to manage several different funds (e.g., SuperStar Asset Management might manage SuperStar Credit Fund, SuperStar Commodities Fund, and SuperStar Multi-Strategy Fund).

The growing popularity of hedge funds is illustrated in Exhibit 4, which shows assets under management and net asset flows for the period of 1990 through 2010. Assets under management grew from approximately $39 billion in 1990 to $491 billion in 2000 to $1,868 billion in 2007. Comparing net asset flows to the change in assets under management indicates that much of the growth in assets under management was because of performance. In 2008, assets under management declined because of withdrawals (a negative net asset flow) and a decline in the value of the assets under management. In 2009, a negative net asset flow was offset by an increase in the value of the assets under management. In 2010, assets under management exceeded assets under management in 2007.

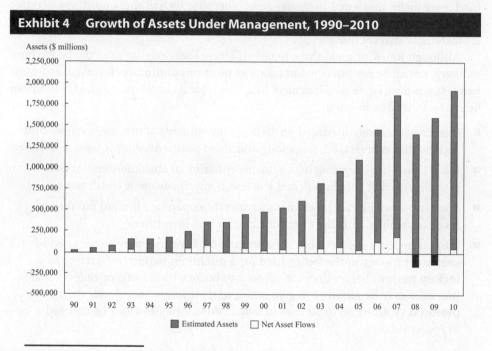

Exhibit 4   Growth of Assets Under Management, 1990–2010

Assets ($ millions)

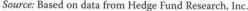

Source: Based on data from Hedge Fund Research, Inc.

Exhibit 5 illustrates the returns *net of fees* to hedge funds based on data provided by Hedge Fund Research, Inc. (HFRI). The HFRI family of indices includes the HFRI Fund Weighted Composite Index and the HFRI Fund of Funds Index. The HFRI Fund Weighted Composite Index is an equally weighted performance index based on the self-reported data of over 2,000 individual funds included in the HFR database. The HFRI Fund of Funds Index is an equally weighted performance index of funds of hedge funds included in the HFR database. Both indices suffer from issues related to self-reporting, but the HFRI Fund of Funds Index reflects the actual performance of portfolios of hedge funds. This index may show a lower reported return because of the added layer of fees,[15] but it may be a more realistic representation of average hedge fund performance. The cumulative performance of the HFRI Fund of Funds Index exceeds that of the Barclays Capital Global Aggregate Bond Index[16] and the MSCI All Country World Index[17] (a global equity index) over the period of 1990 to 2009.

---

15 A fund of funds has an extra layer of fees. Each hedge fund in which a fund of funds invests is structured to receive a management fee plus a performance fee, and the fund of funds is also structured to receive a management fee plus a performance fee.
16 The Barclays Capital Global Aggregate Bond Index provides a broad-based measure of the global investment grade fixed-rate debt markets.
17 The MSCI All Country World Index is based on equity indices of 45 countries: 24 developed and 21 emerging. It is a free float-adjusted market capitalization weighted index.

Exhibit 5   Performance of Funds of Hedge Funds, Global Bonds, and Global Stocks, 1990–2009

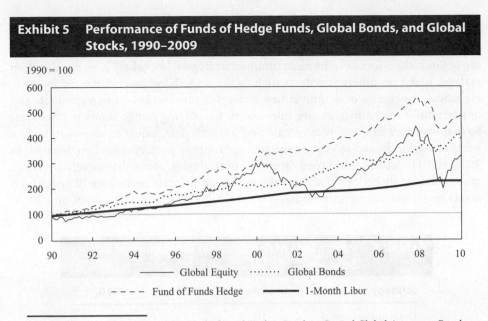

Sources: Based on data from HFRI Fund of Funds Index, Barclays Capital Global Aggregate Bond Index, and MSCI All Country World Index.

Exhibit 6 compares the return and a variety of risk and performance measures of the HFRI Fund of Funds Index, the MSCI Global Total Return Index, the Barclays Capital Global Aggregate Bond Index, and Libor. As shown in Exhibit 5, the "worst drawdown" reflecting the period of largest cumulative negative returns for hedge funds and global equities was over the period that began in 2007 (when each peaked) and ended in 2009. Over the 20-year period, hedge funds had a higher average annualized return and a lower annualized volatility and so appeared to dominate equities in both return and risk. Note that the returns and volatilities (standard deviations) represent an average and are not representative of any single year. Over this period, global bonds appear to have superior returns compared with global stocks. This result is surprising given the expected risk–return relationships. In fact, this outcome is primarily because of the poor performance of stocks over the years 2008 and 2009 (see Exhibit 2).

Exhibit 6   Risk–Return Characteristics of Hedge Funds and Other Investments, 1990–2009

	FoF Hedge	Global Stocks	Global Bonds	1-Mo. Libor
Annualized return	8.2%	6.2%	7.2%	4.2%
Annualized volatility	6.4%	16.8%	6.0%	0.6%
Sharpe Ratio	0.62	0.12	0.50	
% Positive months	71.7%	61.3%	63.8%	100.0%
Best month	6.9%	11.9%	6.2%	0.7%
Worst month	−7.5%	−19.8%	−3.8%	0.0%
Worst drawdown	−22.2%	−54.6%	−10.1%	0.0%

Sources: FoF Hedge data are from HFRI Fund of Funds Weighted Composite Index; global stocks data are from MSCI World All Country Total Returns Index; global bonds data are from Barclays Capital Global Aggregate Bond Index.

3.1 Hedge Fund Strategies

Hedge funds are typically classified by strategy, but categorizations vary. Many classifying organizations focus on the most common strategies, but others have classification systems based on different criteria such as the underlying assets invested in. Also, classifications change over time as new strategies, often based on new products and opportunities in the market, are introduced. Classifying hedge funds is important so that investors can review aggregate performance data, select strategies to build a portfolio of funds, and select or construct appropriate performance benchmarks. In 2008, HFRI identified four broad categories of strategies: event-driven, relative value, macro, and equity hedge.[18] Exhibit 7 shows the approximate percentage of hedge fund assets under management by strategy, according to HFRI, for 1990, 2008, and 2010.

Exhibit 7	Percentage of Assets under Management by Strategy		
Strategy	1990	2008	2010
Event-driven	10	25	26
Relative value	14	25	24
Macro	39	16	20
Equity hedge	37	34	30

3.1.1 Event-Driven Strategies

Event-driven strategies seek to profit from short-term events, typically involving potential changes in corporate structure such as an acquisition or restructuring, that are expected to affect individual companies. This strategy is considered "bottom up" (company level analysis followed by aggregation and analysis of a larger group, such as an industry) as opposed to "top down" (global macro analysis followed by sectoral/regional analysis followed by company analysis). Investments may include long and short positions in common and preferred stocks, as well as debt securities and options. Further subdivisions of this category by HFRI include the following:

- Merger Arbitrage: Generally, these strategies involve going long (buying) the stock of the company being acquired and going short (selling) the stock of the acquiring company when the merger/acquisition is announced. The manager expects the acquirer to ultimately overpay for the acquisition and perhaps suffer from an increased debt load. The primary risk in this strategy is that the announced merger or acquisition does not occur, and the hedge fund has not closed its positions on a timely basis.

- Distressed/Restructuring: These strategies focus on the securities of companies either in bankruptcy or perceived to be near to bankruptcy. There are a variety of ways hedge funds attempt to profit from distressed securities. The hedge fund may simply purchase fixed income securities trading at a significant discount to par. This transaction is done in anticipation of the company restructuring and the fund earning a profit from the subsequent sale of the securities. The hedge fund may also use a more complicated approach and buy senior debt and short junior debt or buy preferred stock and short common stock. This

---

18 The Chartered Alternative Investment Analyst (CAIA)® Association® classifies hedge funds into four broad categories: corporate restructuring, convergence trading, opportunistic, and market directional. These approximately coincide with event-driven, relative value, macro, and equity hedge, respectively.

transaction is done in expectation of a profit as the spread between the securities widens. The fund may also short sell the company's stock, but this transaction involves considerable risk given the potential for loss if the company's prospects improve.

- Activist: The term activist is a shortened form of "activist shareholder." These strategies focus on the purchase of sufficient equity in order to influence a company's policies or direction. For example, the activist hedge fund may advocate for divestitures, restructuring, capital distributions to shareholders, and/or changes in management and company strategy. These hedge funds are distinct from private equity because they operate in the public equity market.

- Special Situations: These strategies focus on opportunities in the equity of companies that are currently engaged in restructuring activities other than merger/acquisitions and bankruptcy. These activities include security issuance/repurchase, special capital distributions, and asset sales/spin-offs.

3.1.2 *Relative Value Strategies*

Relative value funds seek to profit from a pricing discrepancy (an unusual short-term relationship) between related securities. The expectation is that the pricing discrepancy will be resolved in time. This strategy typically involves buying and selling related securities. Examples of relative value strategies include the following:

- Fixed Income Convertible Arbitrage: These are market neutral (a zero beta portfolio, at least in theory) investment strategies that seek to exploit a perceived mispricing between a convertible bond and its component parts (the underlying bond and the embedded stock option). The strategy typically involves buying convertible debt securities and simultaneously selling the same issuer's common stock.

- Fixed Income Asset Backed: These strategies focus on the relative value between a variety of asset-backed securities (ABS) and mortgage-backed securities (MBS) and seek to take advantage of mispricing across different asset-backed securities.

- Fixed Income General: These strategies focus on the relative value within the fixed income markets. Strategies may incorporate trades between two corporate issuers, between corporate and government issuers, between different parts of the same issuer's capital structure, or between different parts of an issuer's yield curve. Currency dynamics and government yield curve considerations may also come into play when managing these fixed income instruments.

- Volatility: These strategies typically use options to go long or short market volatility either in a specific asset class or across asset classes.

- Multi-Strategy: These strategies trade relative value within and across asset classes or instruments. The strategy does not focus upon one type of trade (e.g., convertible arbitrage), a single basis for trade (e.g., volatility), or a particular asset class (e.g., fixed income) but instead looks for investment opportunities wherever they might exist.

3.1.3 *Macro Strategies*

Macro hedge funds emphasize a "top down" approach to identify economic trends evolving across the world. Trades are made based on expected movements in economic variables. Generally, these funds trade opportunistically in the fixed income, equity, currency, and commodity markets. Macro hedge funds use long and/or short positions to potentially profit from a view on overall market direction as influenced by major economic trends and/or events.

3.1.4 *Equity Hedge Strategies*

Equity hedge strategies can be thought of as the original hedge fund category. They are focused on public equity markets and take long and short positions in equity and equity derivative securities. They are not focused on equity trades categorized as consistent with Event-driven or Macro strategies. Equity hedge strategies use a "bottom up" as opposed to "top down" approach. Others, not structured as hedge funds, may use some similar strategies. Examples of equity hedge strategies include the following:

- Market Neutral: These strategies use quantitative (technical) and/or fundamental analysis to identify under- and over-valued equity securities. The hedge fund takes long positions in securities it has identified as undervalued and short positions in securities it has identified as overvalued. The hedge fund tries to maintain a net position that is neutral with respect to market risk. Ideally, the portfolio should have a beta of approximately zero. The intent is to profit from individual securities movements while hedging against market risk.

- Fundamental Growth: These strategies use fundamental analysis to identify companies expected to exhibit high growth and capital appreciation. The hedge fund takes long positions in identified companies.

- Fundamental Value: These strategies use fundamental analysis to identify companies that are undervalued. The hedge fund takes long positions in identified companies.

- Quantitative Directional: These strategies use technical analysis to identify companies that are under- and overvalued and to ascertain relationships between securities. The hedge fund takes long positions in securities identified as undervalued and short positions in securities identified as overvalued. The hedge fund typically varies levels of net long or short exposure depending upon the anticipated direction of the market and stage in the market cycle. Similar long/short approaches exist that are based upon fundamental analysis.

- Short Bias: These strategies use quantitative (technical) and/or fundamental analysis to identify overvalued equity securities. The hedge fund takes short positions in securities identified as overvalued. The fund typically varies its net short exposure based upon market expectations, going fully short in declining markets.

- Sector Specific: These strategies exploit expertise in a particular sector and use quantitative (technical) and fundamental analysis to identify opportunities in the sector.

Many hedge funds start as a focused operation, specializing in one strategy or asset class and if successful, diversify and over time become multi-strategy funds. Large, multi-strategy funds are an alternative to funds of hedge funds. Although funds of hedge funds may offer advantages (for example, access by smaller investors, diversified hedge fund portfolio, better redemption terms, and/or due diligence expertise) that multi-strategy funds do not have, a primary difference between a multi-strategy hedge fund and a fund of hedge funds is the extra layer of fees associated with a fund of funds. Each hedge fund in which a fund of hedge funds invests is structured to receive a management fee plus an incentive fee, and the fund of hedge funds is also structured to receive a management fee plus an incentive fee.

3.2 Hedge Funds and Diversification Benefits

Given the broad range of strategies across hedge funds, general statements about hedge fund performance are not necessarily meaningful. Further, there is a general lack of performance persistence; hedge fund strategies that generate the highest returns in some years can be the ones to perform the most poorly in subsequent years.

The general premise of hedge funds is that they can make money (in other words, earn absolute returns) regardless of the stock market's direction. Their flexibility and the fact that they are not typically restricted to long only positions gives them the opportunity to respond to market fluctuations. In addition, hedge funds have traditionally been thought of as "arbitrage" players, meaning that they seek to earn returns while hedging against risks. Of course, in efficient markets, it is hard to find true arbitrage opportunities. In fact, one of the benefits some hedge funds provide to the financial marketplace is that they help make the markets more efficient by providing liquidity with contrarian views. As the hedge fund market has grown, many traditional hedge fund strategies have become increasingly crowded, forcing funds to take on more risk to generate competitive returns.

Less than perfect correlation with the stock market may provide diversification benefits. However, the sometimes claim that hedge fund performance is uncorrelated, not just less than perfectly correlated, with stock market performance is unsubstantiated. Looking at Exhibit 8, the claims of lack of correlation with the stock market appear to be supported in the period of 2000 to 2002, but are not supported in the subsequent period of 2003 to 2009. Further, during periods of financial crisis, the correlation between hedge fund and stock market performances may increase.

Exhibit 8	Returns for Hedge Fund, Global Stocks and Bonds, and Libor, 2000–2009

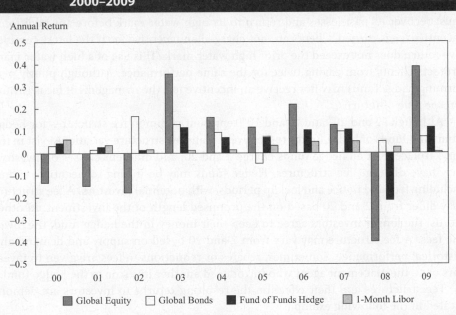

3.3 Hedge Fund Fees and Other Considerations

Hedge fund assets under management have grown over the 10-year period of 2000 through 2009, but they remain a small percentage of the asset management business overall. Hedge funds, however, earn a significantly higher percentage of fees. For example, in 2007 hedge funds managed 3 percent of total managed funds (hedge funds plus mutual funds) but earned 28 percent of managed fund revenue (fees).[19]

3.3.1 *Fees and Returns*

It is important to consider a hedge fund's fee structure prior to making an investment. The hedge fund fee structure accounts for the disproportionately high revenues earned relative to mutual funds and affects the returns to investors. A common fee structure in the hedge fund market is "2 and 20," which reflects a 2 percent management fee and a 20 percent incentive fee. Additionally, funds of hedge funds typically charge a 1 percent management fee and a 10 percent incentive fee. The incentive fee may be calculated on profits net of management fees or on profits before management fees (in other words, the incentive fee is calculated independent of management fees).

Sometimes, the fee structure specifies that the incentive fee is only earned after the fund achieves a specified return known as a hurdle rate. The hurdle rate is frequently set based on a risk-free rate proxy (e.g., Libor or a specified Treasury bill rate) plus a premium but may be set as an absolute, nominal, or real return target. The incentive fee can be based on returns in excess of the hurdle rate (hard hurdle rate) or on the entire return (soft hurdle rate).

The fee structure may specify that before an incentive fee is paid, following a year in which the fund's value has declined, the fund's value must return to a previous high water mark. Note that the high water mark is typically the highest value reported by the fund; the amount reported is net of fees. High water marks reflect the highest cumulative return used to calculate an incentive fee. In other words, the hedge fund must recover its past losses and return to its high water mark before any additional incentive fee is earned. Clients are not charged an incentive fee if the latest cumulative return does not exceed the prior high water mark. This use of a high water mark protects clients from paying twice for the same performance. Although poorly performing hedge funds may not receive an incentive fee, the management fee is earned irrespective of returns.

Although "2 and 20" and "1 and 10" represent common fee structures for hedge funds and funds of hedge funds, respectively, many fee structure variations exist in the marketplace. Not all hedge funds charge 2 and 20, and different classes of investors may have different fee structures. Hedge funds may be willing to negotiate terms, including fees and notice and lockup periods, with potential investors. A fee structure may differ from 2 and 20 based on the promised length of the investment. In other words, the longer investors agree to keep their money in the hedge fund, the lower the fees. A fee structure may vary from 2 and 20 based on supply and demand and historical performance. Sometimes, rebates or reductions in fees are given to investors or to the placement agent who introduced another investor to the hedge fund.

Fee structures and their effect on the resulting returns to investors are demonstrated in the following example.

---

[19] International Financial Services London estimates based on Watson Wyatt, Bridgewell, Merrill Lynch, ICI, SwissRe, and Hennessee Group data.

EXAMPLE 2

Fee and Return Calculations

AWJ Capital is a hedge fund with $100 million of initial investment capital. They charge a 2 percent management fee based on assets under management at year-end and a 20 percent incentive fee. In its first year, AWJ Capital has a 30 percent return. Assume management fees are calculated using end-of-period valuation.

1   What are the fees earned by AWJ if the incentive and management fees are calculated independently? What is an investor's effective return given this fee structure?

2   What are the fees earned by AWJ assuming that the incentive fee is calculated based on return net of the management fee? What is an investor's net return given this fee structure?

3   If the fee structure specifies a hurdle rate of 5 percent and the incentive fee is based on returns in excess of the hurdle rate, what are the fees earned by AWJ assuming the performance fee is calculated net of the management fee? What is an investor's net return given this fee structure?

In the second year, the fund value declines to $110 million.

4   The fee structure is as specified for question 1 but also includes the use of a high water mark. What are the fees earned by AWJ in the second year? What is an investor's net return for the second year given this fee structure?

In the third year, the fund value increases to $128 million.

5   The fee structure is as specified in questions 1 and 4. What are the fees earned by AWJ in the third year? What is an investor's net return for the third year given this fee structure?

6   What are the arithmetic and geometric mean annual returns over the three-year period based on the fee structure specified in questions 1, 4, and 5? What is the capital gain to the investor over the three-year period? What are the total fees paid to AWJ over the three-year period?

Solution to 1:

AWJ fees

$130 million × 2% = $2.6 million management fee

($130 − $100) million × 20% = $6 million incentive fee

Total fees to AWJ Capital = $8.6 million

Investor return: ($130 − $100 − $8.6)/$100 = 21.40%

Solution to 2:

$130 million × 2% = $2.6 million management fee

($130 − $100 − $2.6) million × 20% = $5.48 million incentive fee

Total fees to AWJ Capital = $8.08 million

Investor return: ($130 − $100 − $8.08)/$100 = 21.92%

Solution to 3:

$130 million × 2% = $2.6 million management fee

($130 − $100 − $5 − $2.6) million × 20% = $4.48 million incentive fee

Total fees to AWJ Capital = $7.08 million

Investor return: ($130 − $100 − $7.08)/$100 = 22.92%

Solution to 4:

$110 million × 2% = $2.2 million management fee

No incentive fee because the fund has declined in value.

Total fees to AWJ Capital = $2.2 million

Investor return: ($110 − $2.2 − $121.4)/$121.4 = −11.20%. The beginning capital position in the second year for the investors is ($130 − $8.6) million = $121.4 million. The ending capital position at the end of the second year is ($110 − $2.2) million= $107.8 million.

Solution to 5:

$128 million × 2% = $2.56 million management fee

($128 − $121.4) million× 20% = $1.32 million incentive fee. The $121.4 million represents the high-water mark established at the end of Year 1.

Total fees to AWJ Capital = $3.88 million

Investor return: ($128 − $3.88 − $107.8)/$107.8 = 15.14%. The ending capital position at the end of Year 3 is $124.12 million. This is the new high-water mark.

Solution to 6:

Arithmetic mean annual return = (21.4% − 11.20% + 15.14%)/3 = 8.45%

Geometric mean annual return = [cube root of (124.12/100)] − 1 = 7.47%

Capital gain to the investor = ($124.12 − $100) million = $24.12 million

Total fees = ($8.6 + $2.2 + $3.88) million = $14.68 million

As can be seen from the example, the return to an investor in a fund is significantly different from the return to the fund. Hedge fund indices generally report performance net of fees. However, if fee structures vary, the net-of-fees returns may vary among investors and from that included in the index. The multilayered fee structure of funds of hedge funds has the effect of further diluting returns to the investor, but this disadvantage is balanced with several attractive features. Funds of hedge funds may provide a diversified portfolio of hedge funds, may provide access to hedge funds that may otherwise be closed to direct investments, and may offer expertise in and conduct due diligence in selecting the individual hedge funds. Fund-of-funds money is considered "fast" money by hedge fund managers because fund-of-funds managers tend to be the first to redeem their money when hedge funds start to perform poorly, and they may also have negotiated redemption terms that are more favorable (for example, a shorter lockup period and/or notice period).

EXAMPLE 3

Comparison of Returns—Investment Directly into a Hedge Fund or through a Fund of Hedge Funds

An investor is contemplating investing €100 million in either the ABC Hedge Fund (ABC HF) or the XYZ Fund of Funds (XYZ FOF). XYZ FOF has a "1 and 10" fee structure and invests 10 percent of its assets under management in ABC HF. ABC HF has a standard "2 and 20" fee structure with no hurdle rate. Management fees are calculated on an annual basis on assets under management at the beginning of the year. Management fees and incentive fees are calculated independently. ABC HF has a 20 percent return for the year before management and incentive fees.

1 Calculate the return to the investor of investing directly in ABC HF.

2 Calculate the return to the investor of investing in XYZ FOF. Assume that the other investments in the XYZ FOF portfolio generate the same return before management fees as ABC HF and have the same fee structure as ABC HF.

3 Why would the investor choose to invest in an FOF instead of an HF given the effect of the "double fee" as demonstrated in the answers to questions 1 and 2?

Solution to 1:

ABC HF has a profit before fees on a €100 million investment of €20 million (= 100 million × 20%). The management fee is €2 million (= €100 million × 2%) and the incentive fee is €4 million (= 20 million × 20%). The return to the investor is 14 percent [= (20 − 2 − 4)/100].

Solution to 2:

XYZ FOF earns a 14 percent return or €14 million profit after fees on €100 million invested with hedge funds. XYZ FOF charges the investor a management fee of €1 million (= €100 million × 1%) and an incentive fee of €1.4 million (= €14 million × 10%). The return to the investor is 11.6 percent [= (14 − 1 − 1.4)/100].

Solution to 3:

This scenario assumed that returns were the same for all underlying hedge funds. In practice, this result will not likely be the case, and XYZ FOF may provide due diligence expertise and potentially valuable diversification.

The hedge fund business is attractive to portfolio managers because the management fee of 2 percent alone can generate significant revenue if assets under management are large. Throughout the late 1990s and the early 2000s, many new hedge funds were launched. However, not all hedge funds launched remain in business long. One study suggests that more than a quarter of all hedge funds fail within the first three years because of performance problems.[20] This outcome is one of the reasons survivorship bias is such a problem in hedge fund indices. Because of the survivorship and backfill biases, hedge fund indices may not reflect actual average hedge fund performance but rather the performance of hedge funds that are performing well.

---

20 Brooks and Kat, 2002.

3.3.2 *Other Considerations*

Hedge funds may use leverage to seek higher returns on their investments. Leverage has the effect of magnifying gains or losses because the hedge fund can take a large position relative to the capital committed. Hedge funds may leverage their portfolios by borrowing capital and/or using derivatives.

For example, if a hedge fund expects the price of Nestlé SA (SIX Swiss Exchange: NESN) to increase, it can take a number of actions to benefit from the expected price increase. The fund can buy a thousand shares of Nestlé, buy 10 futures contracts on Nestlé on the NYSE Euronext, buy calls on a thousand shares of Nestlé, or sell puts on a thousand shares of Nestlé to profit from the expected price increase. The profit or loss from holding the futures will be similar to the profit or loss from holding the shares, but the capital requirement for the investment in the futures is far lower. If the hedge fund had bought calls on a thousand shares of Nestlé, the fund would have paid a relatively small premium and potentially experienced a significant profit if Nestlé had increased in price. The maximum loss to the fund would have been the premium paid. If the hedge fund had sold puts on a thousand shares of Nestlé expecting the price to rise and the puts to not be exercised, the fund would have a maximum profit equal to the relatively small premium received. However, if Nestlé declined in price, the potential loss is extremely large.

Investors, including hedge funds, may be required to put up some collateral when using derivatives if they are going to be exposed to potential losses on their positions. This collateral requirement helps to protect against default on the position and helps to protect the counterparty (or clearinghouse) on the derivative. The amount of collateral depends on the riskiness of the investment and the creditworthiness of the hedge fund or other investor.

The borrowing of capital also leverages a portfolio. It often takes the form of buying on margin. By borrowing, a hedge fund is able to invest a larger amount than was invested in the fund. Hedge funds normally trade through **prime brokers**, who provide services including custody, administration, lending, short borrowing, and trading. A hedge fund will normally negotiate its margin requirements with its prime broker(s). The prime broker effectively lends the hedge fund money to make investments, and the hedge fund puts money or other collateral into a margin account with the prime broker. The margin account represents the hedge fund's equity in the position. The margin requirement depends on the riskiness of the investment and the creditworthiness of the hedge fund.

The smaller the margin requirement, the more leverage is available to the hedge fund. Leverage is a large part of the reason that hedge funds make either larger than normal returns or significant losses; the leverage magnifies both gains and losses. If the margin account or the hedge fund's equity in a position declines below a certain level, the lender initiates a margin call and requests the hedge fund put up more collateral. Margin calls can have the effect of magnifying losses because in order to meet a margin call, the hedge fund may liquidate (close) the losing position. This liquidation can lead to further losses if the order size is sufficiently large to move the security's market price.

Another factor that can magnify losses for hedge funds is investor redemptions. **Redemptions** frequently occur when a hedge fund is performing poorly. In the hedge fund industry, a **drawdown** is a reduction in net asset value (NAV).[21] When drawdowns occur, investors may decide to exit the fund or redeem at least a portion of their shares. Redemptions may require the hedge fund manager to liquidate some positions and incur transaction costs. As stated above, the liquidation of a position

---

21 Net asset value is the value of the fund's total assets minus liabilities, divided by the number of shares outstanding.

may further magnify the losses on the position. Redemption fees may serve to discourage redemption and to help the hedge fund managers recover transaction costs. Notice periods may allow the hedge fund manager to liquidate a position in an orderly fashion without magnifying the losses. Lockup periods give the hedge fund manager time to implement and potentially realize the expected results of a strategy. If the hedge fund is unlucky enough to experience a drawdown after the fund launch, the lockup period will force investors to stay in the fund rather than withdraw. The ability for a hedge fund to demand a long lockup period and still raise a significant amount of money depends a great deal on the reputation of either the firm or the hedge fund manager. Funds of hedge funds may offer more redemption flexibility than afforded by direct investment in hedge funds because of special redemption arrangements with the underlying hedge fund managers, maintenance of a cash fund, or access to temporary financing.

Whereas hedge funds are not subject to extensive regulation globally, there have been calls for more oversight. Hedge funds in the United Kingdom are required to be registered with the Financial Services Authority (FSA),[22] and some hedge funds in the United States are registered with the Securities and Exchange Commission (SEC). The lack of regulation explains why hedge funds are not transparent to outsiders or proactive in communicating their strategies and reporting their returns. In response to the calls for oversight, the European Union (EU) has adopted the Directive on Alternative Investment Fund Managers (AIFM Directive), which must be implemented by mid-2013 by EU members.

Offshore jurisdictions (for example, the Cayman Islands) are often the locale for registering funds, whether managed in the United States, Europe, or Asia. However, some hedge funds choose to register domestically. The choice to register, for example, in the United States or the United Kingdom, may be because of the added credibility of registering with the SEC or the FSA, respectively. Sometimes, onshore hedge funds set up complementary offshore funds to attract additional capital.

EXAMPLE 4

Effect of Redemption

A European credit hedge fund has a very short notice period of a week because the fund believes that it invests in highly liquid asset classes and is market neutral. The fund has a small number of holdings that represent a significant portion of the outstanding issue of each holding. The fund's lockup period has expired. Unfortunately, in one particular month, because of the downgrades of two large holdings, the hedge fund has a drawdown (decline in NAV) of over 5 percent. The declines in value of the two holdings result in margin calls from their prime broker, and the drawdown results in requests to redeem 50 percent of total partnership interests. The combined requests are *most likely* to:

A   force the hedge fund to liquidate or unwind 50 percent of its positions in an orderly fashion throughout the week.

B   have little impact on the prices received when liquidating the positions because it has a week before the partnership interests are redeemed.

C   result in a forced liquidation, which will drive prices down further and result in a bigger drawdown, so that the remaining investors will redeem their partnership interests leading to fund liquidation and closure.

---

22 A new regulatory authority is expected to succeed the FSA in the United Kingdom as of 2012.

Solution:

C is correct. One week may not be enough time to unwind the fund's positions in an orderly fashion so that the unwinding does not further drive down prices. A downgrading is not likely to have a temporary effect, so even if other non-losing positions are liquidated to meet the redemption requests, it is unlikely that the two large holdings will return to previous or higher values. Also, the hedge fund may have a week to satisfy the requests for redemptions, but the margin call must be met immediately. Thus, it is most likely that a forced liquidation will drive down prices, resulting in further drawdowns and redemption requests so that ultimately the fund will liquidate and cease to exist.

3.4 Hedge Fund Valuation Issues

Valuations are important for calculating performance and meeting redemptions. The frequency with which and how hedge funds are valued varies among funds. Hedge funds are generally valued on a daily, weekly, monthly, and/or quarterly basis. The valuation may use market or estimated values of underlying positions. When market prices or quotes are used for valuation, funds may differ in which price or quote they use (for example, bid price, ask price, average quote, and median quote). A common practice is to use the average quote [(bid + ask)/2]. A more conservative and theoretically accurate approach is to use bid prices for longs and ask prices for shorts; these are the prices at which the positions could be closed.

The underlying positions may be in highly illiquid or non-traded investments and therefore, it is necessary to estimate values because there are no reliable market values. Estimated values may be computed using statistical models. Any model should be independently tested, benchmarked, and calibrated to industry-accepted standards to ensure a consistency of approach. Because of the potential for conflicts of interests affecting estimates of value, procedures for in-house valuations should be developed and adhered to.

Liquidity is an important issue for valuation, but becomes particularly so for strategies involving convertible bonds, collateralized debt obligations, distressed debt, and emerging markets fixed income securities, which may be relatively illiquid. If a quoted market price is available, the use of liquidity discounts or "haircuts" is actually inconsistent with valuation guidance under most generally accepted accounting standards. However, many practitioners believe that liquidity discounts are necessary to reflect fair value. This assumption has resulted in some funds having two NAVs—trading and reporting. The trading NAV incorporates liquidity discounts, based on the size of the position held relative to the total amount outstanding in the issue and its trading volume. The reporting NAV is based on quoted market prices.

EXAMPLE 5

Hedge Fund Valuation

A hedge fund with a market neutral strategy restricts its investment universe to domestic publicly traded equity securities that are actively traded. In calculating net asset value, the fund is most likely to use which of the following to value underlying positions?

A   Average quotes

B   Average quotes adjusted for liquidity

C   Bid price for shorts and ask price for longs

> **Solution:**
>
> A is correct. The fund is most likely to use average quotes. The securities are actively traded so no liquidity adjustment is required. If the fund uses bid/ask prices, the fund would use ask prices for shorts and bid prices for longs; these are the prices at which the positions could be closed.

3.5 Due Diligence for Investing in Hedge Funds

There are many issues to consider when investing in hedge funds. A basic question is whether one wants to rely upon the expertise of a manager of a fund of hedge funds to invest in a portfolio of hedge funds or whether one has the expertise to undertake the hedge fund investment selection process. Funds of hedge funds potentially offer the benefits of providing a diversified portfolio of hedge funds, supplying expertise in conducting due diligence, and negotiating favorable redemption terms. These potential benefits come at the cost of an additional layer of fees. Also, although a fund of hedge funds may provide expertise in due diligence, the investor should still conduct due diligence when choosing a fund of hedge funds.

Investors in hedge funds should consider many factors in their decision-making process. This section highlights some of the key due diligence points to consider, but does not provide an exhaustive list of factors to consider. Key factors to consider include investment strategy, investment process, competitive advantage, track record, size and longevity, management style, key-person risk, reputation, investor relations, plans for growth, and systems risk management.

Investment strategy and process are challenging to fully assess because hedge funds may limit disclosure in order to maintain their competitive advantage and to not give away information that is considered proprietary. However, it should be possible to identify in which markets the hedge fund invests, the general investment strategy (for example, long/short, relative arbitrage, etc.) and the basic process to implement this strategy, and the benchmark against which the fund gauges its performance.

Track record is a commonly viewed consideration because it should be readily available and is often assumed to be an indicator of future performance and risk (perhaps incorrectly, based on studies of performance persistence).[23] Investors should establish how the returns are calculated (e.g., based on estimates of value or market prices) and reported (e.g., before or after fees) and how the returns and risks compare with some benchmark. The investor should inquire about the fee structure because this information will have an impact, as demonstrated earlier, on the return to the investor.

Size and longevity are also common items for review.[24] The older a fund, the more likely it has not caused significant losses to its investors (otherwise, it is likely to have experienced redemptions, been unable raise further capital, and been liquidated). As a result, older funds are likely to have experienced growth in assets under management through both capital appreciation and additional investments (capital injections). Many investors require hedge funds to have a minimum track record of two years before they will invest. This requirement makes it particularly difficult for start-up funds to raise money as their managers need capital to invest before they can build a track record. In many cases, start-up funds receive money from seed investors who want a share of the business for their investment.

---

[23] For a discussion on the record of institutional investors' record at selecting managers, see Stewart, Heisler, Knittel, and Neumann, 2009.

[24] For a discussion of quantitative factors investors use to select investment managers, see Heisler, Knittel, Neumann, and Stewart, 2007.

A hedge fund's size is an important consideration for investors because many investors set a minimum size on their investments and restrict the percentage of a fund's overall assets under management that their investment can represent. For example, if an investor's minimum investment size is $10 million and the investor's maximum percentage of a fund is 10 percent, the minimum hedge fund size the investor can consider is $100 million (= $10 million/0.1).

The hedge fund due diligence process also focuses on many qualitative factors. These include management style, key person risk, reputation, investor relations, and plans for growth. A thorough due diligence process will also include a review of management procedures, including leverage, brokerage, and diversification policies. The use of leverage and counterparty risk can significantly affect a fund's risk and performance. In addition to gathering information about the fund's prime broker and custody arrangements for securities, the investor should identify the auditor of the hedge fund and ensure that the auditor is independent and known for conducting competent audits.

Systems risk management is an important consideration for reviewing a hedge fund. Relevant risk management questions to ask are varied and related to the type of securities in which the hedge fund invests. Ultimately, the answers should provide comfort to investors that the risk management of the fund is performed in a rigorous fashion. In many cases, particularly with smaller funds or those that invest in more unusual or illiquid assets, the answers to these questions may indicate that the systems and processes are simplistic or that the answers may be very complex. Commonly, hedge funds believe that their strategies, systems, and processes are proprietary and are not willing to provide too much information to potential investors. This reluctance means that conducting due diligence can be very challenging. Regulation of hedge funds is likely to increase in the future, which may help with the due diligence process.

EXAMPLE 6

Due Diligence

HF Alpha and HF Beta invest in the same asset class using a similar investment strategy. A potential investor has gathered the following data from the hedge funds:

Characteristic	HF Alpha	HF Beta
Annualized returns	15%	10%
Sharpe Ratio	1.3	1.6
Size (US$ millions)	200	500
Fees	1.5 and 15	2 and 20
Track Record	2 years	5 years

Based on the above information, the investor is *most likely* to:

A   invest in HF Beta because of its higher Sharpe ratio.

B   question how the annualized returns are calculated.

C   invest in HF Alpha because of its higher returns and lower fees.

Solution:

B is correct. It is important to know how returns are calculated and if they are comparable before making any decision. If the returns are both reported net-of-fees, the higher fees on HF Beta may account for most of the difference in returns.

PRIVATE EQUITY

Private equity generally means investing in privately owned companies or in public companies with the intent to take them private. There are different stages and types of private equity investing. The focus of private equity firms may change through time as business conditions and the availability of financing change. A possible categorization of private equity identifies leveraged buyouts, venture capital, development capital, and distressed investing as primary private equity strategies.

Leveraged buyouts (LBOs) or highly leveraged transactions refer to private equity firms establishing buyout funds (or LBO funds) that acquire public companies or established private companies with a significant percentage of the purchase price financed through debt. The assets of the target company typically serve as the collateral for the debt, and the cash flows of the target company are expected to be sufficient to service the debt. The debt becomes part of the capital structure of the target company if the buyout goes through. The target company after the buyout becomes or remains a privately owned company.

Venture capital entails investing in or providing financing to private companies with high growth potential. Typically, these are start-up or young companies, but venture capital can be provided at a variety of stages.

Development capital generally refers to minority equity investments in more mature companies that are looking for capital to expand or restructure operations, enter new markets, or finance major acquisitions.

Distressed investing typically entails buying the debt of mature companies in financial difficulties. These companies may be in bankruptcy proceedings, have defaulted on debt, or seem likely to default on debt. Some investors attempt to identify companies with a temporary cash flow problem but a good business plan that will help the company survive and in the end flourish. These investors buy the company's debt in expectation of the company and its debt increasing in value. Turnaround investors buy debt and plan to be more active in the management and direction of the company. They seek distressed companies to restructure and revive.

The level of activity in private equity is cyclical. The cyclicality is shown visually over a relatively short period in Exhibit 9. It should be noted that detailed information on private equity activity is not always readily available.

Exhibit 9　Private Equity Funds Raised, 1998–2008

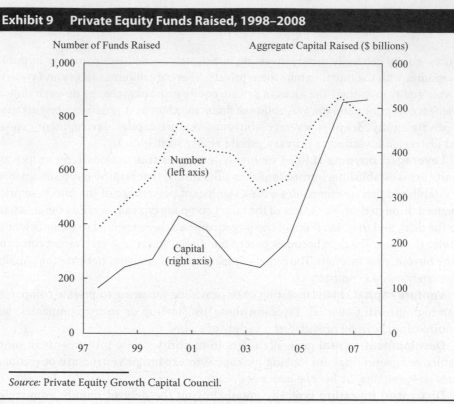

Number of Funds Raised　　　　　　　　　Aggregate Capital Raised ($ billions)

Source: Private Equity Growth Capital Council.

4.1 Private Equity Structure and Fees

Like hedge funds, private equity funds are typically structured as partnerships where outside investors are Limited Partners (LPs) and the private equity firm, which may manage a number of funds, is the General Partner (GP). Most private equity firms charge both a management fee and an incentive fee on a fund basis. The management fees generally range from 1 to 3 percent of **committed capital**. Committed capital is the amount that the LPs have agreed to provide to the private equity fund. Private equity funds raise committed capital, and draw down on those commitments over 3 to 5 years when they have a specific investment to make. Until the committed capital is fully drawn down and invested, the management fee is based on committed capital, *not* invested capital. The committed capital basis for management fees is an important distinction from hedge funds where management fees are based on assets under management. After the committed capital is fully invested, the fees are paid only on the funds remaining in the investment vehicle; as investments are exited, capital is paid back to the investors, and they no longer pay fees on that portion of their investment.

For most private equity funds, the GP does not earn an incentive fee until the LPs have received their initial investment back. The GP typically receives 20 percent of the total profit of the private equity fund as an incentive or profit sharing fee.[25] The LPs receive 80 percent of the total profit of the equity fund plus the return of their initial investment. If distributions are made based on profits earned over time rather than at exit from investments of the fund, the distributions may result in receipts by the GP of more than 20 percent of the total profit. Most private equity partnership agreements include policies that protect the LPs from this contingency. These policies include prohibiting distributions of incentive fees to the GP until the LPs have

---

25 The incentive fee may also be calculated on a deal-by-deal basis.

received back their invested capital, setting up an escrow account for a portion of the incentive fees, and incorporating a **clawback** provision that requires the GP to return any funds distributed as incentive fees until the LPs have received back their initial investment and 80 percent of the total profit.

In addition to management and incentive (profit sharing) fees, LBO firms may receive other fees. These include a fee for arranging the buyout of a company based upon the selling (buyout) price of the company, a fee if a deal falls through, and a fee for arranging for divestitures of assets after the buyout is complete.

4.2 Private Equity Strategies

There are many private equity strategies. A common categorization, as indicated earlier, identifies leveraged buyouts, venture capital, development capital, and distressed investing as the primary strategies. However, leveraged buyouts and venture capital are the dominant strategies.

4.2.1 *Leveraged Buyouts*

LBOs are sometimes referred to as "going private" transactions because, after the acquisition of a publicly traded company, the target company's equity is generally no longer publicly traded. When the target company is an established private company, it is not a "going private" transaction. The LBO may also be of a specific type. In MBOs (**management buyouts**), the current management team is involved in the acquisition, and in MBIs (**management buy-ins**), the current management team is being replaced and the acquiring team will be involved in managing the company. LBO managers seek to add value—from improving company operations and growing revenue and ultimately increasing profits and cash flows. The sources of growth in earnings before interest, taxes, depreciation, and amortization (EBITDA), in order of contribution to growth, include organic revenue growth, cost reduction/restructuring, acquisition, and other.[26] However, the potential returns in this category are to a large extent due to the use of leverage. If debt financing is unavailable or costly, LBOs are less likely to occur.

4.2.1.1 LBO Financing   Debt is central to the structure and feasibility of buyouts in private equity. Target companies are rarely purchased using only the equity of the buyout company. In order to potentially increase equity returns and increase the number of transactions a particular fund can make, private equity firms use debt to finance a significant proportion of each deal (in other words, they use leverage). For example, in a buyout deal, a private equity firm may invest equity representing 30 percent of the purchase price and raise the rest of the purchase price in the debt markets. They may use a combination of bank loans, often called leveraged loans because of the amount of the capital structure of the company they represent, and high yield bonds.

Leveraged loans often carry covenants intended to protect the investors. The covenants may require or restrict certain actions. The covenants may require the company to maintain specified financial ratios within certain limits, submit information so that the bank can monitor performance, or operate within certain parameters. The covenants may restrict the company from further borrowing (in other words, no additional bonds can be issued and no additional funds can be borrowed from banks or other sources), or impose limits on paying dividends or making operating decisions. Similarly, bond terms may include covenants intended to protect the bondholders. However, one of the key differences between leveraged loans and the bonds is that leveraged loans are generally senior secured debt and the bonds are unsecured in the case of bankruptcy.

---

26 Source: Private Equity Growth Council.

Therefore, even given covenants, because of the amount of leverage employed, the bonds issued to finance an LBO are usually high yield bonds that receive low quality ratings and must offer high coupons to attract investors.

A typical LBO capital structure includes equity, bank debt (leveraged loans), and high yield bonds. Leveraged loans often provide a larger amount of capital than either equity or high yield bonds. As an alternative to high yield bonds, **mezzanine financing** may also be used.[27] Mezzanine financing refers to debt or preferred shares with a relationship to common equity due to a feature such as attached warrants or conversion options. Being subordinate to both senior and high yield debt, mezzanine financing typically pays a higher coupon rate. In addition to interest or dividends, this type of financing offers a potential return based on increases in the value of common equity.

The variety of available financing choices provides flexibility for a target company to match its repayment schedules with expected inflows and permits higher levels of leverage compared with traditional bank debt. The optimal capital structure takes into account a variety of factors, including the company's projected cash flows, investor willingness to purchase different types of debt and accept different levels of leverage, the availability of equity, and the required rates of return for equity and different types of debt considering leverage. The optimal capital structure will be different for every deal.

4.2.1.2 Characteristics of Attractive Target Companies for LBOs

Private equity firms invest in companies across many sectors, although an individual private equity firm may specialize in a certain sector or sectors. Whatever the targeted sector(s), there are several characteristics, any one of which may make a company particularly attractive as an LBO target. The characteristics include:

- Undervalued/depressed stock price: The intrinsic value of the company is perceived by the private equity firm to exceed its market price. Private equity firms are therefore willing to pay a premium to the market price to secure shareholder approval. Firms try to buy assets/companies cheaply, and may focus on companies that are out of favor in the public markets and have stock prices that reflect this perception.

- Willing management: Existing management is looking for a deal. Management may have identified opportunities but do not have access to the resources to make substantial investments in new processes, personnel, equipment, etc. to drive long-term growth. Also, private equity may provide management with the time and capital to turn a company around.

- Inefficient companies: Private equity firms seek to generate attractive returns on equity by creating value in the companies they buy. They achieve this goal by identifying companies that are inefficiently managed and that have the potential to perform well if managed better.

- Strong and sustainable cash flow: Companies that generate strong cash flow are attractive because in an LBO transaction, the target company will be taking on a significant portion of debt. Cash flow is necessary to make interest payments on the increased debt load.

---

[27] This type of loan is referred to as *mezzanine financing* because of its location on the balance sheet and is a *type* of financing.

- Low leverage: Private equity firms focus on target companies that do not currently have a significant portion of debt on their balance sheets. This characteristic makes it easier to utilize debt to finance a large portion of the purchase price.

- Assets: Private equity managers like companies that have a significant amount of physical assets. These physical assets can be used as security, and secured debt is cheaper than unsecured debt.

4.2.2 *Venture Capital*

Venture capital (VC) is often categorized by the stage at which the venture capital is provided to the company of interest. The company that is being invested in is often called the **portfolio company** because it will become part of the portfolio of the VC fund. The stages range from inception of an idea for a company to the point when the company is about to make an initial public offering (IPO) or be acquired—most typically, by a strategic buyer. The investment return required varies based on the stage of development of the company. Investors in early stage companies will demand higher expected returns relative to later stage investors. The ultimate returns realized depend on the portfolio company's success in transitioning from a start-up to a going and growing concern.

Venture capitalists are not passive investors. They are actively involved with the companies in which they invest. The VC fund typically gets an equity interest in the company in which it is investing. The VC fund may also provide some debt financing.

1   Formative-stage financing occurs when the company is still in the process of being formed and encompasses several financing steps, which are described as follows:

   a   Angel investing is capital provided at the idea stage. Funds may be used to transform the idea into a business plan and to assess market potential. The amount of financing at this stage is typically small and provided by individuals (often friends and family) rather than by VC funds.

   b   Seed-stage financing or seed capital generally supports product development and/or marketing efforts, including market research. This point is generally the first stage at which VC funds invest.

   c   Early stage financing (early stage venture capital) is provided to companies moving toward operation but before commercial production and sales have occurred. Early stage financing may be provided to initiate commercial production and sales.

2   Later-stage financing (expansion venture capital) is provided after commercial production and sales have begun but before any IPO. Funds may be used for initial expansion of a company already producing and selling a product or for major expansion, such as physical plant expansion, product improvement, or a major marketing campaign.

3   Mezzanine-stage financing[28] (mezzanine venture capital) is provided to prepare to go public and represents the bridge between the expanding company and the IPO.

Formative-stage financing generally is done via ordinary or convertible preferred share transfers to the investor (VC fund), and management retains control of the company. Later-stage financing generally involves management selling control of the

---

28 The term, "mezzanine-stage financing" is used because this financing is provided at the stage between being a private and public company. The focus is on *when* the financing occurs.

company to the venture capital investor; financing is provided through equity and debt (the fund may also use convertible bonds or convertible preferred shares). The debt financing is not intended for income generation to the VC fund but rather, it is for the recovery and control of assets in a bankruptcy situation. Simply put, it provides more protection to the VC fund than equity.

In order to make an investment, a venture capitalist needs to be convinced that the management team of the portfolio company is competent and that there is a solid business plan with strong prospects for growth and development. Because these investments are not in mature businesses with years of operational and financial performance history, the complexity involved with venture capital involves accurately estimating company valuation based on future prospects. This estimation is more of an unknown than in LBO investing, which targets mature, underperforming public companies. As the portfolio company matures and moves into later-stage financing, there is more certainty around valuation but less so than with an LBO investment.

4.2.3 Other Private Equity Strategies

There are several other specialties for private equity firms. These specialties include development capital, also called minority equity investing, which earns profits from funding business growth or restructuring. Many times, minority equity investing is initiated and sought by management, who are interested in realizing earnings from selling a portion of their shares before they are able to go public. Although this scenario occurs most commonly with private companies, publicly quoted companies sometimes seek private equity capital, in opportunities called PIPEs (private investment in public equities).

Distressed investing by a private equity firm typically involves purchasing the debt of troubled companies (companies that are bankrupt, in default, or likely to default). The distressed debt often trades at prices significantly less than the face value of the debt. If the company can be turned around, the debt may recover its value. The return on investment is a function of the ability of the turnaround investor to restructure the company either operationally or financially. Distressed debt investors may be involved in the turnaround and may assume an active role in the management and direction of the company or in the reorganization of the company. Some distressed investors are passive investors who simply try to identify companies that they expect to increase in value; debt holders will benefit from the increase before equity holders. Distressed debt investors are sometimes referred to as vulture investors.

Other private equity strategies exist. These strategies may involve the provision of specific financing (for example, mezzanine funds) or investing in companies in specific industries. As the financial environment changes and evolves, additional strategies may emerge.

4.2.4 Exit Strategies

The ultimate goal for private equity is to improve new or underperforming businesses and exit them at high valuations. Private equity firms buy and hold companies for an average of five years. However, the time to exit can range from less than six months to over 10 years. Before deciding on an exit strategy, private equity managers take into account the dynamics of the industry in which the portfolio company competes, overall economic cycles, interest rates, and company performance.

Below are common exit strategies pursued by private equity portfolio managers:

■ Trade sale: This strategy refers to the sale of a company to a strategic buyer such as a competitor. A trade sale can be conducted through an auction process or by private negotiation. Benefits of a trade sale include (a) an immediate cash exit for the private equity fund; (b) potential for high valuation of the asset because strategic buyers may be willing and able to pay more than other potential buyers because of anticipated synergies; (c) fast and simple execution; (d) lower transaction costs than an IPO; and (e) lower levels of disclosure and higher confidentiality because the private equity firm is generally only dealing with one other party. Disadvantages of trade sales include (a) possible opposition by management; (b) lower attractiveness to employees of the portfolio company; (c) a limited number of potential trade buyers; and (d) a possible lower price than in an IPO.

- IPO: This approach involves the portfolio company selling its shares, including some or all of those held by the private equity firm, to public investors through an IPO. Advantages for an IPO exit include (a) potential for the highest price; (b) management approval since they are retained; (c) publicity for the private equity firm; and (d) potential ability to retain future upside potential as the private equity firm may choose to remain a large shareholder. Disadvantages for an IPO exit include (a) high transaction costs paid to investment banks and lawyers; (b) long lead times; (c) risk of stock market volatility; (d) high disclosure requirements; (e) potential lock-up period, which requires the private equity firm to retain an equity position for a specified period after the IPO; and (f) the fact that an IPO is usually only appropriate for larger companies with attractive growth profiles.

- Recapitalization: A recapitalization is not a true exit strategy as the private equity firm typically maintains control; however, it does allow the private equity investor to extract money from the company. Recapitalization is a very popular strategy when interest rates are low as the private equity firm re-leverages or introduces leverage to the company and pays itself a dividend. A recapitalization is often a prelude to a later exit.

- Secondary Sales: This approach represents a sale to another private equity firm or other group of investors.

- Write-off/Liquidation: A write-off occurs when a transaction has not gone well, and the private equity firm is updating its value of the investment or liquidating the portfolio company to move on to other projects.

The above exit strategies may be pursued individually, combined together, or used for a partial exit strategy. For example, it is not unusual to see a private equity fund sell a portion of a portfolio company to a competitor via a trade sale and then complete a secondary sale to another private equity firm for the remaining portion.

4.3 Private Equity: Diversification Benefits, Performance, and Risk

Private equity funds may provide higher return opportunities relative to traditional investments through their ability to invest in private companies, their influence on portfolio companies' management and operations, and/or their use of leverage. Investments in private equity funds can add diversity to a portfolio comprised of publicly traded stocks and bonds because they may have less than perfect correlation with those investments.

Exhibit 10 shows the mean annual returns for the Thomson Reuters US Private Equity Performance Index (PEPI) and the NASDAQ and S&P 500 indices for a variety of periods ending 31 March 2010. Over the 3-, 5-, 10-, and 20-year periods ending 31 March 2010, US private equity funds, based on the PEPI, on average outperformed stocks based on the NASDAQ and S&P 500 indices. The returns to the PEPI were less than the returns to the NASDAQ and S&P 500 indices for the 1-year period ending 31 March 2010.

Exhibit 10	Comparison of Annual Returns with US Private Equity and US Stocks				
	1 year	**3 years**	**5 years**	**10 years**	**20 years**
All private equity	21.9	0.6	5.8	2.8	11.3
NASDAQ	51.5	−0.3	3.6	−6.2	9.1
S&P 500	42.3	−6.1	−0.2	−2.4	6.5

Note: All periods end 31 March 2010.
Source: Thomson Reuters' 10 August 2010 Press Release, "US Private Equity Short-Term Performance Turns Sharply Positive."

However, the PEPI may not be a reliable measure of performance because of challenges in measuring the historical performance of private equity investing. As with hedge funds, private equity return indices rely on self-reporting and are subject to survivorship, backfill, and other biases. These characteristics typically lead to overstatement of published returns. Moreover, in the absence of a liquidity event, private equity firms may not regularly mark to market their investments. This failure to mark to market leads to understatement of measures of volatility and correlations with other investments. Thus, data adjustments are required to more reliably measure the benefits of private equity investing.

Exhibit 11 lists annualized standard deviations of published quarterly and annual returns of private equity investments for the period of 1981 to 2009. The volatility based on published quarterly returns reflects few liquidity events and results in much lower volatility estimates than using annual returns. Note that the difference between the two measures (quarterly and annual) using MSCI World is insignificant because the stocks in the index are marked to market on a regular basis. In July 2009, private equity firms began reporting investments at their estimated fair values; these estimates are frequently based on market multiples. This change in valuation methodology is reflected in the new International Private Equity and Venture Capital Valuation Guidelines.

Exhibit 11	Annualized Standard Deviations of Returns to Private Equity Investments, 1981–2009	
	Quarterly	**Annual**
Venture capital*	23.0	40.4
Private equity*	15.6	25.9
MSCI World	19.0	19.8

*Thomson Venture Economics, June 1981 to June 2009

According to the historical, standard deviations of annual returns shown in Exhibit 11, private equity investments, including venture capital, are riskier than investing in common stocks. Investors should require a higher return from accepting a higher risk, including illiquidity and leverage risks.

Recognizing its higher risk, private equity, including venture capital investing, may provide benefits to a diversified portfolio. If investors believe they can identify skillful private equity fund managers (managers who can identify attractive portfolio companies and invest in them at reasonable valuations, as well as improve their operations and profitability), investors may benefit from superior returns (returns in excess of those expected given the additional leverage, market, and liquidity risks). Kaplan and Schoar (2005) find significant differences in the returns to the top quartile of funds compared with the bottom quartile of funds for the period; the cash flow internal rate of return (IRR) is 22 percent per year for the top quartile compared with 3 percent per year for the bottom quartile. Further, Kaplan and Schoar find evidence of performance persistence. Identifying top performing funds appears to be critical.

4.4 Portfolio Company Valuation

In order to identify and invest in attractive portfolio companies, private equity professionals must be able to value those companies. There are three common approaches used in the private equity industry to value a company: market or comparable, discounted cash flow (DCF), and asset-based.

A market or comparables approach values a company or its equity using multiples of different measures. For example, an earnings before interest, taxes, depreciation, and amortization (EBITDA) multiple is commonly used in valuing large, mature private companies. For other types of companies, multiples of measures based on net income or revenue may be more appropriate. The EBITDA multiple may be determined by looking at the market value of a similar publicly traded company or the price recently paid for a comparable business, divided by EBITDA. Net income and revenue multiples may be based on the multiples from transactions in comparable companies but are frequently based on heuristics.[29]

EXAMPLE 7

Portfolio Company Valuation

A private equity fund is considering purchasing a radio broadcaster that had an EBITDA of $200 million. In the past year, three radio broadcasting companies were sold for 8x EBITDA, 10x EBITDA, and 9x EBITDA. Based on this information, the maximum value the private equity fund is most likely to assign to the broadcaster is:

A $1,600 million.

B $1,800 million.

C $2,000 million.

Solution:

C is correct. The maximum value the private equity fund is most likely to assign is that using the highest multiple ($10 \times \$200$ million = $2,000 million). The minimum value the seller may be willing to accept is that using the lowest multiple. Of course, in negotiations, growth prospects, risk, size, current market conditions, etc. will be considered.

A discounted cash flow (DCF) approach values a company or its equity as the present value of the relevant expected future cash flows. Future free cash flow projections may be discounted to compute a present value of the portfolio company or its equity. Free cash flow to the firm and the weighted average cost of capital may be used to estimate the value of the company. Free cash flow to equity and the cost of equity may

---

29 Heuristics are mental shortcuts based on experience and knowledge that simplify decision making. They are sometimes called "rules of thumb."

be used to estimate the value of the company's equity. One simple approach takes a measure such as income or cash flow and divides it by a capitalization rate to arrive at an estimate of value. This is conceptually different but practically similar to using an income or cash-based multiple. If the value estimated using a DCF approach is higher than the current price of the investment, the opportunity may be an attractive one.

An asset-based approach values a company based on the values of its underlying assets less the value of any related liabilities. In effect, this approach arrives at the value of the company to the equity holders. This approach assumes that the value of a company is equal to the sum of the values of a company's assets minus its liabilities. The valuations can be arrived at using market (fair) values or other values such as liquidation values. Fair values assume an orderly transaction, whereas liquidation values assume a distressed transaction. The liquidation value is an estimate of how much money could be raised if a company's assets were sold in a liquidation scenario. Liquidation value is the net amount that will be realized if the business is terminated, the assets are sold, and the liabilities are satisfied. In a weak economic environment, liquidation values will most likely be far lower than the immediately previous fair values because there will tend to be many assets for sale and fewer potential buyers.

4.5 Private Equity: Investment Considerations and Due Diligence

Current and anticipated economic conditions, including interest rate and capital availability expectations, are critical factors to consider when evaluating an investment in private equity. Refinancing risk must also be evaluated. If refinancing becomes unavailable, a lack of financing can result in default. The extent to which there is undrawn but committed capital can also affect the private equity sector and the returns to investors.

Investing in private equity firms requires patience. Investors who are comfortable with long-term commitment of funds and illiquidity are best suited to considering private equity investing. Private equity typically requires a long-term commitment on the part of an LP because of the long time lag between investments in and exits from portfolio companies. Once a commitment has been made and an investor becomes an LP, the investor has very limited liquidity options. As many investors are averse to illiquidity, there should be a liquidity risk premium for private equity investors.

Assuming these characteristics are acceptable, the investor must consider the choice of GP. In this regard, many of the due diligence questions for hedge fund selection are relevant to private equity. Some of the important issues to investigate are the GP's experience and knowledge—financial and operating, the valuation methodology used, the alignment of the GP's incentives with the interests of the LPs, the plan to draw on committed capital, and the planned exit strategies.

REAL ESTATE

Real estate investing is often thought of as direct or indirect ownership (equity investing) in real estate property such as land and buildings. However, real estate investing also includes lending (debt investing) against real estate property (for example, providing a mortgage loan or purchasing mortgage-backed securities). The property generally serves as collateral for the lending.

Key reasons for investing in real estate include the following:

■ Potential for competitive long-term total returns driven by both income generation and capital appreciation.

- Prospect that multiple-year leases with fixed rents for some property types may lessen cash flow impact from economic shocks.

- Likelihood that diversification benefits may be provided by less than perfect correlation with other asset classes.

- Potential to provide an inflation hedge if rents can be adjusted quickly for inflation.

Real estate property ownership is represented by a title and may reflect access to air rights, mineral rights, and surface rights in addition to the rights of use of buildings and land. Titles can be purchased, leased, sold, mortgaged, or transferred together or separately, in whole or in part. Real estate investments may also be in the form of partnerships, equity, or debt. Much real estate is residential, but if it is owned with the intention to let, lease, or rent it in order to generate income, it is classified as commercial (i.e., income producing) real estate. In addition to residential real estate classified as commercial, commercial real estate includes other types of real estate properties such as office and retail properties. Some real estate properties may be farmed, provide forest products, or have natural resources that can be obtained by extraction to generate income; the resulting products, such as wheat, timber, gold, and oil, are considered commodities. As a result, some investors include timberland and farmland in their commodities portfolio rather than in their real estate portfolio. Other investors simply treat farmland and timberland as a separate category.

Institutional ownership of commercial property totaled over $2 trillion as of 2008, as shown in Exhibit 12.

Exhibit 12	Institutionally Owned Global Real Estate Property Assets Under Management (US$ millions)
Europe	1,135,881
North America	710,994
Australasia	143,280
Asia	94,440
Latin America	10,075
Middle East	190
Africa	164
Total	**2,095,024**

Source: Based on data from Property Funds Research, 2008.

Real estate property exhibits unique features compared with other investment asset classes. The basic indivisibility, unique characteristics (i.e., no two properties are identical), and the fixed location of real estate property has implications for investors. For example, the size of investment may have to be large and may be relatively illiquid. Also, real estate property typically requires operational management. Real estate may be subject to government regulations affecting what can be done to modify the existing land or property, to whom and how ownership can be transferred, and to other restrictions on ownership. Local or regional markets and real estate property values can be independent of country-wide or global price movements as local factors may override wider market trends. Cross-border investment in real estate is increasingly common and requires knowledge of country, regional, and local markets.

5.1 Forms of Real Estate Investment

Real estate investing may take a variety of forms. Real estate investments may be classified along two dimensions: debt or equity based, and in private or public markets. Equity investments in real estate that occur in the private markets are often referred to as direct investments in real estate. The money to finance real estate property purchases comes from many sources. A well known form of debt financing of real estate purchases is mortgages. Private investors—institutional and individual, real estate corporations, and real estate investment trusts (REITs)—may provide the equity financing for the purchase.

REITs sell shares to raise funds to make property purchases. The shares of REITs are typically publicly traded and represent an indirect investment in real estate property. Similarly, mortgages may be packaged and securitized into asset-backed securitized debt obligations (mortgage-backed securities) that represent rights to receive cash flows from portfolios of mortgage loans. Exhibit 13 shows some examples of the basic forms of real estate investments.

Exhibit 13	Basic Forms of Real Estate Investments and Examples	
	Debt	**Equity**
Private	▪ Mortgages ▪ Construction lending	▪ Direct ownership of real estate. Ownership can be through, sole ownership, joint ventures, real estate limited partnerships, or other commingled funds.
Public	▪ Mortgage-backed securities (residential and commercial) ▪ Collateralized mortgage obligations	▪ Shares in real estate corporations ▪ Shares of real estate investment trusts

Within the basic forms, there can be many variations.

- Direct ownership can be free and clear, where the title to the property is transferred to the owner unencumbered by any financing lien, such as from a mortgage. Initial purchase costs associated with direct ownership may include legal expenses, survey costs, engineering/environmental studies, and valuation (appraisal) fees. Of course, ongoing maintenance and refurbishment charges are also incurred. The property must be managed, which has related costs. The owner may manage the property or may employ a local managing agent.

- Leveraged ownership occurs where the property title is obtained through an equity purchase combined with mortgage financing. In addition to the initial purchase costs above, there are mortgage arrangement fees. A mortgage is secured by the property and in the event of a breach of lending terms, the creditor can petition for the title. Any appreciation (depreciation) of the value of the property plus the net operating income in excess of the debt servicing costs provides investors with a leveraged gain (loss) on their equity.

- Financing provided to leveraged owners is frequently in the form of stand-alone mortgage loans. These loans represent passive investments where the lender expects to receive a predefined stream of payments over the finite life of the mortgage. The loan may become a form of property ownership if the borrower defaults. Investments may be in the form of "whole" loans based on specific properties (typically, direct investment through private markets) or through participation in a pool of mortgage loans (typically, indirect investment in real estate through publicly traded securities such as mortgage-backed securities).

■ Real estate equity investors may utilize different types of pooled vehicles arranged by an intermediary. These vehicles include the following:

● Real estate limited partnerships offer exposure to real estate projects while preserving limited liability (to the amount of the initial investment) and leaving management and liability to general partners who specialize in real estate management.

● REITs issue shares that are typically publicly traded. REITs invest in various types of real estate and provide retail investors with access to a diversified real estate property portfolio and professional management. REITs are required to distribute most of their taxable income to their shareholders.

■ Securitization of residential and commercial mortgages provides retail and institutional investors with access to a diversified portfolio of mortgages and allows the original lenders to alter their portfolio of investments. Mortgages are combined into pools and then into slices (called tranches) by investment banks. The tranches, each having different payment characteristics, are then sold to investors. These securities are generally not considered alternative investments but are held as part of the fixed income (or credit) portfolio.

REITs and partnerships have fees for managing the assets embedded in their valuations. Fee structures for investment funds can be similar to those in private equity, with investment management fees based on committed capital or invested capital. These fees typically range from 1 to 2 percent of capital per annum. Funds also charge performance-based fees, similar to a private equity fund.

5.2 Real Estate Investment Categories

The majority of real estate property may be classified as either commercial or residential. In this reading, residential properties are defined narrowly to include only owner-occupied, single residences (often referred to as single-family residential property). Residential properties owned with the intention to let, lease, or rent them are classified as commercial. Commercial properties also include office, retail, industrial and warehouse, and hospitality (e.g., hotels and motels) properties. Commercial properties may also have mixed uses. Commercial properties generate returns from income (e.g., rent) and capital appreciation. Opportunities for capital appreciation will be affected by several factors, including development strategies, market conditions, and property-specific features.

5.2.1 *Residential Property*

For many individuals and families, real estate investment takes the form of direct equity investment (i.e., ownership) in a residence with the intent to occupy.[30] In other words, a home is purchased. Given the price of homes, most purchasers cannot provide the entire financing (i.e., pay cash) and must borrow funds to make the purchase. Any appreciation (depreciation) in the value of the home increases (decreases) the owner's equity in the home.

Financial institutions are the main providers (originators) of debt financing (typically, through mortgages) for home ownership. The originators of single-family residential mortgages are making a direct, debt investment in the home. Before offering

---

30 Residential properties (single or multi-family) are considered commercial property if they are maintained as rental properties.

a mortgage, the due diligence process should include ensuring that the borrower is making an appropriate equity investment in the home (in other words, paying an adequate proportion of the purchase price), conducting a credit review of the borrower, establishing that the borrower has sufficient cash flows to make the required payments on the mortgage and to maintain the home, appraising (estimating the value of) the home, and ensuring that adequate and appropriate insurance is in place on the home. Home loans may be held on the originator's balance sheet or securitized and offered to the financial markets. Securitization provides indirect, debt investment opportunities in residential property via securitized debt products, such as residential mortgage-backed securities (RMBS), to other investors.

5.2.2 *Commercial Real Estate*

Commercial property has traditionally been considered an appropriate direct investment—equity and debt—for institutional funds or high-net-worth individuals with long time horizons and limited liquidity needs. This perception of appropriateness for only certain types of investors was primarily because of the complexity of the investments, the large investments required, and the relative illiquidity of the investments. Direct, equity investing (i.e., ownership) is further complicated because commercial property requires active and experienced, professional management. The success of the equity investment is a function of a variety of factors, including how well the property is managed, general economic and specific real estate market conditions, and the extent of and terms of any debt financing.

In order to provide direct debt financing, the lender (investor) will conduct financial analyses to establish the creditworthiness of the borrower, to ensure that the property will generate cash flows sufficient to service the debt, to estimate the value of the property, and to evaluate economic conditions. The estimate of the value of the property is critical because the loan-to-value ratio is a critical factor in the lending decision. The borrower's equity in the property is an indicator of commitment to the success of the project and provides a cushion to the lender because the property is generally used as collateral for the loan.

Indirect investment vehicles provide individual investors with the opportunity to invest in real estate. For example, shares of REITs provide indirect, equity investment opportunities in real estate and commercial mortgage-backed securities (CMBS) provide indirect, debt investment opportunities in real estate.

5.2.3 *REIT Investing*

The risk and return characteristics of REITs depend on the type of investment they make. Mortgage REITs, which invest primarily in mortgages, are similar to fixed income investments. Equity REITs, which invest primarily in commercial or residential properties and employ leverage, are similar to direct equity investments in leveraged real estate.

Gross income from rents represents a relatively predictable income stream and, after servicing the debt, is a source of return to equity REITs. Although the regulations with respect to REITs vary among countries, in general, equity REITs have an obligation to distribute the majority of their income to shareholders to retain their regulatory tax-advantaged status. At least 90 percent of revenue (including rent and realized capital gains), net of expenses, must often be distributed in the form of dividends.

The business strategy for equity REITs is simple: maximize property occupancy rates and rents in order to maximize income and dividends. Equity REITs, like other public companies, must report earnings per share based on net income as defined by generally accepted accounting principles (GAAP).

5.2.4 *Mortgage-Backed Securities (MBS)*

The MBS structure is based on the securitization model of buying a pool of assets and assigning the income and principal returns into individual security tranches, as illustrated in Exhibit 14 for commercial mortgage-backed securities (CMBS). On the right hand side of the exhibit, the ranking of losses is indicative of the priority of claims against the real estate property. MBS may be issued privately or publicly. These securities are often included in broad fixed income indices and in indices that are used to indicate the performance of real estate investments.

Exhibit 14   CMBS Security Structure

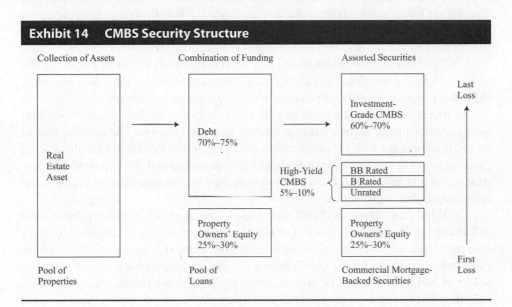

5.2.5 *Timberland and Farmland*

Timberland offers an income stream based on the sale of timber products as a component of total return and has historically provided a return that is not highly correlated with other asset classes. Timberland functions as both a factory and a warehouse. Timber can be grown and easily stored by not harvesting. This feature offers the flexibility of harvesting more trees when timber prices are up, and delaying harvests when prices are down. Timberland has three primary return drivers: biological growth, commodity price changes, and land price changes.

Farmland is often perceived to provide a hedge against inflation. Its returns include an income component related to harvest quantities and agricultural commodity prices. Farmland consists of two main property types: row crops that are planted and harvested annually (i.e., more than one planting and harvesting can occur in a year depending upon the crop and the climate) and permanent crops that grow on trees or vines. Unlike with timberland, there is little flexibility in harvesting, and farm products must be harvested when ripe. Farmland may also be used as pastureland for livestock. Similar to timberland, farmland has three primary return drivers: harvest quantities, commodity prices, and land price changes.

5.3 Real Estate Performance and Diversification Benefits

There are a variety of indices globally that are intended to measure returns to real estate. However, these indices vary in the selection and valuation of components and longevity. A real estate index can generally be categorized as an appraisal index, a repeat sales (transactions-based) index, or a REIT index. Appraisal indices use estimates of value (appraisals) as inputs to the indices. These appraisals, which are conducted by experts, rely on comparable sales and cash flow analysis techniques. Even though the appraisals are done by experts, they are still subjective. The appraisals are done periodically, often annually, but some appraised values included in an index may be from more than one year earlier. This factor, and the way appraisals are done, may result in indices that understate volatility.

Repeat sales indices use repeat sales of properties to construct the indices. The change in prices of properties with repeat sales are measured and used to construct the index. These indices suffer from a sample selection bias because the properties that sell in each period vary and may not be representative. Also, the properties that transact are not a random sample and may be biased towards those that have increased in value or decreased in value depending on current economic conditions. The higher the number of sales, the more reliable and relevant is the index.

REIT indices use the prices of publicly traded shares of REITs to construct the indices. The more frequently the shares trade, the more reliable is the index. However, the index is not necessarily representative of the properties of interest to the investor.

An investor will find a variety of indices to choose from and may find one that seems representative of the market of interest to them. However, the investor should be aware of how the index is constructed and the inherent limitations resulting from the construction method. Investors should also be aware that the apparent low correlation of real estate with other asset classes may be because of limitations in the real estate index construction.

A comparison of returns on US real estate based on different indices is provided in Exhibit 15. The National Council of Real Estate Investment Fiduciaries (NCREIF) constructs a variety of appraisal-based indices. The National Association of Real Estate Investment Trusts (NAREIT) constructs a variety of indices based on the prices of shares of REITs. The NAREIT returns based on REIT share prices are clearly more volatile—displaying higher standard deviations and a lower worst calendar year return—than the NCREIF returns based on appraisals. The NCREIF Farmland index shows the least reported volatility. The lowest annualized return shown is that of commercial property based on appraisals (NCREIF Property index).

Exhibit 15	Historical Returns of US Real Estate Indices, 1992–3Q2010			
	NCREIF Data			**NAREIT**
	Property*	**Timber**	**Farmland**	**All REITs**
Annualized return	7.6%	10.9%	10.9%	10.1%
Ann. standard deviation	8.2%	11.4%	7.6%	18.6%
Worst calendar year	−16.9%	−5.2%	2.0%	−37.3%

*Commercial real estate property

Global and regional REIT returns are displayed in Exhibit 16. The table shows the disparity among regional returns and demonstrates the importance of knowledge of country, local, and regional markets. However, a cursory examination indicates a significant degree of correlation among the regional returns.

| Exhibit 16 | Historical Returns of Global REITs | | | | | | | | | | | |

	Global Composite Return Components			North America Return Components			Asia Return Components			Europe Return Components		
Year	Total	Price	Income	Total	Price	Income	Total	Price	Income	Total	Price	Income
1998	−8.2	−12.5	4.4	−17.7	−22.7	5.0	−3.2	−6.9	3.7	5.0	1.5	3.5
1999	8.9	3.7	5.2	−4.4	−11.3	6.9	32.2	28.2	3.9	−3.2	−6.9	3.7
2000	13.2	7.9	5.3	31.2	22.7	8.6	1.2	−1.9	3.1	8.1	4.2	3.9
2001	−3.8	−7.9	4.0	10.0	4.1	5.9	−17.2	−19.6	2.3	−6.1	−9.4	3.3
2002	2.8	−2.4	5.2	2.4	−3.8	6.2	−7.2	−10.6	3.4	21.7	16.8	4.9
2003	40.7	33.5	7.2	37.7	29.7	8.1	44.8	38.5	6.4	44.7	38.7	6.0
2004	38.0	32.0	6.0	33.5	26.9	6.6	36.9	32.2	4.6	52.7	47.0	5.8
2005	15.4	10.7	4.7	13.2	8.1	5.1	23.4	18.6	4.7	9.4	6.0	3.4
2006	42.4	37.5	4.9	36.3	30.9	5.4	36.5	32.2	4.3	67.0	62.8	4.2
2007	−7.0	−10.0	3.0	−14.9	−18.3	3.3	14.8	11.7	3.1	−24.5	−26.6	2.1
2008	−55.0	−56.9	1.9	−51.0	−53.3	2.3	−58.1	−59.6	1.5	−56.0	−57.9	1.9

Note: Data are as of 3 December 2008.
Source: Based on data from NAREIT.

During 1990–2009, the correlations of global REITs (NAREIT Global composite) and global stocks (MSCI All Country World Index) and global REITs and global bonds (Barclays Capital Global Aggregate Bond Index) were 0.597 and 0.068, respectively. Correlations of global real estate and equity returns are relatively high, and correlation of global real estate and bond returns are relatively low. The returns from investing in REITs and investing in equities are more highly correlated with each other than with bonds because both are affected similarly by the business cycle.

5.4 Real Estate Valuation

Until a property is actually sold, real estate values need to be estimated. This process is often referred to as appraising the property. There are a variety of approaches used to value real estate property. Common techniques for appraising real estate property include comparable sales, income, and cost approaches.

- Comparable sales approach: This approach involves determining an approximate value based on recent sales of similar properties. Adjustments are made for differences in key characteristics of the property being appraised and the sold properties identified as similar. Key characteristics include condition, age, location, and size. Adjustments are also made for price changes in the relevant real estate market between dates of sales.

- Income approach: Direct capitalization and discounted cash flow approaches are two income-based approaches to appraisal of an income-producing property.

  The direct capitalization approach estimates the value of an income-producing property based upon the level and quality of its net operating income (NOI). NOI is similar to EBITDA and represents the income to the property after deducting operating expenses, including property taxes, insurance, maintenance, utilities, and repairs but before depreciation, financing costs, and income taxes. NOI is a proxy for property level operating cash flow. The expected annual NOI is divided by a capitalization rate (or cap rate) to estimate the value of the property. A cap rate is a discount rate less a growth rate. The reciprocal of the cap rate is a multiple that can be applied to NOI. The cap rate is estimated for a given property based on relevant information, including cap rates on sales of comparable properties, general business conditions, property quality, and assessment of management. The analysis might include assessing the strength of tenants, the level of landlord involvement, the extent and adequacy of repairs and improvements, the vacancy rate, management and operating costs, and expected inflation of costs and rent.

The discounted cash flow approach discounts future projected cash flows to arrive at a present value of the property. Typically, the analysis involves projections of annual operating cash flows for a finite number of periods and a resale or reversion value at the end of that total period. The projected resale value is often estimated using a direct capitalization approach.

■ Cost approach: This approach evaluates the replacement cost of the property by estimating the value of the land and the costs of rebuilding using current construction costs and standards. Costs include building materials, labor to build, tenant improvements, and various "soft" costs, including architectural and engineering costs, legal, insurance and brokerage fees, and environmental assessment costs. The cost of rebuilding is the replacement cost of the building(s) in new condition and is adjusted to take into account the location and condition of the existing building(s).

A combination and reconciliation of these approaches may be used to increase confidence in the appraisal.

5.4.1 REIT Valuations

REITs are composed of a portfolio of real estate properties or mortgages and as a result, a REIT security's valuation depends on the characteristics of the entire pool. There are two basic approaches to estimating the intrinsic value of a REIT: income-based and asset-based. The estimates of value can be compared with the observed market price of the REIT.

Income-based approaches for REITs are typically similar to the direct capitalization approach. A measure of income, which is a cash flow proxy, is capitalized into a value indication by using a cap rate (an alternative calculation could multiply the income measure by the reciprocal of the cap rate). Two common measures used are funds from operations (FFO) and adjusted funds from operations (AFFO). FFO, in its most basic form, equals net income plus depreciation charges on real estate property less gains from sales of real estate property plus losses on sales of real estate property. These adjustments to net income effectively exclude depreciation and the gains and losses from sales of real estate property from the FFO. Depreciation is excluded because it represents a non-cash charge and is often unrelated to changes in the value of the property. Gains and losses from sales are excluded because these are assumed to be non-recurring. AFFO adjusts the FFO for recurring capital expenditures. It is similar to a free cash flow measure.

The cap rate and its reciprocal multiple are estimated based on a variety of factors, including market cap rates and multiples of recent transactions, current market and economic conditions, expectations for growth in the relevant measure, risks associated with the REIT's underlying properties, and the financial leverage of the REIT.

Asset-based approaches calculate a REIT's NAV. Generally, a REIT's NAV is calculated as the estimated market value of a REIT's total assets minus the value of its total liabilities. REIT shares frequently trade at prices that differ from its NAV per share. Both premiums and discounts to the NAV are observed in the market.

5.5 Real Estate Investment Risks

Real estate investments, like any investment, may fail to perform in accordance with expectations. Property values are subject to variability based on national and global economic conditions, local real estate conditions, and interest rate levels. Other risks inherent to real estate investments include the ability of fund management to select, finance, and manage real properties, and changes in government regulations. Management of the underlying properties includes handling rentals or leasing of the property, controlling expenses, directing maintenance and improvements, and ultimately disposing of the property. Expenses may increase because of circumstances beyond the control of management. Returns to both debt and equity investors in real estate depend to a large extent on the ability of the owners or their agents to successfully operate the underlying properties.

Investments in distressed properties and property development are subject to greater risks than investments in properties with stable operations and/or sound financial condition. Property development is subject to special risks, including regulatory issues, construction delays, and cost overruns. Regulatory issues include the failure to receive zoning, occupancy and other approvals and permits, and the impact of environmental regulation. Economic conditions can also change over the development and disposition period, which can be very lengthy. Acquisitions and developments may be financed with lines of credit or other forms of temporary financing rather than long-term debt financing. There is a risk that long-term financing with acceptable terms might not be available when desired. Financing problems with one property may cause further activity by the same owner to be curtailed.

It is important to recognize that many equity investment real estate funds pursue leverage to potentially increase returns to their investors. Leverage magnifies the impact of gains and losses, because of operations and changes in property value, on the equity investors. Leverage increases the risk to equity investors and also increases the risk to debt investors. Leverage increases the risk that there will be insufficient funds to make expected interest payments and that principal will be not be recovered in its entirety. As the loan-to-value ratio increases, the latter risk increases.

COMMODITIES

Commodities are physical products. Returns on commodity investments are based on changes in price rather than on an income stream such as interest, dividends, or rent. In fact, holding commodities (i.e., the physical products) incurs costs for transportation and storage. Thus, most commodity investors do not trade actual physical commodities, but rather trade commodity derivatives. The underlying for a commodity derivative may be a single commodity or an index of commodities.

Trading in physical commodities is primarily limited to a smaller group of entities that are part of the physical supply chain. Some investors that are not part of the supply chain may invest in physical commodities, but the commodities are typically those that are non-perishable, of high value relative to weight and volume, and easily stored at relatively low cost. Most investors invest in commodities using commodity derivatives. However, because the prices of commodity derivatives are, to a significant extent, a function of the underlying commodity prices, it is important to understand the physical supply chain and general supply–demand dynamics of a commodity. The supply chain consists of entities that actually produce the commodities, users of the commodities, and participants in between. These entities may trade commodity derivatives for hedging purposes. Other investors, sometimes referred to as speculators, trade commodity derivatives in search of profit based largely on changes or expected changes in the price of the underlying commodities. Non-hedging investors include retail and institutional investors, hedge funds, proprietary desks within financial institutions, and trading desks operating within the physical supply chain.

Commodities include precious and base (i.e., industrial) metals, energy products, and agricultural products. Some examples of each type are shown in Exhibit 17. The relative importance, amount, and price of individual commodities evolve with society's preferences and needs. The increasing industrialization of China, India, and other emerging markets has driven strong global demand for commodities. Developing markets need increasing amounts of oil, steel, and other materials to support manufacturing, infrastructure development, and consumption demands of their populations. Emerging technologies, such as advanced cell phones and electric vehicles, may create demand for new materials to meet manufacturing needs. Thus, commodities of interest evolve over time.

Exhibit 17	Examples of Commodities
Sector	**Sample Commodities**
Energy	Oil, natural gas, electricity, coal
Base Metals	Copper, aluminum, zinc, lead, tin, nickel
Precious Metals	Gold, silver, platinum
Agriculture	Grains, livestock, coffee
Other	Carbon credits, freight, forest products

Commodities may be further classified based on a variety of factors, including physical location and grade or quality. For example, there are many grades and locations of oil. Similarly, there are many grades and locations of wheat. Commodity derivative contracts specify terms such as quantity, quality, maturity date, and delivery location.

Commodity derivatives may be attractive to investors not only for the potential profits but also because of the perceptions that commodities are effective hedges against inflation (i.e., commodity prices historically have been correlated with inflation) and that commodities are effective for portfolio diversification (i.e., commodity returns have historically low correlations with returns of other investments in the portfolio). Institutional investors, particularly endowments, foundations, and increasingly corporate and public pension funds and sovereign wealth funds are allocating more of their portfolios to investments in commodities and commodity derivatives. There were $354 billion of commodity investments under management in 2010, compared with less than $20 billion in 2001.[31]

6.1 Commodity Derivatives and Indices

The majority of commodities investing is implemented through derivatives, and commodity index futures are a popular derivative.[32] Commodity derivatives include futures, forwards, options, and swaps. These contracts may trade on exchanges (exchange-traded products, or ETPs) or over the counter (OTC). They are described as follows:

▪ Futures and forward contracts are obligations to buy or sell a specific amount of a given commodity at a fixed price, location, and date in the future. Futures contracts are ETPs, marked to market daily, and generally are not settled with

---

31 Barclays Capital, November 2010.
32 Stoll & Whaley (2009) report commodities indexing totaling $174 billion as of July 2009.

delivery and receipt of the physical commodity. Forward contracts trade OTC, and the expectation is that delivery and receipt of the physical commodity will occur. Counterparty risk is higher for forward contracts.

- Options contracts for commodities give their holders the right, but not the obligation, to buy or sell a specific amount of a given commodity at a specified price and delivery location on or before a specified date in the future. Options can be ETPs or OTC traded.

- Swaps contracts are agreements to exchange streams of cash flows between two parties based on future commodity or commodity index prices. One party typically makes fixed payments in exchange for payments that depend on a specified commodity or commodity index price.

Commodity indices typically use the price of futures contracts on the commodities included in them rather than the prices of the commodities themselves. As a result, the performance of a commodity index can be quite different from the performance of the underlying commodities. Commodity indices also vary in the commodities included in them and the weighting methods used. Thus, they vary in their exposures to specific commodities or commodity sectors.

6.2 Other Commodity Investment Vehicles

Commodity exposure can be achieved through other means than direct investment in commodities or commodity derivatives. Although commodity exposure is most commonly accessed via commodity derivatives, either directly or through an investment manager, alternative means are becoming increasingly popular. Alternative means of achieving commodity exposure include the following:

- Exchange traded funds (ETFs) may be suitable for investors who can only buy equity shares or seek the simplicity of trading them. ETFs may invest in commodities or futures of commodities (often, specializing in a particular sector) seeking to track the performance of the commodities. For example, the SPDR Gold Trust ETF (NYSE: GLD) attempts to track the price of gold and owned over $50 billion in gold bullion as of November 2010. There are also commodity index-linked ETFs. ETFs may use leverage. Like mutual funds or unit trusts, ETFs charge fees that are included in their expense ratios, although the ETF expense ratios are generally lower than those of most mutual funds.

- Common stock of companies exposed to a particular commodity, such as Royal Dutch Shell, which is exposed to oil, may be purchased. Investors may consider owning shares in a few commodity-exposed companies in order to have a small exposure to commodities. However, it is unclear that the performance of these stocks closely tracks the performance of the underlying commodity(ies).

- Managed futures funds are actively managed investment funds. Professional money managers invest in the futures market (and forwards market sometimes) on behalf of the funds. These funds historically focused on commodity futures, but today they may invest in other futures contracts as well. The funds may concentrate on specific commodity sectors or may be broadly diversified. They are similar to hedge funds in that each fund has a general partner, and fees typically follow a 2 and 20 structure. The funds may operate similarly to mutual funds with shares that are available to the general public, or they may operate like hedge funds and restrict sales to high net worth and institutional investors. The former may be appealing to retail investors because of the professional management, low minimum investment, and relatively high liquidity.

- Individual managed accounts are managed by chosen professional money managers with expertise in commodities and futures on behalf of high net worth individuals or institutional investors.

- Funds exist that specialize in specific commodity sectors. For example, private energy partnerships, like private equity funds, are a popular way for institutions to gain exposure to the energy sector. Management fees can range from 1 to 3 percent of committed capital with a lockup period of 10 years and extensions of 1- and 2-year periods. Publicly available energy mutual funds and unit trusts typically focus on the oil and gas sector. They may focus on upstream (drilling), midstream (refineries), or downstream (chemicals). Management fees for these funds are in line with those of other public equity managers and range from 0.4 to 1 percent.

6.3 Commodity Performance and Diversification Benefits

The arguments for investing in commodities include the potential for returns, portfolio diversification, and inflation protection. Investors may invest in commodities if they believe prices will increase in the short or intermediate terms. If commodity prices determine inflation index levels, then over time, on average, commodities should yield a zero real return. Commodity futures contracts may offer liquidity or other premiums, creating the opportunity for a real return different from zero.

The portfolio diversification argument is based on the observation that commodities historically have behaved differently during the business cycle from stocks and bonds. Panel A of Exhibit 18 shows the correlation between selected commodities, global equity, and global bond indices. Panel B shows returns, standard deviations, and Sharpe ratios for different investments. In the 20-year period of 1990–2009, commodities exhibited a low correlation with traditional assets; the correlations of commodities with global stocks and global bonds were 0.160 and 0.133, respectively. The correlations of stocks, bonds, and commodities are expected to be positive because each of the assets has some exposure to the global business cycle. Note that the selected commodity index (S&P GSCI Commodity Index) is heavily weighted toward the energy sector and that each commodity may exhibit unique behavior.

Exhibit 18	Commodities Return Correlations and Volatility

Panel A: Monthly Return Correlations, 1990–2009

	Global Stocks	Global Bonds	Commodities	1-mo. Libor	US CPI
Global stocks	1.000	0.274	0.160	−0.057	−0.016
Global bonds		1.000	0.133	−0.020	−0.054
Commodities			1.000	0.025	0.336
1-mo. Libor				1.000	0.116

Exhibit 18   (Continued)

Panel B: Annualized Risk and Return, 1990–2009

	Global Stocks	Global Bonds	Commodities	1-mo. Libor	US CPI
Return	6.2%	7.2%	4.5%	4.2%	2.7%
Volatility	16.8%	6.0%	23.4%	0.6%	1.2%
Sharpe ratio	0.12	0.50	0.01	0.00	NA

Sources: Global stocks = MSCI All Country World Index; Global bonds = Barclays Capital Global Aggregate Bond Index; Commodities = S&P GSCI Commodity Index.

The argument for commodities as a hedge against inflation is related to the fact that commodity prices affect inflation calculations. Commodities, especially energy and food, impact the cost of living for consumers. The positive correlation of 0.336 between monthly commodity price changes and monthly changes in the US CPI supports this assertion. The correlations between the US CPI and global stocks and global bonds are negative. The volatility of commodity prices, especially energy and food, is much higher than that of reported consumer inflation. Consumer inflation is computed from many products used by consumers, including housing, that change more slowly than commodity prices. Commodity investments, especially when combined with leverage, exhibit high volatility, and have led to many well-publicized losses among commodity players. A sample of these losses is provided in Exhibit 19.

Exhibit 19   Large Commodity Investor Losses

Affected Company	Loss
Bank of Montreal (2007)	Wrong-way bets on natural gas led to a pre-tax loss of C$680 million (US$663 million)
Amaranth Advisors LLC (2006)	Bad bets on natural gas triggered US$6.6 billion of losses
China Aviation Oil (Singapore) Corp. (2004)	Loss of US$550 million on speculative oil futures trades, forcing debt restructuring

Source: "The 20 Biggest Trading Disasters," The Telegraph, January 2008.

6.4 Commodity Prices and Investments

Commodity spot prices are a function of supply and demand, costs of production and storage, value to users, and global economic conditions. Non-hedging investors with positions in physical commodities may be accumulating or divesting a particular commodity. Supplies of commodities are determined by production and inventory levels and the actions of non-hedging investors. Demand for commodities is determined by the needs of end users and the actions of non-hedging investors.

Supplies of commodities cannot be altered quickly by producers because extended lead times may exist and affect production levels. For example, agricultural output may be altered by planting more and changing farming techniques, but at least a growing cycle is required before the actual output occurs. However, for agricultural products, at least one factor, which is outside of the control of the producer, the weather, will have a significant effect on output. Increased oil and mining production may require a number of years. Weather can also have significant effect on oil production in parts of the world. For commodities, the inability of suppliers to quickly respond to changes in demand levels may result in supply levels that are too low in times of economic growth and too high in times of economic slowing. In addition, despite advancing technology, the cost of new supply may grow over time. For example, the cost of new energy and mineral exploration tends to exceed that of past finds because easy discoveries tend to be exploited first. If the costs of production are high, the producers are unlikely to produce more than what is needed to meet anticipated demand and to maintain more than modest levels of inventory.

Overall demand levels are influenced by global manufacturing dynamics and economic growth. Manufacturing needs can change in a period of months as orders and inventories vary. Investors seek to anticipate these changes by monitoring economic events, including government policy, inventory levels, and forecasts for growth. When demand levels and investors' orders to buy and sell over a given period of time change quickly, the resulting mismatch of supply and demand may lead to price volatility.

6.4.1 *Pricing of Commodity Futures Contracts*

It is important to understand futures contracts and the sources of return for each commodity futures contract because commodity investments often involve the use of futures contracts. These contracts trade on exchanges. The buyer (i.e., the long side) of a futures contract is obligated to take delivery of the commodity or its cash equivalent based on the spot price at expiration and will pay a settlement price. The settlement price is an amount specified in the contract or the previous mark-to-market price if the contract has been marked to market. In other words, the long side is obligated to buy the commodity at the settlement price. The long side of a futures contract increases in value when the value of the underlying commodity increases in value. The seller of a futures contract (i.e., the short side) is obligated to deliver the commodity or its cash equivalent based on the spot price at expiration and will receive the settlement price.

Futures positions are often closed over the life of the contract by taking the opposite position to that originally entered into. In other words, the long side will sell an identical futures contract, and the short side will buy an identical futures contract. If a contract is outstanding at expiration, it is typically not settled by delivery and receipt of the physical commodity but rather, it is settled by cash equal to the difference between the cash equivalent and settlement price. If a contract is physically settled, there are specific rules defining the characteristics of acceptable delivery, such as the quality of the commodity and the location of the delivery.

Parties to a futures contract are required to make an initial margin payment on the contract; each party has a separate margin account. Futures contracts and margin accounts are typically marked to market daily. On a daily basis, the futures exchange calculates price changes in the contract and the values of the margin accounts given the new price. If the value in a margin account declines sufficiently, the investor will receive a margin call and will be required to make an additional payment into the margin account. If the investor is unable or unwilling to do so, the investor's position will be closed.

Given the characteristics of a commodity, the price of a futures contract (futures price) may be approximated by the following formula:[33]

Futures price ≈ Spot price (1 + r) + Storage costs − Convenience yield

where r is the period's short-term risk-free interest rate. Arbitrage opportunities would exist if the futures price differs from the spot price compounded at the risk-free rate. For example, if the spot price of a commodity is 100 and the risk-free interest rate is

---

[33] Futures pricing is discussed in greater detail in Level II of the CFA Program curriculum.

5 percent and the 1-year futures price is 107 as opposed to 105, an arbitrageur can buy the commodity for 100 and sell a futures contract for 107. Assuming no storage costs, when the commodity is delivered for 107, the arbitrageur earns 2 in excess of that earned investing in the risk-free asset. However, commodities typically incur a storage cost. The buyer of a futures contract, in effect, gains access to the commodity in the future without buying it now and incurring storage costs. The futures price includes an amount for storage costs of the underlying commodity over the life of the contract. The storage and interest costs together are sometimes referred to as "the cost of carry" or "the carry." Finally, the buyer of the futures contract does not have immediate access to the commodity but will receive it in the future. The buyer has given up the convenience of having physical possession of the commodity and having it immediately available for use. The futures price is adjusted for the loss of convenience; the convenience yield is subtracted to arrive at the futures price. The value of convenience may vary over time and across users. For example, the convenience yield to having heating oil in January in Canada is higher than the convenience yield to having heating oil in Canada in July or to having heating oil in Australia in January.

Futures prices may be higher or lower than spot prices depending upon the convenience yield. When futures prices are higher than the spot price, the commodity forward curve is upward sloping, and the prices are referred to as being in contango. *Contango* occurs when there is little or no convenience yield. When futures prices are lower than the spot price, the commodity forward curve is downward sloping, and the prices are referred to as being in backwardation. *Backwardation* occurs when the convenience yield is high.

There are three sources of return for each commodity futures contract: the roll yield, the collateral yield, and the change in spot prices for the underlying commodity.

Roll Yield: The term "roll yield" refers to the difference between the spot price of a commodity and the price specified by its futures contract (or the difference between two futures contracts with different expiration dates). The formula shows that, with a convenience yield high enough to position the futures price below the spot price, the price of the futures contract generally rolls up to the spot price as the expiry date of the futures contract approaches. This price convergence earns the bearer of the futures contract a positive roll yield. This explanation is called the *theory of storage*. An alternative theory, called the *hedging pressure hypothesis*, suggests the difference between the spot and futures price is determined by user preferences and risk premiums.

Collateral Yield: The collateral yield component of the commodity index returns is the interest earned on the collateral (plus invested cash up to the value of the underlying asset) posted as a good-faith deposit for the futures contracts. In measuring this component of return, index managers typically assume that futures contracts are fully collateralized and that the collateral is invested in risk-free assets. Thus, the returns on a passive investment in commodity futures are expected to equal the return on the collateral plus a risk premium (i.e., the hedging pressure hypothesis) or the convenience yield net of storage costs (i.e., the theory of storage).

Spot Prices: The primary determinant of spot (or current) prices is the relationship between current supply and demand, as discussed earlier.

OTHER ALTERNATIVE INVESTMENTS

There are numerous other investments that do not fit within the definition of traditional investments (i.e., long-only investments in stocks, bonds, and cash) and may be considered alternative investments. Many of these other investments are categorized as collectibles.

Collectibles are tangible assets such as antiques and fine art, fine wine, rare stamps and coins, jewelry and watches, and sports memorabilia. Collectibles do not provide current income, but they can potentially provide long-term capital appreciation, diversify a portfolio, and be a source of enjoyment while held. However, there is no guarantee that any of these benefits will be realized. Collectibles can fluctuate dramatically in value and be highly illiquid with potential difficulty in realizing gains. Transactions can occur in a number of ways and settings, including through professional auctioneers; in local flea markets, online auctions, garage sales, and antique stores; or directly with personal collectors. Investors must have a degree of expertise, otherwise one may be vulnerable to fads, fakes, and fraud. Also, some collectibles must be stored in appropriate conditions to preserve their condition and avoid declines in value because of deterioration of the asset. Wine should be cellared, art should be kept in a humidity- and temperature-controlled environment, and coins and stamps must be handled with care to preserve their values. Although some collectibles (e.g., some great wines; fine art; and rare stamps, coins, and trading cards) have experienced great appreciation, this result is by no means the norm.

There are a number of indices that provide information about returns to these investments. Any of these indices are not necessarily reliable or representative of performance of a collectibles asset class as a whole. The Stanley Gibbons' SG 100 Stamp Index measures the performance, using retail and auction prices, of the 100 most traded stamps in the world. This index has increased from 291.50 at the end of 2000 to 475.78 at the end of 2010. This increase equals a 5 percent return per year over the 10-year period. This return, however, does not represent the return to the overall population of traded stamps.

The popularity of art as an investment has led to the creation of a number of art price indices. For example, Artprice provides statistics, econometric data, and indices to help measure returns on artworks. Another company that develops indices, Art Market Research, does not restrict itself to art but has over 500 indices in three broad categories: Painting; Antiques, Collectibles, Etc.; and Other Markets. The indices range from very broad [e.g., Painting (General) and Antiques (General)] to more specific [e.g., Chinese Ceramics (General) and Ancient Coins (General)] to very specific (e.g., Wrist-Watches Patek Philippe, Continental Flint-lock Pistols 1700–1800, and in wine, Château Lafite 1961). Subscribers are even able to specify parameters and create their own indices. Christie's first published an index of wine auction prices (listed by château) in 1972.

Collectors have no doubt been trading sports memorabilia since sporting events began to take place. One can only imagine the market for a piece of equipment or a keepsake of a martial artist in ancient China, an Olympian in ancient Greece, or a gladiator in ancient Rome. Trading cards—sports and other—have been swapped and sold in the United States since the early 1900s and are increasing in popularity elsewhere.[34] As is the case with any collectible, considerable expertise and perhaps a little luck are required to invest successfully in sports memorabilia.

8 RISK MANAGEMENT OVERVIEW

Alternative investments pose unusual challenges for investors seeking to manage risk. They are often characterized by asymmetric risk and return profiles, limited portfolio transparency, and illiquidity. Because of the active use of derivatives by many alternatives managers, operational risk, financial risk, counterparty risk, and liquidity

---

34 The most valuable baseball card in history, T206 Honus Wagner, was sold in 2007 for $2.35 million.

risk are key considerations for prospective investors. The returns to some types of alternatives, such as private equity, may rely to a great extent on manager skill rather than on general asset class performance. For these reasons, traditional risk and return measures (such as mean return, standard deviation of returns, and beta) may not provide an adequate picture of characteristics of alternative investments. Moreover, these measures may not be reliable or representative of specific investments.

8.1 Investment and Risk Management Process

Investment risk management is not solely the responsibility of either the investor or the manager of an investment portfolio. The investor, possibly in consultation with others, decides on an allocation to alternative investments. The investor then needs to decide the vehicles and managers of the investments and the amounts that will be allocated to each alternative investment class and manager. Risk has to be taken into account and due diligence conducted in making these decisions. The manager of an investment portfolio makes investment decisions consistent with the portfolio's established investment policies, taking risk into account. Investor due diligence should be used to ensure portfolio risk is effectively managed by the portfolio manager. Pension consultants, wealth managers, and individual investors all recognize that risk management processes can differ substantially between different alternative investment categories.

8.1.1 *Risk Management Issues*

Risks vary across alternative investments. The risks associated with investing in private markets (e.g., private equity funds and real estate ownership) differ from the risks associated with investing in publicly traded markets (e.g., commodity futures and REITs). Private equity and direct real estate ownership may involve selecting companies or properties, managing them, and then selling them years later. Private equity and hedge funds may have long lockup periods. As a result, investors' funds may be tied up for years. Intermediate valuations are challenging. As a result, any malfeasance or mismanagement may go undetected for years, so due diligence on the part of the investor is critical. The illiquid nature of alternative investments also means that poor manager selection can create a lingering drag on the portfolio. Limited partnership vehicles may limit the visibility of underlying holdings and liquidity to investor assets.

Portfolios of publicly traded securities are more liquid, with prices that are more timely and observable. For those who seek liquidity, publicly traded securities, such as shares of REITs, ETFs, and publicly traded private equity firms, may serve as the means for investing in alternatives.

8.1.2 *Risk Issues for Implementation*

For allocation purposes, the investor should recognize that historical returns and the standard deviation of those returns using indices may not be representative of the returns and volatility of alternative investments. Further, the reported correlations of those investments with other investments may vary from the actual correlations. As is always the case, even if these are relevant and representative measures of historical performance, past performance is not necessarily representative of future performance. The performance of alternative investments can be highly correlated with the business cycle, especially commodities and real estate investments, and may be susceptible to bubbles (i.e., much higher prices than justified by fundamentals). Investors should consider valuation before making allocation changes.

When selecting managers or funds, the investor should recognize that there may be significant differences in returns and risks among individual managers or funds and the overall investment class. Large institutional investors deal with this challenge by diversifying across managers or funds, but this approach may not be practical for smaller investors. As a result, these smaller investors may invest in (publicly traded) or with (private) a few large, diversified funds.

There are several risks of which alternative investment portfolio managers need to be mindful. In the case of illiquid investments, most notably in private equity or venture capital, there is a real possibility of 100 percent loss of equity on individual investments. As a result, portfolios should be diversified sufficiently to reduce the possibility of this outcome happening to all investments. At the same time, the manager should avoid diluting the opportunity for making substantial returns by arbitrarily identifying a target number of investments and, in the process, selecting inferior investments. Managers should consider and manage the risk associated with the use of leverage.

Performance fee structures, while high, may encourage alignment of interests between investors and managers. However, established portfolio managers may seek to attract large amounts of capital and to profit from the management fees based on assets under management or committed capital without seeking superior performance. Performance fees may also encourage hedge fund managers who experience a large loss to liquidate their funds instead of working them back to par.

8.1.3 *Due Diligence Issues Regarding Risk*

Due diligence of alternative investment managers necessitates special procedures, over and above the process required for a manager of a portfolio of publicly traded securities. Historical measures of performance may not be reliable or representative as a result of intermediate valuation estimates and narrow portfolio diversification. With limited transparency and long horizons, the honesty of the company's staff needs to be carefully reviewed.

Hedge funds will have trading desks much like long-only investment firms, but private equity and real estate companies usually make investment decisions via an investment committee of partners. These may or may not include external non-executive directors or subject matter experts. The committee votes on the rationale, analysis, and suitability of every investment and requires a majority in favour before investor funds are committed. This committee may also oversee and vote on exit strategies of investments, including timing and realization price.

Independent valuation of illiquid underlying assets should be performed on a regular basis. Often, this analysis is done in conjunction with a portfolio review explaining the performance of every transaction in detail, its status, and future strategy for the portfolio. Limits on security type, leverage, sector, geography, and individual positions should be well defined in the offering memorandum, and the positions should be carefully monitored by the manager and regularly reported to clients.

Hedge fund risk is often monitored by a chief risk officer, who should be separated from the investment process. As part of the risk management process, a hedge fund needs to establish and maintain limits on leverage, sector, and individual positions. Investments in commodities may be subject to counterparty risks as well as leverage risks. The exposure to counterparty risk and leverage risk should be regularly monitored and reported. Policies limiting leverage, positions, and sectors as well as counterparty exposures may be adopted.

One issue for investors is that hedge and commodity funds may seek to keep their positions and strategies private. This lack of transparency makes it difficult for the investor to effectively manage diversification across funds and to conduct adequate due diligence.

8.2 Risk–Return Measures

The Sharpe ratio is a risk–return measure frequently reported because of its ease of calculation and understandability. The Sharpe ratio may not be the appropriate risk–return measure for alternative investments because measures of return and standard deviation may not be relevant and reliable given the illiquid nature of the assets. The illiquid nature of the assets means that estimates, rather than observable transaction prices, may be used for valuation purposes. As a result, returns may be smoothed and/or overstated and the volatility of returns understated. Also, the use of standard deviation as the measure of risk ignores the diversification impact for a broad portfolio of managers and alternative investments.

Many alternative investments do not exhibit close-to-normal distributions of returns, which is a crucial assumption for the validity of a standard deviation as a comprehensive risk measure. Alternative investment returns tend to be leptokurtic, negatively skewed (i.e., they have fat tails characterized by positive average returns and long-tails downside characterized by potential extreme losses). For this reason, a measure of downside risk, ideally non-normal, would be useful. Downside risk measures focus on the left side of the return distribution curve where losses occur. For example, value at risk (VaR) is a measure of the minimum amount of loss expected over a given time period at a given level of probability. In other words, this measure answers a question such as, "What is the minimum amount expected to be lost in a year with a 5 percent probability?" However, this measure, if it is calculated using standard deviation, will underestimate the VaR for a negatively skewed distribution. Shortfall or safety-first risk measures the probability that the portfolio value will fall below some minimum acceptable level over a given time period. In other words, this measure answers a question such as, "What is the probability of losing 20 percent of principal in any given year?" This measure also uses standard deviation as the measure of risk. The Sortino ratio, another measure of downside risk, uses downside deviation rather than standard deviation as a measure of risk. Assuming normal probability distributions when calculating these measures will lead to an underestimation of downside risk for a negatively skewed distribution.

Understanding and evaluating "tail events"—low probability, high severity instances of stress—is an important, yet extraordinarily difficult aspect of the risk management process. Stress testing/scenario analysis is often used as a complement to VaR to develop a better understanding of the potential loss of a portfolio under both normal and stressed market conditions. Stress testing involves estimating losses under extremely unfavourable conditions.

8.3 Due Diligence Overview

Manager selection is a critical factor in portfolio performance. A manager should have a verifiable track record and display a high level of expertise and experience with the asset type. The asset management team should be assigned an appropriate workload and provided sufficient resources. Moreover, they should be rewarded with an effective compensation package to ensure alignment of interest, continuity, motivation, and thoughtful oversight of assets.

Fraud, while infrequent, is always a possibility. The investor should be skeptical of unusually good and overly consistent reported performance. Third-party custody of assets and independent verification of results can help reduce the chance of an investor being defrauded. Diversification across mangers is also wise.

For a new investor, a proper due diligence process should be carried out to ensure that the targeted investment is in compliance with its prospectus and that it will meet his/her investment strategy, risk and return objectives, and restrictions. Existing investors should monitor results and fund holdings to determine whether a fund has performed in line with expectations and continues to comply with its prospectus.

Exhibit 20 lists key items that should be considered in a typical due diligence process.

Exhibit 20	A Typical Due Diligence Process
Organization:	▪ Experience and quality of management team, compensation, and staffing
	▪ Analysis of prior and current funds
	▪ Track record/alignment of interests
	▪ Reputation and quality of third-party service providers, e.g., lawyers, auditors, prime brokers
Portfolio Management:	▪ Investment process
	▪ Target markets/asset types/strategies
	▪ Sourcing of investments
	▪ Role of operating partners
	▪ Underwriting
	▪ Environmental and engineering review process
	▪ Integration of asset management/acquisitions/dispositions
	▪ Disposition process, including how initiated and executed
Operations and Controls:	▪ Reporting and accounting methodology
	▪ Audited financial statements and other internal controls
	▪ Valuations—frequency and approach(es)
	▪ Insurance and contingency plans
Risk Management:	▪ Fund policies and limits
	▪ Risk management policy
	▪ Portfolio risk and key risk factors
	▪ Leverage and currency—risks/constraints/hedging
Legal Review:	▪ Fund structure
	▪ Registrations
	▪ Existing/prior litigation
Fund Terms:	▪ Fees (management and performance) and expenses
	▪ Contractual terms
	▪ Investment period and fund term and extensions
	▪ Carried interest
	▪ Distributions
	▪ Conflicts
	▪ Limited partners' rights
	▪ "Key Person" and/or other termination procedures

Alternative investing may add value to an investor's portfolio. However, to be effective, alternative investing requires thoughtful implementation, including consideration of the amount to allocate to alternative investments and of diversification among alternative investments. Valuation issues, manager selection, and risk management are other items to be considered.

SUMMARY

This reading has provided an overview of the characteristics, potential benefits, and risks of alternative investments. Features of some categories of alternative investments were described. Including alternative investments in an investor's portfolio may result in benefits, such as diversification benefits. However, these benefits do not come without associated risks. It is important that investors understand these risks before including alternative investments in their portfolios. Some key points of the reading are summarized below:

- Alternative investments are alternatives to long-only positions in stocks, bonds, and cash. Alternative investments include investments in assets such as real estate and commodities and investments in special vehicles such as private equity and hedge funds.

- Characteristics, common to many alternative investments compared with traditional investments, include lower liquidity, less regulation, lower transparency; higher fees; and limited and potentially problematic historical risk and return data.

- Alternative investments often have unique legal and tax considerations and may be highly leveraged.

- Alternative investments are attractive to investors because of potential for diversification and higher returns when added to a portfolio of traditional investments.

- The risks associated with alternative investments must be factored into the decision-making process.

- Many alternative investments are valued for performance reporting purposes, including reporting to index providers, using estimated values rather than actual market prices. As a result, the volatility of returns and correlation of returns with the returns to traditional investments will tend to be underestimated. It is important to identify and understand how alternative investments are valued.

- Indices for alternative investments may be subject to a variety of biases, including survivorship and backfill biases.

- Alternative investment strategies are typically active, alpha-seeking strategies.

- Many alternative investments, such as hedge and private equity funds, use a partnership structure with a general partner (the fund) that manages the business and bears unlimited liability and limited partners (investors) who own fractional interests in the partnership.

- The general partner (the fund) typically receives a management fee based on assets under management or committed capital (the former is common to hedge funds and the latter is common to private equity funds) and an incentive fee based on realized profits.

■ Hurdle rates, high water marks, lockup and notice periods, side pockets, and clawback provisions may also be specified in a partnership agreement.

■ The fee structure affects the returns to investors (limited partners) in alternative investments such as hedge and private equity funds.

■ Hedge funds are typically classified by strategy. One such classification includes four broad categories of strategies: event-driven, relative value, macro, and equity hedge.

■ Primary private equity fund strategies include leveraged buyouts, venture capital, development capital, and distressed investing. Leveraged buyouts and venture capital are the dominant strategies.

■ Real estate investing includes direct and indirect ownership of real estate property and lending against real estate properties.

■ Real estate property has some unique features, including basic indivisibility, heterogeneity (no two properties are identical), and fixed location.

■ The required amount to directly invest in real estate may be large, and the investment may be relatively illiquid. Different investment forms, such as REITs and mortgage securitizations, partially accommodate these issues.

■ Commodity investments may involve investing in actual physical commodities or in producers of commodities, but more typically, commodity investing is done using commodity derivatives.

■ Returns to commodity investing are based on changes in price and do not include an income stream such as dividends, interest, or rent.

■ Managing risks associated with alternative investments can be challenging because these investments are often characterized by asymmetric risk and return profiles, limited portfolio transparency, and illiquidity.

■ Traditional risk and return measures (such as mean return, standard deviation of returns, and beta) may not provide an adequate picture of characteristics of alternative investments. Moreover, these measures may not be reliable or representative of specific investments.

■ Operational, financial, counterparty, and liquidity risks may be key considerations for those investing in alternative investments.

■ It is critical to do due diligence to assess whether (a) a potential investment is in compliance with its prospectus; (b) the appropriate organizational structure and policies for managing investments, operations, risk, and compliance are in place; and (c) the fund terms appear reasonable.

■ The inclusion of alternative investments in a portfolio, including the amounts to allocate, should be considered in the context of an investor's risk–return objectives, constraints, and preferences.

REFERENCES

Brooks, C., and H. Kat. 2002. "The Statistical Properties of Hedge Fund Index Returns and Their Implications for Investors." *Journal of Alternative Investments*, vol. 5, no. 25: 44.

Hall, Robert, and Susan Woodward. 2004. "Benchmarking the Returns to Venture." National Bureau of Economic Research. January, 2004.

Heisler, J., C. Knittel, J. Neumann, and S. Stewart. 2007. "Why do Institutional Plan Sponsors Hire and Fire Their Investment Managers?" *Journal of Business and Economic Studies*, vol. 13, no. 1: 88–118.

Kaplan, Steven N., and Antoinette Schoar. 2005. "Private Equity Performance, Returns, Persistence, and Capital Flows." *Journal of Finance*, vol. 60, no. 4: 1791–1823.

Stewart, S., J. Heisler, C. Knittel, and J. Neumann. 2009. "Absence of Value: an Analysis of Investment Allocation Decisions by Institutional Plan Sponsors." *Financial Analysts Journal*, vol. 65, no. 6: 34–51.

Stoll, Hans R., and Robert E. Whaley. 2009. "Commodity Index Investing and Commodity Futures Prices." Working paper, Vanderbilt University.

PRACTICE PROBLEMS

1   Which of the following is *least likely* to be considered an alternative investment?

    A Real estate

    B Commodities

    C Long-only equity funds

2   An investor is seeking an investment that can take long and short positions, may use multi-strategies, and historically exhibits low correlation with a traditional investment portfolio. The investor's goals will be *best* satisfied with an investment in:

    A real estate.

    B a hedge fund.

    C a private equity fund.

3   Relative to traditional investments, alternative investments are *least likely* to be characterized by:

    A high levels of transparency.

    B limited historical return data.

    C significant restrictions on redemptions.

4   Alternative investment funds are typically managed:

    A actively.

    B to generate positive beta return.

    C assuming that markets are efficient.

5   An investor is most likely to consider adding alternative investments to a traditional investment portfolio because:

    A of their historically higher returns.

    B of their historically lower standard deviation of returns.

    C their inclusion is expected to reduce the portfolio's Sharpe ratio.

6   An investor may prefer a single hedge fund to a fund of funds if he seeks:

    A due diligence expertise.

    B better redemption terms.

    C a less complex fee structure.

7   Hedge funds are similar to private equity funds in that both:

    A are typically structured as partnerships.

    B assess management fees based on assets under management.

    C do not earn an incentive fee until the initial investment is repaid.

8   An investor seeks a current income stream as a component of total return, and desires an investment that historically has low correlation with other asset classes. The investment *most likely* to achieve the investor's goals is:

    A timberland.

    B collectibles.

    C commodities.

Developed by Jennie I. Sanders, CFA (Austin, TX, USA). Copyright © 2012 CFA Institute

9 A hedge fund invests primarily in distressed debt. Quoted market prices are available for the underlying holdings but they trade infrequently. Which of the following will the hedge fund *most likely* use in calculating net asset value for trading purposes?

    A Average quotes

    B Average quotes adjusted for liquidity

    C Bid prices for short positions and ask prices for long positions

10 Angel investing capital is typically provided in which stage of financing?

    A Later-stage.

    B Formative-stage.

    C Mezzanine-stage.

11 If a commodity's forward curve is in contango, the component of a commodities futures return *most likely* to reflect this is:

    A spot prices.

    B the roll yield.

    C the collateral yield.

12 United Capital is a hedge fund with $250 million of initial capital. United charges a 2% management fee based on assets under management at year end, and a 20% incentive fee based on returns in excess of an 8% hurdle rate. In its first year, United appreciates 16%. Assume management fees are calculated using end-of-period valuation. The investor's net return assuming the performance fee is calculated net of the management fee is *closest* to:

    A 11.58%.

    B 12.54%.

    C 12.80%.

13 Capricorn Fund of Funds invests GBP 100 million in each of Alpha Hedge Fund and ABC Hedge Fund. Capricorn FOF has a "1 and 10" fee structure. Management fees and incentive fees are calculated independently at the end of each year. After one year, net of their respective management and incentive fees, the investment in Alpha is valued at GBP80 million and the investment in ABC is valued at GBP140 million. The annual return to an investor in Capricorn, net of fees assessed at the fund of funds level, is *closest* to:

    A 7.9%.

    B 8.0%.

    C 8.1%.

14 An analyst wanting to assess the downside risk of an alternative investment is *least likely* to use the investment's:

    A Sortino ratio.

    B value at risk (VaR).

    C standard deviation of returns.

SOLUTIONS

1 C is correct. Long-only equity funds are typically considered traditional investments and real estate and commodities are typically classified as alternative investments.

2 B is correct. Hedge funds may use a variety of strategies (event-driven, relative value, macro and equity hedge), generally have a low correlation with traditional investments, and may take long and short positions.

3 A is correct. Alternative investments are characterized as typically having low levels of transparency.

4 A is correct. There are many approaches to managing alternative investment funds but typically these funds are actively managed and aim to generate positive alpha return.

5 A is correct. The historically higher returns to most categories of alternative investments compared with traditional investments result in potentially higher returns to a portfolio containing alternative investments. The less than perfect correlation with traditional investments results in portfolio risk (standard deviation) being less than the weighted average of the standard deviations of the investments. This has potential to increase the Sharpe ratio in spite of the historically higher standard deviation of returns of most categories of alternative investments.

6 C is correct. Hedge funds of funds have multi-layered fee structures, while the fee structure for a single hedge fund is less complex. Funds of funds presumably have some expertise in conducting due diligence on hedge funds and may be able to negotiate more favorable redemption terms than could an individual investor in a single hedge fund.

7 A is correct. Private equity funds and hedge funds are typically structured as partnerships where investors are limited partners (LP) and the fund is the general partner (GP). The management fee for private equity funds is based on committed capital whereas for hedge funds the management fees are based on assets under management. For most private equity funds, the general partner does not earn an incentive fee until the limited partners have received their initial investment back.

8 A is correct. Timberland offers an income stream based on the sale of timber products as a component of total return and has historically generated returns not highly correlated with other asset classes.

9 B is correct. Many practitioners believe that liquidity discounts are necessary to reflect fair value. This has resulted in some funds having two NAVs - for trading and reporting. The fund may use average quotes for reporting purposes but apply liquidity discounts for trading purposes.

10 B is correct. Formative-stage financing occurs when the company is still in the process of being formed and encompasses several financing steps. Angel investing capital is typically raised in this early stage of financing.

11 B is correct. Roll yield refers to the difference between the spot price of a commodity and the price specified by its futures contract (or the difference between two futures contracts with different expiration dates). When futures prices are higher than the spot price, the commodity forward curve is upward sloping, and the prices are referred to as being in contango. Contango occurs when there is little or no convenience yield.

12 B is correct. The net investor return is 12.54%, calculated as:

End of year capital = $250 million × 1.16 = $290 million

Management fee = $290 million × 2% = $5.8 million

Hurdle amount = 8% of $250 million = $20 million;

Incentive fee = ($290 − $250 − $20 − $5.8) million × 20% = $2.84 million

Total fees to United Capital = ($5.8 + $2.84) million = $8.64 million

Investor net return: ($290 − $250 − $8.64) / $250 = 12.54%

13 A is correct because the net investor return is 7.9%, calculated as:

First, note that "1 and 10" refers to a 1% management fee, and a 10% incentive fee.

End of year capital = GBP140 million + GBP80 million = GBP220 million

Management fee = GBP220 million × 1% = GBP2.2 million

Incentive fee = (GBP220 − GBP200) million × 10% = GBP2 million

Total fees to Capricorn = (GBP2.2 + GBP2) million = GBP4.2 million

Investor net return: (GBP220 − GBP200 − GBP4.2) / GBP200 = 7.9%

14 C is correct. Downside risk measures focus on the left side of the return distribution curve where losses occur. The standard deviation of returns assumes that returns are normally distributed. Many alternative investments do not exhibit close-to-normal distribution of returns, which is a crucial assumption for the validity of a standard deviation as a comprehensive risk measure. Assuming normal probability distributions when calculating these measures will lead to an underestimation of downside risk for a negatively skewed distribution. Both the Sortino ratio and the value-at-risk measure are both measures of downside risk.

Glossary

A priori probability   A probability based on logical analysis rather than on observation or personal judgment.

Abnormal profit   Equal to accounting profit less the implicit opportunity costs not included in total accounting costs; the difference between total revenue (TR) and total cost (TC).

Abnormal return   The amount by which a security's actual return differs from its expected return, given the security's risk and the market's return.

Absolute advantage   A country's ability to produce a good or service at a lower absolute cost than its trading partner.

Absolute dispersion   The amount of variability present without comparison to any reference point or benchmark.

Absolute frequency   The number of observations in a given interval (for grouped data).

Accelerated book build   An offering of securities by an investment bank acting as principal that is accomplished in only one or two days.

Accelerated methods   Depreciation methods that allocate a relatively large proportion of the cost of an asset to the early years of the asset's useful life.

Account   With the accounting systems, a formal record of increases and decreases in a specific asset, liability, component of owners' equity, revenue, or expense.

Accounting (or explicit) costs   Payments to non-owner parties for services or resources they supply to the firm.

Accounting loss   When accounting profit is negative.

Accounting profit   Income as reported on the income statement, in accordance with prevailing accounting standards, before the provisions for income tax expense. Also called *income before taxes* or *pretax income*.

Accounts payable   Amounts that a business owes to its vendors for goods and services that were purchased from them but which have not yet been paid.

Accounts receivable   Amounts customers owe the company for products that have been sold as well as amounts that may be due from suppliers (such as for returns of merchandise). Also called *commercial receivables* or *trade receivables*.

Accounts receivable turnover   Ratio of sales on credit to the average balance in accounts receivable.

Accrued expenses   Liabilities related to expenses that have been incurred but not yet paid as of the end of an accounting period—an example of an accrued expense is rent that has been incurred but not yet paid, resulting in a liability "rent payable." Also called *accrued liabilities*.

Accrued interest   Interest earned but not yet paid.

Accrued revenue   Revenue that has been earned but not yet billed to customers as of the end of an accounting period.

Accumulated depreciation   An offset to property, plant, and equipment (PPE) reflecting the amount of the cost of PPE that has been allocated to current and previous accounting periods.

Acid-test ratio   A stringent measure of liquidity that indicates a company's ability to satisfy current liabilities with its most liquid assets, calculated as (cash + short-term marketable investments + receivables) divided by current liabilities.

Acquisition method   A method of accounting for a business combination where the acquirer is required to measure each identifiable asset and liability at fair value. This method was the result of a joint project of the IASB and FASB aiming at convergence in standards for the accounting of business combinations.

Action lag   Delay from policy decisions to implementation.

Active investment   An approach to investing in which the investor seeks to outperform a given benchmark.

Active return   The return on a portfolio minus the return on the portfolio's benchmark.

Active strategy   In reference to short-term cash management, an investment strategy characterized by monitoring and attempting to capitalize on market conditions to optimize the risk and return relationship of short-term investments.

Activity ratio   The ratio of the labor force to total population of working age. Also called *participation ratio*.

Activity ratios   Ratios that measure how efficiently a company performs day-to-day tasks, such as the collection of receivables and management of inventory. Also called *asset utilization ratios* or *operating efficiency ratios*.

Add-on rates   Bank certificates of deposit, repos, and indices such as Libor and Euribor are quoted on an add-on rate basis (bond equivalent yield basis).

Addition rule for probabilities   A principle stating that the probability that *A* or *B* occurs (both occur) equals the probability that *A* occurs, plus the probability that *B* occurs, minus the probability that both *A* and *B* occur.

Agency RMBS   In the United States, securities backed by residential mortgage loans and guaranteed by a federal agency or guaranteed by either of the two GSEs (Fannie Mae and Freddie Mac).

Agency bonds   See *quasi-government bond*.

Aggregate demand   The quantity of goods and services that households, businesses, government, and foreign customers want to buy at any given level of prices.

Aggregate demand curve   Inverse relationship between the price level and real output.

Aggregate income   The value of all the payments earned by the suppliers of factors used in the production of goods and services.

Aggregate output   The value of all the goods and services produced in a specified period of time.

Aggregate supply   The quantity of goods and services producers are willing to supply at any given level of price.

Aggregate supply curve   The level of domestic output that companies will produce at each price level.

Aging schedule   A breakdown of accounts into categories of days outstanding.

All-or-nothing (AON) orders   An order that includes the instruction to trade only if the trade fills the entire quantity (size) specified.

Allocationally efficient   Said of a market, a financial system, or an economy that promotes the allocation of resources to their highest value uses.

Allowance for bad debts   An offset to accounts receivable for the amount of accounts receivable that are estimated to be uncollectible.

Alternative investment markets   Market for investments other than traditional securities investments (i.e., traditional common and preferred shares and traditional fixed income instruments). The term usually encompasses direct and indirect investment in real estate (including timberland and farmland) and commodities (including precious metals); hedge funds, private equity, and other investments requiring specialized due diligence.

Alternative trading systems   Trading venues that function like exchanges but that do not exercise regulatory authority over their subscribers except with respect to the conduct of the subscribers' trading in their trading systems. Also called *electronic communications networks* or *multilateral trading facilities*.

American depository receipt   A US dollar-denominated security that trades like a common share on US exchanges.

American depository share   The underlying shares on which American depository receipts are based. They trade in the issuing company's domestic market.

American-style   Said of an option contract that can be exercised at any time up to the option's expiration date.

Amortisation   The process of allocating the cost of intangible long-term assets having a finite useful life to accounting periods; the allocation of the amount of a bond premium or discount to the periods remaining until bond maturity.

Amortised cost   The historical cost (initially recognised cost) of an asset, adjusted for amortisation and impairment.

Amortizing bond   Bond with a payment schedule that calls for periodic payments of interest and repayments of principal.

Amortizing loans   Loan with a payment schedule that calls for periodic payments of interest and repayments of principal.

Annual percentage rate   The cost of borrowing expressed as a yearly rate.

Annuity   A finite set of level sequential cash flows.

Annuity due   An annuity having a first cash flow that is paid immediately.

Anticipation stock   Excess inventory that is held in anticipation of increased demand, often because of seasonal patterns of demand.

Antidilutive   With reference to a transaction or a security, one that would increase earnings per share (EPS) or result in EPS higher than the company's basic EPS—antidilutive securities are not included in the calculation of diluted EPS.

Arbitrage   1) The simultaneous purchase of an undervalued asset or portfolio and sale of an overvalued but equivalent asset or portfolio, in order to obtain a riskless profit on the price differential. Taking advantage of a market inefficiency in a risk-free manner. 2) The condition in a financial market in which equivalent assets or combinations of assets sell for two different prices, creating an opportunity to profit at no risk with no commitment of money. In a well-functioning financial market, few arbitrage opportunities are possible. 3) A risk-free operation that earns an expected positive net profit but requires no net investment of money.

Arbitrage-free pricing   The overall process of pricing derivatives by arbitrage and risk neutrality. Also called the *principle of no arbitrage*.

Arbitrageurs   Traders who engage in arbitrage. See *arbitrage*.

Arc elasticity   An elasticity based on two points, in contrast with (point) elasticity. With reference to price elasticity, the percentage change in quantity demanded divided by the percentage change in price between two points for price.

Arithmetic mean   The sum of the observations divided by the number of observations.

Arms index   A flow of funds indicator applied to a broad stock market index to measure the relative extent to which money is moving into or out of rising and declining stocks.

Ascending price auction   An auction in which an auctioneer calls out prices for a single item and potential buyers bid directly against each other, with each subsequent bid being higher than the previous one.

Asian call option   A European-style option with a value at maturity equal to the difference between the stock price at maturity and the average stock price during the life of the option, or $0, whichever is greater.

Ask   The price at which a dealer or trader is willing to sell an asset, typically qualified by a maximum quantity (ask size). See *offer*.

Ask size   The maximum quantity of an asset that pertains to a specific ask price from a trader. For example, if the ask for a share issue is $30 for a size of 1,000 shares, the trader is offering to sell at $30 up to 1,000 shares.

Asset allocation   The process of determining how investment funds should be distributed among asset classes.

Asset beta   The unlevered beta; reflects the business risk of the assets; the asset's systematic risk.

Asset class   A group of assets that have similar characteristics, attributes, and risk/return relationships.

Asset swap   Converts the periodic fixed coupon of a specific bond to a Libor plus or minus a spread.

Asset utilization ratios   Ratios that measure how efficiently a company performs day-to-day tasks, such as the collection of receivables and management of inventory.

Asset-backed securities   A type of bond issued by a legal entity called a *special purpose vehicle* (SPV), on a collection of assets that the SPV owns. Also, securities backed by receivables and loans other than mortgage loans.

Asset-based loan   A loan that is secured with company assets.

Asset-based valuation models   Valuation based on estimates of the market value of a company's assets.

Assets   Resources controlled by an enterprise as a result of past events and from which future economic benefits to the enterprise are expected to flow.

Assignment of accounts receivable   The use of accounts receivable as collateral for a loan.

At the money   An option in which the underlying's price equals the exercise price.

At-the-money   Said of an option in which the underlying's price equals the exercise price.

Auction   A type of bond issuing mechanism often used for sovereign bonds that involves bidding.

Autarkic price   The price of a good or service in an autarkic economy.

Autarky   A state in which a country does not trade with other countries.

Automated Clearing House (ACH)   An electronic payment network available to businesses, individuals, and financial institutions in the United States, US Territories, and Canada.

Automatic stabilizer   A countercyclical factor that automatically comes into play as an economy slows and unemployment rises.

Available-for-sale Debt and equity securities not classified as either held-to-maturity or held-for-trading securities. The investor is willing to sell but not actively planning to sell. In general, available-for-sale securities are reported at fair value on the balance sheet.

Average fixed cost Total fixed cost divided by quantity.

Average life See *weighted average life*.

Average product Measures the productivity of inputs on average and is calculated by dividing total product by the total number of units for a given input that is used to generate that output.

Average revenue Quantity sold divided into total revenue.

Average total cost Total costs divided by quantity.

Average variable cost Total variable cost divided by quantity.

Back simulation Another term for the historical method of estimating VAR. This term is somewhat misleading in that the method involves not a *simulation* of the past but rather what *actually happened* in the past, sometimes adjusted to reflect the fact that a different portfolio may have existed in the past than is planned for the future.

Back-testing With reference to portfolio strategies, the application of a strategy's portfolio selection rules to historical data to assess what would have been the strategy's historical performance.

Backup lines of credit A type of credit enhancement provided by a bank to an issuer of commercial paper to ensure that the issuer will have access to sufficient liquidity to repay maturing commercial paper if issuing new paper is not a viable option.

Balance of payments A double-entry bookkeeping system that summarizes a country's economic transactions with the rest of the world for a particular period of time, typically a calendar quarter or year.

Balance of trade deficit When the domestic economy is spending more on foreign goods and services than foreign economies are spending on domestic goods and services.

Balance sheet The financial statement that presents an entity's current financial position by disclosing resources the entity controls (its assets) and the claims on those resources (its liabilities and equity claims), as of a particular point in time (the date of the balance sheet). Also called *statement of financial position* or *statement of financial condition*.

Balance sheet ratios Financial ratios involving balance sheet items only.

Balanced With respect to a government budget, one in which spending and revenues (taxes) are equal.

Balloon payment Large payment required at maturity to retire a bond's outstanding principal amount.

Bank discount basis A quoting convention that annualizes, on a 360-day year, the discount as a percentage of face value.

Bar chart A price chart with four bits of data for each time interval—the high, low, opening, and closing prices. A vertical line connects the high and low. A cross-hatch left indicates the opening price and a cross-hatch right indicates the close.

Barter economy An economy where economic agents as house-holds, corporations, and governments "pay" for goods and services with another good or service.

Base rates The reference rate on which a bank bases lending rates to all other customers.

Basic EPS Net earnings available to common shareholders (i.e., net income minus preferred dividends) divided by the weighted average number of common shares outstanding.

Basis point Used in stating yield spreads, one basis point equals one-hundredth of a percentage point, or 0.01%.

Basket of listed depository receipts An exchange-traded fund (ETF) that represents a portfolio of depository receipts.

Bearer bonds Bonds for which ownership is not recorded; only the clearing system knows who the bond owner is.

Behavioral equations With respect to demand and supply, equations that model the behavior of buyers and sellers.

Behavioral finance A field of finance that examines the psychological variables that affect and often distort the investment decision making of investors, analysts, and portfolio managers.

Behind the market Said of prices specified in orders that are worse than the best current price; e.g., for a limit buy order, a limit price below the best bid.

Benchmark A comparison portfolio; a point of reference or comparison.

Benchmark issue The latest sovereign bond issue for a given maturity. It serves as a benchmark against which to compare bonds that have the same features but that are issued by another type of issuer.

Benchmark rate Typically the yield-to-maturity on a government bond having the same, or close to the same, time-to-maturity.

Benchmark spread The yield spread over a specific benchmark, usually measured in basis points.

Bermuda-style Said of an option contract that can be exercised on specified dates up to the option's expiration date.

Bernoulli random variable A random variable having the outcomes 0 and 1.

Bernoulli trial An experiment that can produce one of two outcomes.

Best bid The highest bid in the market.

Best effort offering An offering of a security using an investment bank in which the investment bank, as agent for the issuer, promises to use its best efforts to sell the offering but does not guarantee that a specific amount will be sold.

Best offer The lowest offer (ask price) in the market.

Beta A measure of systematic risk that is based on the covariance of an asset's or portfolio's return with the return of the overall market.

Bid The price at which a dealer or trader is willing to buy an asset, typically qualified by a maximum quantity.

Bid size The maximum quantity of an asset that pertains to a specific bid price from a trader.

Bid–ask spread The difference between the prices at which dealers will buy from a customer (bid) and sell to a customer (offer or ask). It is often used as an indicator of liquidity.

Bid–offer spread The difference between the prices at which dealers will buy from a customer (bid) and sell to a customer (offer or ask). It is often used as an indicator of liquidity.

Bilateral loan A loan from a single lender to a single borrower.

Binomial model A model for pricing options in which the underlying price can move to only one of two possible new prices.

Binomial random variable The number of successes in n Bernoulli trials for which the probability of success is constant for all trials and the trials are independent.

Binomial tree The graphical representation of a model of asset price dynamics in which, at each period, the asset moves up with probability p or down with probability $(1 - p)$.

Block brokers A broker (agent) that provides brokerage services for large-size trades.

Blue chip Widely held large market capitalization companies that are considered financially sound and are leaders in their respective industry or local stock market.

Bollinger Bands A price-based technical analysis indicator consisting of a moving average plus a higher line representing the moving average plus a set number of standard deviations from average price (for the same number of periods as used to calculate the moving average) and a lower line that is a moving average minus the same number of standard deviations.

Bond Contractual agreement between the issuer and the bondholders.

Bond equivalent yield A calculation of yield that is annualized using the ratio of 365 to the number of days to maturity. Bond equivalent yield allows for the restatement and comparison of securities with different compounding periods.

Bond indenture The governing legal credit agreement, typically incorporated by reference in the prospectus.

Bond market vigilantes Bond market participants who might reduce their demand for long-term bonds, thus pushing up their yields.

Bond yield plus risk premium approach An estimate of the cost of common equity that is produced by summing the before-tax cost of debt and a risk premium that captures the additional yield on a company's stock relative to its bonds. The additional yield is often estimated using historical spreads between bond yields and stock yields.

Bonus issue of shares A type of dividend in which a company distributes additional shares of its common stock to shareholders instead of cash.

Book building Investment bankers' process of compiling a "book" or list of indications of interest to buy part of an offering.

Book value The net amount shown for an asset or liability on the balance sheet; book value may also refer to the company's excess of total assets over total liabilities. Also called *carrying value*.

Boom An expansionary phase characterized by economic growth "testing the limits" of the economy.

Bottom-up analysis With reference to investment selection processes, an approach that involves selection from all securities within a specified investment universe, i.e., without prior narrowing of the universe on the basis of macroeconomic or overall market considerations.

Break point In the context of the weighted average cost of capital (WACC), a break point is the amount of capital at which the cost of one or more of the sources of capital changes, leading to a change in the WACC.

Breakeven point The number of units produced and sold at which the company's net income is zero (revenues = total costs); in the case of perfect competition, the quantity where price, average revenue, and marginal revenue equal average total cost.

Bridge financing Interim financing that provides funds until permanent financing can be arranged.

Broad money Encompasses narrow money plus the entire range of liquid assets that can be used to make purchases.

Broker 1) An agent who executes orders to buy or sell securities on behalf of a client in exchange for a commission. 2) See *futures commission merchants*.

Brokered market A market in which brokers arrange trades among their clients.

Broker–dealer A financial intermediary (often a company) that may function as a principal (dealer) or as an agent (broker) depending on the type of trade.

Budget constraint A constraint on spending or investment imposed by wealth or income.

Budget surplus/deficit The difference between government revenue and expenditure for a stated fixed period of time.

Business risk The risk associated with operating earnings. Operating earnings are uncertain because total revenues and many of the expenditures contributed to produce those revenues are uncertain.

Buy-side firm An investment management company or other investor that uses the services of brokers or dealers (i.e., the client of the sell side firms).

Buyback A transaction in which a company buys back its own shares. Unlike stock dividends and stock splits, share repurchases use corporate cash.

Buyout fund A fund that buys all the shares of a public company so that, in effect, the company becomes private.

CBOE Volatility Index A measure of near-term market volatility as conveyed by S&P 500 stock index option prices.

CD equivalent yield A yield on a basis comparable to the quoted yield on an interest-bearing money market instrument that pays interest on a 360-day basis; the annualized holding period yield, assuming a 360-day year.

Call An option that gives the holder the right to buy an underlying asset from another party at a fixed price over a specific period of time.

Call market A market in which trades occur only at a particular time and place (i.e., when the market is called).

Call money rate The interest rate that buyers pay for their margin loan.

Call option An option that gives the holder the right to buy an underlying asset from another party at a fixed price over a specific period of time.

Call protection The time during which the issuer of the bond is not allowed to exercise the call option.

Callable bond A bond containing an embedded call option that gives the issuer the right to buy the bond back from the investor at specified prices on pre-determined dates.

Callable common shares Shares that give the issuing company the option (or right), but not the obligation, to buy back the shares from investors at a call price that is specified when the shares are originally issued.

Candlestick chart A price chart with four bits of data for each time interval. A candle indicates the opening and closing price for the interval. The body of the candle is shaded if the opening price was higher than the closing price, and the body is clear if the opening price was lower than the closing price. Vertical lines known as wicks or shadows extend from the top and bottom of the candle to indicate the high and the low prices for the interval.

Cannibalization Cannibalization occurs when an investment takes customers and sales away from another part of the company.

Capacity The ability of the borrower to make its debt payments on time.

Capital account A component of the balance of payments account that measures transfers of capital.

Capital allocation line (CAL) A graph line that describes the combinations of expected return and standard deviation of return available to an investor from combining the optimal portfolio of risky assets with the risk-free asset.

Capital asset pricing model (CAPM) An equation describing the expected return on any asset (or portfolio) as a linear function of its beta relative to the market portfolio.

Capital budgeting The allocation of funds to relatively long-range projects or investments.

Capital consumption allowance A measure of the wear and tear (depreciation) of the capital stock that occurs in the production of goods and services.

Capital deepening investment Increases the stock of capital relative to labor.

Capital expenditure Expenditure on physical capital (fixed assets).

Capital lease See *finance lease*.

Capital market expectations An investor's expectations concerning the risk and return prospects of asset classes.

Capital market line (CML) The line with an intercept point equal to the risk-free rate that is tangent to the efficient frontier of risky assets; represents the efficient frontier when a risk-free asset is available for investment.

Capital market securities Securities with maturities at issuance longer than one year.

Capital markets Financial markets that trade securities of longer duration, such as bonds and equities.

Capital rationing A capital rationing environment assumes that the company has a fixed amount of funds to invest.

Capital restrictions Controls placed on foreigners' ability to own domestic assets and/or domestic residents' ability to own foreign assets.

Capital stock The accumulated amount of buildings, machinery, and equipment used to produce goods and services.

Capital structure The mix of debt and equity that a company uses to finance its business; a company's specific mixture of long-term financing.

Capital-indexed bonds Type of index-linked bond. The coupon rate is fixed but is applied to a principal amount that increases in line with increases in the index during the bond's life.

Captive finance subsidiary A wholly-owned subsidiary of a company that is established to provide financing of the sales of the parent company.

Carry The net of the costs and benefits of holding, storing, or "carrying" an asset.

Carrying amount The amount at which an asset or liability is valued according to accounting principles.

Carrying value The net amount shown for an asset or liability on the balance sheet; book value may also refer to the company's excess of total assets over total liabilities. For a bond, the purchase price plus (or minus) the amortized amount of the discount (or premium).

Cartel Participants in collusive agreements that are made openly and formally.

Cash In accounting contexts, cash on hand (e.g., petty cash and cash not yet deposited to the bank) and demand deposits held in banks and similar accounts that can be used in payment of obligations.

Cash conversion cycle A financial metric that measures the length of time required for a company to convert cash invested in its operations to cash received as a result of its operations; equal to days of inventory on hand + days of sales outstanding − number of days of payables. Also called *net operating cycle*.

Cash equivalents Very liquid short-term investments, usually maturing in 90 days or less.

Cash flow additivity principle The principle that dollar amounts indexed at the same point in time are additive.

Cash flow from operating activities The net amount of cash provided from operating activities.

Cash flow from operations The net amount of cash provided from operating activities.

Cash flow yield The internal rate of return on a series of cash flows.

Cash market securities Money market securities settled on a "same day" or "cash settlement" basis.

Cash markets See *spot markets*.

Cash prices See *spot prices*.

Cash-settled forwards See *non-deliverable forwards*.

Central bank funds market The market in which deposit-taking banks that have an excess reserve with their national central bank can loan money to banks that need funds for maturities ranging from overnight to one year. Called the Federal or Fed funds market in the United States.

Central bank funds rates Interest rates at which central bank funds are bought (borrowed) and sold (lent) for maturities ranging from overnight to one year. Called Federal or Fed funds rates in the United States.

Central banks The dominant bank in a country, usually with official or semi-official governmental status.

Certificate of deposit An instrument that represents a specified amount of funds on deposit with a bank for a specified maturity and interest rate. It is issued in small or large denominations, and can be negotiable or non-negotiable.

Change in polarity principle A tenet of technical analysis that once a support level is breached, it becomes a resistance level. The same holds true for resistance levels; once breached, they become support levels.

Change in quantity supplied A movement along a given supply curve.

Change in supply A shift in the supply curve.

Change of control put A covenant giving bondholders the right to require the issuer to buy back their debt, often at par or at some small premium to par value, in the event that the borrower is acquired.

Character The quality of a debt issuer's management.

Chart of accounts A list of accounts used in an entity's accounting system.

Classified balance sheet A balance sheet organized so as to group together the various assets and liabilities into subcategories (e.g., current and noncurrent).

Clawback A requirement that the GP return any funds distributed as incentive fees until the LPs have received back their initial investment and a percentage of the total profit.

Clearing The process by which the exchange verifies the execution of a transaction and records the participants' identities.

Clearing instructions Instructions that indicate how to arrange the final settlement ("clearing") of a trade.

Clearinghouse An entity associated with a futures market that acts as middleman between the contracting parties and guarantees to each party the performance of the other.

Closed economy An economy that does not trade with other countries; an *autarkic economy*.

Closed-end fund A mutual fund in which no new investment money is accepted. New investors invest by buying existing shares, and investors in the fund liquidate by selling their shares to other investors.

Coefficient of variation (CV) The ratio of a set of observations' standard deviation to the observations' mean value.

Coincident economic indicators Turning points that are usually close to those of the overall economy; they are believed to have value for identifying the economy's present state.

Collateral The quality and value of the assets supporting an issuer's indebtedness.

Collateral manager Buys and sells debt obligations for and from the CDO's portfolio of assets (i.e., the collateral) to generate sufficient cash flows to meet the obligations to the CDO bondholders.

Collateral trust bonds Bonds secured by securities such as common shares, other bonds, or other financial assets.

Collateralized bond obligations A structured asset-backed security that is collateralized by a pool of bonds.

Collateralized debt obligation Generic term used to describe a security backed by a diversified pool of one or more debt obligations.

Collateralized debt obligations A securitized pool of fixed-income assets.

Collateralized loan obligations A structured asset-backed security that is collateralized by a pool of loans.

Collateralized mortgage obligation A security created through the securitization of a pool of mortgage-related products (mortgage pass-through securities or pools of loans).

Collateralized mortgage obligation (CMO) A structured asset-backed security that is collateralized by a pool of mortgages.

Collaterals Assets or financial guarantees underlying a debt obligation above and beyond the issuer's promise to pay.

Combination A listing in which the order of the listed items does not matter.

Commercial paper A short-term, negotiable, unsecured promissory note that represents a debt obligation of the issuer.

Commercial receivables Amounts customers owe the company for products that have been sold as well as amounts that may be due from suppliers (such as for returns of merchandise). Also called *trade receivables* or *accounts receivable*.

Committed capital The amount that the limited partners have agreed to provide to the private equity fund.

Committed lines of credit A bank commitment to extend credit up to a pre-specified amount; the commitment is considered a short-term liability and is usually in effect for 364 days (one day short of a full year).

Commodity swap A swap in which the underlying is a commodity such as oil, gold, or an agricultural product.

Common market Level of economic integration that incorporates all aspects of the customs union and extends it by allowing free movement of factors of production among members.

Common shares A type of security that represent an ownership interest in a company.

Common stock See *common shares*.

Common value auction An auction in which the item being auctioned has the same value to each auction participant, although participants may be uncertain as to what that value is.

Common-size analysis The restatement of financial statement items using a common denominator or reference item that allows one to identify trends and major differences; an example is an income statement in which all items are expressed as a percent of revenue.

Company analysis Analysis of an individual company.

Comparable company A company that has similar business risk; usually in the same industry and preferably with a single line of business.

Comparative advantage A country's ability to produce a good or service at a lower relative cost, or opportunity cost, than its trading partner.

Competitive strategy A company's plans for responding to the threats and opportunities presented by the external environment.

Complements Said of goods which tend to be used together; technically, two goods whose cross-price elasticity of demand is negative.

Complete markets Informally, markets in which the variety of distinct securities traded is so broad that any desired payoff in a future state-of-the-world is achievable.

Complete preferences The assumption that a consumer is able to make a comparison between any two possible bundles of goods.

Completed contract A method of revenue recognition in which the company does not recognize any revenue until the contract is completed; used particularly in long-term construction contracts.

Component cost of capital The rate of return required by suppliers of capital for an individual source of a company's funding, such as debt or equity.

Compounding The process of accumulating interest on interest.

Comprehensive income The change in equity of a business enterprise during a period from nonowner sources; includes all changes in equity during a period except those resulting from investments by owners and distributions to owners; comprehensive income equals net income plus other comprehensive income.

Conditional expected value The expected value of a stated event given that another event has occurred.

Conditional probability The probability of an event given (conditioned on) another event.

Conditional variances The variance of one variable, given the outcome of another.

Consistent With reference to estimators, describes an estimator for which the probability of estimates close to the value of the population parameter increases as sample size increases.

Conspicuous consumption Consumption of high status goods, such as a luxury automobile or a very expensive piece of jewelry.

Constant returns to scale The characteristic of constant per-unit costs in the presence of increased production.

Constant-cost industry When firms in the industry experience no change in resource costs and output prices over the long run.

Constant-yield price trajectory A graph that illustrates the change in the price of a fixed-income bond over time assuming no change in yield-to-maturity. The trajectory shows the "pull to par" effect on the price of a bond trading at a premium or a discount to par value.

Constituent securities With respect to an index, the individual securities within an index.

Consumer choice theory The theory relating consumer demand curves to consumer preferences.

Consumer surplus The difference between the value that a consumer places on units purchased and the amount of money that was required to pay for them.

Consumption   The purchase of final goods and services by individuals.

Consumption basket   A specific combination of the goods and services that a consumer wants to consume.

Consumption bundle   A specific combination of the goods and services that a consumer wants to consume.

Contingency provision   Clause in a legal document that allows for some action if a specific event or circumstance occurs.

Contingent claims   Derivatives in which the payoffs occur if a specific event occurs; generally referred to as options.

Contingent convertible bonds   Bonds that automatically convert into equity if a specific event or circumstance occurs, such as the issuer's equity capital falling below the minimum requirement set by the regulators. Also called *CoCos*.

Continuation patterns   A type of pattern used in technical analysis to predict the resumption of a market trend that was in place prior to the formation of a pattern.

Continuous random variable   A random variable for which the range of possible outcomes is the real line (all real numbers between $-\infty$ and $+\infty$ or some subset of the real line).

Continuous time   Time thought of as advancing in extremely small increments.

Continuous trading market   A market in which trades can be arranged and executed any time the market is open.

Continuously compounded return   The natural logarithm of 1 plus the holding period return, or equivalently, the natural logarithm of the ending price over the beginning price.

Contra account   An account that offsets another account.

Contract rate   See *mortgage rate*.

Contraction   The period of a business cycle after the peak and before the trough; often called a *recession* or, if exceptionally severe, called a *depression*.

Contraction risk   The risk that when interest rates decline, the security will have a shorter maturity than was anticipated at the time of purchase because borrowers refinance at now-available lower interest rates.

Contractionary   Tending to cause the real economy to contract.

Contractionary fiscal policy   A fiscal policy that has the objective to make the real economy contract.

Contracts for differences   See *non-deliverable forwards*.

Contribution margin   The amount available for fixed costs and profit after paying variable costs; revenue minus variable costs.

Convenience yield   A non-monetary advantage of holding an asset.

Conventional bond   See *plain vanilla bond*.

Conventional cash flow   A conventional cash flow pattern is one with an initial outflow followed by a series of inflows.

Convergence   The tendency for differences in output per capita across countries to diminish over time; in technical analysis, a term that describes the case when an indicator moves in the same manner as the security being analyzed.

Conversion price   For a convertible bond, the price per share at which the bond can be converted into shares.

Conversion ratio   For a convertible bond, the number of common shares that each bond can be converted into.

Conversion value   For a convertible bond, the current share price multiplied by the conversion ratio.

Convertible bond   Bond that gives the bondholder the right to exchange the bond for a specified number of common shares in the issuing company.

Convertible preference shares   A type of equity security that entitles shareholders to convert their shares into a specified number of common shares.

Convexity adjustment   For a bond, one half of the annual or approximate convexity statistic multiplied by the change in the yield-to-maturity squared.

Core inflation   The inflation rate calculated based on a price index of goods and services except food and energy.

Correlation   A number between -1 and $+1$ that measures the comovement (linear association) between two random variables.

Correlation coefficient   A number between -1 and $+1$ that measures the consistency or tendency for two investments to act in a similar way. It is used to determine the effect on portfolio risk when two assets are combined.

Cost averaging   The periodic investment of a fixed amount of money.

Cost of capital   The rate of return that suppliers of capital require as compensation for their contribution of capital.

Cost of carry   See *carry*.

Cost of debt   The cost of debt financing to a company, such as when it issues a bond or takes out a bank loan.

Cost of goods sold   For a given period, equal to beginning inventory minus ending inventory plus the cost of goods acquired or produced during the period.

Cost of preferred stock   The cost to a company of issuing preferred stock; the dividend yield that a company must commit to pay preferred stockholders.

Cost recovery method   A method of revenue recognition in which the seller does not report any profit until the cash amounts paid by the buyer—including principal and interest on any financing from the seller—are greater than all the seller's costs for the merchandise sold.

Cost structure   The mix of a company's variable costs and fixed costs.

Cost-push   Type of inflation in which rising costs, usually wages, compel businesses to raise prices generally.

Counterparty risk   The risk that the other party to a contract will fail to honor the terms of the contract.

Coupon rate   The interest rate promised in a contract; this is the rate used to calculate the periodic interest payments.

Cournot assumption   Assumption in which each firm determines its profit-maximizing production level assuming that the other firms' output will not change.

Covariance   A measure of the co-movement (linear association) between two random variables.

Covariance matrix   A matrix or square array whose entries are covariances; also known as a variance–covariance matrix.

Covenants   The terms and conditions of lending agreements that the issuer must comply with; they specify the actions that an issuer is obligated to perform (affirmative covenant) or prohibited from performing (negative covenant).

Covered bond   Debt obligation secured by a segregated pool of assets called the cover pool. The issuer must maintain the value of the cover pool. In the event of default, bondholders have recourse against both the issuer and the cover pool.

Covered call   An option strategy involving the holding of an asset and sale of a call on the asset.

Credit   With respect to double-entry accounting, a credit records increases in liability, owners' equity, and revenue accounts or decreases in asset accounts; with respect to borrowing, the willingness and ability of the borrower to make promised payments on the borrowing.

Credit analysis   The evaluation of credit risk; the evaluation of the creditworthiness of a borrower or counterparty.

Credit curve   A curve showing the relationship between time to maturity and yield spread for an issuer with comparable bonds of various maturities outstanding, usually upward sloping.

Credit default swap (CDS)   A type of credit derivative in which one party, the credit protection buyer who is seeking credit protection against a third party, makes a series of regularly scheduled payments to the other party, the credit protection seller. The seller makes no payments until a credit event occurs.

Credit derivatives   A contract in which one party has the right to claim a payment from another party in the event that a specific credit event occurs over the life of the contract.

Credit enhancements   Provisions that may be used to reduce the credit risk of a bond issue.

Credit migration risk   The risk that a bond issuer's creditworthiness deteriorates, or migrates lower, leading investors to believe the risk of default is higher. Also called *downgrade risk*.

Credit risk   The risk of loss caused by a counterparty's or debtor's failure to make a promised payment. Also called *default risk*.

Credit scoring model   A statistical model used to classify borrowers according to creditworthiness.

Credit spread option   An option on the yield spread on a bond.

Credit tranching   A structure used to redistribute the credit risk associated with the collateral; a set of bond classes created to allow investors a choice in the amount of credit risk that they prefer to bear.

Credit-linked coupon bond   Bond for which the coupon changes when the bond's credit rating changes.

Credit-linked note   Fixed-income security in which the holder of the security has the right to withhold payment of the full amount due at maturity if a credit event occurs.

Credit-worthiness   The perceived ability of the borrower to pay what is owed on the borrowing in a timely manner; it represents the ability of a company to withstand adverse impacts on its cash flows.

Cross-default provisions   Provisions whereby events of default such as non-payment of interest on one bond trigger default on all outstanding debt; implies the same default probability for all issues.

Cross-price elasticity of demand   The percent change in quantity demanded for a given small change in the price of another good; the responsiveness of the demand for Product A that is associated with the change in price of Product B.

Cross-sectional analysis   Analysis that involves comparisons across individuals in a group over a given time period or at a given point in time.

Cross-sectional data   Observations over individual units at a point in time, as opposed to time-series data.

Crossing networks   Trading systems that match buyers and sellers who are willing to trade at prices obtained from other markets.

Crowding out   The thesis that government borrowing may divert private sector investment from taking place.

Cumulative distribution function   A function giving the probability that a random variable is less than or equal to a specified value.

Cumulative preference shares   Preference shares for which any dividends that are not paid accrue and must be paid in full before dividends on common shares can be paid.

Cumulative relative frequency   For data grouped into intervals, the fraction of total observations that are less than the value of the upper limit of a stated interval.

Cumulative voting   Voting that allows shareholders to direct their total voting rights to specific candidates, as opposed to having to allocate their voting rights evenly among all candidates.

Currencies   Monies issued by national monetary authorities.

Currency option bonds   Bonds that give the bondholder the right to choose the currency in which he or she wants to receive interest payments and principal repayments.

Currency swap   A swap in which each party makes interest payments to the other in different currencies.

Current account   A component of the balance of payments account that measures the flow of goods and services.

Current assets   Assets that are expected to be consumed or converted into cash in the near future, typically one year or less. Also called *liquid assets*.

Current cost   With reference to assets, the amount of cash or cash equivalents that would have to be paid to buy the same or an equivalent asset today; with reference to liabilities, the undiscounted amount of cash or cash equivalents that would be required to settle the obligation today.

Current government spending   With respect to government expenditures, spending on goods and services that are provided on a regular, recurring basis including health, education, and defense.

Current liabilities   Short-term obligations, such as accounts payable, wages payable, or accrued liabilities, that are expected to be settled in the near future, typically one year or less.

Current ratio   A liquidity ratio calculated as current assets divided by current liabilities.

Current yield   The sum of the coupon payments received over the year divided by the flat price; also called the *income* or *interest yield* or *running yield*.

Curve duration   The sensitivity of the bond price (or the market value of a financial asset or liability) with respect to a benchmark yield curve.

Customs union   Extends the free trade area (FTA) by not only allowing free movement of goods and services among members, but also creating a common trade policy against nonmembers.

Cyclical   See *cyclical companies*.

Cyclical companies   Companies with sales and profits that regularly expand and contract with the business cycle or state of economy.

Daily settlement   See *mark to market* and *marking to market*.

Dark pools   Alternative trading systems that do not display the orders that their clients send to them.

Data mining   The practice of determining a model by extensive searching through a dataset for statistically significant patterns. Also called *data snooping*.

Data snooping   See *data mining*.

Date of book closure   The date that a shareholder listed on the corporation's books will be deemed to have ownership of the shares for purposes of receiving an upcoming dividend; two business days after the ex-dividend date.

Date of record   The date that a shareholder listed on the corporation's books will be deemed to have ownership of the shares for purposes of receiving an upcoming dividend; two business days after the ex-dividend date.

Day order   An order that is good for the day on which it is submitted. If it has not been filled by the close of business, the order expires unfilled.

Days in receivables   Estimate of the average number of days it takes to collect on credit accounts.

Days of inventory on hand (DOH)   An activity ratio equal to the number of days in the period divided by inventory turnover over the period.

Day's sales outstanding   Estimate of the average number of days it takes to collect on credit accounts.

Dead cross   A technical analysis term that describes a situation where a short-term moving average crosses from above a longer-term moving average to below it; this movement is considered bearish.

Deadweight loss   A net loss of total (consumer and producer) surplus.

Dealers   A financial intermediary that acts as a principal in trades.

Dealing securities   Securities held by banks or other financial intermediaries for trading purposes.

Debentures   Type of bond that can be secured or unsecured.

Debit   With respect to double-entry accounting, a debit records increases of asset and expense accounts or decreases in liability and owners' equity accounts.

Debt incurrence test   A financial covenant made in conjunction with existing debt that restricts a company's ability to incur additional debt at the same seniority based on one or more financial tests or conditions.

Debt-rating approach   A method for estimating a company's before-tax cost of debt based upon the yield on comparably rated bonds for maturities that closely match that of the company's existing debt.

Debt-to-assets ratio   A solvency ratio calculated as total debt divided by total assets.

Debt-to-capital ratio   A solvency ratio calculated as total debt divided by total debt plus total shareholders' equity.

Debt-to-equity ratio   A solvency ratio calculated as total debt divided by total shareholders' equity.

Declaration date   The day that the corporation issues a statement declaring a specific dividend.

Decreasing returns to scale   Increase in cost per unit resulting from increased production.

Decreasing-cost industry   An industry in which per-unit costs and output prices are lower when industry output is increased in the long run.

Deductible temporary differences   Temporary differences that result in a reduction of or deduction from taxable income in a future period when the balance sheet item is recovered or settled.

Default probability   The probability that a borrower defaults or fails to meet its obligation to make full and timely payments of principal and interest, according to the terms of the debt security. Also called *default risk*.

Default risk   The probability that a borrower defaults or fails to meet its obligation to make full and timely payments of principal and interest, according to the terms of the debt security. Also called *default probability*.

Default risk premium   An extra return that compensates investors for the possibility that the borrower will fail to make a promised payment at the contracted time and in the contracted amount.

Defensive companies   Companies with sales and profits that have little sensitivity to the business cycle or state of the economy.

Defensive interval ratio   A liquidity ratio that estimates the number of days that an entity could meet cash needs from liquid assets; calculated as (cash + short-term marketable investments + receivables) divided by daily cash expenditures.

Deferred coupon bond   Bond that pays no coupons for its first few years but then pays a higher coupon than it otherwise normally would for the remainder of its life. Also called *split coupon bond*.

Deferred income   A liability account for money that has been collected for goods or services that have not yet been delivered; payment received in advance of providing a good or service.

Deferred revenue   A liability account for money that has been collected for goods or services that have not yet been delivered; payment received in advance of providing a good or service.

Deferred tax assets   A balance sheet asset that arises when an excess amount is paid for income taxes relative to accounting profit. The taxable income is higher than accounting profit and income tax payable exceeds tax expense. The company expects to recover the difference during the course of future operations when tax expense exceeds income tax payable.

Deferred tax liabilities   A balance sheet liability that arises when a deficit amount is paid for income taxes relative to accounting profit. The taxable income is less than the accounting profit and income tax payable is less than tax expense. The company expects to eliminate the liability over the course of future operations when income tax payable exceeds tax expense.

Defined benefit pension plans   Plan in which the company promises to pay a certain annual amount (defined benefit) to the employee after retirement. The company bears the investment risk of the plan assets.

Defined contribution pension plans   Individual accounts to which an employee and typically the employer makes contributions, generally on a tax-advantaged basis. The amounts of contributions are defined at the outset, but the future value of the benefit is unknown. The employee bears the investment risk of the plan assets.

Defined-benefit plan   A pension plan that specifies the plan sponsor's obligations in terms of the benefit to plan participants.

Defined-contribution plan   A pension plan that specifies the sponsor's obligations in terms of contributions to the pension fund rather than benefits to plan participants.

Deflation   Negative inflation.

Degree of confidence   The probability that a confidence interval includes the unknown population parameter.

Degree of financial leverage   (DFL) The ratio of the percentage change in net income to the percentage change in operating income; the sensitivity of the cash flows available to owners when operating income changes.

Degree of operating leverage   (DOL) The ratio of the percentage change in operating income to the percentage change in units sold; the sensitivity of operating income to changes in units sold.

Degree of total leverage   The ratio of the percentage change in net income to the percentage change in units sold; the sensitivity of the cash flows to owners to changes in the number of units produced and sold.

Degrees of freedom (df)   The number of independent observations used.

Demand The willingness and ability of consumers to purchase a given amount of a good or service at a given price.

Demand and supply analysis The study of how buyers and sellers interact to determine transaction prices and quantities.

Demand curve Graph of the inverse demand function.

Demand function A relationship that expresses the quantity demanded of a good or service as a function of own-price and possibly other variables.

Demand shock A typically unexpected disturbance to demand, such as an unexpected interruption in trade or transportation.

Demand-pull Type of inflation in which increasing demand raises prices generally, which then are reflected in a business's costs as workers demand wage hikes to catch up with the rising cost of living.

Dependent With reference to events, the property that the probability of one event occurring depends on (is related to) the occurrence of another event.

Depository bank A bank that raises funds from depositors and other investors and lends it to borrowers.

Depository institutions Commercial banks, savings and loan banks, credit unions, and similar institutions that raise funds from depositors and other investors and lend it to borrowers.

Depository receipt A security that trades like an ordinary share on a local exchange and represents an economic interest in a foreign company.

Depreciation The process of systematically allocating the cost of long-lived (tangible) assets to the periods during which the assets are expected to provide economic benefits.

Depression See *contraction*.

Derivative pricing rule A pricing rule used by crossing networks in which a price is taken (derived) from the price that is current in the asset's primary market.

Derivatives A financial instrument whose value depends on the value of some underlying asset or factor (e.g., a stock price, an interest rate, or exchange rate).

Descending price auction An auction in which the auctioneer begins at a high price, then lowers the called price in increments until there is a willing buyer for the item being auctioned.

Descriptive statistics The study of how data can be summarized effectively.

Development capital Minority equity investments in more mature companies that are looking for capital to expand or restructure operations, enter new markets, or finance major acquisitions.

Diffuse prior The assumption of equal prior probabilities.

Diffusion index Reflects the proportion of the index's components that are moving in a pattern consistent with the overall index.

Diluted EPS The EPS that would result if all dilutive securities were converted into common shares.

Diluted shares The number of shares that would be outstanding if all potentially dilutive claims on common shares (e.g., convertible debt, convertible preferred stock, and employee stock options) were exercised.

Diminishing balance method An accelerated depreciation method, i.e., one that allocates a relatively large proportion of the cost of an asset to the early years of the asset's useful life.

Diminishing marginal productivity Describes a state in which each additional unit of input produces less output than previously.

Direct debit program An arrangement whereby a customer authorizes a debit to a demand account; typically used by companies to collect routine payments for services.

Direct financing leases A type of finance lease, from a lessor perspective, where the present value of the lease payments (less receivable) equals the carrying value of the leased asset. The revenues earned by the lessor are financing in nature.

Direct format With reference to the cash flow statement, a format for the presentation of the statement in which cash flow from operating activities is shown as operating cash receipts less operating cash disbursements. Also called *direct method*.

Direct method See *direct format*.

Direct taxes Taxes levied directly on income, wealth, and corporate profits.

Direct write-off method An approach to recognizing credit losses on customer receivables in which the company waits until such time as a customer has defaulted and only then recognizes the loss.

Disbursement float The amount of time between check issuance and a check's clearing back against the company's account.

Discount To reduce the value of a future payment in allowance for how far away it is in time; to calculate the present value of some future amount. Also, the amount by which an instrument is priced below its face (par) value.

Discount interest A procedure for determining the interest on a loan or bond in which the interest is deducted from the face value in advance.

Discount margin See *required margin*.

Discount rates In general, the interest rate used to calculate a present value. In the money market, however, discount rate is a specific type of quoted rate.

Discounted cash flow models Valuation models that estimate the intrinsic value of a security as the present value of the future benefits expected to be received from the security.

Discouraged worker A person who has stopped looking for a job or has given up seeking employment.

Discrete random variable A random variable that can take on at most a countable number of possible values.

Discriminatory pricing rule A pricing rule used in continuous markets in which the limit price of the order or quote that first arrived determines the trade price.

Diseconomies of scale Increase in cost per unit resulting from increased production.

Dispersion The variability around the central tendency.

Display size The size of an order displayed to public view.

Distressed investing Investing in securities of companies in financial difficulties. Private equity funds typically buy the debt of mature companies in financial difficulties.

Divergence In technical analysis, a term that describes the case when an indicator moves differently from the security being analyzed.

Diversification ratio The ratio of the standard deviation of an equally weighted portfolio to the standard deviation of a randomly selected security.

Dividend A distribution paid to shareholders based on the number of shares owned.

Dividend discount model (DDM) A present value model that estimates the intrinsic value of an equity share based on the present value of its expected future dividends.

Dividend discount model based approach An approach for estimating a country's equity risk premium. The market rate of return is estimated as the sum of the dividend yield and the growth rate in dividends for a market index. Subtracting the risk-free rate of return from the estimated market return produces an estimate for the equity risk premium.

Dividend payout ratio The ratio of cash dividends paid to earnings for a period.

Dividend yield Annual dividends per share divided by share price.

Divisor A number (denominator) used to determine the value of a price return index. It is initially chosen at the inception of an index and subsequently adjusted by the index provider, as necessary, to avoid changes in the index value that are unrelated to changes in the prices of its constituent securities.

Domestic content provisions Stipulate that some percentage of the value added or components used in production should be of domestic origin.

Double bottoms In technical analysis, a reversal pattern that is formed when the price reaches a low, rebounds, and then sells off back to the first low level; used to predict a change from a downtrend to an uptrend.

Double coincidence of wants A prerequisite to barter trades, in particular that both economic agents in the transaction want what the other is selling.

Double declining balance depreciation An accelerated depreciation method that involves depreciating the asset at double the straight-line rate. This rate is multiplied by the book value of the asset at the beginning of the period (a declining balance) to calculate depreciation expense.

Double top In technical analysis, a reversal pattern that is formed when an uptrend reverses twice at roughly the same high price level; used to predict a change from an uptrend to a downtrend.

Double-entry accounting The accounting system of recording transactions in which every recorded transaction affects at least two accounts so as to keep the basic accounting equation (assets = liabilities + owners' equity) in balance.

Down transition probability The probability that an asset's value moves down in a model of asset price dynamics.

Downgrade risk The risk that a bond issuer's creditworthiness deteriorates, or migrates lower, leading investors to believe the risk of default is higher. Also called *credit migration risk*.

Drag on liquidity When receipts lag, creating pressure from the decreased available funds.

Drawdown A reduction in net asset value (NAV).

DuPont analysis An approach to decomposing return on investment, e.g., return on equity, as the product of other financial ratios.

Dual-currency bonds Bonds that make coupon payments in one currency and pay the par value at maturity in another currency.

Duration gap A bond's Macaulay duration minus the investment horizon.

Dutch Book theorem A result in probability theory stating that inconsistent probabilities create profit opportunities.

Dutch auction An auction in which the auctioneer begins at a high price, then lowers the called price in increments until there is a willing buyer for the item being auctioned.

Early repayment option See *prepayment option*.

Earnings per share The amount of income earned during a period per share of common stock.

Earnings surprise The portion of a company's earnings that is unanticipated by investors and, according to the efficient market hypothesis, merits a price adjustment.

Economic costs All the remuneration needed to keep a productive resource in its current employment or to acquire the resource for productive use; the sum of total accounting costs and implicit opportunity costs.

Economic indicator A variable that provides information on the state of the overall economy.

Economic loss The amount by which accounting profit is less than normal profit.

Economic order quantity–reorder point (EOQ–ROP) An approach to managing inventory based on expected demand and the predictability of demand; the ordering point for new inventory is determined based on the costs of ordering and carrying inventory, such that the total cost associated with inventory is minimized.

Economic profit Equal to accounting profit less the implicit opportunity costs not included in total accounting costs; the difference between total revenue (TR) and total cost (TC). Also called *abnormal profit* or *supernormal profit*.

Economic rent The surplus value that results when a particular resource or good is fixed in supply and market price is higher than what is required to bring the resource or good onto the market and sustain its use.

Economic stabilization Reduction of the magnitude of economic fluctuations.

Economic union Incorporates all aspects of a common market and in addition requires common economic institutions and coordination of economic policies among members.

Economics The study of the production, distribution, and consumption of goods and services; the principles of the allocation of scarce resources among competing uses. Economics is divided into two broad areas of study: macroeconomics and microeconomics.

Economies of scale Reduction in cost per unit resulting from increased production.

Effective annual rate The amount by which a unit of currency will grow in a year with interest on interest included.

Effective annual yield (EAY) An annualized return that accounts for the effect of interest on interest; EAY is computed by compounding 1 plus the holding period yield forward to one year, then subtracting 1.

Effective convexity A *curve convexity* statistic that measures the secondary effect of a change in a benchmark yield curve on a bond's price.

Effective duration The sensitivity of a bond's price to a change in a benchmark yield curve.

Effective interest rate The borrowing rate or market rate that a company incurs at the time of issuance of a bond.

Efficient market A market in which asset prices reflect new information quickly and rationally.

Elastic Said of a good or service when the magnitude of elasticity is greater than one.

Elasticity The percentage change in one variable for a percentage change in another variable; a measure of how sensitive one variable is to a change in the value of another variable.

Elasticity of supply A measure of the sensitivity of quantity supplied to a change in price.

Electronic communications networks See *alternative trading systems*.

Electronic funds transfer (EFT) The use of computer networks to conduct financial transactions electronically.

Elliott wave theory   A technical analysis theory that claims that the market follows regular, repeated waves or cycles.

Embedded option   Contingency provisions that provide the issuer or the bondholders the right, but not the obligation, to take action. These options are not part of the security and cannot be traded separately.

Empirical probability   The probability of an event estimated as a relative frequency of occurrence.

Employed   The number of people with a job.

Endogenous variables   Variables whose equilibrium values are determined within the model being considered.

Enterprise value   A measure of a company's total market value from which the value of cash and short-term investments have been subtracted.

Equal weighting   An index weighting method in which an equal weight is assigned to each constituent security at inception.

Equilibrium condition   A condition necessary for the forces within a system to be in balance.

Equipment trust certificates   Bonds secured by specific types of equipment or physical assets.

Equity   Assets less liabilities; the residual interest in the assets after subtracting the liabilities.

Equity risk premium   The expected return on equities minus the risk-free rate; the premium that investors demand for investing in equities.

Equity swap   A swap transaction in which at least one cash flow is tied to the return to an equity portfolio position, often an equity index.

Equity-linked note   Type of index-linked bond for which the final payment is based on the return of an equity index.

Estimate   The particular value calculated from sample observations using an estimator.

Estimation   With reference to statistical inference, the subdivision dealing with estimating the value of a population parameter.

Estimator   An estimation formula; the formula used to compute the sample mean and other sample statistics are examples of estimators.

Eurobonds   Type of bond issued internationally, outside the jurisdiction of the country in whose currency the bond is denominated.

European-style   Said of an option contract that can only be exercised on the option's expiration date.

Event   Any outcome or specified set of outcomes of a random variable.

Ex-date   The first date that a share trades without (i.e. "ex") the dividend.

Ex-dividend date   The first date that a share trades without (i.e. "ex") the dividend.

Excess kurtosis   Degree of peakedness (fatness of tails) in excess of the peakedness of the normal distribution.

Excess supply   A condition in which the quantity ready to be supplied is greater than the quantity demanded.

Exchanges   Places where traders can meet to arrange their trades.

Execution instructions   Instructions that indicate how to fill an order.

Exercise   The process of using an option to buy or sell the underlying.

Exercise price   The fixed price at which an option holder can buy or sell the underlying. Also called *strike price*, *striking price*, or *strike*.

Exercise value   The value obtained if an option is exercised based on current conditions. Also known as *intrinsic value*.

Exhaustive   Covering or containing all possible outcomes.

Exogenous variables   Variables whose equilibrium values are determined outside of the model being considered.

Expansion   The period of a business cycle after its lowest point and before its highest point.

Expansionary   Tending to cause the real economy to grow.

Expansionary fiscal policy   Fiscal policy aimed at achieving real economic growth.

Expected inflation   The level of inflation that economic agents expect in the future.

Expected loss   Default probability times Loss severity given default.

Expected value   The probability-weighted average of the possible outcomes of a random variable.

Expenses   Outflows of economic resources or increases in liabilities that result in decreases in equity (other than decreases because of distributions to owners); reductions in net assets associated with the creation of revenues.

Experience curve   A curve that shows the direct cost per unit of good or service produced or delivered as a typically declining function of cumulative output.

Export subsidy   Paid by the government to the firm when it exports a unit of a good that is being subsidized.

Exports   Goods and services that an economy sells to other countries.

Extension risk   The risk that when interest rates rise, fewer prepayments will occur because homeowners are reluctant to give up the benefits of a contractual interest rate that now looks low. As a result, the security becomes longer in maturity than anticipated at the time of purchase.

Externality   An effect of a market transaction that is borne by parties other than those who transacted.

Extra dividend   A dividend paid by a company that does not pay dividends on a regular schedule, or a dividend that supplements regular cash dividends with an extra payment.

FIFO method   The first in, first out, method of accounting for inventory, which matches sales against the costs of items of inventory in the order in which they were placed in inventory.

FX swap   The combination of a spot and a forward FX transaction.

Face value   The amount of cash payable by a company to the bondholders when the bonds mature; the promised payment at maturity separate from any coupon payment.

Factor   A common or underlying element with which several variables are correlated.

Factor markets   Markets for the purchase and sale of factors of production.

Fair value   The amount at which an asset could be exchanged, or a liability settled, between knowledgeable, willing parties in an arm's-length transaction; the price that would be received to sell an asset or paid to transfer a liability in an orderly transaction between market participants.

Fed funds rate   The US interbank lending rate on overnight borrowings of reserves.

Federal funds rate   The US interbank lending rate on overnight borrowings of reserves.

Fiat money   Money that is not convertible into any other commodity.

Fibonacci sequence   A sequence of numbers starting with 0 and 1, and then each subsequent number in the sequence is the sum of the two preceding numbers. In Elliott Wave Theory, it is believed that market waves follow patterns that are the ratios of the numbers in the Fibonacci sequence.

Fiduciary call   A combination of a European call and a risk-free bond that matures on the option expiration day and has a face value equal to the exercise price of the call.

Fill or kill   See *immediate or cancel order*.

Finance lease   Essentially, the purchase of some asset by the buyer (lessee) that is directly financed by the seller (lessor). Also called *capital lease*.

Financial account   A component of the balance of payments account that records investment flows.

Financial flexibility   The ability to react and adapt to financial adversities and opportunities.

Financial leverage   The extent to which a company can effect, through the use of debt, a proportional change in the return on common equity that is greater than a given proportional change in operating income; also, short for the financial leverage ratio.

Financial leverage ratio   A measure of financial leverage calculated as average total assets divided by average total equity.

Financial risk   The risk that environmental, social, or governance risk factors will result in significant costs or other losses to a company and its shareholders; the risk arising from a company's obligation to meet required payments under its financing agreements.

Financing activities   Activities related to obtaining or repaying capital to be used in the business (e.g., equity and long-term debt).

Firm commitment offering   See *underwritten offering*.

First lien debt   Debt secured by a pledge of certain assets that could include buildings, but may also include property and equipment, licenses, patents, brands, etc.

First mortgage debt   Debt secured by a pledge of a specific property.

First price sealed bid auction   An auction in which envelopes containing bids are opened simultaneously and the item is sold to the highest bidder.

First-degree price discrimination   Where a monopolist is able to charge each customer the highest price the customer is willing to pay.

Fiscal multiplier   The ratio of a change in national income to a change in government spending.

Fiscal policy   The use of taxes and government spending to affect the level of aggregate expenditures.

Fisher effect   The thesis that the real rate of interest in an economy is stable over time so that changes in nominal interest rates are the result of changes in expected inflation.

Fisher index   The geometric mean of the Laspeyres index.

Fixed charge coverage   A solvency ratio measuring the number of times interest and lease payments are covered by operating income, calculated as (EBIT + lease payments) divided by (interest payments + lease payments).

Fixed costs   Costs that remain at the same level regardless of a company's level of production and sales.

Fixed price tender offer   Offer made by a company to repurchase a specific number of shares at a fixed price that is typically at a premium to the current market price.

Fixed rate perpetual preferred stock   Nonconvertible, non-callable preferred stock that has a fixed dividend rate and no maturity date.

Fixed-for-floating interest rate swap   An interest rate swap in which one party pays a fixed rate and the other pays a floating rate, with both sets of payments in the same currency. Also called *plain vanilla swap* or *vanilla swap*.

Flags   A technical analysis continuation pattern formed by parallel trendlines, typically over a short period.

Flat price   The full price of a bond minus the accrued interest; also called the *quoted* or *clean* price.

Float   In the context of customer receipts, the amount of money that is in transit between payments made by customers and the funds that are usable by the company.

Float factor   An estimate of the average number of days it takes deposited checks to clear; average daily float divided by average daily deposit.

Float-adjusted market-capitalization weighting   An index weighting method in which the weight assigned to each constituent security is determined by adjusting its market capitalization for its market float.

Floaters   See *floating-rate notes*.

Floating-rate notes   A note on which interest payments are not fixed, but instead vary from period to period depending on the current level of a reference interest rate.

Flotation cost   Fees charged to companies by investment bankers and other costs associated with raising new capital.

Foreclosure   Allows the lender to take possession of a mortgaged property if the borrower defaults, and then sell it to recover funds.

Foreign currency reserves   Holding by the central bank of non-domestic currency deposits and non-domestic bonds.

Foreign direct investment   Direct investment by a firm in one country (the source country) in productive assets in a foreign country (the host country).

Foreign exchange gains (or losses)   Gains (or losses) that occur when the exchange rate changes between the investor's currency and the currency that foreign securities are denominated in.

Foreign portfolio investment   Shorter-term investment by individuals, firms, and institutional investors (e.g., pension funds) in foreign financial instruments such as foreign stocks and foreign government bonds.

Forward commitments   Class of derivatives that provides the ability to lock in a price to transact in the future at a previously agreed-upon price.

Forward contract   An agreement between two parties in which one party, the buyer, agrees to buy from the other party, the seller, an underlying asset at a later date for a price established at the start of the contract.

Forward curve   A series of forward rates, each having the same timeframe.

Forward market   For future delivery, beyond the usual settlement time period in the cash market.

Forward price   The fixed price or rate at which the transaction scheduled to occur at the expiration of a forward contract will take place. This price is agreed on at the initiation date of the contract.

Forward rate   The interest rate on a bond or money market instrument traded in a forward market. A forward rate can be interpreted as an incremental, or marginal, return for extending the time-to-maturity for an additional time period.

Forward rate agreements   A forward contract calling for one party to make a fixed interest payment and the other to make an interest payment at a rate to be determined at the contract expiration.

Fractile   A value at or below which a stated fraction of the data lies.

Fractional reserve banking   Banking in which reserves constitute a fraction of deposits.

Free cash flow   The actual cash that would be available to the company's investors after making all investments necessary to maintain the company as an ongoing enterprise (also referred to as free cash flow to the firm); the internally generated funds that can be distributed to the company's investors (e.g., shareholders and bondholders) without impairing the value of the company.

Free cash flow to equity (FCFE)   The cash flow available to a company's common shareholders after all operating expenses, interest, and principal payments have been made, and necessary investments in working and fixed capital have been made.

Free cash flow to the firm (FCFF)   The cash flow available to the company's suppliers of capital after all operating expenses have been paid and necessary investments in working capital and fixed capital have been made.

Free float   The number of shares that are readily and freely tradable in the secondary market.

Free trade   When there are no government restrictions on a country's ability to trade.

Free trade areas   One of the most prevalent forms of regional integration, in which all barriers to the flow of goods and services among members have been eliminated.

Free-cash-flow-to-equity models   Valuation models based on discounting expected future free cash flow to equity.

Frequency distribution   A tabular display of data summarized into a relatively small number of intervals.

Frequency polygon   A graph of a frequency distribution obtained by drawing straight lines joining successive points representing the class frequencies.

Full price   The price of a security with accrued interest; also called the *invoice* or *dirty* price.

Fundamental analysis   The examination of publicly available information and the formulation of forecasts to estimate the intrinsic value of assets.

Fundamental value   The underlying or true value of an asset based on an analysis of its qualitative and quantitative characteristics. Also called *intrinsic value*.

Fundamental weighting   An index weighting method in which the weight assigned to each constituent security is based on its underlying company's size. It attempts to address the disadvantages of market-capitalization weighting by using measures that are independent of the constituent security's price.

Funds of hedge funds   Funds that hold a portfolio of hedge funds.

Future value (FV)   The amount to which a payment or series of payments will grow by a stated future date.

Futures contract   A variation of a forward contract that has essentially the same basic definition but with some additional features, such as a clearinghouse guarantee against credit losses, a daily settlement of gains and losses, and an organized electronic or floor trading facility.

Futures price   The agreed-upon price of a futures contract.

G-spread   The yield spread in basis points over an actual or interpolated government bond.

GDP deflator   A gauge of prices and inflation that measures the aggregate changes in prices across the overall economy.

Gains   Asset inflows not directly related to the ordinary activities of the business.

Game theory   The set of tools decision makers use to incorporate responses by rival decision makers into their strategies.

General equilibrium analysis   An analysis that provides for equilibria in multiple markets simultaneously.

General partner   The partner that runs the business and theoretically bears unlimited liability.

Geometric mean   A measure of central tendency computed by taking the nth root of the product of n non-negative values.

Giffen good   A good that is consumed more as the price of the good rises.

Gilts   Bonds issued by the UK government.

Giro system   An electronic payment system used widely in Europe and Japan.

Global depository receipt   A depository receipt that is issued outside of the company's home country and outside of the United States.

Global minimum-variance portfolio   The portfolio on the minimum-variance frontier with the smallest variance of return.

Global registered share   A common share that is traded on different stock exchanges around the world in different currencies.

Gold standard   With respect to a currency, if a currency is on the gold standard a given amount can be converted into a prespecified amount of gold.

Golden cross   A technical analysis term that describes a situation where a short-term moving average crosses from below a longer-term moving average to above it; this movement is considered bullish.

Good-on-close   An execution instruction specifying that an order can only be filled at the close of trading. Also called *market on close*.

Good-on-open   An execution instruction specifying that an order can only be filled at the opening of trading.

Good-till-cancelled order   An order specifying that it is valid until the entity placing the order has cancelled it (or, commonly, until some specified amount of time such as 60 days has elapsed, whichever comes sooner).

Goods markets   Markets for the output of production.

Goodwill   An intangible asset that represents the excess of the purchase price of an acquired company over the value of the net assets acquired.

Government equivalent yield   A yield that restates a yield-to-maturity based on 30/360 day-count to one based on actual/actual.

Greenmail   The purchase of the accumulated shares of a hostile investor by a company that is targeted for takeover by that investor, usually at a substantial premium over market price.

Grey market   The forward market for bonds about to be issued. Also called "when issued" market.

Gross domestic product   The market value of all final goods and services produced within the economy in a given period of time (output definition) or, equivalently, the aggregate income earned by all households, all companies, and the government within the economy in a given period of time (income definition).

Gross margin   Sales minus the cost of sales (i.e., the cost of goods sold for a manufacturing company).

Gross profit   Sales minus the cost of sales (i.e., the cost of goods sold for a manufacturing company).

Gross profit margin   The ratio of gross profit to revenues.

Grouping by function   With reference to the presentation of expenses in an income statement, the grouping together of expenses serving the same function, e.g. all items that are costs of goods sold.

Grouping by nature   With reference to the presentation of expenses in an income statement, the grouping together of expenses by similar nature, e.g., all depreciation expenses.

Growth cyclical   A term sometimes used to describe companies that are growing rapidly on a long-term basis but that still experience above-average fluctuation in their revenues and profits over the course of a business cycle.

Growth investors   With reference to equity investors, investors who seek to invest in high-earnings-growth companies.

Haircut   See *repo margin*.

Harmonic mean   A type of weighted mean computed by averaging the reciprocals of the observations, then taking the reciprocal of that average.

Head and shoulders pattern   In technical analysis, a reversal pattern that is formed in three parts: a left shoulder, head, and right shoulder; used to predict a change from an uptrend to a downtrend.

Headline inflation   The inflation rate calculated based on the price index that includes all goods and services in an economy.

Hedge funds   Private investment vehicles that typically use leverage, derivatives, and long and short investment strategies.

Hedge portfolio   A hypothetical combination of the derivative and its underlying that eliminates risk.

Held for trading   Debt or equity financial assets bought with the intention to sell them in the near term, usually less than three months; securities that a company intends to trade. Also called *trading securities*.

Held-to-maturity   Debt (fixed-income) securities that a company intends to hold to maturity; these are presented at their original cost, updated for any amortization of discounts or premiums.

Herding   Clustered trading that may or may not be based on information.

Hidden order   An order that is exposed not to the public but only to the brokers or exchanges that receive it.

High water marks   The highest value, net of fees, which a fund has reached. It reflects the highest cumulative return used to calculate an incentive fee.

Histogram   A bar chart of data that have been grouped into a frequency distribution.

Historical cost   In reference to assets, the amount paid to purchase an asset, including any costs of acquisition and/or preparation; with reference to liabilities, the amount of proceeds received in exchange in issuing the liability.

Historical equity risk premium approach   An estimate of a country's equity risk premium that is based upon the historical averages of the risk-free rate and the rate of return on the market portfolio.

Historical simulation   Another term for the historical method of estimating VAR. This term is somewhat misleading in that the method involves not a *simulation* of the past but rather what *actually happened* in the past, sometimes adjusted to reflect the fact that a different portfolio may have existed in the past than is planned for the future.

Holder-of-record date   The date that a shareholder listed on the corporation's books will be deemed to have ownership of the shares for purposes of receiving an upcoming dividend; two business days after the ex-dividend date.

Holding period return   The return that an investor earns during a specified holding period; a synonym for total return.

Holding period yield (HPY)   The return that an investor earns during a specified holding period; holding period return with reference to a fixed-income instrument.

Homogeneity of expectations   The assumption that all investors have the same economic expectations and thus have the same expectations of prices, cash flows, and other investment characteristics.

Horizon yield   The internal rate of return between the total return (the sum of reinvested coupon payments and the sale price or redemption amount) and the purchase price of the bond.

Horizontal analysis   Common-size analysis that involves comparing a specific financial statement with that statement in prior or future time periods; also, cross-sectional analysis of one company with another.

Horizontal demand schedule   Implies that at a given price, the response in the quantity demanded is infinite.

Household   A person or a group of people living in the same residence, taken as a basic unit in economic analysis.

Hurdle rate   The rate of return that must be met for a project to be accepted.

Hypothesis   With reference to statistical inference, a statement about one or more populations.

Hypothesis testing   With reference to statistical inference, the subdivision dealing with the testing of hypotheses about one or more populations.

I-spread   The yield spread of a specific bond over the standard swap rate in that currency of the same tenor.

IRR rule   An investment decision rule that accepts projects or investments for which the IRR is greater than the opportunity cost of capital.

Iceberg order   An order in which the display size is less than the order's full size.

If-converted method   A method for accounting for the effect of convertible securities on earnings per share (EPS) that specifies what EPS would have been if the convertible securities had been converted at the beginning of the period, taking account of the effects of conversion on net income and the weighted average number of shares outstanding.

Immediate or cancel order   An order that is valid only upon receipt by the broker or exchange. If such an order cannot be filled in part or in whole upon receipt, it cancels immediately. Also called *fill or kill*.

Impact lag   The lag associated with the result of actions affecting the economy with delay.

Imperfect competition   A market structure in which an individual firm has enough share of the market (or can control a certain segment of the market) such that it is able to exert some influence over price.

Implicit price deflator for GDP   A gauge of prices and inflation that measures the aggregate changes in prices across the overall economy.

Implied forward rates   Calculated from spot rates, an implied forward rate is a break-even reinvestment rate that links the return on an investment in a shorter-term zero-coupon bond to the return on an investment in a longer-term zero-coupon bond.

Implied volatility   The volatility that option traders use to price an option, implied by the price of the option and a particular option-pricing model.

Import license   Specifies the quantity of a good that can be imported into a country.

Imports Goods and services that a domestic economy (i.e., house-holds, firms, and government) purchases from other countries.

In the money Options that, if exercised, would result in the value received being worth more than the payment required to exercise.

In-the-money Options that, if exercised, would result in the value received being worth more than the payment required to exercise.

Incentive fee (or performance fee) Funds distributed by the general partner to the limited partner(s) based on realized profits.

Income Increases in economic benefits in the form of inflows or enhancements of assets, or decreases of liabilities that result in an increase in equity (other than increases resulting from contributions by owners).

Income constraint The constraint on a consumer to spend, in total, no more than his income.

Income elasticity of demand A measure of the responsiveness of demand to changes in income, defined as the percentage change in quantity demanded divided by the percentage change in income.

Income statement A financial statement that provides information about a company's profitability over a stated period of time. Also called *statement of operations* or *profit and loss statement*.

Income tax paid The actual amount paid for income taxes in the period; not a provision, but the actual cash outflow.

Income tax payable The income tax owed by the company on the basis of taxable income.

Income trust A type of equity ownership vehicle established as a trust issuing ownership shares known as units.

Increasing marginal returns Where the marginal product of a resource increases as additional units of that input are employed.

Increasing returns to scale Reduction in cost per unit resulting from increased production.

Increasing-cost industry An industry in which per-unit costs and output prices are higher when industry output is increased in the long run.

Incremental cash flow The cash flow that is realized because of a decision; the changes or increments to cash flows resulting from a decision or action.

Indenture Legal contract that describes the form of a bond, the obligations of the issuer, and the rights of the bondholders. Also called the *trust deed*.

Independent With reference to events, the property that the occurrence of one event does not affect the probability of another event occurring.

Independent projects Independent projects are projects whose cash flows are independent of each other.

Independently and identically distributed (IID) With respect to random variables, the property of random variables that are independent of each other but follow the identical probability distribution.

Index of Leading Economic Indicators A composite of economic variables used by analysts to predict future economic conditions.

Index-linked bond Bond for which coupon payments and/or principal repayment are linked to a specified index.

Indexing An investment strategy in which an investor constructs a portfolio to mirror the performance of a specified index.

Indifference curve A curve representing all the combinations of two goods or attributes such that the consumer is entirely indifferent among them.

Indifference curve map A group or family of indifference curves, representing a consumer's entire utility function.

Indirect format With reference to cash flow statements, a format for the presentation of the statement which, in the operating cash flow section, begins with net income then shows additions and subtractions to arrive at operating cash flow. Also called *indirect method*.

Indirect method See *indirect format*.

Indirect taxes Taxes such as taxes on spending, as opposed to direct taxes.

Industry A group of companies offering similar products and/or services.

Industry analysis The analysis of a specific branch of manufacturing, service, or trade.

Inelastic Insensitive to price changes.

Inelastic supply Said of supply that is insensitive to the price of goods sold.

Inferior goods A good whose consumption decreases as income increases.

Inflation The percentage increase in the general price level from one period to the next; a sustained rise in the overall level of prices in an economy.

Inflation Reports A type of economic publication put out by many central banks.

Inflation premium An extra return that compensates investors for expected inflation.

Inflation rate The percentage change in a price index—that is, the speed of overall price level movements.

Inflation uncertainty The degree to which economic agents view future rates of inflation as difficult to forecast.

Inflation-linked bond Type of index-linked bond that offers investors protection against inflation by linking the bond's coupon payments and/or the principal repayment to an index of consumer prices. Also called *linkers*.

Information cascade The transmission of information from those participants who act first and whose decisions influence the decisions of others.

Information-motivated traders Traders that trade to profit from information that they believe allows them to predict future prices.

Informationally efficient market A market in which asset prices reflect new information quickly and rationally.

Initial margin The amount that must be deposited in a clearinghouse account when entering into a futures contract.

Initial margin requirement The margin requirement on the first day of a transaction as well as on any day in which additional margin funds must be deposited.

Initial public offering (IPO) The first issuance of common shares to the public by a formerly private corporation.

Installment method With respect to revenue recognition, a method that specifies that the portion of the total profit of the sale that is recognized in each period is determined by the percentage of the total sales price for which the seller has received cash.

Installment sales With respect to revenue recognition, a method that specifies that the portion of the total profit of the sale that is recognized in each period is determined by the percentage of the total sales price for which the seller has received cash.

Intangible assets Assets lacking physical substance, such as patents and trademarks.

Interbank market The market of loans and deposits between banks for maturities ranging from overnight to one year.

Interbank money market The market of loans and deposits between banks for maturities ranging from overnight to one year.

Interest Payment for lending funds.

Interest coverage A solvency ratio calculated as EBIT divided by interest payments.

Interest rate A rate of return that reflects the relationship between differently dated cash flows; a discount rate.

Interest rate swap A swap in which the underlying is an interest rate. Can be viewed as a currency swap in which both currencies are the same and can be created as a combination of currency swaps.

Interest-only mortgage A loan in which no scheduled principal repayment is specified for a certain number of years.

Intergenerational data mining A form of data mining that applies information developed by previous researchers using a dataset to guide current research using the same or a related dataset.

Intermarket analysis A field within technical analysis that combines analysis of major categories of securities—namely, equities, bonds, currencies, and commodities—to identify market trends and possible inflections in a trend.

Intermediate goods and services Goods and services purchased for use as inputs to produce other goods and services.

Internal rate of return (IRR) The discount rate that makes net present value equal 0; the discount rate that makes the present value of an investment's costs (outflows) equal to the present value of the investment's benefits (inflows).

Interpolated spread The yield spread of a specific bond over the standard swap rate in that currency of the same tenor.

Interquartile range The difference between the third and first quartiles of a dataset.

Interval With reference to grouped data, a set of values within which an observation falls.

Interval scale A measurement scale that not only ranks data but also gives assurance that the differences between scale values are equal.

Intrinsic value See *exercise value*.

Inventory The unsold units of product on hand.

Inventory blanket lien The use of inventory as collateral for a loan. Though the lender has claim to some or all of the company's inventory, the company may still sell or use the inventory in the ordinary course of business.

Inventory investment Net change in business inventory.

Inventory turnover An activity ratio calculated as cost of goods sold divided by average inventory.

Inverse demand function A restatement of the demand function in which price is stated as a function of quantity.

Investing activities Activities which are associated with the acquisition and disposal of property, plant, and equipment; intangible assets; other long-term assets; and both long-term and short-term investments in the equity and debt (bonds and loans) issued by other companies.

Investment banks Financial intermediaries that provide advice to their mostly corporate clients and help them arrange transactions such as initial and seasoned securities offerings.

Investment opportunity schedule A graphical depiction of a company's investment opportunities ordered from highest to lowest expected return. A company's optimal capital budget is found where the investment opportunity schedule intersects with the company's marginal cost of capital.

Investment policy statement (IPS) A written planning document that describes a client's investment objectives and risk tolerance over a relevant time horizon, along with constraints that apply to the client's portfolio.

Investment property Property used to earn rental income or capital appreciation (or both).

January effect Calendar anomaly that stock market returns in January are significantly higher compared to the rest of the months of the year, with most of the abnormal returns reported during the first five trading days in January. Also called *turn-of-the-year effect*.

Joint probability The probability of the joint occurrence of stated events.

Joint probability function A function giving the probability of joint occurrences of values of stated random variables.

Just-in-time (JIT) method Method of managing inventory that minimizes in-process inventory stocks.

Key rate duration A method of measuring the interest rate sensitivities of a fixed-income instrument or portfolio to shifts in key points along the yield curve.

Keynesians Economists who believe that fiscal policy can have powerful effects on aggregate demand, output, and employment when there is substantial spare capacity in an economy.

Kondratieff wave A 54-year long economic cycle postulated by Nikolai Kondratieff.

Kurtosis The statistical measure that indicates the peakedness of a distribution.

LIFO layer liquidation With respect to the application of the LIFO inventory method, the liquidation of old, relatively low-priced inventory; happens when the volume of sales rises above the volume of recent purchases so that some sales are made from relatively old, low-priced inventory. Also called *LIFO liquidation*.

LIFO method The last in, first out, method of accounting for inventory, which matches sales against the costs of items of inventory in the reverse order the items were placed in inventory (i.e., inventory produced or acquired last are assumed to be sold first).

Labor force The portion of the working age population (over the age of 16) that is employed or is available for work but not working (unemployed).

Labor markets Markets for labor services.

Labor productivity The quantity of goods and services (real GDP) that a worker can produce in one hour of work.

Laddering strategy A form of active strategy which entails scheduling maturities on a systematic basis within the investment portfolio such that investments are spread out equally over the term of the ladder.

Lagging economic indicators Turning points that take place later than those of the overall economy; they are believed to have value in identifying the economy's past condition.

Laspeyres index A price index created by holding the composition of the consumption basket constant.

Law of demand The principle that as the price of a good rises, buyers will choose to buy less of it, and as its price falls, they will buy more.

Law of diminishing returns The smallest output that a firm can produce such that its long run average costs are minimized.

Law of one price   The condition in a financial market in which two equivalent financial instruments or combinations of financial instruments can sell for only one price. Equivalent to the principle that no arbitrage opportunities are possible.

Law of supply   The principle that a rise in price usually results in an increase in the quantity supplied.

Lead underwriter   The lead investment bank in a syndicate of investment banks and broker–dealers involved in a securities underwriting.

Leading economic indicators   Turning points that usually precede those of the overall economy; they are believed to have value for predicting the economy's future state, usually near-term.

Legal tender   Something that must be accepted when offered in exchange for goods and services.

Lender of last resort   An entity willing to lend money when no other entity is ready to do so.

Leptokurtic   Describes a distribution that is more peaked than a normal distribution.

Lessee   The party obtaining the use of an asset through a lease.

Lessor   The owner of an asset that grants the right to use the asset to another party.

Letter of credit   Form of external credit enhancement whereby a financial institution provides the issuer with a credit line to reimburse any cash flow shortfalls from the assets backing the issue.

Level of significance   The probability of a Type I error in testing a hypothesis.

Leverage   In the context of corporate finance, leverage refers to the use of fixed costs within a company's cost structure. Fixed costs that are operating costs (such as depreciation or rent) create operating leverage. Fixed costs that are financial costs (such as interest expense) create financial leverage.

Leveraged buyout   (LBO) A transaction whereby the target company management team converts the target to a privately held company by using heavy borrowing to finance the purchase of the target company's outstanding shares.

Liabilities   Present obligations of an enterprise arising from past events, the settlement of which is expected to result in an outflow of resources embodying economic benefits; creditors' claims on the resources of a company.

Life-cycle stage   The stage of the life cycle: embryonic, growth, shakeout, mature, declining.

Likelihood   The probability of an observation, given a particular set of conditions.

Limit down   A limit move in the futures market in which the price at which a transaction would be made is at or below the lower limit.

Limit order   Instructions to a broker or exchange to obtain the best price immediately available when filling an order, but in no event accept a price higher than a specified (limit) price when buying or accept a price lower than a specified (limit) price when selling.

Limit order book   The book or list of limit orders to buy and sell that pertains to a security.

Limit up   A limit move in the futures market in which the price at which a transaction would be made is at or above the upper limit.

Limitations on liens   Meant to put limits on how much secured debt an issuer can have.

Limited partners   Partners with limited liability. Limited partnerships in hedge and private equity funds are typically restricted to investors who are expected to understand and to be able to assume the risks associated with the investments.

Line chart   In technical analysis, a plot of price data, typically closing prices, with a line connecting the points.

Linear interpolation   The estimation of an unknown value on the basis of two known values that bracket it, using a straight line between the two known values.

Linear scale   A scale in which equal distances correspond to equal absolute amounts. Also called *arithmetic scale*.

Linker   See *inflation-linked bond*.

Liquid market   Said of a market in which traders can buy or sell with low total transaction costs when they want to trade.

Liquidating dividend   A dividend that is a return of capital rather than a distribution from earnings or retained earnings.

Liquidation   To sell the assets of a company, division, or subsidiary piecemeal, typically because of bankruptcy; the form of bankruptcy that allows for the orderly satisfaction of creditors' claims after which the company ceases to exist.

Liquidity   The ability to purchase or sell an asset quickly and easily at a price close to fair market value. The ability to meet short-term obligations using assets that are the most readily converted into cash.

Liquidity premium   An extra return that compensates investors for the risk of loss relative to an investment's fair value if the investment needs to be converted to cash quickly.

Liquidity ratios   Financial ratios measuring the company's ability to meet its short-term obligations.

Liquidity trap   A condition in which the demand for money becomes infinitely elastic (horizontal demand curve) so that injections of money into the economy will not lower interest rates or affect real activity.

Load fund   A mutual fund in which, in addition to the annual fee, a percentage fee is charged to invest in the fund and/or for redemptions from the fund.

Loan-to-value ratio   The ratio of a property's purchase price to the amount of its mortgage.

Lockbox system   A payment system in which customer payments are mailed to a post office box and the banking institution retrieves and deposits these payments several times a day, enabling the company to have use of the fund sooner than in a centralized system in which customer payments are sent to the company.

Locked limit   A condition in the futures markets in which a transaction cannot take place because the price would be beyond the limits.

Lockup period   The minimum period before investors are allowed to make withdrawals or redeem shares from a fund.

Logarithmic scale   A scale in which equal distances represent equal proportional changes in the underlying quantity.

London Interbank Offered Rate   (Libor) Collective name for multiple rates at which a select set of banks believe they could borrow unsecured funds from other banks in the London interbank market for different currencies and different borrowing periods ranging from overnight to one year.

London interbank offered rate   (Libor or LIBOR) Collective name for multiple rates at which a select set of banks believe they could borrow unsecured funds from other banks in the London interbank market for different currencies and different borrowing periods ranging from overnight to one year.

Long   The buyer of a derivative contract. Also refers to the position of owning a derivative.

Long position   A position in an asset or contract in which one owns the asset or has an exercisable right under the contract.

Long-lived assets   Assets that are expected to provide economic benefits over a future period of time, typically greater than one year. Also called *long-term assets*.

Long-run average total cost curve   The curve describing average total costs when no costs are considered fixed.

Long-run industry supply curve   A curve describing the relationship between quantity supplied and output prices when no costs are considered fixed.

Long-term contract   A contract that spans a number of accounting periods.

Longitudinal data   Observations on characteristic(s) of the same observational unit through time.

Look-ahead bias   A bias caused by using information that was unavailable on the test date.

Loss severity   Portion of a bond's value (including unpaid interest) an investor loses in the event of default.

Losses   Asset outflows not directly related to the ordinary activities of the business.

Lower bound   The lowest possible value of an option.

M^2   A measure of what a portfolio would have returned if it had taken on the same total risk as the market index.

Macaulay duration   The approximate amount of time a bond would have to be held for the market discount rate at purchase to be realized if there is a single change in interest rate. It indicates the point in time when the coupon reinvestment and price effects of a change in yield-to- maturity offset each other.

Macroeconomics   The branch of economics that deals with aggregate economic quantities, such as national output and national income.

Maintenance covenants   Covenants in bank loan agreements that require the borrower to satisfy certain financial ratio tests while the loan is outstanding.

Maintenance margin   The minimum amount that is required by a futures clearinghouse to maintain a margin account and to protect against default. Participants whose margin balances drop below the required maintenance margin must replenish their accounts.

Maintenance margin requirement   The margin requirement on any day other than the first day of a transaction.

Management buy-ins   Leveraged buyout in which the current management team is being replaced and the acquiring team will be involved in managing the company.

Management buyout   (MBO) An event in which a group of investors consisting primarily of the company's existing management purchase all of its outstanding shares and take the company private.

Management fee   A fee based on assets under management or committed capital, as applicable. Also called *base fee*.

Manufacturing resource planning (MRP)   The incorporation of production planning into inventory management. A MRP analysis provides both a materials acquisition schedule and a production schedule.

Margin   The amount of money that a trader deposits in a margin account. The term is derived from the stock market practice in which an investor borrows a portion of the money required to purchase a certain amount of stock. In futures markets, there is no borrowing so the margin is more of a down payment or performance bond.

Margin bond   A cash deposit required by the clearinghouse from the participants to a contract to provide a credit guarantee. Also called a *performance bond*.

Margin call   A request for the short to deposit additional funds to bring their balance up to the initial margin.

Margin loan   Money borrowed from a broker to purchase securities.

Marginal cost   The cost of producing an additional unit of a good.

Marginal probability   The probability of an event *not* conditioned on another event.

Marginal product   Measures the productivity of each unit of input and is calculated by taking the difference in total product from adding another unit of input (assuming other resource quantities are held constant).

Marginal propensity to consume   The proportion of an additional unit of disposable income that is consumed or spent; the change in consumption for a small change in income.

Marginal propensity to save   The proportion of an additional unit of disposable income that is saved (not spent).

Marginal rate of substitution   The rate at which one is willing to give up one good to obtain more of another.

Marginal revenue   The change in total revenue divided by the change in quantity sold; simply, the additional revenue from selling one more unit.

Marginal revenue product   The amount of additional revenue received from employing an additional unit of an input.

Marginal value   The added value from an additional unit of a good.

Marginal value curve   A curve describing the highest price consumers are willing to pay for each additional unit of a good.

Mark to market   The revaluation of a financial asset or liability to its current market value or fair value.

Market   A means of bringing buyers and sellers together to exchange goods and services.

Market anomaly   Change in the price or return of a security that cannot directly be linked to current relevant information known in the market or to the release of new information into the market.

Market bid–ask spread   The difference between the best bid and the best offer.

Market discount rate   The rate of return required by investors given the risk of the investment in a bond; also called the *required yield* or the *required rate of return*.

Market equilibrium   The condition in which the quantity willingly offered for sale by sellers at a given price is just equal to the quantity willingly demanded by buyers at that same price.

Market float   The number of shares that are available to the investing public.

Market liquidity risk   The risk that the price at which investors can actually transact—buying or selling—may differ from the price indicated in the market.

Market mechanism   The process by which price adjusts until there is neither excess supply nor excess demand.

Market model   A regression equation that specifies a linear relationship between the return on a security (or portfolio) and the return on a broad market index.

Market multiple models   Valuation models based on share price multiples or enterprise value multiples.

Market order   Instructions to a broker or exchange to obtain the best price immediately available when filling an order.

Market rate of interest   The rate demanded by purchases of bonds, given the risks associated with future cash payment obligations of the particular bond issue.

Market structure   The competitive environment (perfect competition, monopolistic competition, oligopoly, and monopoly).

Market value   The price at which an asset or security can currently be bought or sold in an open market.

Market-capitalization weighting   An index weighting method in which the weight assigned to each constituent security is determined by dividing its market capitalization by the total market capitalization (sum of the market capitalization) of all securities in the index. Also called *value weighting*.

Market-on-close   An execution instruction specifying that an order can only be filled at the close of trading.

Market-oriented investors   With reference to equity investors, investors whose investment disciplines cannot be clearly categorized as value or growth.

Marketable limit order   A buy limit order in which the limit price is placed above the best offer, or a sell limit order in which the limit price is placed below the best bid. Such orders generally will partially or completely fill right away.

Markowitz efficient frontier   The graph of the set of portfolios offering the maximum expected return for their level of risk (standard deviation of return).

Matching principle   The accounting principle that expenses should be recognized when the associated revenue is recognized.

Matching strategy   An active investment strategy that includes intentional matching of the timing of cash outflows with investment maturities.

Matrix pricing   Process of estimating the market discount rate and price of a bond based on the quoted or flat prices of more frequently traded comparable bonds.

Maturity premium   An extra return that compensates investors for the increased sensitivity of the market value of debt to a change in market interest rates as maturity is extended.

Maturity structure   A factor explaining the differences in yields on similar bonds; also called *term structure*.

Mean absolute deviation   With reference to a sample, the mean of the absolute values of deviations from the sample mean.

Mean excess return   The average rate of return in excess of the risk-free rate.

Mean–variance analysis   An approach to portfolio analysis using expected means, variances, and covariances of asset returns.

Measure of central tendency   A quantitative measure that specifies where data are centered.

Measure of value   A standard for measuring value; a function of money.

Measurement scales   A scheme of measuring differences. The four types of measurement scales are nominal, ordinal, interval, and ratio.

Measures of location   A quantitative measure that describes the location or distribution of data; includes not only measures of central tendency but also other measures such as percentiles.

Median   The value of the middle item of a set of items that has been sorted into ascending or descending order; the 50th percentile.

Medium of exchange   Any asset that can be used to purchase goods and services or to repay debts; a function of money.

Medium-term note   A corporate bond offered continuously to investors by an agent of the issuer, designed to fill the funding gap between commercial paper and long-term bonds.

Menu costs   A cost of inflation in which businesses constantly have to incur the costs of changing the advertised prices of their goods and services.

Mesokurtic   Describes a distribution with kurtosis identical to that of the normal distribution.

Mezzanine financing   Debt or preferred shares with a relationship to common equity due to a feature such as attached warrants or conversion options and that is subordinate to both senior and high yield debt. It is referred to as mezzanine because of its location on the balance sheet.

Microeconomics   The branch of economics that deals with markets and decision making of individual economic units, including consumers and businesses.

Minimum efficient scale   The smallest output that a firm can produce such that its long run average cost is minimized.

Minimum-variance portfolio   The portfolio with the minimum variance for each given level of expected return.

Minsky moment   Named for Hyman Minksy: A point in a business cycle when, after individuals become overextended in borrowing to finance speculative investments, people start realizing that something is likely to go wrong and a panic ensues leading to asset sell-offs.

Mismatching strategy   An active investment strategy whereby the timing of cash outflows is not matched with investment maturities.

Modal interval   With reference to grouped data, the most frequently occurring interval.

Mode   The most frequently occurring value in a set of observations.

Modern portfolio theory   (MPT) The analysis of rational portfolio choices based on the efficient use of risk.

Modified duration   A measure of the percentage price change of a bond given a change in its yield-to-maturity.

Momentum oscillators   A graphical representation of market sentiment that is constructed from price data and calculated so that it oscillates either between a high and a low or around some number.

Monetarists   Economists who believe that the rate of growth of the money supply is the primary determinant of the rate of inflation.

Monetary policy   Actions taken by a nation's central bank to affect aggregate output and prices through changes in bank reserves, reserve requirements, or its target interest rate.

Monetary transmission mechanism   The process whereby a central bank's interest rate gets transmitted through the economy and ultimately affects the rate of increase of prices.

Monetary union   An economic union in which the members adopt a common currency.

Money   A generally accepted medium of exchange and unit of account.

Money convexity   For a bond, the annual or approximate convexity multiplied by the full price.

Money creation   The process by which changes in bank reserves translate into changes in the money supply.

Money duration   A measure of the price change in units of the currency in which the bond is denominated given a change in its yield-to-maturity.

Money market   The market for short-term debt instruments (one-year maturity or less).

Money market securities Fixed-income securities with maturities at issuance of one year or less.

Money market yield A yield on a basis comparable to the quoted yield on an interest-bearing money market instrument that pays interest on a 360-day basis; the annualized holding period yield, assuming a 360-day year.

Money multiplier Describes how a change in reserves is expected to affect the money supply; in its simplest form, 1 divided by the reserve requirement.

Money neutrality The thesis that an increase in the money supply leads in the long-run to an increase in the price level, while leaving real variables like output and employment unaffected.

Money-weighted return The internal rate of return on a portfolio, taking account of all cash flows.

Moneyness The relationship between the price of the underlying and an option's exercise price.

Monopolist Said of an entity that is the only seller in its market.

Monopolistic competition Highly competitive form of imperfect competition; the competitive characteristic is a notably large number of firms, while the monopoly aspect is the result of product differentiation.

Monopoly In pure monopoly markets, there are no substitutes for the given product or service. There is a single seller, which exercises considerable power over pricing and output decisions.

Monte Carlo simulation An approach to estimating a probability distribution of outcomes to examine what might happen if particular risks are faced. This method is widely used in the sciences as well as in business to study a variety of problems.

Mortgage loan A loan secured by the collateral of some specified real estate property that obliges the borrower to make a predetermined series of payments to the lender.

Mortgage pass-through security A security created when one or more holders of mortgages form a pool of mortgages and sell shares or participation certificates in the pool.

Mortgage rate The interest rate on a mortgage loan; also called *contract rate*.

Mortgage-backed securities Debt obligations that represent claims to the cash flows from pools of mortgage loans, most commonly on residential property.

Mortgage-backed security Debt obligations that represent claims to the cash flows from pools of mortgage loans, most commonly on residential property.

Moving average The average of the closing price of a security over a specified number of periods. With each new period, the average is recalculated.

Moving-average convergence/divergence oscillator (MACD) A momentum oscillator that is constructed based on the difference between short-term and long-term moving averages of a security's price.

Multi-factor model A model that explains a variable in terms of the values of a set of factors.

Multi-market indices Comprised of indices from different countries, designed to represent multiple security markets.

Multi-step format With respect to the format of the income statement, a format that presents a subtotal for gross profit (revenue minus cost of goods sold).

Multilateral trading facilities See *alternative trading systems*.

Multinational corporation A company operating in more than one country or having subsidiary firms in more than one country.

Multiplication rule for probabilities The rule that the joint probability of events A and B equals the probability of A given B times the probability of B.

Multiplier models Valuation models based on share price multiples or enterprise value multiples.

Multivariate distribution A probability distribution that specifies the probabilities for a group of related random variables.

Multivariate normal distribution A probability distribution for a group of random variables that is completely defined by the means and variances of the variables plus all the correlations between pairs of the variables.

Muni A type of non-sovereign bond issued by a state or local government in the United States. It very often (but not always) offers income tax exemptions.

Municipal bonds A type of non-sovereign bond issued by a state or local government in the United States. It very often (but not always) offers income tax exemptions.

Mutual fund A professionally managed investment pool in which investors in the fund typically each have a pro-rata claim on the income and value of the fund.

Mutually exclusive projects Mutually exclusive projects compete directly with each other. For example, if Projects A and B are mutually exclusive, you can choose A or B, but you cannot choose both.

n Factorial For a positive integer n, the product of the first n positive integers; 0 factorial equals 1 by definition. n factorial is written as $n!$.

NPV rule An investment decision rule that states that an investment should be undertaken if its NPV is positive but not undertaken if its NPV is negative.

Narrow money The notes and coins in circulation in an economy, plus other very highly liquid deposits.

Nash equilibrium When two or more participants in a non-coop-erative game have no incentive to deviate from their respective equilibrium strategies given their opponent's strategies.

National income The income received by all factors of production used in the generation of final output. National income equals gross domestic product (or, in some countries, gross national product) minus the capital consumption allowance and a statistical discrepancy.

Natural rate of unemployment Effective unemployment rate, below which pressure emerges in labor markets.

Negative externality A negative effect (e.g., pollution) of a market transaction that is borne by parties other than those who transacted; a spillover cost.

Neo-Keynesians A group of dynamic general equilibrium models that assume slow-to-adjust prices and wages.

Net book value The remaining (undepreciated) balance of an asset's purchase cost. For liabilities, the face value of a bond minus any unamortized discount, or plus any unamortized premium.

Net exports The difference between the value of a country's exports and the value of its imports (i.e., value of exports minus imports).

Net income The difference between revenue and expenses; what remains after subtracting all expenses (including depreciation, interest, and taxes) from revenue.

Net operating cycle An estimate of the average time that elapses between paying suppliers for materials and collecting cash from the subsequent sale of goods produced.

Net present value (NPV) The present value of an investment's cash inflows (benefits) minus the present value of its cash outflows (costs).

Net profit margin An indicator of profitability, calculated as net income divided by revenue; indicates how much of each dollar of revenues is left after all costs and expenses. Also called *profit margin* or *return on sales*.

Net realisable value Estimated selling price in the ordinary course of business less the estimated costs necessary to make the sale.

Net revenue Revenue after adjustments (e.g., for estimated returns or for amounts unlikely to be collected).

Net tax rate The tax rate net of transfer payments.

Neutral rate of interest The rate of interest that neither spurs on nor slows down the underlying economy.

New Keynesians A group of dynamic general equilibrium models that assume slow-to-adjust prices and wages.

New classical macroeconomics An approach to macroeconomics that seeks the macroeconomic conclusions of individuals maximizing utility on the basis of rational expectations and companies maximizing profits.

New-issue DRP Dividend reinvestment plan in which the company meets the need for additional shares by issuing them instead of purchasing them.

No-load fund A mutual fund in which there is no fee for investing in the fund or for redeeming fund shares, although there is an annual fee based on a percentage of the fund's net asset value.

Node Each value on a binomial tree from which successive moves or outcomes branch.

Nominal GDP The value of goods and services measured at current prices.

Nominal rate A rate of interest based on the security's face value.

Nominal risk-free interest rate The sum of the real risk-free interest rate and the inflation premium.

Nominal scale A measurement scale that categorizes data but does not rank them.

Non-accelerating inflation rate of unemployment Effective unemployment rate, below which pressure emerges in labor markets.

Non-agency RMBS In the United States, securities issued by private entities that are not guaranteed by a federal agency or a GSE.

Non-cumulative preference shares Preference shares for which dividends that are not paid in the current or subsequent periods are forfeited permanently (instead of being accrued and paid at a later date).

Non-current assets Assets that are expected to benefit the company over an extended period of time (usually more than one year).

Non-current liabilities Obligations that broadly represent a probable sacrifice of economic benefits in periods generally greater than one year in the future.

Non-current liability Obligations that broadly represent a probably sacrifice of economic benefits in periods generally greater than one year in the future.

Non-cyclical A company whose performance is largely independent of the business cycle.

Non-deliverable forwards Cash-settled forward contracts, used predominately with respect to foreign exchange forwards. Also called *contracts for differences*.

Non-participating preference shares Preference shares that do not entitle shareholders to share in the profits of the company. Instead, shareholders are only entitled to receive a fixed dividend payment and the par value of the shares in the event of liquidation.

Non-recourse loan Loan in which the lender does not have a shortfall claim against the borrower, so the lender can look only to the property to recover the outstanding mortgage balance.

Non-renewable resources Finite resources that are depleted once they are consumed, such as oil and coal.

Non-satiation The assumption that the consumer could never have so much of a preferred good that she would refuse any more, even if it were free; sometimes referred to as the "more is better" assumption.

Non-sovereign bonds A bond issued by a government below the national level, such as a province, region, state, or city.

Non-sovereign government bonds A bond issued by a government below the national level, such as a province, region, state, or city.

Nonconventional cash flow In a nonconventional cash flow pattern, the initial outflow is not followed by inflows only, but the cash flows can flip from positive (inflows) to negative (outflows) again (or even change signs several times).

Noncurrent assets Assets that are expected to benefit the company over an extended period of time (usually more than one year).

Nonparametric test A test that is not concerned with a parameter, or that makes minimal assumptions about the population from which a sample comes.

Nonsystematic risk Unique risk that is local or limited to a particular asset or industry that need not affect assets outside of that asset class.

Normal distribution A continuous, symmetric probability distribution that is completely described by its mean and its variance.

Normal good A good that is consumed in greater quantities as income increases.

Normal profit The level of accounting profit needed to just cover the implicit opportunity costs ignored in accounting costs.

Notching Ratings adjustment methodology where specific issues from the same borrower may be assigned different credit ratings.

Notes payable Amounts owed by a business to creditors as a result of borrowings that are evidenced by (short-term) loan agreements.

Notice period The length of time (typically 30 to 90 days) in advance that investors may be required to notify a fund of their intent to redeem.

Notional principal An imputed principal amount.

Number of days of inventory An activity ratio equal to the number of days in a period divided by the inventory ratio for the period; an indication of the number of days a company ties up funds in inventory.

Number of days of payables An activity ratio equal to the number of days in a period divided by the payables turnover ratio for the period; an estimate of the average number of days it takes a company to pay its suppliers.

Number of days of receivables Estimate of the average number of days it takes to collect on credit accounts.

Objective probabilities Probabilities that generally do not vary from person to person; includes a priori and objective probabilities.

Off-the-run Seasoned government bonds are off-the-run securities; they are not the most recently issued or the most actively traded.

Offer The price at which a dealer or trader is willing to sell an asset, typically qualified by a maximum quantity (ask size).

Official interest rate An interest rate that a central bank sets and announces publicly; normally the rate at which it is willing to lend money to the commercial banks. Also called *official policy rate* or *policy rate.*

Official policy rate An interest rate that a central bank sets and announces publicly; normally the rate at which it is willing to lend money to the commercial banks.

Oligopoly Market structure with a relatively small number of firms supplying the market.

On-the-run The most recently issued and most actively traded sovereign securities.

One-sided hypothesis test A test in which the null hypothesis is rejected only if the evidence indicates that the population parameter is greater than (smaller than) θ_0. The alternative hypothesis also has one side.

One-tailed hypothesis test A test in which the null hypothesis is rejected only if the evidence indicates that the population parameter is greater than (smaller than) θ_0. The alternative hypothesis also has one side.

Open economy An economy that trades with other countries.

Open interest The number of outstanding contracts in a clearinghouse at any given time. The open interest figure changes daily as some parties open up new positions, while other parties offset their old positions.

Open market operations The purchase or sale of bonds by the national central bank to implement monetary policy. The bonds traded are usually sovereign bonds issued by the national government.

Open-end fund A mutual fund that accepts new investment money and issues additional shares at a value equal to the net asset value of the fund at the time of investment.

Open-market DRP Dividend reinvestment plan in which the company purchases shares in the open market to acquire the additional shares credited to plan participants.

Operating activities Activities that are part of the day-to-day business functioning of an entity, such as selling inventory and providing services.

Operating breakeven The number of units produced and sold at which the company's operating profit is zero (revenues = operating costs).

Operating cash flow The net amount of cash provided from operating activities.

Operating cycle A measure of the time needed to convert raw materials into cash from a sale; it consists of the number of days of inventory and the number of days of receivables.

Operating efficiency ratios Ratios that measure how efficiently a company performs day-to-day tasks, such as the collection of receivables and management of inventory.

Operating lease An agreement allowing the lessee to use some asset for a period of time; essentially a rental.

Operating leverage The use of fixed costs in operations.

Operating profit A company's profits on its usual business activities before deducting taxes. Also called *operating income.*

Operating profit margin A profitability ratio calculated as operating income (i.e., income before interest and taxes) divided by revenue. Also called *operating margin.*

Operating risk The risk attributed to the operating cost structure, in particular the use of fixed costs in operations; the risk arising from the mix of fixed and variable costs; the risk that a company's operations may be severely affected by environmental, social, and governance risk factors.

Operational independence A bank's ability to execute monetary policy and set interest rates in the way it thought would best meet the inflation target.

Operationally efficient Said of a market, a financial system, or an economy that has relatively low transaction costs.

Opportunity cost The value that investors forgo by choosing a particular course of action; the value of something in its best alternative use.

Option A financial instrument that gives one party the right, but not the obligation, to buy or sell an underlying asset from or to another party at a fixed price over a specific period of time. Also referred to as *contingent claim* or *option contract.*

Option contract See *option.*

Option premium The amount of money a buyer pays and seller receives to engage in an option transaction.

Option-adjusted price The value of the embedded option plus the flat price of the bond.

Option-adjusted spread OAS = Z-spread – Option value (in basis points per year).

Option-adjusted yield The required market discount rate whereby the price is adjusted for the value of the embedded option.

Order A specification of what instrument to trade, how much to trade, and whether to buy or sell.

Order precedence hierarchy With respect to the execution of orders to trade, a set of rules that determines which orders execute before other orders.

Order-driven markets A market (generally an auction market) that uses rules to arrange trades based on the orders that traders submit; in their pure form, such markets do not make use of dealers.

Ordinal scale A measurement scale that sorts data into categories that are ordered (ranked) with respect to some characteristic.

Ordinary annuity An annuity with a first cash flow that is paid one period from the present.

Ordinary shares Equity shares that are subordinate to all other types of equity (e.g., preferred equity). Also called *common stock* or *common shares.*

Organized exchange A securities marketplace where buyers and seller can meet to arrange their trades.

Other comprehensive income Items of comprehensive income that are not reported on the income statement; comprehensive income minus net income.

Other receivables Amounts owed to the company from parties other than customers.

Out of the money Options that, if exercised, would require the payment of more money than the value received and therefore would not be currently exercised.

Out-of-sample test A test of a strategy or model using a sample outside the time period on which the strategy or model was developed.

Out-of-the-money Options that, if exercised, would require the payment of more money than the value received and therefore would not be currently exercised.

Outcome A possible value of a random variable.

Over-the-counter (OTC) markets   A decentralized market where buy and sell orders initiated from various locations are matched through a communications network.

Overbought   A market condition in which market sentiment is thought to be unsustainably bullish.

Oversold   A market condition in which market sentiment is thought to be unsustainably bearish.

Own-price   The price of a good or service itself (as opposed to the price of something else).

Own-price elasticity of demand   The percentage change in quantity demanded for a percentage change in own price, holding all other things constant.

Owner-of-record date   The date that a shareholder listed on the corporation's books will be deemed to have ownership of the shares for purposes of receiving an upcoming dividend; two business days after the ex-dividend date.

Owners' equity   The excess of assets over liabilities; the residual interest of shareholders in the assets of an entity after deducting the entity's liabilities. Also called *shareholders' equity*.

Paasche index   An index formula using the current composition of a basket of products.

Paired comparisons test   A statistical test for differences based on paired observations drawn from samples that are dependent on each other.

Paired observations   Observations that are dependent on each other.

Pairs arbitrage trade   A trade in two closely related stocks involving the short sale of one and the purchase of the other.

Panel data   Observations through time on a single characteristic of multiple observational units.

Par curve   A sequence of yields-to-maturity such that each bond is priced at par value. The bonds are assumed to have the same currency, credit risk, liquidity, tax status, and annual yields stated for the same periodicity.

Par value   The amount of principal on a bond.

Parallel shift   A parallel yield curve shift implies that all rates change by the same amount in the same direction.

Parameter   A descriptive measure computed from or used to describe a population of data, conventionally represented by Greek letters.

Parametric test   Any test (or procedure) concerned with parameters or whose validity depends on assumptions concerning the population generating the sample.

Pari passu   On an equal footing.

Partial duration   See *key rate duration*.

Partial equilibrium analysis   An equilibrium analysis focused on one market, taking the values of exogenous variables as given.

Participating preference shares   Preference shares that entitle shareholders to receive the standard preferred dividend plus the opportunity to receive an additional dividend if the company's profits exceed a pre-specified level.

Pass-through rate   The coupon rate of a mortgage pass-through security.

Passive investment   A buy and hold approach in which an investor does not make portfolio changes based on short-term expectations of changing market or security performance.

Passive strategy   In reference to short-term cash management, it is an investment strategy characterized by simple decision rules for making daily investments.

Payable date   The day that the company actually mails out (or electronically transfers) a dividend payment.

Payment date   The day that the company actually mails out (or electronically transfers) a dividend payment.

Payments system   The system for the transfer of money.

Payout   Cash dividends and the value of shares repurchased in any given year.

Payout policy   A company's set of principles guiding payouts.

Peak   The highest point of a business cycle.

Peer group   A group of companies engaged in similar business activities whose economics and valuation are influenced by closely related factors.

Pennants   A technical analysis continuation pattern formed by trendlines that converge to form a triangle, typically over a short period.

Per capita real GDP   Real GDP divided by the size of the population, often used as a measure of the average standard of living in a country.

Per unit contribution margin   The amount that each unit sold contributes to covering fixed costs—that is, the difference between the price per unit and the variable cost per unit.

Percentage-of-completion   A method of revenue recognition in which, in each accounting period, the company estimates what percentage of the contract is complete and then reports that percentage of the total contract revenue in its income statement.

Percentiles   Quantiles that divide a distribution into 100 equal parts.

Perfect competition   A market structure in which the individual firm has virtually no impact on market price, because it is assumed to be a very small seller among a very large number of firms selling essentially identical products.

Perfectly elastic   Said of a good or service that is infinitely sensitive to a change in the value of a specified variable (e.g., price).

Perfectly inelastic   Said of a good or service that is completely insensitive to a change in the value of a specified variable (e.g., price).

Performance appraisal   The evaluation of risk-adjusted performance; the evaluation of investment skill.

Performance bond   See *margin bond*.

Performance evaluation   The measurement and assessment of the outcomes of investment management decisions.

Performance measurement   The calculation of returns in a logical and consistent manner.

Period costs   Costs (e.g., executives' salaries) that cannot be directly matched with the timing of revenues and which are thus expensed immediately.

Periodicity   The assumed number of periods in the year, typically matches the frequency of coupon payments.

Permanent differences   Differences between tax and financial reporting of revenue (expenses) that will not be reversed at some future date. These result in a difference between the company's effective tax rate and statutory tax rate and do not result in a deferred tax item.

Permutation   An ordered listing.

Perpetual bonds   Bonds with no stated maturity date.

Perpetuity   A perpetual annuity, or a set of never-ending level sequential cash flows, with the first cash flow occurring one period from now. A bond that does not mature.

Personal consumption expenditures   All domestic personal consumption; the basis for a price index for such consumption called the PCE price index.

Personal disposable income   Equal to personal income less personal taxes.

Personal income   A broad measure of household income that includes all income received by households, whether earned or unearned; measures the ability of consumers to make purchases.

Plain vanilla bond   Bond that makes periodic, fixed coupon payments during the bond's life and a lump-sum payment of principal at maturity. Also called *conventional bond*.

Planning horizon   A time period in which all factors of production are variable, including technology, physical capital, and plant size.

Platykurtic   Describes a distribution that is less peaked than the normal distribution.

Point and figure chart   A technical analysis chart that is constructed with columns of X's alternating with columns of O's such that the horizontal axis represents only the number of changes in price without reference to time or volume.

Point estimate   A single numerical estimate of an unknown quantity, such as a population parameter.

Point of sale (POS)   Systems that capture transaction data at the physical location in which the sale is made.

Policy rate   An interest rate that a central bank sets and announces publicly; normally the rate at which it is willing to lend money to the commercial banks.

Population   All members of a specified group.

Population mean   The arithmetic mean value of a population; the arithmetic mean of all the observations or values in the population.

Population standard deviation   A measure of dispersion relating to a population in the same unit of measurement as the observations, calculated as the positive square root of the population variance.

Population variance   A measure of dispersion relating to a population, calculated as the mean of the squared deviations around the population mean.

Portfolio company   In private equity, the company that is being invested in.

Portfolio demand for money   The demand to hold speculative money balances based on the potential opportunities or risks that are inherent in other financial instruments.

Portfolio planning   The process of creating a plan for building a portfolio that is expected to satisfy a client's investment objectives.

Position   The quantity of an asset that an entity owns or owes.

Positive externality   A positive effect (e.g., improved literacy) of a market transaction that is borne by parties other than those who transacted; a spillover benefit.

Posterior probability   An updated probability that reflects or comes after new information.

Potential GDP   The level of real GDP that can be produced at full employment; measures the productive capacity of the economy.

Power of a test   The probability of correctly rejecting the null—that is, rejecting the null hypothesis when it is false.

Precautionary money balances   Money held to provide a buffer against unforeseen events that might require money.

Precautionary stocks   A level of inventory beyond anticipated needs that provides a cushion in the event that it takes longer to replenish inventory than expected or in the case of greater than expected demand.

Preference shares   A type of equity interest which ranks above common shares with respect to the payment of dividends and the distribution of the company's net assets upon liquidation. They have characteristics of both debt and equity securities. Also called *preferred stock*.

Preferred stock   See *preference shares*.

Premium   In the case of bonds, premium refers to the amount by which a bond is priced above its face (par) value. In the case of an option, the amount paid for the option contract.

Prepaid expense   A normal operating expense that has been paid in advance of when it is due.

Prepayment option   Contractual provision that entitles the borrower to prepay all or part of the outstanding mortgage principal prior to the scheduled due date the principal must be repaid. Also called *early repayment option*.

Prepayment penalty mortgages   Mortgages that stipulate a monetary penalty if a borrower prepays within a certain time period after the mortgage is originated.

Prepayment risk   The uncertainty that the cash flows will be different from the scheduled cash flows as set forth in the loan agreement due to the borrowers' ability to alter payments.

Present value (PV)   The present discounted value of future cash flows: For assets, the present discounted value of the future net cash inflows that the asset is expected to generate; for liabilities, the present discounted value of the future net cash outflows that are expected to be required to settle the liabilities.

Present value models   Valuation models that estimate the intrinsic value of a security as the present value of the future benefits expected to be received from the security. Also called *discounted cash flow models*.

Pretax margin   A profitability ratio calculated as earnings before taxes divided by revenue.

Price   The market price as established by the interactions of the market demand and supply factors.

Price elasticity of demand   Measures the percentage change in the quantity demanded, given a percentage change in the price of a given product.

Price floor   A minimum price for a good or service, typically imposed by government action and typically above the equilibrium price.

Price index   Represents the average prices of a basket of goods and services.

Price limits   Limits imposed by a futures exchange on the price change that can occur from one day to the next.

Price multiple   A ratio that compares the share price with some sort of monetary flow or value to allow evaluation of the relative worth of a company's stock.

Price priority   The principle that the highest priced buy orders and the lowest priced sell orders execute first.

Price relative   A ratio of an ending price over a beginning price; it is equal to 1 plus the holding period return on the asset.

Price return   Measures *only* the price appreciation or percentage change in price of the securities in an index or portfolio.

Price return index   An index that reflects *only* the price appreciation or percentage change in price of the constituent securities. Also called *price index*.

Price stability   In economics, refers to an inflation rate that is low on average and not subject to wide fluctuation.

Price takers   Producers that must accept whatever price the market dictates.

Price to book value   A valuation ratio calculated as price per share divided by book value per share.

Price to cash flow   A valuation ratio calculated as price per share divided by cash flow per share.

Price to earnings ratio   (P/E ratio or P/E) The ratio of share price to earnings per share.

Price to sales   A valuation ratio calculated as price per share divided by sales per share.

Price value of a basis point   A version of money duration, it is an estimate of the change in the full price of a bond given a 1 basis point change in the yield-to-maturity.

Price weighting   An index weighting method in which the weight assigned to each constituent security is determined by dividing its price by the sum of all the prices of the constituent securities.

Priced risk   Risk for which investors demand compensation for bearing (e.g. equity risk, company-specific factors, macroeconomic factors).

Primary bond markets   Markets in which issuers first sell bonds to investors to raise capital.

Primary capital markets (primary markets)   The market where securities are first sold and the issuers receive the proceeds.

Primary dealers   Financial institutions that are authorized to deal in new issues of sovereign bonds and that serve primarily as trading counterparties of the office responsible for issuing sovereign bonds.

Primary market   The market where securities are first sold and the issuers receive the proceeds.

Prime brokers   Brokers that provide services including custody, administration, lending, short borrowing, and trading.

Principal   The amount of funds originally invested in a project or instrument; the face value to be paid at maturity.

Principal amount   Amount that an issuer agrees to repay the debt holders on the maturity date.

Principal business activity   The business activity from which a company derives a majority of its revenues and/or earnings.

Principal value   Amount that an issuer agrees to repay the debt holders on the maturity date.

Principle of no arbitrage   See *arbitrage-free pricing*.

Prior probabilities   Probabilities reflecting beliefs prior to the arrival of new information.

Priority of claims   Priority of payment, with the most senior or highest ranking debt having the first claim on the cash flows and assets of the issuer.

Private equity securities   Securities that are not listed on public exchanges and have no active secondary market. They are issued primarily to institutional investors via non-public offerings, such as private placements.

Private investment in public equity   An investment in the equity of a publicly traded firm that is made at a discount to the market value of the firm's shares.

Private placement   Typically a non-underwritten, unregistered offering of securities that are sold only to an investor or a small group of investors. It can be accomplished directly between the issuer and the investor(s) or through an investment bank.

Private value auction   An auction in which the value of the item being auctioned is unique to each bidder.

Probability   A number between 0 and 1 describing the chance that a stated event will occur.

Probability density function   A function with non-negative values such that probability can be described by areas under the curve graphing the function.

Probability distribution   A distribution that specifies the probabilities of a random variable's possible outcomes.

Probability function   A function that specifies the probability that the random variable takes on a specific value.

Producer price index   Reflects the price changes experienced by domestic producers in a country.

Producer surplus   The difference between the total revenue sellers receive from selling a given amount of a good and the total variable cost of producing that amount.

Production function   Provides the quantitative link between the level of output that the economy can produce and the inputs used in the production process.

Production opportunity frontier   Curve describing the maximum number of units of one good a company can produce, for any given number of the other good that it chooses to manufacture.

Productivity   The amount of output produced by workers in a given period of time—for example, output per hour worked; measures the efficiency of labor.

Profit   The return that owners of a company receive for the use of their capital and the assumption of financial risk when making their investments.

Profit and loss (P&L) statement   A financial statement that provides information about a company's profitability over a stated period of time.

Profit margin   An indicator of profitability, calculated as net income divided by revenue; indicates how much of each dollar of revenues is left after all costs and expenses.

Profitability ratios   Ratios that measure a company's ability to generate profitable sales from its resources (assets).

Project sequencing   To defer the decision to invest in a future project until the outcome of some or all of a current project is known. Projects are sequenced through time, so that investing in a project creates the option to invest in future projects.

Promissory note   A written promise to pay a certain amount of money on demand.

Property, plant, and equipment   Tangible assets that are expected to be used for more than one period in either the production or supply of goods or services, or for administrative purposes.

Prospectus   The document that describes the terms of a new bond issue and helps investors perform their analysis on the issue.

Protective put   An option strategy in which a long position in an asset is combined with a long position in a put.

Pseudo-random numbers   Numbers produced by random number generators.

Public offer   See *public offering*.

Public offering   An offering of securities in which any member of the public may buy the securities. Also called *public offer*.

Pull on liquidity   When disbursements are paid too quickly or trade credit availability is limited, requiring companies to expend funds before they receive funds from sales that could cover the liability.

Pure discount bonds   See *zero-coupon bonds*.

Pure discount instruments   Instruments that pay interest as the difference between the amount borrowed and the amount paid back.

Pure-play method   A method for estimating the beta for a company or project; it requires using a comparable company's beta and adjusting it for financial leverage differences.

Put   An option that gives the holder the right to sell an underlying asset to another party at a fixed price over a specific period of time.

Put option An option that gives the holder the right to sell an underlying asset to another party at a fixed price over a specific period of time.

Put/call ratio A technical analysis indicator that evaluates market sentiment based upon the volume of put options traded divided by the volume of call options traded for a particular financial instrument.

Putable bonds Bonds that give the bondholder the right to sell the bond back to the issuer at a predetermined price on specified dates.

Putable common shares Common shares that give investors the option (or right) to sell their shares (i.e., "put" them) back to the issuing company at a price that is specified when the shares are originally issued.

Put–call parity An equation expressing the equivalence (parity) of a portfolio of a call and a bond with a portfolio of a put and the underlying, which leads to the relationship between put and call prices.

Put–call–forward parity The relationship among puts, calls, and forward contracts.

Quantile A value at or below which a stated fraction of the data lies. Also called *fractile*.

Quantitative easing An expansionary monetary policy based on aggressive open market purchase operations.

Quantity The amount of a product that consumers are willing and able to buy at each price level.

Quantity demanded The amount of a product that consumers are willing and able to buy at each price level.

Quantity equation of exchange An expression that over a given period, the amount of money used to purchase all goods and services in an economy, $M \times V$, is equal to monetary value of this output, $P \times Y$.

Quantity theory of money Asserts that total spending (in money terms) is proportional to the quantity of money.

Quartiles Quantiles that divide a distribution into four equal parts.

Quasi-fixed cost A cost that stays the same over a range of production but can change to another constant level when production moves outside of that range.

Quasi-government bonds A bond issued by an entity that is either owned or sponsored by a national government. Also called *agency bond*.

Quick assets Assets that can be most readily converted to cash (e.g., cash, short-term marketable investments, receivables).

Quick ratio A stringent measure of liquidity that indicates a company's ability to satisfy current liabilities with its most liquid assets, calculated as (cash + short-term marketable investments + receivables) divided by current liabilities.

Quintiles Quantiles that divide a distribution into five equal parts.

Quota rents Profits that foreign producers can earn by raising the price of their goods higher than they would without a quota.

Quotas Government policies that restrict the quantity of a good that can be imported into a country, generally for a specified period of time.

Quote-driven market A market in which dealers acting as principals facilitate trading.

Quoted interest rate A quoted interest rate that does not account for compounding within the year. Also called *stated annual interest rate*.

Quoted margin The specified yield spread over the reference rate, used to compensate an investor for the difference in the credit risk of the issuer and that implied by the reference rate.

Random number An observation drawn from a uniform distribution.

Random number generator An algorithm that produces uniformly distributed random numbers between 0 and 1.

Random variable A quantity whose future outcomes are uncertain.

Range The difference between the maximum and minimum values in a dataset.

Ratio scales A measurement scale that has all the characteristics of interval measurement scales as well as a true zero point as the origin.

Real GDP The value of goods and services produced, measured at base year prices.

Real income Income adjusted for the effect of inflation on the purchasing power of money.

Real interest rate Nominal interest rate minus the expected rate of inflation.

Real risk-free interest rate The single-period interest rate for a completely risk-free security if no inflation were expected.

Realizable (settlement) value With reference to assets, the amount of cash or cash equivalents that could currently be obtained by selling the asset in an orderly disposal; with reference to liabilities, the undiscounted amount of cash or cash equivalents expected to be paid to satisfy the liabilities in the normal course of business.

Rebalancing Adjusting the weights of the constituent securities in an index.

Rebalancing policy The set of rules that guide the process of restoring a portfolio's asset class weights to those specified in the strategic asset allocation.

Recession A period during which real GDP decreases (i.e., negative growth) for at least two successive quarters, or a period of significant decline in total output, income, employment, and sales usually lasting from six months to a year.

Recognition lag The lag in government response to an economic problem resulting from the delay in confirming a change in the state of the economy.

Record date The date that a shareholder listed on the corporation's books will be deemed to have ownership of the shares for purposes of receiving an upcoming dividend; two business days after the ex-dividend date.

Recourse loan Loan in which the lender has a claim against the borrower for any shortfall between the mortgage balance outstanding and the proceeds received from the sale of the property.

Redemption yield See *yield to maturity*.

Redemptions Withdrawals of funds by investors.

Refinancing rate A type of central bank policy rate.

Registered bonds Bonds for which ownership is recorded by either name or serial number.

Relative dispersion The amount of dispersion relative to a reference value or benchmark.

Relative frequency With reference to an interval of grouped data, the number of observations in the interval divided by the total number of observations in the sample.

Relative price The price of a specific good or service in comparison with those of other goods and services.

Relative strength analysis   A comparison of the performance of one asset with the performance of another asset or a benchmark based on changes in the ratio of the securities' respective prices over time.

Relative strength index   A technical analysis momentum oscillator that compares a security's gains with its losses over a set period.

Renewable resources   Resources that can be replenished, such as a forest.

Rent   Payment for the use of property.

Reorganization   Agreements made by a company in bankruptcy under which a company's capital structure is altered and/or alternative arrangements are made for debt repayment; US Chapter 11 bankruptcy. The company emerges from bankruptcy as a going concern.

Replication   The creation of an asset or portfolio from another asset, portfolio, and/or derivative.

Repo   A form of collateralized loan involving the sale of a security with a simultaneous agreement by the seller to buy the same security back from the purchaser at an agreed-on price and future date. The party who sells the security at the inception of the repurchase agreement and buys it back at maturity is borrowing money from the other party, and the security sold and subsequently repurchased represents the collateral.

Repo margin   The difference between the market value of the security used as collateral and the value of the loan. Also called *haircut*.

Repo rate   The interest rate on a repurchase agreement.

Repurchase agreement   A form of collateralized loan involving the sale of a security with a simultaneous agreement by the seller to buy the same security back from the purchaser at an agreed-on price and future date. The party who sells the security at the inception of the repurchase agreement and buys it back at maturity is borrowing money from the other party, and the security sold and subsequently repurchased represents the collateral.

Repurchase date   The date when the party who sold the security at the inception of a repurchase agreement buys the security back from the cash lending counterparty.

Repurchase price   The price at which the party who sold the security at the inception of the repurchase agreement buys the security back from the cash lending counterparty.

Required margin   The yield spread over, or under, the reference rate such that an FRN is priced at par value on a rate reset date.

Required rate of return   See *market discount rate*.

Required yield   See *market discount rate*.

Required yield spread   The difference between the yield-to-maturity on a new bond and the benchmark rate; additional compensation required by investors for the difference in risk and tax status of a bond relative to a government bond. Sometimes called the *spread over the benchmark*.

Reservation prices   The highest price a buyer is willing to pay for an item or the lowest price at which a seller is willing to sell it.

Reserve requirement   The requirement for banks to hold reserves in proportion to the size of deposits.

Residual claim   The owners' remaining claim on the company's assets after the liabilities are deducted.

Resistance   In technical analysis, a price range in which selling activity is sufficient to stop the rise in the price of a security.

Restricted payments   A bond covenant meant to protect creditors by limiting how much cash can be paid out to shareholders over time.

Retail method   An inventory accounting method in which the sales value of an item is reduced by the gross margin to calculate the item's cost.

Retracement   In technical analysis, a reversal in the movement of a security's price such that it is counter to the prevailing longterm price trend.

Return on assets (ROA)   A profitability ratio calculated as net income divided by average total assets; indicates a company's net profit generated per dollar invested in total assets.

Return on equity (ROE)   A profitability ratio calculated as net income divided by average shareholders' equity.

Return on sales   An indicator of profitability, calculated as net income divided by revenue; indicates how much of each dollar of revenues is left after all costs and expenses.

Return on total capital   A profitability ratio calculated as EBIT divided by the sum of short- and long-term debt and equity.

Return-generating model   A model that can provide an estimate of the expected return of a security given certain parameters and estimates of the values of the independent variables in the model.

Revaluation model   The process of valuing long-lived assets at fair value, rather than at cost less accumulated depreciation. Any resulting profit or loss is either reported on the income statement and/or through equity under revaluation surplus.

Revenue   The amount charged for the delivery of goods or services in the ordinary activities of a business over a stated period; the inflows of economic resources to a company over a stated period.

Reversal patterns   A type of pattern used in technical analysis to predict the end of a trend and a change in direction of the security's price.

Reverse repo   A repurchase agreement viewed from the perspective of the cash lending counterparty.

Reverse repurchase agreement   A repurchase agreement viewed from the perspective of the cash lending counterparty.

Reverse stock split   A reduction in the number of shares outstanding with a corresponding increase in share price, but no change to the company's underlying fundamentals.

Revolving credit agreements   The strongest form of short-term bank borrowing facilities; they are in effect for multiple years (e.g., 3–5 years) and may have optional medium-term loan features.

Ricardian equivalence   An economic theory that implies that it makes no difference whether a government finances a deficit by increasing taxes or issuing debt.

Risk averse   The assumption that an investor will choose the least risky alternative.

Risk aversion   The degree of an investor's inability and unwillingness to take risk.

Risk budgeting   The establishment of objectives for individuals, groups, or divisions of an organization that takes into account the allocation of an acceptable level of risk.

Risk management   The process of identifying the level of risk an entity wants, measuring the level of risk the entity currently has, taking actions that bring the actual level of risk to the desired level of risk, and monitoring the new actual level of risk so that it continues to be aligned with the desired level of risk.

Risk premium   An extra return expected by investors for bearing some specified risk.

Risk tolerance The amount of risk an investor is willing and able to bear to achieve an investment goal.

Risk-neutral pricing Sometimes said of derivatives pricing, uses the fact that arbitrage opportunities guarantee that a risk-free portfolio consisting of the underlying and the derivative must earn the risk-free rate.

Risk-neutral probabilities Weights that are used to compute a binomial option price. They are the probabilities that would apply if a risk-neutral investor valued an option.

Robust The quality of being relatively unaffected by a violation of assumptions.

Rule of 72 The principle that the approximate number of years necessary for an investment to double is 72 divided by the stated interest rate.

Running yield See *current yield*.

Safety stock A level of inventory beyond anticipated needs that provides a cushion in the event that it takes longer to replenish inventory than expected or in the case of greater than expected demand.

Safety-first rules Rules for portfolio selection that focus on the risk that portfolio value will fall below some minimum acceptable level over some time horizon.

Sales Generally, a synonym for revenue; "sales" is generally understood to refer to the sale of goods, whereas "revenue" is understood to include the sale of goods or services.

Sales returns and allowances An offset to revenue reflecting any cash refunds, credits on account, and discounts from sales prices given to customers who purchased defective or unsatisfactory items.

Sales risk Uncertainty with respect to the quantity of goods and services that a company is able to sell and the price it is able to achieve; the risk related to the uncertainty of revenues.

Sales-type leases A type of finance lease, from a lessor perspective, where the present value of the lease payments (less receivable) exceeds the carrying value of the leased asset. The revenues earned by the lessor are operating (the profit on the sale) and financing (interest) in nature.

Salvage value The amount the company estimates that it can sell the asset for at the end of its useful life. Also called *residual value*.

Sample A subset of a population.

Sample excess kurtosis A sample measure of the degree of a distribution's peakedness in excess of the normal distribution's peakedness.

Sample kurtosis A sample measure of the degree of a distribution's peakedness.

Sample mean The sum of the sample observations, divided by the sample size.

Sample selection bias Bias introduced by systematically excluding some members of the population according to a particular attribute—for example, the bias introduced when data availability leads to certain observations being excluded from the analysis.

Sample skewness A sample measure of degree of asymmetry of a distribution.

Sample standard deviation The positive square root of the sample variance.

Sample statistic A quantity computed from or used to describe a sample.

Sample variance A sample measure of the degree of dispersion of a distribution, calculated by dividing the sum of the squared deviations from the sample mean by the sample size minus 1.

Sampling The process of obtaining a sample.

Sampling distribution The distribution of all distinct possible values that a statistic can assume when computed from samples of the same size randomly drawn from the same population.

Sampling error The difference between the observed value of a statistic and the quantity it is intended to estimate.

Sampling plan The set of rules used to select a sample.

Saving In economics, income not spent.

Say's law Named for French economist J.B. Say: All that is produced will be sold because supply creates its own demand.

Scenario analysis Analysis that shows the changes in key financial quantities that result from given (economic) events, such as the loss of customers, the loss of a supply source, or a catastrophic event; a risk management technique involving examination of the performance of a portfolio under specified situations. Closely related to stress testing.

Screening The application of a set of criteria to reduce a set of potential investments to a smaller set having certain desired characteristics.

Scrip dividend schemes Dividend reinvestment plan in which the company meets the need for additional shares by issuing them instead of purchasing them.

Sealed bid auction An auction in which bids are elicited from potential buyers, but there is no ability to observe bids by other buyers until the auction has ended.

Search costs Costs incurred in searching; the costs of matching buyers with sellers.

Seasoned offering An offering in which an issuer sells additional units of a previously issued security.

Second lien A secured interest in the pledged assets that ranks below first lien debt in both collateral protection and priority of payment.

Second price sealed bid An auction (also known as a Vickery auction) in which bids are submitted in sealed envelopes and opened simultaneously. The winning buyer is the one who submitted the highest bid, but the price paid is equal to the second highest bid.

Second-degree price discrimination When the monopolist charges different per-unit prices using the quantity purchased as an indicator of how highly the customer values the product.

Secondary bond markets Markets in which existing bonds are traded among investors.

Secondary market The market where securities are traded among investors.

Secondary precedence rules Rules that determine how to rank orders placed at the same time.

Sector A group of related industries.

Sector indices Indices that represent and track different economic sectors—such as consumer goods, energy, finance, health care, and technology—on either a national, regional, or global basis.

Secured bonds Bonds secured by assets or financial guarantees pledged to ensure debt repayment in case of default.

Secured debt Debt in which the debtholder has a direct claim—a pledge from the issuer—on certain assets and their associated cash flows.

Securitization A process that involves moving assets into a special legal entity, which then uses the assets as guarantees to secure a bond issue.

Securitized assets Assets that are typically used to create asset backed bonds, for example when a bank securitizes a pool of loans the loans are said to be securitized.

Securitized bonds Bonds created from a process that involves moving assets into a special legal entity, which then uses the assets as guarantees to secure a bond issue.

Security characteristic line A plot of the excess return of a security on the excess return of the market.

Security market index A portfolio of securities representing a given security market, market segment, or asset class.

Security market line (SML) The graph of the capital asset pricing model.

Security selection The process of selecting individual securities; typically, security selection has the objective of generating superior risk-adjusted returns relative to a portfolio's benchmark.

Self-investment limits With respect to investment limitations applying to pension plans, restrictions on the percentage of assets that can be invested in securities issued by the pension plan sponsor.

Sell-side firm A broker or dealer that sells securities to and provides independent investment research and recommendations to investment management companies.

Semi-strong-form efficient market A market in which security prices reflect all publicly known and available information.

Semiannual bond basis yield An annual rate having a periodicity of two; also known as a *semiannual bond equivalent yield*.

Semiannual bond equivalent yield See *semiannual bond basis yield*.

Semideviation The positive square root of semivariance (sometimes called *semistandard deviation*).

Semilogarithmic Describes a scale constructed so that equal intervals on the vertical scale represent equal rates of change, and equal intervals on the horizontal scale represent equal amounts of change.

Semivariance The average squared deviation below the mean.

Seniority ranking Priority of payment of various debt obligations.

Sensitivity analysis Analysis that shows the range of possible outcomes as specific assumptions are changed.

Separately managed account (SMA) An investment portfolio managed exclusively for the benefit of an individual or institution.

Serial maturity structure Structure for a bond issue in which the maturity dates are spread out during the bond's life; a stated number of bonds mature and are paid off each year before final maturity.

Settlement The process that occurs after a trade is completed, the securities are passed to the buyer, and payment is received by the seller.

Settlement date Date when the buyer makes cash payment and the seller delivers the security.

Settlement price The official price, designated by the clearinghouse, from which daily gains and losses will be determined and marked to market.

Share repurchase A transaction in which a company buys back its own shares. Unlike stock dividends and stock splits, share repurchases use corporate cash.

Shareholder wealth maximization To maximize the market value of shareholders' equity.

Shareholder-of-record date The date that a shareholder listed on the corporation's books will be deemed to have ownership of the shares for purposes of receiving an upcoming dividend; two business days after the ex-dividend date.

Shareholders' equity Assets less liabilities; the residual interest in the assets after subtracting the liabilities.

Sharpe ratio The average return in excess of the risk-free rate divided by the standard deviation of return; a measure of the average excess return earned per unit of standard deviation of return.

Shelf registration Type of public offering that allows the issuer to file a single, all-encompassing offering circular that covers a series of bond issues.

Short The seller of an asset or derivative contract. Also refers to the position of being short an asset or derivative contract.

Short position A position in an asset or contract in which one has sold an asset one does not own, or in which a right under a contract can be exercised against oneself.

Short selling A transaction in which borrowed securities are sold with the intention to repurchase them at a lower price at a later date and return them to the lender.

Short-run average total cost curve The curve describing average total costs when some costs are considered fixed.

Short-run supply curve The section of the marginal cost curve that lies above the minimum point on the average variable cost curve.

Shortfall risk The risk that portfolio value will fall below some minimum acceptable level over some time horizon.

Shutdown point The point at which average revenue is less than average variable cost.

Simple interest The interest earned each period on the original investment; interest calculated on the principal only.

Simple random sample A subset of a larger population created in such a way that each element of the population has an equal probability of being selected to the subset.

Simple random sampling The procedure of drawing a sample to satisfy the definition of a simple random sample.

Simple yield The sum of the coupon payments plus the straight-line amortized share of the gain or loss, divided by the flat price.

Simulation Computer-generated sensitivity or scenario analysis that is based on probability models for the factors that drive outcomes.

Simulation trial A complete pass through the steps of a simulation.

Single price auction A Dutch auction variation, also involving a single price, is used in selling US Treasury securities.

Single-step format With respect to the format of the income statement, a format that does not subtotal for gross profit (revenue minus cost of goods sold).

Sinking fund arrangement Provision that reduces the credit risk of a bond issue by requiring the issuer to retire a portion of the bond's principal outstanding each year.

Skewed Not symmetrical.

Skewness A quantitative measure of skew (lack of symmetry); a synonym of skew.

Small country A country that is a price taker in the world market for a product and cannot influence the world market price.

Solvency With respect to financial statement analysis, the ability of a company to fulfill its long-term obligations.

Solvency ratios Ratios that measure a company's ability to meet its long-term obligations.

Sovereign bonds A bond issued by a national government.

Sovereign yield spread An estimate of the country spread (country equity premium) for a developing nation that is based on a comparison of bonds yields in country being analyzed and a developed country. The sovereign yield spread is the difference between a government bond yield in the country being analyzed, denominated in the currency of the developed country, and the Treasury bond yield on a similar maturity bond in the developed country.

Sovereigns   A bond issued by a national government.

Spearman rank correlation coefficient   A measure of correlation applied to ranked data.

Special dividend   A dividend paid by a company that does not pay dividends on a regular schedule, or a dividend that supplements regular cash dividends with an extra payment.

Special purpose entity   A non-operating entity created to carry out a specified purpose, such as leasing assets or securitizing receivables; can be a corporation, partnership, trust, limited liability, or partnership formed to facilitate a specific type of business activity. Also called *special purpose vehicle* or *variable interest entity*.

Special purpose vehicle   See *special purpose entity*.

Specific identification method   An inventory accounting method that identifies which specific inventory items were sold and which remained in inventory to be carried over to later periods.

Speculative demand for money   The demand to hold speculative money balances based on the potential opportunities or risks that are inherent in other financial instruments. Also called *portfolio demand for money*.

Speculative money balances   Monies held in anticipation that other assets will decline in value.

Split coupon bond   See *deferred coupon bond*.

Sponsored   A type of depository receipt in which the foreign company whose shares are held by the depository has a direct involvement in the issuance of the receipts.

Spot curve   A sequence of yields-to-maturity on zero-coupon bonds. Sometimes called *zero* or *strip curve* because coupon payments are "stripped" off of the bonds.

Spot markets   Markets in which assets are traded for immediate delivery.

Spot prices   The price of an asset for immediately delivery.

Spot rates   A sequence of market discount rates that correspond to the cash flow dates; yields-to-maturity on zero-coupon bonds maturing at the date of each cash flow.

Spread   In general, the difference in yield between different fixed income securities. Often used to refer to the difference between the yield-to-maturity and the benchmark.

Spread over the benchmark   See *required yield spread*.

Spread risk   Bond price risk arising from changes in the yield spread on credit-risky bonds; reflects changes in the market's assessment and/or pricing of credit migration (or downgrade) risk and market liquidity risk.

Stable   With reference to an equilibrium, one in which price, when disturbed away from the equilibrium, tends to converge back to it.

Stackelberg model   A prominent model of strategic decision-making in which firms are assumed to make their decisions sequentially.

Stagflation   When a high inflation rate is combined with a high level of unemployment and a slowdown of the economy.

Standard cost   With respect to inventory accounting, the planned or target unit cost of inventory items or services.

Standard deviation   The positive square root of the variance; a measure of dispersion in the same units as the original data.

Standard normal distribution   The normal density with mean (μ) equal to 0 and standard deviation (σ) equal to 1.

Standardizing   A transformation that involves subtracting the mean and dividing the result by the standard deviation.

Standing limit orders   A limit order at a price below market and which therefore is waiting to trade.

Stated annual interest rate   A quoted interest rate that does not account for compounding within the year. Also called *quoted interest rate*.

Statement of cash flows   A financial statement that reconciles beginning-of-period and end-of-period balance sheet values of cash; provides information about an entity's cash inflows and cash outflows as they pertain to operating, investing, and financing activities. Also called *cash flow statement*.

Statement of changes in equity   (statement of owners' equity) A financial statement that reconciles the beginning-of-period and end-of-period balance sheet values of shareholders' equity; provides information about all factors affecting shareholders' equity. Also called *statement of owners' equity*.

Statement of financial condition   The financial statement that presents an entity's current financial position by disclosing resources the entity controls (its assets) and the claims on those resources (its liabilities and equity claims), as of a particular point in time (the date of the balance sheet).

Statement of financial position   The financial statement that presents an entity's current financial position by disclosing resources the entity controls (its assets) and the claims on those resources (its liabilities and equity claims), as of a particular point in time (the date of the balance sheet).

Statement of operations   A financial statement that provides information about a company's profitability over a stated period of time.

Statement of owners' equity   A financial statement that reconciles the beginning of-period and end-of-period balance sheet values of shareholders' equity; provides information about all factors affecting shareholders' equity. Also called *statement of changes in shareholders' equity*.

Statement of retained earnings   A financial statement that reconciles beginning-of-period and end-of-period balance sheet values of retained income; shows the linkage between the balance sheet and income statement.

Statistic   A quantity computed from or used to describe a sample of data.

Statistical inference   Making forecasts, estimates, or judgments about a larger group from a smaller group actually observed; using a sample statistic to infer the value of an unknown population parameter.

Statistically significant   A result indicating that the null hypothesis can be rejected; with reference to an estimated regression coefficient, frequently understood to mean a result indicating that the corresponding population regression coefficient is different from 0.

Statutory voting   A common method of voting where each share represents one vote.

Step-up coupon bond   Bond for which the coupon, which may be fixed or floating, increases by specified margins at specified dates.

Stock dividend   A type of dividend in which a company distributes additional shares of its common stock to shareholders instead of cash.

Stock-out losses   Profits lost from not having sufficient inventory on hand to satisfy demand.

Stop order   An order in which a trader has specified a stop price condition. Also called *stop-loss order*.

Stop-loss order   See *stop order*.

Store of value   The quality of tending to preserve value.

Store of wealth Goods that depend on the fact that they do not perish physically over time, and on the belief that others would always value the good.

Straight-line method A depreciation method that allocates evenly the cost of a long-lived asset less its estimated residual value over the estimated useful life of the asset.

Strategic analysis Analysis of the competitive environment with an emphasis on the implications of the environment for corporate strategy.

Strategic asset allocation The set of exposures to IPS-permissible asset classes that is expected to achieve the client's long-term objectives given the client's investment constraints.

Strategic groups Groups sharing distinct business models or catering to specific market segments in an industry.

Street convention Yield measure that neglects weekends and holidays; the internal rate of return on cash flows assuming payments are made on the scheduled dates, even when the scheduled date falls on a weekend or holiday.

Stress testing A set of techniques for estimating losses in extremely unfavorable combinations of events or scenarios.

Strong-form efficient market A market in which security prices reflect all public and private information.

Structural (or cyclically adjusted) budget deficit The deficit that would exist if the economy was at full employment (or full potential output).

Structural subordination Arises in a holding company structure when the debt of operating subsidiaries is serviced by the cash flow and assets of the subsidiaries before funds can be passed to the holding company to service debt at the parent level.

Subjective probability A probability drawing on personal or subjective judgment.

Subordinated debt A class of unsecured debt that ranks below a firm's senior unsecured obligations.

Subordination A common structure in securitization, which leads to the creation of more than one bond class or tranche. Bond classes differ as to how they will share any losses resulting from defaults of the borrowers whose loans are in the pool of loans.

Substitutes Said of two goods or services such that if the price of one increases the demand for the other tends to increase, holding all other things equal (e.g., butter and margarine).

Sunk cost A cost that has already been incurred.

Supernormal profit Equal to accounting profit less the implicit opportunity costs not included in total accounting costs; the difference between total revenue (TR) and total cost (TC).

Supply The willingness of sellers to offer a given quantity of a good or service for a given price.

Supply curve The graph of the inverse supply function.

Supply function The quantity supplied as a function of price and possibly other variables.

Supply shock A typically unexpected disturbance to supply.

Support In technical analysis, a price range in which buying activity is sufficient to stop the decline in the price of a security.

Support tranche A class or tranche in a CMO that protects the PAC tranche from prepayment risk.

Supranational bonds A bond issued by a supranational agency such as the World Bank.

Surety bond Form of external credit enhancement whereby a rated and regulated insurance company guarantees to reimburse bondholders for any losses incurred up to a maximum amount if the issuer defaults.

Survey approach An estimate of the equity risk premium that is based upon estimates provided by a panel of finance experts.

Survivorship bias The bias resulting from a test design that fails to account for companies that have gone bankrupt, merged, or are otherwise no longer reported in a database.

Sustainable growth rate The rate of dividend (and earnings) growth that can be sustained over time for a given level of return on equity, keeping the capital structure constant and without issuing additional common stock.

Sustainable rate of economic growth The rate of increase in the economy's productive capacity or potential GDP.

Swap contract An agreement between two parties to exchange a series of future cash flows.

Syndicated loans Loans from a group of lenders to a single borrower.

Syndicated offering A bond issue that is underwritten by a group of investment banks.

Systematic risk Risk that affects the entire market or economy; it cannot be avoided and is inherent in the overall market. Systematic risk is also known as non diversifiable or market risk.

Systematic sampling A procedure of selecting every kth member until reaching a sample of the desired size. The sample that results from this procedure should be approximately random.

t-Test A hypothesis test using a statistic (t-statistic) that follows a t-distribution.

TRIN A flow of funds indicator applied to a broad stock market index to measure the relative extent to which money is moving into or out of rising and declining stocks.

Tactical asset allocation The decision to deliberately deviate from the strategic asset allocation in an attempt to add value based on forecasts of the near-term relative performance of asset classes.

Target balance A minimum level of cash to be held available—estimated in advance and adjusted for known funds transfers, seasonality, or other factors.

Target capital structure A company's chosen proportions of debt and equity.

Target independent A bank's ability to determine the definition of inflation that they target, the rate of inflation that they target, and the horizon over which the target is to be achieved.

Target semideviation The positive square root of target semivariance.

Target semivariance The average squared deviation below a target value.

Tariffs Taxes that a government levies on imported goods.

Tax base The amount at which an asset or liability is valued for tax purposes.

Tax expense An aggregate of an entity's income tax payable (or recoverable in the case of a tax benefit) and any changes in deferred tax assets and liabilities. It is essentially the income tax payable or recoverable if these had been determined based on accounting profit rather than taxable income.

Tax loss carry forward A taxable loss in the current period that may be used to reduce future taxable income.

Taxable income The portion of an entity's income that is subject to income taxes under the tax laws of its jurisdiction.

Taxable temporary differences Temporary differences that result in a taxable amount in a future period when determining the taxable profit as the balance sheet item is recovered or settled.

Technical analysis A form of security analysis that uses price and volume data, which is often displayed graphically, in decision making.

Technology The process a company uses to transform inputs into outputs.

Technology of production The "rules" that govern the transformation of inputs into finished goods and services.

Tenor The time-to-maturity for a bond or derivative contract. Also called *term to maturity*.

Term maturity structure Structure for a bond issue in which the bond's notional principal is paid off in a lump sum at maturity.

Term structure See *maturity structure*.

Term structure of credit spreads The relationship between the spreads over the "risk-free" (or benchmark) rates and times-to-maturity.

Term structure of yield volatility The relationship between the volatility of bond yields-to-maturity and times-to-maturity.

Terminal stock value The expected value of a share at the end of the investment horizon—in effect, the expected selling price. Also called *terminal value*.

Terminal value The expected value of a share at the end of the investment horizon—in effect, the expected selling price.

Terms of trade The ratio of the price of exports to the price of imports, representing those prices by export and import price indices, respectively.

Theory of the consumer The branch of microeconomics that deals with consumption—the demand for goods and services—by utility-maximizing individuals.

Theory of the firm The branch of microeconomics that deals with the supply of goods and services by profit-maximizing firms.

Third-degree price discrimination When the monopolist segregates customers into groups based on demographic or other characteristics and offers different pricing to each group.

Time tranching The creation of classes or tranches in an ABS/MBS that possess different (expected) maturities.

Time value The difference between the market price of the option and its intrinsic value, determined by the uncertainty of the underlying over the remaining life of the option.

Time value decay Said of an option when, at expiration, no time value remains and the option is worth only its exercise value.

Time value of money The principles governing equivalence relationships between cash flows with different dates.

Time-period bias The possibility that when we use a time-series sample, our statistical conclusion may be sensitive to the starting and ending dates of the sample.

Time-series data Observations of a variable over time.

Time-weighted rate of return The compound rate of growth of one unit of currency invested in a portfolio during a stated measurement period; a measure of investment performance that is not sensitive to the timing and amount of withdrawals or additions to the portfolio.

Top-down analysis With reference to investment selection processes, an approach that starts with macro selection (i.e., identifying attractive geographic segments and/or industry segments) and then addresses selection of the most attractive investments within those segments.

Total comprehensive income The change in equity during a period resulting from transaction and other events, other than those changes resulting from transactions with owners in their capacity as owners.

Total costs The summation of all costs, where costs are classified according to fixed or variable.

Total expenditure The total amount spent over a time period.

Total factor productivity A scale factor that reflects the portion of growth that is not accounted for by explicit factor inputs (e.g. capital and labor).

Total fixed cost The summation of all expenses that do not change when production varies.

Total invested capital The sum of market value of common equity, book value of preferred equity, and face value of debt.

Total probability rule A rule explaining the unconditional probability of an event in terms of probabilities of the event conditional on mutually exclusive and exhaustive scenarios.

Total probability rule for expected value A rule explaining the expected value of a random variable in terms of expected values of the random variable conditional on mutually exclusive and exhaustive scenarios.

Total product The aggregate sum of production for the firm during a time period.

Total return Measures the price appreciation, or percentage change in price of the securities in an index or portfolio, plus any income received over the period.

Total return index An index that reflects the price appreciation or percentage change in price of the constituent securities plus any income received since inception.

Total return swap A swap in which one party agrees to pay the total return on a security. Often used as a credit derivative, in which the underlying is a bond.

Total revenue Price times the quantity of units sold.

Total surplus The difference between total value to buyers and the total variable cost to sellers; made up of the sum of consumer surplus and producer surplus.

Total variable cost The summation of all variable expenses.

Tracking error The standard deviation of the differences between a portfolio's returns and its benchmark's returns; a synonym of active risk.

Tracking risk The standard deviation of the differences between a portfolio's returns and its benchmark's returns; a synonym of active risk. Also called *tracking error*.

Trade creation When regional integration results in the replacement of higher cost domestic production by lower cost imports from other members.

Trade credit A spontaneous form of credit in which a purchaser of the goods or service is financing its purchase by delaying the date on which payment is made.

Trade diversion When regional integration results in lower-cost imports from non-member countries being replaced with higher-cost imports from members.

Trade payables Amounts that a business owes to its vendors for goods and services that were purchased from them but which have not yet been paid.

Trade protection Government policies that impose restrictions on trade, such as tariffs and quotas.

Trade receivables   Amounts customers owe the company for products that have been sold as well as amounts that may be due from suppliers (such as for returns of merchandise) Also called *commercial receivables* or *accounts receivable*.

Trade surplus (deficit)   When the value of exports is greater (less) than the value of imports.

Trading securities   Securities held by a company with the intent to trade them. Also called *held-for-trading securities*.

Traditional investment markets   Markets for traditional investments, which include all publicly traded debts and equities and shares in pooled investment vehicles that hold publicly traded debts and/or equities.

Transactions money balances   Money balances that are held to finance transactions.

Transactions motive   In the context of inventory management, the need for inventory as part of the routine production–sales cycle.

Transfer payments   Welfare payments made through the social security system that exist to provide a basic minimum level of income for low-income households.

Transitive preferences   The assumption that when comparing any three distinct bundles, A, B, and C, if A is preferred to B and simultaneously B is preferred to C, then it must be true that A is preferred to C.

Transparency   Said of something (e.g., a market) in which information is fully disclosed to the public and/or regulators.

Treasury Inflation-Protected Securities   A bond issued by the United States Treasury Department that is designed to protect the investor from inflation by adjusting the principal of the bond for changes in inflation.

Treasury shares   Shares that were issued and subsequently repurchased by the company.

Treasury stock   Shares that were issued and subsequently repurchased by the company.

Treasury stock method   A method for accounting for the effect of options (and warrants) on earnings per share (EPS) that specifies what EPS would have been if the options and warrants had been exercised and the company had used the proceeds to repurchase common stock.

Tree diagram   A diagram with branches emanating from nodes representing either mutually exclusive chance events or mutually exclusive decisions.

Trend   A long-term pattern of movement in a particular direction.

Treynor ratio   A measure of risk-adjusted performance that relates a portfolio's excess returns to the portfolio's beta.

Triangle patterns   In technical analysis, a continuation chart pattern that forms as the range between high and low prices narrows, visually forming a triangle.

Trimmed mean   A mean computed after excluding a stated small percentage of the lowest and highest observations.

Triple bottoms   In technical analysis, a reversal pattern that is formed when the price forms three troughs at roughly the same price level; used to predict a change from a downtrend to an uptrend.

Triple tops   In technical analysis, a reversal pattern that is formed when the price forms three peaks at roughly the same price level; used to predict a change from an uptrend to a downtrend.

Trough   The lowest point of a business cycle.

True yield   The internal rate of return on cash flows using the actual calendar including weekends and bank holidays.

Trust deed   See *indenture*.

Trust receipt arrangement   The use of inventory as collateral for a loan. The inventory is segregated and held in trust, and the proceeds of any sale must be remitted to the lender immediately.

Turn-of-the-year effect   Calendar anomaly that stock market returns in January are significantly higher compared to the rest of the months of the year, with most of the abnormal returns reported during the first five trading days in January.

Two-fund separation theorem   The theory that all investors regardless of taste, risk preferences, and initial wealth will hold a combination of two portfolios or funds: a risk-free asset and an optimal portfolio of risky assets.

Two-sided hypothesis test   A test in which the null hypothesis is rejected in favor of the alternative hypothesis if the evidence indicates that the population parameter is either smaller or larger than a hypothesized value.

Two-tailed hypothesis test   A test in which the null hypothesis is rejected in favor of the alternative hypothesis if the evidence indicates that the population parameter is either smaller or larger than a hypothesized value.

Two-week repo rate   The interest rate on a two-week repurchase agreement; may be used as a policy rate by a central bank.

Type I error   The error of rejecting a true null hypothesis.

Type II error   The error of not rejecting a false null hypothesis.

Unanticipated (unexpected) inflation   The component of inflation that is a surprise.

Unbilled revenue   Revenue that has been earned but not yet billed to customers as of the end of an accounting period. Also called *accrued revenue*.

Unclassified balance sheet   A balance sheet that does not show subtotals for current assets and current liabilities.

Unconditional probability   The probability of an event *not* conditioned on another event.

Underemployed   A person who has a job but has the qualifications to work a significantly higher-paying job.

Underlying   An asset that trades in a market in which buyers and sellers meet, decide on a price, and the seller then delivers the asset to the buyer and receives payment. The underlying is the asset or other derivative on which a particular derivative is based. The market for the underlying is also referred to as the *spot market*.

Underwriter   A firm, usually an investment bank, that takes the risk of buying the newly issued securities from the issuer, and then reselling them to investors or to dealers, thus guaranteeing the sale of the securities at the offering price negotiated with the issuer.

Underwritten offering   A type of securities issue mechanism in which the investment bank guarantees the sale of the securities at an offering price that is negotiated with the issuer. Also known as *firm commitment offering*.

Unearned fees   Unearned fees are recognized when a company receives cash payment for fees prior to earning them.

Unearned revenue   A liability account for money that has been collected for goods or services that have not yet been delivered; payment received in advance of providing a good or service. Also called *deferred revenue* or *deferred income*.

Unemployed   People who are actively seeking employment but are currently without a job.

Unemployment rate   The ratio of unemployed to the labor force.

Unexpected inflation   The component of inflation that is a surprise.

Unit elastic   An elasticity with a magnitude of 1.

Unit labor cost   The average labor cost to produce one unit of output.

Unit normal distribution   The normal density with mean (μ) equal to 0 and standard deviation (σ) equal to 1.

Unitary elastic   An elasticity with a magnitude of 1.

Units-of-production method   A depreciation method that allocates the cost of a long-lived asset based on actual usage during the period.

Univariate distribution   A distribution that specifies the probabilities for a single random variable.

Unlimited funds   An unlimited funds environment assumes that the company can raise the funds it wants for all profitable projects simply by paying the required rate of return.

Unsecured debt   Debt which gives the debtholder only a general claim on an issuer's assets and cash flow.

Unsponsored   A type of depository receipt in which the foreign company whose shares are held by the depository has no involvement in the issuance of the receipts.

Unstable   With reference to an equilibrium, one in which price, when disturbed away from the equilibrium, tends not to return to it.

Up transition probability   The probability that an asset's value moves up.

Utility function   A mathematical representation of the satisfaction derived from a consumption basket.

Utils   A unit of utility.

Validity instructions   Instructions which indicate when the order may be filled.

Valuation allowance   A reserve created against deferred tax assets, based on the likelihood of realizing the deferred tax assets in future accounting periods.

Valuation ratios   Ratios that measure the quantity of an asset or flow (e.g., earnings) in relation to the price associated with a specified claim (e.g., a share or ownership of the enterprise).

Value at risk   (VAR) A money measure of the minimum value of losses expected during a specified time period at a given level of probability.

Value investors   With reference to equity investors, investors who are focused on paying a relatively low share price in relation to earnings or assets per share.

Variable costs   Costs that fluctuate with the level of production and sales.

Variable-rate note   Similar to a floating-rate note, except that the spread is variable rather than constant.

Variance   The expected value (the probability-weighted average) of squared deviations from a random variable's expected value.

Variation margin   Additional margin that must be deposited in an amount sufficient to bring the balance up to the initial margin requirement.

Veblen good   A good that increases in desirability with price.

Venture capital   Investments that provide "seed" or start-up capital, early-stage financing, or mezzanine financing to companies that are in the early stages of development and require additional capital for expansion.

Venture capital fund   A fund for private equity investors that provides financing for development-stage companies.

Vertical analysis   Common-size analysis using only one reporting period or one base financial statement; for example, an income statement in which all items are stated as percentages of sales.

Vertical demand schedule   Implies that some fixed quantity is demanded, regardless of price.

Volatility   As used in option pricing, the standard deviation of the continuously compounded returns on the underlying asset.

Voluntarily unemployed   A person voluntarily outside the labor force, such as a jobless worker refusing an available vacancy.

Voluntary export restraint   A trade barrier under which the exporting country agrees to limit its exports of the good to its trading partners to a specific number of units.

Vote by proxy   A mechanism that allows a designated party—such as another shareholder, a shareholder representative, or management—to vote on the shareholder's behalf.

Warehouse receipt arrangement   The use of inventory as collateral for a loan; similar to a trust receipt arrangement except there is a third party (i.e., a warehouse company) that supervises the inventory.

Warrant   Attached option that gives its holder the right to buy the underlying stock of the issuing company at a fixed exercise price until the expiration date.

Waterfall   The provision in an ABS that describes the flow of payments between bond classes.

Weak-form efficient market hypothesis   The belief that security prices fully reflect all past market data, which refers to all historical price and volume trading information.

Wealth effect   An increase (decrease) in household wealth increases (decreases) consumer spending out of a given level of current income.

Weighted average cost method   An inventory accounting method that averages the total cost of available inventory items over the total units available for sale.

Weighted average cost of capital   A weighted average of the aftertax required rates of return on a company's common stock, preferred stock, and long-term debt, where the weights are the fraction of each source of financing in the company's target capital structure.

Weighted average coupon rate   Weighting the mortgage rate of each mortgage loan in the pool by the percentage of the mortgage outstanding relative to the outstanding amount of all the mortgages in the pool.

Weighted average life   Measure that gives investors an indication of how long they can expect to hold the MBS before it is paid off; the convention-based average time to receipt of all principal repayments. Also called *average life*.

Weighted average maturity   Weighting the remaining number of months to maturity for each mortgage loan in the pool by the amount of the outstanding mortgage balance.

Weighted mean   An average in which each observation is weighted by an index of its relative importance.

Wholesale price index   Reflects the price changes experienced by domestic producers in a country.

Winner's curse   The tendency for the winner in certain competitive bidding situations to overpay, whether because of overestimation of intrinsic value, emotion, or information asymmetries.

Winsorized mean   A mean computed after assigning a stated percent of the lowest values equal to one specified low value, and a stated percent of the highest values equal to one specified high value.

Working capital   The difference between current assets and current liabilities.

Working capital management The management of a company's short-term assets (such as inventory) and short-term liabilities (such as money owed to suppliers).

World price The price prevailing in the world market.

Yield The actual return on a debt security if it is held to maturity.

Yield duration The sensitivity of the bond price with respect to the bond's own yield-to-maturity.

Yield to maturity Annual return that an investor earns on a bond if the investor purchases the bond today and holds it until maturity. It is the discount rate that equates the present value of the bond's expected cash flows until maturity with the bond's price. Also called *yield-to-redemption* or *redemption yield*.

Yield to redemption See *yield to maturity*.

Yield-to-worst The lowest of the sequence of yields-to-call and the yield-to-maturity.

Zero volatility spread (Z-spread) Calculates a constant yield spread over a government (or interest rate swap) spot curve.

Zero-coupon bonds Bonds that do not pay interest during the bond's life. It is issued at a discount to par value and redeemed at par. Also called *pure discount bonds*.

Index